The Danish Army of the Napoleonic Wars 1801–1814, Organisation, Uniforms and Equipment

Volume 3: Norwegian Troops and Militia

David A. Wilson

The Royal Arms of Norway
With the Appropation of
His Royal Highness Prince Joachim of Denmark

Helion & Company Ltd

> **Dedications**
>
> To my wife Josette for many years of patience
>
> To Teddy Suren for his original inspiration and 'joie de vivre'
>
> To Jean François Blanc for his constant encouragement.
>
> In memoriam of my dear friend, Lieutenant Colonel Anders Lindström,
> Late of the Royal Swedish Army and of Tradition of Scandinavia.
> 14 October 1941–3 September 2014

Helion & Company Limited
Unit 8 Amherst Business Centre
Budbrooke Road
Warwick
CV34 5WE
England
Tel. 01926 499619
Email: info@helion.co.uk
Website: www.helion.co.uk
Twitter: @helionbooks
Visit our blog at https://helionbooks.wordpress.com/

Published by Helion & Company 2022
Designed and typeset by Serena Jones
Cover designed by Paul Hewitt, Battlefield Design (www.battlefield-design.co.uk)

Text © David A. Wilson 2022
Plates © David A. Wilson 2022
Cover: Oberstløjtnant Andreas Krebs, Akerhusiske Skarpskytter Regiment 1814, original artwork by David Wilson

Every reasonable effort has been made to trace copyright holders and to obtain their permission for the use of copyright material. The author and publisher apologise for any errors or omissions in this work, and would be grateful if notified of any corrections that should be incorporated in future reprints or editions of this book.

ISBN 978-1-914059-81-0

British Library Cataloguing-in-Publication Data.

A catalogue record for this book is available from the British Library.
All rights reserved. No part of this publication may be reproduced, stored in a retrieval system, or transmitted, in any form, or by any means, electronic, mechanical, photocopying, recording or otherwise, without the express written consent of Helion & Company Limited.
For details of other military history titles published by Helion & Company Limited, contact the above address, or visit our website: http://www.helion.co.uk
We always welcome receiving book proposals from prospective authors.

Contents

List of Plates	iv
Foreword	vi
Preface	vi
Acknowledgements	vii

Part I

1	Background	11
2	The Norwegian High Command and The Royal Military Cadet School	13
3	The Norwegian Line Infantry: Organisation	22
4	The Norwegian Line Infantry: Uniforms	31
5	Norwegian Infantry Colours	54
6	The Norwegian *Jægers*, Light Infantry and Ski Troops	64
7	The Norwegian Cavalry	90
8	The Norwegian Dragoon Guidons	104
9	The Norwegian Artillery	108

Part II

10	The Danish Landeværn and Kystmilitsen	128
11	The Danish Volunteer *Jægere*	131
12	The Defence of Bornholm, Including Colours and Standards	140
13	The Citizen or Town Militias (I): The *Borgervæbninger* of Denmark and Norway, and of Copenhagen	173
14	The Citizen or Town Militias (II): The *Borgervæbninger* of Schleswig-Holstein	197
15	The Norwegian Citizen Militia	201

Appendix I: Norwegian Cavalry Active in 1808–1809	213
Appendix II: Norwegian Horses	214
Appendix III: Norwegian Orders of Battle	215
Appendix IV: Det Kongelige Frivillige Røråske Bergjæger Corps	216
Glossary	217
Bibliography	220

List of Plates

Plate 1.	The Norwegian General Staff 1803–1814	14
Plate 2.	The Norwegian Military Cadets, Det Kongelige Norske Landkadet Korps	16
Plate 3.	Norwegian Line Infantry Uniforms I, 1803–1810	24
Plate 4.	Norwegian Line Infantry II, NCOs' Halberds 1803–1810	26
Plate 5.	Norwegian Line Infantry II, Regimental Distinctions 1800–1810	28
Plate 6.	Norwegian Line Infantry Uniforms III, 1810–1814	34
Plate 7.	Norwegian Line Infantry Uniforms IV, Regimental Distinctions 1810–1814	36
Plate 8.	Norwegian Line Infantry Uniforms V, 1800–1810; Grenadier Equipment Details	40
Plate 9.	Norwegian Infantry Colours I, Grenadier Colour	44
Plate 10.	Norwegian Infantry Colours II, Søndenfjeldske & Nordenfjeldske Geworbne Regiments	47
Plate 11.	Norwegian Infantry Colours III, 1st Akershusiske Regiment *Livfane*	48
Plate 12.	Norwegian Infantry Colours IV, *1st Akershusiske Regiment Ordinærfane*	49
Plate 13.	Norwegian Infantry Colours V, 2nd Akershusiske Regiment	51
Plate 14.	Opplandske Nationale Infantry Regiment pre-1810	55
Plate 15.	Norwegian Colours VII	56
Plate 16.	Norwegian Colours VIII	58
Plate 17.	Norwegian Colours IX	60
Plate 18.	Norwegian Colours X	61
Plate 19.	Norwegian Colours XI	63
Plate 20.	Norwegian Colours XII	63
Plate 21.	Norwegian Colours XIII	63
Plate 22.	The Norske Geworbne Jæger Corps (Norwegian Enlisted *Jæger* Corps)	66
Plate 23.	Norwegian Light Infantry (Norske Lette Infanteri)	68
Plate 24.	The Norwegian Sharpshooters (Norske Skarpskyttere) 1810–1815	72
Plate 25.	Norwegian Ski Troops 1790–1814	80
Plate 26.	Norwegian Ski Troops (*Skiløber*) Equipment and Skis	84
Plate 27.	The Norwegian Dragoons and Ridende Jæger Corps 1803–1814	92
Plate 28.	The Norwegian Dragoons and Ridende Jæger Corps 1803–1814, II Details	94
Plate 29.	The Norwegian Dragoons and Ridende Jæger Corps III, Housings and Shabraques	98
Plate 30.	Norwegian Kettle Drummer, Akershusiske Dragonregiment *c.* 1808	100
Plate 31.	Norwegian Dragoon Guidons I, Smaalehnske Dragonregiment	105
Plate 32.	Norwegian Dragoon Guidons II	106
Plate 33.	Norwegian 1-pdr M1766 *Amusette*	110
Plate 34.	A Norwegian 10-pdr Portable Mortar	113
Plate 35.	Norwegian 3-pdr 16 calibre M1687–1757 system *Harboe* field gun	114
Plate 36.	Danish-Norwegian 10-pdr (light) M1789 Howitzer System *Carl af Hessen*.	118
Plate 37.	Norwegian 3-pdr 16 calibre sledge gun, in Trønderlavet M1809.	120
Plate 38.	Norwegian *Kørende* Artillery Limber M1811	122
Plate 39.	Norwegian Artillery uniforms	124
Plate 40.	Landeværn and Coastal Militia	132
Plate 41.	The *Landeværnet* M1801 Colours	135
Plate 42.	Danish Volunteer Foot *Jægere*	142
Plate 43.	Danish Mounted Volunteer *Jægere* I	144
Plate 44.	Danish Mounted Volunteer *Jægere* II	146
Plate 45.	Danish Mounted Volunteer *Jæger* Shabraques	148

Plate 46. Bornholm Nationale Dragoons I	154
Plate 47. Bornholm Nationale Dragoons II	156
Plate 48. Bornholm Nationale Infantry	158
Plate 49. Bornholm Militia	160
Plate 50. Bornholm Volunteer/Militia Artillery	162
Plate 51. 3-pdr 16 calibre M1687/1748/1757 *Harboe* System Field Gun	166
Plate 52. Bornholmske Nationale Dragoner/Dragoon Standards and Infantry Colours	168
Plate 53. *Bornholmske Borger* and *Herreds* Company Colours	170
Plate 54. Danish Militia Units of Copenhagen	174
Plate 55. Danish Volunteer Militia Colours	176
Plate 56. Danish Volunteer Militia Rank Distinctions	178
Plate 57. Samsøe Landeværn and Danish Citizen Militias I	180
Plate 58. Danish Citizen Militias II (*Borgervæbninger*)	190
Plate 59. Danish Militia III	192
Plate 60. Schleswig and Holstein Citizen Militia	198
Plate 61. Norwegian Citizen Militia I	202
Plate 62. Norwegian Citizen Militia II	206

Foreword

In a perfect world, military historians, military collectors, model soldier builders and collectors would have experienced that when new book on military uniforms, banners and ordnance were published, they would concern subjects where not much has already been written. Unfortunately, this is seldom the case. Many books mostly reproduce information that has been easily accessible from other books. Armies from smaller nations will often be more or less forgotten, as little is written on the subject for others to copy, or what is written, is in a language not well known to the English-speaking authors.

It is therefore with great pleasure we received the books by David A. Wilson on the armies of Denmark-Norway during the Napoleonic Wars. These three books are well researched, and they are well illustrated giving the reader not acquainted with these armies an easy guide to all questions about colours, uniforms and ordnance.

For Norwegian readers, the third volume of mention about the Norwegian Army will be especially welcomed. The Danish army has to some extent been the subject of publicity in connection with the warfare in Germany. For the part of the Norwegian Army, all combat operations took place on the border areas to Sweden and have therefore not invoked much interest from others. This volume covers the history of the Norwegian Army's participation in the Napoleonic Wars in an excellent way.

David Wilson refers to this as a uniform book. However, it is much more than that. One thing is the uniform drawings themselves that are based on extensive material that has not previously been widely known. He gives us information about when the different uniform parts and equipment actually came to different units, nor is the equipment of the horses forgotten. The book also goes into what weapons the individual units had at all times, and the tactical use of these weapons, also what artillery material was at their disposal and how it was used. The precise and detailed presentation is impressive not least given the Norwegian Army's extensive reorganisation in 1789 and 1810. These reorganisations have created major challenges when it comes to the colours. A number of older Danish colours were sent to Norway for reuse in the Norwegian army in 1788. It is difficult to document which battalions received which of the regiment's colours of older Norwegians and Danish colours. Things became worse when a number of regiments were disbanded in 1789 and the battalions were transferred to other regiments. But the range of colours presented in the book is convincing. Moreover, David Wilson's reconstructions are exceptional.

It is also important that David Wilson has included the uniforms of Citizen Militia units. Even though few of these units actually saw action during the Napoleonic Wars, these units were of importance as they gave the citizens in both large towns and the many small towns the opportunity to show their will to defend their country. The exercises of these units were also an important opportunity for the citizens to mix and get acquainted. For some young men this have been a chance to acquire important connections, and for some old and established men, a chance through commissions as militia officers to confirm their social position. And as each unit had their particular uniforms, it gives insight into a fascinating world of different uniforms worn at exercises and on social events.

Knut Erik Strøm, Redaktør, Norske Våpenhistorisk Selskap

Erik Aagaard, Norske Våpenhistorisk Selskap

Preface

This the third volume of the series covering the uniforms of both the Danish and Norwegian Armies of the Napoleonic Wars is principally a uniform book, but there is just enough historical information to place the details in their context.

This study started over six years ago as a simple fascicule for some friends, in particular the Colonel Jean-François Blanc, who wanted to paint some Danish Napoleonic model soldiers, but they did not have any information on the subject, but they knew that, thanks to my late friend, Lieutenant Colonel Anders Lindström, I had a couple of books on the subject and could I write them a few lines and make a couple of sketches, this is where the adventure started.

One thing led to another and I became fascinated by all the aspects of this gallant little army, but I also discovered that there was very little written on the subject in English, so I decided to write a little more and as I wanted it to be as accurate as possible I have given pride of place to the closest contemporary source.

Obviously I cannot be dogmatic about all that I have written and I am sure some errors may have crept in. Any other 'interpretations' are my own, based on Danish and Norwegian usages and customs of the time, along with a little bit of logic and a lot of help from friends in both Denmark and Norway.

I must mention Alan Perry of Perry Miniatures who was responsible for putting me in contact with Jørgen Koefoed Larsen and his becoming involved and he has been my guide through this book.

In this volume which covers the Norwegian Army I have left the names in their in their original Danish form.[1]

Concerning the Infantry colours carried in Norway I have only illustrated those which were known to be in use during the period and due to limitations of space I have not illustrated the company pennons, maybe in the future a second edition I could cover these. Again the help from Erik Aagaard was indispensable. Some of the colours I have applied to the illustrations may not be exact as the originals are both faded and discoloured so it is quite difficult to be certain without chemical analysis. Another detail which I have omitted is the fringes on some of the Infantry colours which I feel have been added later to either embellish or reinforce the edges or both, I may be wrong, but they do not look right to me.

Another problem concerned weapons used in Norway, as due to shortages and rare new supplies from Denmark, a lot of weapons which pressed into service were much older than those used in the Danish army, in particular bladed weapons.

Concerning the artillery I have only illustrated the pieces most associated with Norway and the majority of the standard pieces have already been dealt with in Volume 2.

---

1 One has to be extremely careful as in 1800–1814 there was no official 'Norwegian' language; Danish was the only official common language, that variation normally spoken by commoners, a kind of Danish 'dialect'. Only from *c.* 1840, mainly as a nationalistic movement, were experiments made to form a (new) Norwegian language. This had the effect that two kinds of 'Norwegian' developed. After the union with Sweden was dissolved in 1905, this discussion carried on, and only after a lengthy struggle it took its final formal in *c.* 1959. Today two official forms of Norwegian: *Bokmål* (literally 'book tongue') and *Nynorsk* ('new Norwegian'), each with its own variants. *Bokmål* developed from the pre 1814 Dano-Norwegian language, while *Nynorsk* was developed based upon a collective of older spoken Norwegian dialects. Most new history and names are today changed, but not in an 'original' form. As we are writing the story of the Danish-Norwegian army of 1800–1814 we have kept the original form for most names and terms as they were in 1800–1814.

Acknowledgements

A special mention must be made to Jørgen Koefoed Larsen, Honorary member of the Danish military society 'Chakoten', who assisted me with his precious help with this work would not have achieved the degree of authenticity that it has. I must also mention his patience with my very poor Danish and supplying me with many extraordinary documents and putting them into their context and correcting my errors along the way.

I was also assisted by Karsten Skold Petersen senior researcher of the Tøjhusmuseet (now called the Krigsmuseet) of Denmark and Erik Aagaard and Knut Erik Strøm of Norway who have supplied me with material from their private archives.

Not forgetting Trond Wikborg of Norway with his help on arms used in Norway and access to his exceptional personal collection.

Also I would like to extend my thanks to the following researchers for their kind and irreplaceable help and encouragement that they have given me over the years on Danish and Norwegian uniforms.

Mr Torstein Snorrason, for his kindness and patience with my poor Danish.

I must also mention Ola Jonsgaard Moen and Trond Bækkevold of Norway, who helped me to start this project.

Mr Frode Lindgjerdet of the Rustkammeret in Trondheim for his help on sledgeborne artillery

Dr Peter Bunde, who has supplied me with copies of his illustrations based on his own research on this army.

Mr Peter Kristiansen, Curator of Castle Rosenborg Copenhagen.

Mr Lars Kjær, Arkivar og arkivkoordinator, Køge Town History Archive, Køge Museum and Bruno Juul.

Thank you all so much.

Part I

1

Background

In Norway the conditions were somewhat different. After 1762 the Norwegian army did not serve outside of Norway and were used principally in defence of their homeland, facing their principal landward enemy Sweden, and defending the coast from British attacks from 1807 to 1814. They had an extremely long frontier to defend with difficult terrain and generally harsh climatic conditions and an even longer coastline.

Not being a rich country – financed only by agriculture and maritime trades – they were hampered by lack of resources to be able to modernise, train, dress and equip their troops for the harsh climatic conditions they faced, but this did not dampen their will to resist, or their patriotism. Also, food and supply shortages together with crop failures – the one in 1812 being the worst – together with the tight blockade in 1813, meant that many people simply died of hunger. This situation only eased from January 1814, when large amounts of supplies, grain and equipment came across from Denmark before the War of Independence, which started in 1814. All these factors meant that only parts of the army could be mobilised for field service at any one time. In Norway the national recruits would only be exercised for 12 days a year, usually in the summer, and this at company level only. This was due to the great distances between the districts, but also not to avoid laying too heavy a burden on the workforce of the peasant society and on the local economy. Only every fourth year were they formed into the battalions of their parent regiment, when they could be exercised for 16 days in larger formations. In wartime, only one battalion was formed for field service, while the rest formed one battalion which was technically the depot or Landeværn battalion, not a fighting battalion.

In 1808–1809 they used small brigade formations composed normally of a battalion made up of four grenadier divisions each of two grenadier companies, composite units of regimental *skarpskytte*, *jægere* and ski battalions, and sometimes supplemented by regimental 1-pdr *amusettes*[1] which formed the basis of a normal unit used for field service. This structure continued to be used even after the grenadiers had been disbanded and more infantry been converted into sharpshooters and regimental *jægere*. Only from 1810–1814 were two field battalions formed from each regiment under the new organisation; the rest formed a depot/*Landeværn* reserve. Clearly this structure influenced all military decisions.

So when the Norwegians actually went to war they were hampered by the absence of training in large formations, a lack of experienced officers and NCOs, generally obsolete equipment and worst of all, their gunpowder was of an inferior quality compared to that of their enemies. They compensated for these shortcomings to a certain extent, with their patriotism, superior marksmanship, individual training and field craft. The terrain was not suitable for large continental-style warfare, but was perfect for small-scale actions, at which the Norwegians excelled.

From the outbreak of hostilities on land in 1807 and until the 1814 campaign and invasion of Norway, there was a chronic lack of officers, so some older pensioned-off officers, and even some very young cadets (16–17 years old) taken from the Norwegian Cadet Academy, were given temporary positions within the regiments, where some made a very favourable impression. Although a few died in combat, most replaced more experienced depot officers so releasing them for field service. The line musketeers and (dismounted) *dragoner* (dragoons) together with the artillery were mainly used to defend the towns, fortifications and fortresses. They did not take part in many field actions.

---

1 It was mainly Danish artillery officers and later historians who saw the amusette as a useless hindrance, without effect, but most Norwegian artillery officers, gunners and ordinary soldiers saw their use as a blessing. It may have fired a small shot, but it was accurate and light, and the Swedish never had anything like it to support their infantry, as their use of 3-pdr guns were never as effective, because of their weight. They needed eight to 10 men to manoeuvre it and the need for two to four horses to draw them normally confined them to roads and good terrain. The *amusette* could be drawn by just one or two horses, and could even be manhandled by two to four gunners or soldiers for short distances, or even be broken down and carried in two loads in difficult terrain. As General Rye said in 1848 'The *amusettes* were well liked by our soldiers, but hated by the Swedes, as they had none.'

As Norway was (and still is) a difficult country to move about, the Swedish attackers were forced to use narrow roads, winding through hills, valleys and forests, and were often forced to stop or change direction due to well-placed fortifications. As a consequence, their advancing columns were extended, exposing their flanks to attack. Against them, the Norwegians, aided by their knowledge of the terrain and superior field craft, advanced, outflanked and encircled several isolated Swedish formations on more than one occasion with a tactic not unlike the famous *Motti* tactic (literally, 'Chop them up into smaller pieces') as used in Finland in the Winter War of 1939–1940 and took out their opponents piecemeal. This normally forced other Swedish formations that were outflanked to retreat. In 1814 the same tactics were used, but the Norwegians were eventually forced to surrender because of their less than competent high command, even though the troops were well led by skilful officers and were locally successful; so successful in fact that Bernadotte finally offered better terms of surrender than were at first offered to avoid fighting a long, bloody and unpopular war. The fighting ended with a ceasefire and the acceptance of a forced union with Sweden, Norway only gaining their independence in 1905.

When in action against the Swedes, it was the Swedes who usually came off worst and they were only able to beat Norwegians by sheer weight of numbers, a lack of supplies and a far from fully committed Norwegian high command who wished to avoid a bloody conflict which they would have eventually lost. This was fortunate for the Swedes, as the war would probably have ended in a pyrrhic victory for them.

2

The Norwegian High Command and The Royal Military Cadet School

Norway was at this time governed by *stadtholders* (governors) based in Christiana[1] and appointed by Denmark. They were usually a member of the royal family. They were also the overall commander-in-chief of all Norwegian forces.

The first was Prince Christian August (1768–1810) of the Augustenborg line of the Danish royal family, a very capable officer with a great deal of experience which he had gained when he was an officer (brigadier general) with the Austrian army during the revolutionary wars against France. He soon gained both the hearts and minds of the Norwegians and the respect of his Swedish opponents, so much so that after the peace in 1809, they offered him the position of Crown Prince of Sweden, which he accepted, and he left for Sweden. But during subsequent military manoeuvres he was suddenly struck down with a heart attack and died. He was mourned by all, and left the way free for French Marshal Bernadotte, but that is another story.

The next in line was the King's brother-in-law, Prince Frederik of Hessen. His was the hand behind the significant military reforms made in Norway between 1810–1813, and although he was a very capable soldier, he was not much of a politician.

He was succeeded by a third *Stadtholder*, Prince Christian Frederik (1786–1848) who was the son of Frederik VI's uncle, and although he had held several commissions in Danish regiments, he had few abilities as a soldier, but he was a learned and politically knowledgeable man. He was also a man of good looks, and charm, but was plagued with indecision, which would have dire consequences on more than one occasion.

Although he led a revolt against the Treaty of Kiel, following which he was elected King of Norway in 1814 (supported in secret by King Frederik VI of Denmark), his inability to decide on a clear military strategy and his general indecision lost him his crown and Norway.[2] He returned to Denmark in 1839 on the death of Frederik VI, and succeeded him on the Danish throne as Christian VIII. His reign is remembered as one of great hope, but was (again) spoiled by indecision and lost opportunities.

Firstly, to understand the system of command in Norway one must first consider the topography of the country. It was virtually cut in two by a heavily wooded mountain range and by a number of major rivers, which were difficult in the summer months and near impassable in the depths of winter. Effectively this divided Norway in two, a southern region, governed by the capital city of Christiana/Oslo, and a northern part, administered by the city of Trondheim. This Northern Division was more or less an independent command, particularly in winter. From 1808 Norway was divided into two military command districts, the Søndenfjeldske and the Nordenfjeldske, each under a commanding general. The Generals commanding the Northern Division were always chosen among those who were deemed as the best qualified, and the most capable of acting independently.

When Prince Christian Frederik became head of state, and thus also commander-in-chief of all Norwegian forces, no other commanding general was appointed to the Søndenfjeldske, keeping this post for himself. The obvious choice had been General Løjtnant Bernhard Ditlev von Staffeldt (1753–1819). But Christian Frederik had flair in

---

1 At the time the capital of Norway was called Christiania, which was built in the shadow of the fortress of Akerhus in 1624, and Oslo was a simply a village on the outskirts of the capital. The capital was only renamed Oslo in 1924 amid a number of protests.

2 A tale tells us, that after the last Swedish attack on the Norwegian fortifications at Langnes farm on 9 August 1814 was thrown back, after three fruitless direct assaults and the Swedes had to retreat in some disorder with more than 100 casualties, the commander Colonel von Hegermann, was about to pursue the Swedish fugitives. Just as he was ready to advance, the Norwegian King Christian Frederik arrived. The King had been sleeping when the battle started, and woken by the firing, quickly rode to the front. But as he rode to the battle, he passed the body of artillery Lieutenant Hauchs, who had been mortally wounded during the battle and was being carried from the field on a bloody stretcher. This sight unnerved him so much, that he shouted, with sorrow, 'Too much blood for my sake'.

THE DANISH ARMY OF THE NAPOLEONIC WARS VOLUME 3

The Norwegian General Staff 1803–1814

> Facing page
> Plate 1. The Norwegian General Staff 1803–1814
> Top row, from left to right:
> 1. Norwegian General *c.* 1804, based on a portrait of General of Infantry George Frederik von Krogh, commander of the northern division in full dress. Although both orders are shown on his coat, in all probability he would only have worn one in the field. On the left he wears the Order of the Dannebrog and on the right the Order of the Elephant.
> 2. ADC Quartermaster's staff *c.* 1809, in fact an officer of the Akershusiske Dragonregiment wearing regimental dress, but with a yellow-tipped red feather denoting his function
> 3. Staff officer in M1808 uniform *c.* 1808
> 4. Chief of staff of Prince Christian August, Captain von Darre in an officer's M1806 overcoat *overkjole*
> 5. Officer of engineers, loosely based on the portrait of Lieutenant Hans Ditlev Franz von Linstow *c.* 1814 in regimental uniform
>
> Bottom row, from left to right:
> 5. Staff officer *c.* 1810
> 6. General, based on a portrait of Prince Christian August of Augustenborg (1768–1810) in the uniform of the Søndenfjeldske Geworbne Infanteri Regiment, of which he was commander from 1803 to 1808. Note his epaulettes should have been gold with silver stars (the button colour), but his portrait shows these non-regulation epaulettes.
> 7. Stadtholder and commander-in-chief Prince Christian Frederik (1786–1848), in the grey uniform of the Akershusiske Skarpskytte Regiment, based on a portrait *c.* 1813
> 8. Chief of the Norwegian General Staff in 1814, General Lieutenant von Sejersted (1761–1823) wearing the new grey staff officer's uniform M1814
> 9. Staff officer based on a portrait of Kaptajn Gregers Fougner von Lundh in 1814, wearing the M1814 staff officer's uniform. As a special favour, King Christian Frederik allowed the officers of his own staff and those of the general staff to wear epaulettes on this uniform.
> 10. General officer's embroidery, silver for silver-buttoned uniforms and gold for gold-buttoned uniforms

his personality, he often disliked or distrusted people with greater ability than himself, and von Staffeldt was a much better soldier than him. This was to have dire consequences, and as one contemporary noted: 'King Christian Frederik wanted to lead all, give advice to all, but never himself, even saw, the slightest glimpse of a Swedish soldier'. Christian Frederik established a general staff on 22 May 1814. It consisted of an adjutant general and chief of the general staff (Major General von Sejersted), two adjutant generals, one of whom served as general quartermaster (*Oberstløjtnant* von Haffner), four senior adjutants, one (*Major* von Brock) as the King's personal adjutant, four division adjutants as well as a varying number of *adjoints* (aides-de-camp).

According to legend, the answer he got from one of the stretcher bearers was: 'Not too much blood spilled, majesty, but too little!' The King arrived in a rather unnerved state before *Oberst* von Hegermann and ordered him to retreat over the Glomma River and destroy the bridge. When von Hegermann protested, the King replied: 'By god! Have you not yet sacrificed enough of our beautiful people?'

(Norwegian losses had only been six dead and 10 wounded). So, Christian Frederik lost his nerve, missed yet another opportunity, and gave up the war and his Norwegian throne.

Uniforms
The generals, their staff, and officers in general had shorter clothing terms (generally of two years) which meant they often applied new regulations much earlier than the regiments did. In Norway to begin with, all generals, staff and officers' uniforms normally followed the Danish form and style along the basic guidelines issued from Copenhagen as most were also supplied with cloth etc. directly from Denmark, and at favourable prices. But as time went by as the English/Swedish blockade tightened they became more independent, using local suppliers, and they made a number of decisions which distinguished their uniforms from those worn in Denmark.

Although the new 1812 regulations for officer's distinctions abolished the sashes and epaulettes this did not concern the generals who continued to use them. Their staff

THE DANISH ARMY OF THE NAPOLEONIC WARS VOLUME 3

The Norwegian Miltary Cadets
"Det Kongelike Norske Landkadet Korps"

> Facing page
>
> Plate 2. Det Kongelige Norske Landkadet Corps (The Norwegian Military Cadets)
>
> 1. Cadet school staff officer full dress *Stadsuniform* according to the approved drawings of 13 April 1804. It was restricted to the use of the *direktør*/schoolmaster and the three full-time staff officers.
>
> 2. Cadet school staff officer's service uniform according to the approved drawings of 13 April 1804
>
> 3. Full dress *Stadsuniform* for the school commander(*leder/direktør*)and the three full-time administrative officers. This is a first lieutenant's version. Note that they were also allowed yellow trousers as before. The gold embroidery was reused from the previous red uniforms.
>
> 4. Ordinary service uniform 1814 for one of the four *repetenter* of the eldest class, who were chosen to teach the younger cadet classes, with the rank of second lieutenant
>
> 5. The Norwegian cadet parade uniform according to the approved drawings of 13 April 1804
>
> 6. Cadet with the new cadet shako M1809 in 1811, wearing the epaulettes of a third-year cadet. Note: he is shown wearing the M1811 tailed coat as issued in Denmark, but there is no record of them arriving in Norway, so they may have continued to wear the 1804 coat until the issue of the grey uniforms.
>
> 7. Cadet in school dress c. 1813. Due to clothing shortages this grey kersey daily *Hverdagstrøjer* uniform became the norm for everyday classes wearing the epaulettes of a second-year cadet. From 1813 their headwear was a black leather cap with a white plume. From 1811 until 1812 their headwear was an ordinary soldier's hat, with a white plume; the same plume was transferred to the cap when needed.
>
> 8. Cadet wearing the new *Søndagsmundring* (Sunday dress), as it was reserved for church parades, parades and formal service. This dress was authorised in June 1814. The cuff distinctions denote a first-year cadet.
>
> 9. *Landkadetsabel* M1802
>
> 10. *Landkadetsabel* M1789
>
> 11. Shako plate, of which a drawing was made and approved on 23 July 1809. Drawn by J. K. Larsen.
>
> 12. Belt plate for a bandolier. Author's reconstruction.

officers were also permitted to keep their epaulettes, but not the sash. See Volume 1 for a more detailed description of their uniforms.

The New Grey Uniforms of the Generals and Staff Worn in Norway 1814

Because of the difficult economic situation and the difficulty of importing dyed cloth, Denmark had laid down plans that in the next change of uniforms (in 1814) the whole army would change from red into a dark grey cloth, but the war ended before this was implemented in Denmark. In Norway, the issue of grey uniforms had been discussed on several occasions between 1808–1813, leading to its use for mainly *skarpskytte* (sharpshooters). In Norway, *Stadtholder* and commander-in-chief Prince Christian Frederik also wanted to equip the whole Norwegian army in grey, and so just after taking power in Norway in early 1814 he ordered a large quantity of grey English cloth, to be used for the new grey uniform for his whole army. But this was because of Swedish pressure, now held back, so this plan came to nothing. Prince Christian Frederik, as king, had already ordered that all uniforms in Norway would be changed to grey at the first uniform replenishment after July 1814. But this was now impossible, and the stock in Norway of red and white cloth was in fact sufficient for uniform coats and trousers, as was also locally made grey *vadmel* (homespun), for other clothing, until the war ended in the summer of 1814.

But one part of the army had already begun this change; this was the newly elected king (Christian Frederik) and his general staff. After a royal order of 21 February 1814 his general staff were to change into a 'grey uniform coat with one row of buttons, with a (dark) blue collar and cuffs and white lining (some appear to have kept the previous used buff lining), onto which the former embroideries are to be transferred and used. To be worn with a white waistcoat and grey trousers for normal service wear and white trousers for parades'. Already by 22 February, Prince Christian Frederik and his staff had changed into grey uniforms, participating in a parade at Eidsvoll so dressed. So, the change had clearly been both planned and prepared before the official date, so that the Prince and everybody on his personnel staff already had new uniforms ready to wear.

Although according to the orders of August 1812, all epaulettes were to be discontinued, except for generals, evidence from portraits and some contemporary letters, suggests that this allowance was also extended to members of the general staff. Several portraits show that epaulettes were indeed worn by staff officers as late as 1814. Although they all have only one row of buttons the number and size of those buttons were all different on all the uniforms in contemporary portraits which suggests that there was not a standard model, just the basic guidelines and as officer's uniforms were privately commissioned there are a number of variations.

Their headwear was now either a shako or a bicorn. The shako was the standard black leather officer's model with gold and red cords and tassels, a black cockade with a loop and button corresponding to their button colour generally silver or white. Depending on which staff they served, the plume would be red for the general staff or red tipped yellow for the quartermaster's staff.

The generals' bicorns were not laced but were edged in black feathers for general and campaign service and white for parades and formal occasions. The bicorn had a black cockade and a loop (*agraf*) in metallic lace and from 1801 with stars, which were two different-sized stars placed over the loop one above the other. They could be gold or silver corresponding to the button colour. There was also a gold tassel on each horn.

Some Notable General Officers
Lieutenant General Carl Jacob Waldemar Greve von[3] Schmettow (1744–1821). He commanded a brigade from 1808–1809 and in 1814 was made the overall commander of the Nordenfjeldske (the Northern Division). In a portrait dated before 1808, he is shown wearing the uniform of his regiment, 2nd Trondhjemske Nationale Infanteri Regiment.

Prince Christian August of Augustenborg (1768–1810) wore the uniform of the Søndenfjeldske Geworbne Infanteri Regiment of which he was commander from 1803 to 1808. Note that against normal practice, he had white epaulettes with gold stars, although his regiment had yellow buttons, but as the epaulettes are those of a full general, he possibly only had one pair to use on all of his uniforms.

---

3   Between 1761 and 1762, a large part of the Norwegian army had served together with the rest of the Danish army along the southern borders, ready to repel a Russian attack. Here it was felt that the Norwegian officers, might feel inferior, serving along the Danish officers who were mostly of German descent as they were all allowed to use a 'von' in front of their family name. So from 1762, all officers, Norwegians included, were allowed to also use 'von', in front of their family name. This was adopted by all officers in Norway, as their privilege until 1814. After 1814, this usage fell out of use, as it was seen as a Danish royal favour with German overtones and not something to use in the new Norwegian state, being thought to be un-Norwegian. So when writing the names of those officers who served between 1762–1814 most Norwegian historians have by tradition, left out the 'von' from all officer's names, So we have in all cases, used the 'von' prefix, as this would have been used at the time and it would be incorrect not to include them here.

General of Infantry Georg Frederik von Krogh (1732–1818) was commander of the Northern Division until 1814. He was reckoned to be the ablest general in Norway by most of his contemporaries, including King Frederik V.

Major General Bernhard Ditlev von Staffeldt (1753–1819) was probably one of the most able officers in Southern Norway. As *oberst* (colonel) he was commander of the Norske Geworbne Jæger Corps 1803–1814. He fought with distinction during the campaign of 1808–1809, and as a result was promoted major general in 1809. In 1814 he was made a lieutenant general, and all thought he would take command of the army. But the new King Christian Frederik disliked him and kept the command for himself. Instead, he was made a brigade commander on the main front of the fighting in 1814, a post needing a trusted independent commander. But King Christian Frederik and his staff overwhelmed him with useless orders, distrust and bad advice. Also, the situation was not made better by the fact that the Swedes had managed to get a copy of the Norwegian defence plans, written by the Chief of Staff von Sejerstedt. So, first King Christian Frederik, later followed by others, made him one of the main scapegoats for the disappointing end of the war. After the war, the new Norwegian government brought him before a military tribunal, unjustly blaming him, with five others, for the outcome of the war. But he was judged innocent of all charges. So instead, at the direct instigation of parliament, probably needing someone to blame for their own mistakes, he was brought before the civil Norwegian Supreme Court, which promptly condemned him to death. He was quickly pardoned by Crown Prince Carl Johan and was instead imprisoned in the fortress of Frederiksten for five months in 1817, after which he was released. He died in 1808, a broken man.

General Frederik Gottschalk von Haxthausen (1750–1825) was regarded as a very capable and knowledgeable officer. He had held several commands in Norway, Major General in 1802 and from 1803 commander of *Feltkommissariatet for den Danske hær* (quartermaster of supply in Denmark), a job he did very well until 1810. In this year he left the command which was same year the service was reorganised into a branch of the general staff. He was decorated with the Grand Cross of the Order of Dannebrog in 1810. He served both Prince Frederik of Hessen and in particularly Prince Christian Frederik as *generalintendandt* (chief of supply), promoted lieutenant general and later *hofmarskal*; apparently, he had a number of enemies in Norway who were envious of his numerous promotions. In a contemporary portrait dated 1808 he is shown wearing a general's uniform 1808, as commander of the Kongelige Norske Landkadet Corps (The Norwegian Officer Cadet School), of which he was the commander from 1802.

Unjustifiably (like von Staffeldt) he was blamed for the surrender to the Swedish (whose rule he accepted) and of treason by his enemies, but although a military court later found him innocent of all charges, he never really gained favour later on and he left the army in 1817.

The Engineer Staff

In Norway as in Denmark this was an all-officer unit, mainly tasked with improving and maintaining the fortresses and batteries, but also making roads, harbours, canals, town building and mining. They undertook engineer training at either *Det Kongelige Norske Bergseminarium*, or *Kongsberg bergseminar*, which was an academic institution for general engineering education, but in particular specialising in technology, and which existed from 1757 to 1814.

In 1807 there was an engineer regiment with 11 officers and an aide, which in 1814 was referred to as an engineer brigade with 16 officers and an aide. The work itself was carried out by soldiers (during 1808–1809, a *sappør companie* – sapper company – was formed, with a strength of three officers and 153 NCOs and soldiers). Also used were civil contractors or sometimes condemned criminals on hard labour, virtually slave labour. The officers' uniforms were the same as in Denmark,[4] while the sappers wore old infantry uniforms.

But in 1810 Frederik VI, with planning and advice from Prince Frederik of Hessen, reorganised a large portion of the Norwegian army, who were converted into *skarpskytte* (light infantry battalions), and they were all to be clad in grey (although in a lighter grey colour than at first planned), as the light grey cloth supplied to Norway for the production of long grey overcoats was used for the new uniforms instead. Black belts were also issued. At this time larger quantities of grey cloth were available, and for better prices, and the Danish light infantry had also changed into grey uniforms.

The Royal Military Cadet School (Det Kongelige Norske Landkadet Corps)

The education of future officers in Norway started when King Frederik V decided with the Royal Resolution of 16 December 1750, to create the Free Mathematical School (*Den frie matematiske skole*). It was the first institution offering higher education in Norway, but it did not give an extensive military education. The students were recruited from the officer corps or from nobles in military service. In 1798 it was named Det Norske Militaire Institut, and from 1804 renamed Det Kongelige Norske Landkadet Corps. It was reorganised, and from then on the school focused on training future officers and became an independent unit with its own command structure.

The basic staff consisted of a school headmaster/commander (*leder*). In theory this was General Frederik von Haxthausen, but he was absent in Denmark for most of the period. He was assisted in his duties by three full-time staff officers. He was eventually replaced by Oberst Diderik Hegermann.[5] Uniforms were only for officers of the school staff. Ordinary teachers, at the school were not given a uniform, but used their normal service uniforms or civilian dress in the classroom. Other members of the staff included two drummers.

The teaching staff in 1813–1814 consisted of von Hegermann himself, four other regular officers, one *auditør* (military judge advocate) and five civilian teachers. To this must be added four so-called *repetent(er)* (cadet teacher(s)), the best cadets of the senior class, who were chosen to teach the junior cadet classes. Strangely, there are none included in the list of 1814, but this is probably because they were counted among the cadets. However on the list from 1809 there are four *repetenter*, all with the rank of second lieutenant. Several future well-known Norwegian officers (Schleppegrell, Rye and Helgesen), had their basic schooling here.[6] Some even joined their regiments earlier than usual.[7]

---

4 For a full description see David Wilson, *The Danish Army of the Napoleonic Wars 1801–1814 Volume 2: Cavalry and Artillery*.

5 Oberst Diderik Hegermann (1763–1835). This officer had a deep interest in improving the teaching of cadets in both Denmark and Norway and in 1802 he became *Direktør* (schoolmaster). When the school was renamed Det Kongelige Norske Landkadet Corps and in 1805 he was elected a member of a commission to improve teaching. He was made Leder (school commander) of the Det Kongelige Norske Landkadet Corps in March 1814.

6 The famous Olaf Rye of Telemark and his two lifetime friends and comrades-in-arms, Frederic Adolf Schleppergrell and Hans Helgesen show what kind of boys, later men, these officers were. Two of these extraordinary men became generals, one a colonel. Olaf Rye, together with his two friends fought courageously in 1814, and he is also officially credited with inventing ski jumping. He, like his two fellow officers, took service as officers in the Danish army after 1814. He was, with the rank of major general, killed in action on 6 July 1849 at the battle of Frederica, while leading a successful charge on foot. Frederic Adolf Schleppergrell, who also later became a major general was probably the most able commanding officer of all three, was also killed in action while leading a cavalry charge in 1850 at the Battle of Istedt on 25 July 1850. During the same war Hans Helgesen became a national hero, after his successful performance, at the siege of Friedrichstadt in 1850, and he was made a colonel. His last wish was to be buried beside his best friend Schleppergrell at the cemetery of Flensburg.

7 It is a myth that the cadets went straight into action as mere 15–16-year-old boys, straight from the Kongelige Norske Landkadet Corps. As was normal for the youngest officers in a regiment, they had to do some basic regimental training first before going into action. So during their first months as officers they spent their time mainly drilling recruits, performing guard and coastguard duties, or guarding Swedish prisoners. There they learned their trade, and all

Uniforms

Until 1813, most of the uniforms and other equipment, were received from Denmark, but from 1808, several items, had to be found and produced in Norway to. This naturally, had some influence on the uniforms worn.

In 1804 the school staff wore a black bicorn with a white plume, black cockade with a loop, button and tassels. Their double-breasted long-tailed coat was made in a special poppy red, but they were allowed to use carmine-coloured coats as well. It had a medium blue collar, square cuffs and lining. The turnbacks and lining and the piping were straw yellow. The buttons, epaulettes and embroidery were gold. They had a double-breasted straw yellow waistcoat and yellow breeches (*bukser*) and black hussar boots. They were armed with a sabre carried on a black leather belt and slings with a rectangular buckle. This uniform was the full-dress version and only worn by the director and senior officers. The service dress was the same but with blue breeches.

The cadets' uniform in 1804 consisted of a black hat with a white plume on the side, black cockade with a loop and a brass button. Their double-breasted short-tailed coat was red, and it had a blue collar and square cuffs with gold embroidery and straw yellow lining. The turnbacks and the piping was straw yellow. The buttons were brass. They had a double-breasted straw yellow waistcoat and blue breeches (*bukser*) and black hussar boots. They carried a cadet sabre on a thin black leather shoulder belt with an oval brass plate bearing the crown cypher of Christian VII. They appear to have continued to wear this uniform until the new grey uniforms were issued. Until 1811–1812, the cadets did not wear rank distinctions, but from there on they first adopted simple gold cloth epaulettes with a blue stripe down the centre to show which class they belonged to. The epaulettes of first year cadets had short fringes, second year cadets had medium length fringes and third year cadet students had standard length fringes. This was changed in 1814 at the latest to simple buttons worn over the new cuffs.

Although accurate information concerning their armaments is scarce, it is thought that originally they carried the *Landkadetsabel* M1761 and this was replaced by the *Landkadetsabel* M1789 which was in service in 1804.[8] Probably around 100 of these weapons were received from Denmark and continued to be used until 1806. In turn they were replaced by the *Landkadetsabel* M1802, 72 of which were delivered in 1804 and another 30 sabres in 1805.[9]

After the start of the war in 1807 and the difficulties in ordering and receiving officer's sabres from Denmark, the newly qualified cadet officers were given stored cavalry *pallasker* (broadswords) from the arsenals, which sometimes would have seemed ridiculously large compared to their small size of the cadets for their first weapon, until they could acquire the correct weapon for their arm of service.[10]

When army cadets graduated from the Det Kongelige Norske Landkadet Corps, they were able to buy their first officers sabre with help from the school, but from 1808 this was often difficult and often non-standard sidearms were used. It is possible that a few even may have been allowed to buy some of the surplus *Landkadetsabel* M1802 or the older *Landkadetsabel* M1789.

The cadets received 110 of the M1809 cadet shakos in April 1810 and two shakos for the school's service drummers. The plume, cockade and loop came from their old hats. It also had a brass shako plate with a silver Norwegian lion on it.[11]

The uniforms which were made from after the original pattern proof model from 1804, but it also followed the new style, with a higher collar and higher waistline from 1810. It was normally referred to as *Søndagsmundring* (Sunday dress/full dress), as it was reserved for church parades on Sundays, but also all other type of parades or formal service. The blue appears to have become lighter in hue.

Already in 1808–1809, there had already been problems getting supplies of red cloth for their coats and blue cloth for their trousers from Denmark. Also the new shakos were very expensive to make. So already on 20 August 1810, grey *kirsey* (kersey cloth) was ordered for the production of the *Hverdagstrøjer* ordinary service uniform,[12] which could be worn for the daily schooling and training. Also simple grey trousers were worn, and

---

three excelled in 1814. The same was true of the other young cadets and that is why only one was killed in action between 1808–1809.

8   It is also recognisable on the paper-cut portrait of Officer Cadet Bernt Magnus Kinck, made in 1805.

9   *Hærens Blankvåben på Napoleonskrigens*: Niels M. Saxtorp. Note 46, p.43.

10 The young cadet Jens Christian Schrøder, who was born in 1796 and entered the academy in 1808 when he was 12 years old, says in his memoires: 'The cadets of 4th and 5th Class (16 and 17+ years) were sent to the regiments. I remember that they could not equip themselves as officers, as there was nothing to buy, and that they had to be given large cavalry dragoon *pallasker* (dragoon straight swords) from the arsenal'.

11 A *Kongelig Resolution* approved the plate on 23 July 1809, but in the same document it is stated, that the shield was to have the opposite colours as those shown on the drawing! It states: '… that the plate will be in the colour of the buttons and the arms (Norwegian Lion), in silver upon …'

12 According to information from the FMU archive, found in *Kongens Klæder*, Karsten Skjold Petersen p.582, note 86. Here it is also noted that on 13 March 1813 'new blue collars, blue inside lining and cuffs, all with gold embroidery, were sent from Denmark'. Probably the cuffs were of the new pointed style model, introduced from 1812. The same collar and cuffs were reused on the new M1814 grey *Søndagsmundring* (Sunday dress) uniform.

a simple black leather cap was also issued for ordinary class wear. Furthermore, in May 1811, they requested 100 ordinary soldier's hats to also be used together with the ordinary service uniform, to save the shakos for parades or formal service. In 1813, they instead received *læder cachets* (caps made of black leather), probably of the same model as that used by the levy battalions. In 1811 they received 20 black lacquered cross belts, with a bayonet attachment and another with ammunition pouch and shield. These were probably for drill and guard duties. The shade of the grey of the coats was darker than that of the trousers. The dress version of the trousers (in fact they were in fact closer to cavalry overalls), had two light blue welts down the outside leg.

Uniforms in 1814

Already by 1811–1813 there had been problems getting the correct red uniform coats and other materials from Denmark. With the ties cut from January 1814, delivery from Denmark became impossible. As stocks ran out, the schoolmaster Diderik von Hegermann made plans for the adoption of new locally made grey uniforms, and also forwarded drawings to the new King, Christian Frederik, for approval. These uniforms were approved by him.[13]

These were full dress uniforms, for wear by the schoolmaster and the three staff officers. They were grey single-breasted tailed coats, with light blue collars and cuffs, with the former officer s gold embroidery on them. The coat had tails with buff turnbacks and yellow buttons. They were worn with buff breeches, and short cavalry-style boots.

For service wear, the schoolmaster, the three staff officers and also the four *repetenter*, were allowed a simple uniform in grey with light blue collars and cuffs which had simple square gold embroidery on them. The coat had tails with buff turnbacks and yellow buttons. They were worn with grey *pantalongs* (pantaloons) with double light blue welts down the sides, worn over the boots.

The cadets were allowed basically the same uniform (but only as *Søndagsmundring*), but their coats were in the style of coatees, with light blue turn-ups at the front.

The Academy Colour

The Academy had a colour which was principally carried on formal parades. Its dimension was, more or less, 132 cm square. It was based on a M1785 regimental colour (*Dannebrogsfane*) which bore the crowned arms of the kingdom complete with the wild man supporters and collars of the Order of the Dannebrog and Order of the Elephant in the centre, in each corner there was a gold crown and the King's monogram CVII within green laurel wreaths. The obverse and reverse were identical.

The remains of the original colour of Det Norske Militære Institute (the Military Academy) is conserved in the Forsvarets museum in Oslo. It was made after a drawing approved on 28 August 1801. It was slightly different to the colour of the Danish school in several details (*Krigskolens fane FMU*[14]).

---

13 During his very short reign in Norway, Christian August only approved one known uniform drawing, and it was for these uniforms.

3

The Norwegian Line Infantry: Organisation

The Norwegian army was based on a foundation laid down on 18 February 1628, where it was established that the army should be built on a system called *legdsinndeling*. This system specified that a number of farms would be grouped together to supply a soldier for military service, and to pay for and supply some of his equipment. They would serve alongside the *geworbne* (enlisted) as *Nationale* (conscripted) and when their first eight-year period of service was completed they would continue to serve further in the *Landeværnet* as a reserve and local defence force.

Up to 1789 there had been 13 infantry regiments, these being:

1st Akershusiske Nationale Infanteri Regiment
2nd Akershusiske Nationale Infanteri Regiment
1st Trondhjemske Nationale Infanteri Regiment
2nd Trondhjemske Nationale Infanteri Regiment
3rd Trondhjemske Nationale Infanteri Regiment (disbanded in 1789)
1st Smaalehnske Nationale Infanteri Regiment (disbanded in 1789)
2nd Smaalehnske Nationale Infanteri Regiment (disbanded in 1789)
1st Oplandske Nationale Infanteri Regiment.
2nd Oplandske Nationale Infanteri Regiment (disbanded in 1789)
1st Bergenhusiske Nationale Infanteri Regiment
2nd Bergenhusiske Nationale Infanteri Regiment (disbanded in 1789)
1st Westerlehnske Infanteri Regiment
2nd Westerlehnske Infanteri Regiment (disbanded in 1789)

The Norwegian army underwent two major reforms and several minor ones during the period 1785–1813 and these can appear somewhat confusing. Even the chief of staff of the Norwegian general staff von Sejersted was so frustrated by the enormous amount work facing him and his staff to make the army ready for war in 1814 that he wrote on 3 September 1814, to the Norwegian War Commission: 'The greatest and most significant shortcoming is, in my mind, to look at the Army's organisation to date; for here you need more than human power to sort out this Chaos'.

But in many ways, in such a geographically large area, with a very dispersed population, hampered by the very lay of the land, where nearly 90 percent of the population were peasants, where tradition, religion, finance and often hard conditions prevailed, much of the systems were sound and basically the best options found from experience. But most importantly, many of the system's shortcomings were overcome by the fact that this formed together soldiers willing to defend their homeland and created a will and pride in being a soldier.

In a letter to King Frederik VI from Prince Frederik of Hessen, Christiania (Oslo), 22 December 1811 he wrote:

> But I can assure that I know no nation that can be so hastily trained into a soldier than the Norwegians, as every Norwegian seems to have been born a soldier, and have myself this year, had the personal experience, that National companies, who had only exercised for 12 days and even had their new recruits, as part of the companies, were as good, in all parts of the drill, as the best Geworbne companies could be.

From 1785 several reforms had begun in the army, and these had been completed by 1789, and these were essentially those used until 1810. Although technically these reforms were like those which were carried out in Denmark, there were however a number of local differences. The outcome of these reforms was some regiments were disbanded or amalgamated and new regiments were formed. Their strengths were altered, and a number of battalions and companies were either used to create the new regiments or transferred into the existing ones.

The infantry regiments of the Norwegian army formed two enlisted or semi-regular regiments (*geworbne infanteri regimenter*), with each two Nationale battalions attached had the following strength:

The two *geworbne* regiments had a total of 1,600 *geworbne,* 2,400 Nationale and 1,200 Landeværn soldiers.

In peacetime the *geworbne* battalions each had eight companies and each company had three officers, seven NCOs, two *tambourer* (drummers) and 80 men, and 80 more soldiers were on leave but could be recalled when needed. Each company had 10 *skarpskyttere* (sharpshooters) A further 80 more *geworbne* were on furlough (*permiterede*), to be recalled when needed.

The *geworbne grenader* companies each had three officers, seven NCOs, two *tambourer*, one *piber* and 80 men. The same number of men were on leave but could be added when needed. Each *grenader* company also had 10 *skarpskyttere*.

A peacetime Nationale battalion in Norway normally had six companies (the 1st battalion of the 2nd Akershusiske and 2nd battalion of the Oplandske only had four companies). The strength of each peacetime company was two officers, five NCOs, two *tambourer,* on *tømmermand* and 76 soldiers. Each company had four *skarpskyttere* as well. Another 50 soldiers who were ex-Landeværn (those soldiers which had served their first eight years of service) could be added when needed.

The eight Nationale *infanteri regimenter* or territorial regiments formed mainly with conscripts and reservists, but with a few *geworbne* companies, originally two *grenader* companies, later converted to one *geworbne jæger* enlisted light company and one *geworbne musketeer liv companie* (enlisted life company). The Nationale regiments had a total of 1,920 *geworbne,* 13,200 Nationale and 6,600 Landeværn troops available.

The Nationale recruits in Norway exercised for only 12 days a year in peacetime in company drill. This was largely because of the great distance between the districts, but also so as not to lay too heavy a burden on the workforce of the peasant society. But every fourth year they had to form into the battalions of their parent regiment, in order to undertake exercises for 16 days on larger manoeuvres.

After a Royal Resolution of 1799, the *legdsinndeling* responsibility to enlist soldiers ceased. This was the consequence of the Danish reform abolishing of the former serf-like institution and the agricultural and military reforms from 1788 (*Stavnsbåndets ophævelse*). From then on the 80–100 recruits were to be enlisted by lot within the district of the company, regardless of residence. By the same resolution to order the recruitment of more men, the age of enlistment was lowered to 20 years.

As the *geworbne grenader* companies of the Nationale regiments had experienced difficulties in enlisting the *geworbne grenaderer*, they were by a Royal Resolution of 10 March 1804, made part of the normal structure of the Nationale regiments and would consequently be conscripted in the same way as the musketeers, but they were to be chosen first, from the ablest, fittest and tallest (minimum height was set as low as 165 cm/5 ft 5 in) recruits available, between the ages of 20 and 22 years. They were to serve for eight years, the first two years performing sentry and other duties in towns and fortresses. The organisation was to be the same, but all Nationale companies, would have three reserves, ready for the *grenaderer*, when needed. They were also in the future to be called *tjenestegørende grenaderer* (serving grenadiers) not *geworbne*.

The following are the peacetime regiments, with their composition and the location of the companies, at the start of the campaign of 1808:

The Søndenfjeldske Geworbne Infanteri Regiment formed in 1789 (garrison: Halden)
It contained the 1st and 2nd company of the Geworbene Søndenfjeldske Grenaderer
A *geworben* battalion of eight companies of *geworbne* musketeers
1st Nationale Bataljon, of six companies: Skjeberg, Berg, Idd, Nordre Rakkestad, Marker, Vestre Rakkestad
2nd Nationale Bataljon, of six companies: Tune, Hobøl, Onsø, Skibtvedt, Rygge, Borge

The Nordenfjeldske Geworbne Infanteri Regiment formed in 1789 (garrison: Frederikstad)
The 1st and 2nd companies of the Geworbne Nordenfjeldske Grenaderer
A *geworben* battalion of eight companies composed of *geworbne* musketeers
1st Nationale Bataljon, of six companies: Hurum, Lier, Aker, Hougsund, Asker, Skedsmo
2nd Nationale Bataljon, of six companies: Søndre Follo, Trøgstad, Eidsberg, Enebakk, Høland, Nordre Follo

The 1st Akershusiske Nationale Infanteri Regiment (garrison: Frederikstad)
The 1st and 2nd companies of the Tjenestegørende 1st Akershusiske Grenaderer
1st Nationale Bataljon of six companies: Sigdal, Hadeland, Modum, Ytre Hallingdal, Ringerike, Østre
2nd Nationale Bataljon of six companies: Land, Midtre Valdres, Eidsvold, Ytre Valdres, Toten, Østre Valdres

Norwegian Line Infantry Uniforms (I), 1803–1810

THE NORWEGIAN LINE INFANTRY: ORGANISATION

Facing page
Plate 3. Norwegian Line Infantry Uniforms I, 1803–1810

The grenadiers and musketeers are mainly shown wearing the M1799 coat, white cloth knee-length M1789 breeches and black gaiters. Most musketeers wear the M1797 hat, a rather low top hat with a fairly flat brim. It was worn by the men until c. 1810. The M1802 hat was worn by the musketeers of the *geworbne* regiments and by most NCOs as they had shorter clothing terms and received their uniforms from Denmark more often. The grenadiers originally wore the M1789 grenadier hat, which had two wide cloth *flyers* in the facing colour on the top of the hat.

1. Officer of musketeers or *grenaders* 1st Trondhjemske Nationale Infanteri Regiment. The *grenader* officers did not wear grenadier caps and are shown here wearing an M1804 officer's hat, with M1806 cords. As far as we know, officers at first did not have blue tips to their plumes, but some, at least from 1809, did adopt blue tops.
2. *Grenader*, 2nd Akershusiske Nationale Infanteri Regiment
3. *Grenader*, Bergenhusiske Nationale Infanteri Regiment. He wears blue gaiter trousers, which the two *geworbne* regiments received from Denmark, so were allowed to use them. He is seen from the rear in full marching order with a cowskin knapsack (hairy side out) slung over one shoulder, copper canteen and bread-bag.
4. Sergeant of grenadiers, Westerlenske Nationale Infanteri Regiment. Note that sergeants had two M1769 epaulettes. He is armed with an M1769 *Korsgevær for underofficer*/NCO partisan, today generally known as a *Lilje*/lily, after the form of the blade.
5. *Løjtnant* of 1st Trondhjemske Grenaderbataillon 1809. After a self portrait made by *Løjtnant* C. A. F. T. von Tischendorff in 1809. Note his new M1808 shako worn with old model cords. He has added a blue tip to his new plume.
6. Officer of sharpshooters, 1st Akershusiske Infanteri Regiment, wearing M1806 hat
7. Sharpshooters, Bergenhusiske Nationale Infanteri Regiment, wearing white gaiter trousers and wearing an M1797 hat
8. *Sergent* of musketeers, 2nd Trondhjemske Nationale Infanteri Regiment, wearing an M1802 hat. He is armed with an M1725 *Korsgevær for Underofficerer*/NCO's halberd. This was model was still used in Norway, mainly by some of the Nationale regiments.
9. *Tamboure* of musketeers, Oplandske Infanteri Regiment, with a brass drum, but a painted wooden model was just as common. The drum's rims are painted blue, designating the reign of Christian VII.
10. Musketeer, Telemarkske Nationale Infanteri Regiment

The 2nd Akershusiske Nationale Infanteri Regiment (garrison: Aggershus in Oslo)
The 1st and 2nd companies of the Tjenestegørende, 2nd Akershusiske Grenaderer
1st Nationale Bataljon, four companies: Eker, Laurdal, Kongsberg, Numedal
2nd Nationale Bataljon, six companies: Vestre Laurvig, Vestre Jarlsberg, Nordre Laurvig, Østre Jarlsberg, Søndre Jarlsberg, Østre Laurvig

The Oplandske Nationale Infanteri Regiment (garrison: Kongsvinger)
The 1st and 2nd companies of the Tjenestegørende Oplandske Grenaderer
1st Nationale Bataljon, of six companies: Stange, Vestre Hedmark, Nordre Hedmark, Løiten, Vang, Gausdal
2nd Nationale Bataljon, of four companies: Ringebu, Fron, Kvam, Vågå, Lesja

The Westerlehnske Nationale Infanteri Regiment (garrison: Kristiansand)
The 1st and 2nd companies of the Tjenestegørende Westerlehnske Grenaderer
1st Nationale Bataljon, six companies: 1st Mandal, 2nd Mandal, 1st Råbygdelag, 2nd Råbygdelag, 2nd Nedenes, 3rd Nedenes
2nd Nationale Bataljon, six companies: 1st Stavanger, 2nd Stavanger, 1st Lister, 2nd Lister, 3rd Lister, 4th Lister
3rd Nationale Bataljon, six companies: Erna, 3rd Stavanger, 1st Ryfylke, 2nd Ryfylke, 3rd Ryfylke, Skånevig

The Telemarkske Nationale Infanteri Regiment formed in 1789 (garrison: Frederiksværn)
The 1st and 2nd companies of the Tjenestegørende Telemarkske Grenaderer
1st Nationale Bataljon, six companies: Hitterdal, Gierpen, Hierdal, Eidanger, Bøherred, Tinn

Norwegian Line Infantry II, NCOs' Halberds 1803–1810

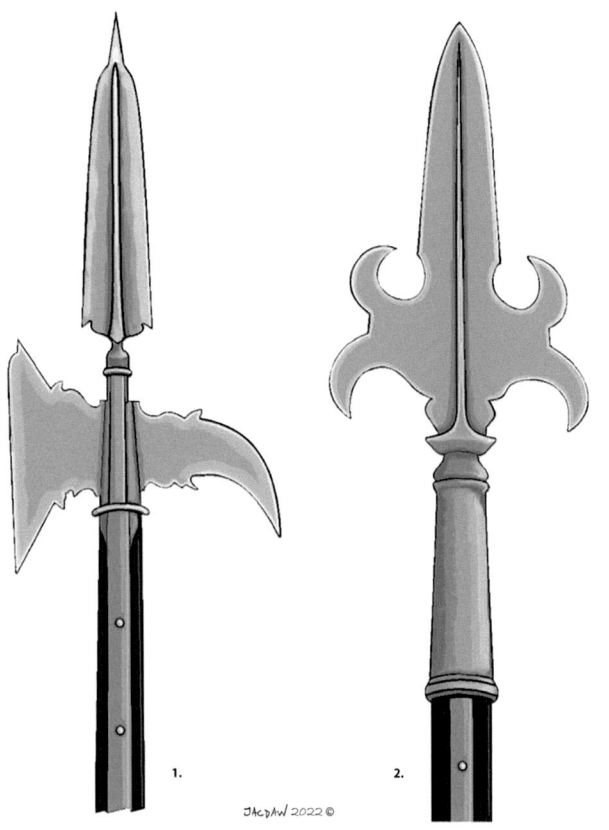

Plate 4. Norwegian Line Infantry II NCOs' Halberds 1803–1810

Due to a shortage of suitable muskets, line infantry NCOs (*sergenter* and *corporaler*) continued to carry halberds and partisans until 1808/1810, when enough light infantry muskets became available

1. Halberd M1725 *Korsgevær for Underofficerer*, a more rustic polearm made for combat with steel runners for attachment to the two-metre haft. The tip was probably ground to a point at this time.

2. The M1769 *Korsgevær for Underofficer* generally referred to as a *Lilje* (lily), a more modern arm. They were used as in the British army, not so much intended to fight with, but as a clear indication of where the NCOs were placed, and most importantly to be used to physically to dress the lines, so the soldiers stood correctly aligned.

To differentiate the *sergenter* from the *corporaler*, as in the collection in the Defence Museum, Rustkammeret, Trondheim, there appear to be two different lengths to the hafts. Generally the wood used would have been ash (*asketræ/asketre*).

2nd Nationale Bataljon, six companies: Nordre Telemark, 1st Vestfield, 2nd Vestfield, 3rd Vestfield, 1st Nedenes, Bamle

The Bergenhusiske Nationale Infanteri Regiment, formed in 1789 (garrison: Bergen)
The 1st and 2nd companies of the Tjenestegørende Bergenhusiske Grenaderer
Bergenske Nationale Bataljon, six companies: Søndre søndhordlen, Nordhordlen, Søndre Nordhordlen, Opdal, Nordre Nordhordlen, Nordre Søndhordlen
Vossiske Nationale Bataljon, six companies: Nordre Hardanger, Voss, Midtre Nordhordlen, Urland, Søndre Hardanger, Tiugum
Sognske Nationale Bataljonn, seven companies including a light company: Sogndal, Nordre Søndfjord, Søndre Søndfjord, Ytre Sogn, Vig, Lyster, Lærdalske (light company)
Nordfjordske Nationale Bataljon, six companies: Nordre Søndmør, Søndre Nordmør, Gloppen, Søndre Søndfjord, Nordre Nordfjord, Stryn

The 1st (Nordre) Trondhjemske Nationale Infanteri Regiment (garrison: Trondhjem)
The 1st and 2nd companies of the Tjenestegørende 1st Trondhjemske Grenaderer
1st Nationale Bataljon, six companies: Overhalden, Fosnes, Beitstad, Sparbu, Stod, Nærø
2nd Nationale Bataljon, six companies: Skogn, Stjørdal, Ytterøen, Værdal, Frosta, Inderøy
3rd Nationale Bataljon, six companies: Ritsen, Melhus, Strinden, Stadsbygd, Selbu, Biørnør.
Nordenfieldske Skiløberbataljon, which consisted of three companies: Snåsa, Haltålen, Meråker

The 2nd (Søndre) Trondhjemske Nationale Infanteri Regiment (garrison: Trondhjem)
The 1st and 2nd companies of the Tjenestegørende 2nd Trondhjemske Grenaderer
1st Nationale Bataljon, six companies: Gimnes, Havne, Meldal, Surendal, Brøske, Vig
2nd Nationale Bataljon, six companies: Buvik, Børsen, Rennebu, Ørkedal, Støren, Opdal
3rd Nationale Bataljon, six companies: Sundal, Vestnes, Eresfjord, Fanoting, Gagnat, Romsdal

Each *geworbne/tjenestegørende grenader* company had a field strength of *c.* 150–180 *grenaders*
Each Nationale musketeer company had a field strength of *c.* 120–160 soldiers
Each Nationale light/*skiløber* company had a field strength of *c.* 100–120 soldiers

In peacetime however the regiments, companies and battalions of both the *geworbne* and Nationale battalions were purely administrative formations. On mobilisation, they were totally reorganised into two field battalions for each *geworbne* regiment and normally just one field battalion for each Nationale regiment (normally the first battalion). These field battalions were formed by each peacetime company, forming a new field company with a strength of 75 soldiers, chosen from the youngest, fittest and preferably unmarried men, often from several companies. Two such companies were merged into what were called divisions. Field battalions were to consist of four such divisions.

The rest of the regiment were organised into a depot battalion and a Landeværn battalion, which were used to enlist and supply new manpower, to defend the arsenals/fortresses and for local defence. The *geworbne* regiments (grenadiers included) and the *tjenestegørende grenader* companies were normally raised the quickest, while the ordinary Nationale field battalions, were not ready immediately as the companies took some time to gather because of the great distances within the company/battalion district. They were then amalgamated and reformed, as all of the peacetime companies were not of equal strength, and men who were not fit for service in the field were discharged. When they were ready, they were grouped into all-arms brigades (or battlegroups). The brigade commander took over the direct leadership of the different field battalions, both administratively and more importantly, tactically. This was a uniquely Norwegian practice.

Each field division (including the *grenaderer*) had a detachment of 12 *skarpskyttere*, led by an NCO who were normally combined with those of the other companies to form a separate sharpshooters' detachment (48–72 men) under an officer and a *hornblæser* (hornist), often detached from their parent regiment.

The strength of a field battalion in 1788 was set at approximately 480 soldiers. In 1808 the strength of a field battalion was increased to 600 soldiers, by adding reserves and new recruits.

The strength of a field battalion was again increased in 1809 to 700–800 soldiers, by adding even more reserves and new recruits.

This general enlargement in time of war was in particular applied to the *tjenestegørende grenader* companies, as they did most of the real fighting between 1808–1809, mainly assisted by the different light infantry companies (see later).

Each field battalion was further reinforced by two 1-pdr guns (*amusettes*) served by trained soldiers of the regiment as battalion artillery. Also, each battalion had an ammunition and supply train. They had either 10 single-horse wagons or five two-horse wagons. The officers had five two-horse wagons for their luggage. A further carriage was for the battalion surgeon and there was a two-horse gunsmith cart.

In winter a number of supply and ammunition sledges were used. In total, there should have been 38 draft horses per battalion and 17 for the ski battalions.

The *Geworbne* Grenadiers, from 1804–1810 called *Tjenestegørende Grenaderer*

If all these different regional organisations were not confusing enough, we now need to look at the details of the enlisted companies and the grenadiers. Only the best most physically fittest, tallest and ablest recruits of the Nationale/territorial regiments could be enlisted as *grenaderer*. They had to perform more service (but were not full-time soldiers like a real regular), which included more sentry duty and formal training, than the ordinary Nationale musketeers, but this also resulted in some extra pay and privileges (such as being ranked as NCOs, in Nationale regiments and better local community jobs).

One of the main functions they had in times of peace was to help the soldiers of the *geworbne* regiments guard the fortresses, harbours, depots, prisons and main cities, and also to perform some police duties. This was done mainly in their local districts or garrison towns and cities. In war they were the first to serve, and as a consequence did most of the fighting in 1808–1809.

Field strengths 1800–1810 of the *geworbne* or *tjenestegørende grenader* field battalions:

> Four *grenader* battalions could be raised for field service, in the Søndenfjeldske (Southern Division).[1]
>
> 1st Grenader Bataljon. Two companies from Søndenfjeldske Geworbne Infanteri Regiment; two companies from Nordenfjeldske [Northern Division] Geworbne Infanteri Regiment. Total strength 600 grenadiers.
>
> 2nd Grenader Bataljon. Two companies from 1st Akershusiske Nationale Infanteri Regiment; two

---

[1] Until 20 January 1808 the Norwegian army was divided into three commands; the Søndenfjeldske General Kommando, Bergenhusiske General Kommando and the Nordenfjeldske General Kommando. After this date the army was divided into two divisions instead: Den Søndenfjeldske Division or 1st Division and Den Nordenfjeldske Division or 2nd Division. This took full effect from January 1809 and remained the formal organisation until after 1814. This was because, as already stated, Norway was divided in two by a mountain range, and the course of major rivers. The southern part was commanded from the main city of Christiana, now called Oslo, and the northern part commanded from the city of Trondheim. The Nordenfjeldske Division was more or less an independent command.

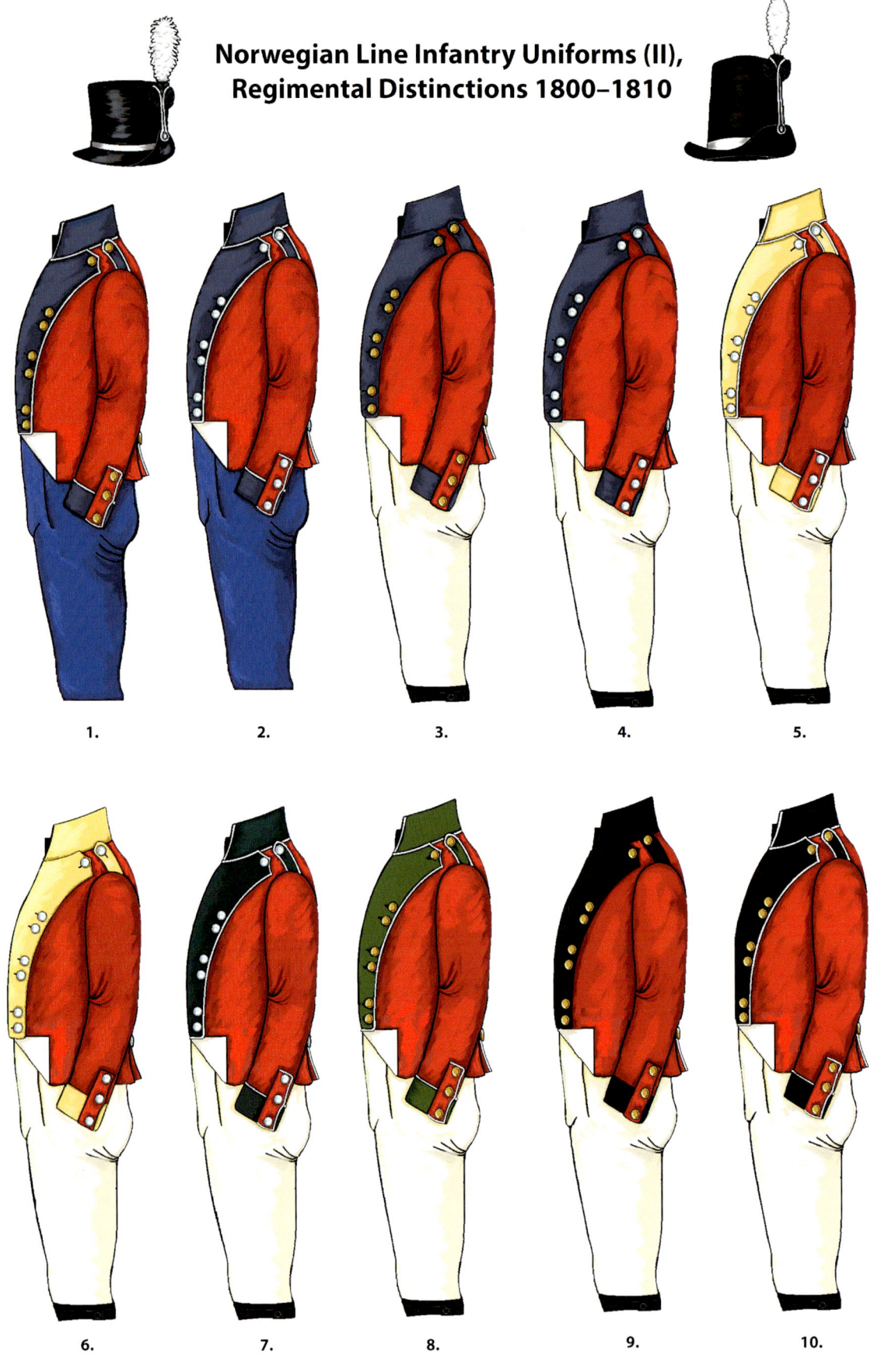

THE NORWEGIAN LINE INFANTRY: ORGANISATION

> Facing page
> Plate 5. Norwegian Line Infantry II, Regimental Distinctions 1800–1810
>
> The men are mainly shown wearing the M1795 coat, white cloth knee-length M1789 breeches (*bukser*) and black gaiters. Most wear the M1797 hat, a rather low top hat with a fairly flat brim. It was worn by the men until *c*. 1810. Inset, on the right the M1802 hat was worn by the musketeers of the *geworbne* regiments and by most NCOs, as they had shorter clothing replacement terms and received their uniforms direct from Denmark.
>
> Only the two *geworbne* regiments are known to have received the new blue trousers. Note that while many illustrations show this shade of blue, contemporary cloth samples show a much darker shade.
>
> 1. Søndenfjeldske Geworbne Infanteri Regiment
> 2. Nordenfjeldske Geworbne Infanteri Regiment
> 3. 1st Akershusiske Nationale Infanteri Regiment, disbanded 1810 and converted into the Akershusiske Skarpskytter Regiment
> 4. 2nd Akershusiske Nationale Infanteri Regiment, disbanded 1810 and converted into the Akershusiske Skarpskytter Regiment
> 5. 1st Trondhjemske Nationale Infanteri Regiment
> 6. 2nd Trondhjemske Nationale Infanteri Regiment
> 7. Oplandske Nationale Infanteri Regiment
> 8. Telemarkske Nationale Infanteri Regiment
> 9. Bergenhusiske Nationale Infanteri Regiment
> 10. Westerlehnske Nationale Infanteri Regiment. In 1809 the regiment changed its facings to green with brass buttons.

companies from Oplandske Nationale Infanteri Regiment. Total strength 600 grenadiers.

3rd Grenader Bataljon. Two companies from 2nd Akershusiske Infanteri Regiment; two companies from Telemarkske Nationale Infanteri Regiment. Total strength 600 *grenaders*.

4th Grenader Bataljon.[2] Two companies from Westerlehnske Nationale Infanteri Regiment; two companies from Bergenhusiske Nationale Infanteri Regiment. Total strength 600 grenadiers.

One battalion was raised in the Nordenfjeldske (Northern Division), but did serve in the south. 5th Grenader Bataljon. Two *grenader* companies from 1st Trondhjemske Nationale Infanteri Regiment; two *grenader* companies from 2nd Trondhjemske Nationale Infanteri Regiment. Total strength 600 men.

In 1809 the organisation was changed again, and the number of battalions now rose to seven. This was done by enlisting new *grenaderer*, and other able reserves, from the parent regiments:

'Søndenfjeldske Gew. Regmt's. Grenaderbataillon Major v. Kjøbing), 16 officers and 600 grenadiers

Nordenfjeldske Gew. Inf. Regmt's. Grenaderbataillon (Major v. Stielau), 17 officers and 622 grenadiers

1st Akershusiske of Oplandske Regmt's Grenaderbataillon (Oberstløjtnant v. Muller), 13 officers and 810 grenadiers.

2nd Akershusiske og Telemarkske Nat. Regmt's, Oberstløjtnant v. Hegermann, 14 officers and 812 grenadiers

Bergenhusiske og Westerlehnske Nat. Regmt's Grenaderbataillon (Oberstløjtnant v. Synnestved), 16 officers and 512 grenadiers

---

2 Technically this battalion was part of the Bergenhusiske General Commando until January 1809.

1st Trondhjemske Nationale/Regmet`s. grenader Bataillon (Major v. Sommerschild), 17 officers and 656 grenadiers

2nd Trondhjemske Nationale/Regmt's Grenader Bataillon (Kapitajn Stang), 17 officers and 656 grenadiers'

Tactics
Most fighting in Norway was carried out in small formations as the 1788 infantry regulations, with latter additions, allowed, and often in two ranks, because of the normally close and difficult terrain, As a consequence, the normal fighting formation, in 1807–1809, was a first line of two war divisions deployed side by side, or in closed terrain one behind the other. They would be formed in three ranks, but as the *skarpskyttere* would normally have already been detached the third rank was sent forward as skirmishers, in accordance with the 1788 (and later) tactical regulations. They would normally be supported by a second line, formed by another two war divisions, formed in three ranks. Most of the fighting was carried out in battalion or brigade-sized formations at most. All fighting employed linear formations, never in column tactics.

4

The Norwegian Line Infantry: Uniforms

Table 1. Norwegian Infantry Regiments Pre-1810				
Regimental Name	Facings, Shoulder Straps and Piping	Hat Band	Button Colour	Particularities
Søndenfjeldskeke Gevorbne Infanteri Regiment	Dark blue/white	Yellow	Brass	They were classed as enlisted because compared to other regiments they had more enlisted men than conscripts.
Nordenfjeldske/ke Gevorbne Infanteri Regiment	Dark blue/white	White	White metal	
1st Akershusiske Nationale Infanteri Regiment	Dark blue	Yellow	Brass	Became the Akershusiske Nationale Skarpskytte Regiment in 1810
2nd Akershusiske Nationale Infanteri Regiment	Dark blue	White	White metal	Became the Akershusiske Nationale Skarpskytte Regiment in 1810
Oplandske Nationale Infanteri Regiment	Grass green/white	White	White metal	Became an enlisted or *geworben* regiment from 1810
Telemarkske Nationale Infanteri Regiment	Grass green/white	Yellow	Brass	
1st Trondhjemske Nationale Infanteri Regiment	Straw yellow/ white	White	White metal	
2nd Trondhjemske Nationale Infanteri Regiment	Straw yellow	White	White metal	
Westerlehnske Nationale Infanteri Regiment	Black/white	Yellow	Brass	
Bergenhusiske Nationale Infanteri Regiment	Black	Yellow	Brass	

Uniform Supplies

All their uniforms were made in Denmark, both for economic and practical reasons.[1] To understand the uniforms used in Norway, one should note that there were two systems of clothing issues (terms), one for the *geworbne* (enlisted) companies, which included all the grenadier companies and the musketeer companies of the two *geworbne* regiments and their uniform issues were normally for the same terms as in Denmark. But the Nationale regiments had much longer terms on most of their clothing. This has led to the long-term myth, that Denmark did not care for the Norwegian soldiers, purely out of financial reasons.

But this is not true, as this was seen as a very practical way to control the issue of clothing both in Denmark and Norway. The Nationale recruits in Norway were only exercised 12 days a year in company drill. This was because of the great distance between the districts, but also not to lay a too heavy a burden on the workforce of the agricultural society and the local economy. Only every fourth year did they have to form into the battalions of their parent regiment, in order to be exercised for 16 days on larger-scale manoeuvres. In time of war, as explained previously, until 1810, only one battalion was formed for actual field service (two in 1811–1814). So, in light of this arrangement it is much easier to understand that the Nationale soldiers in Norway had rather long terms between the issuing of new uniforms, as they were not used much, except for every fourth year and only for 16 days

---

1 Before 1808 Norway did not have a large cloth industry or the capacity to make uniforms on a large, centralised scale. But by necessity and with a massive drive and voluntary spirit they quickly managed to create a large and capable inland centre for uniform and equipment production 1808–1814, an impressive tour de force.

and maybe some few parades, and naturally in wartime. Normally the newest uniforms were, in peacetime, stored in the local arsenals and only taken out when absolutely needed. For the annual 12 days exercise/drill and for the drilling of raw recruits stocks of surplus older uniforms were used. After the normal eight years of service, when they were transferred into the Landeværn, sometimes they were given a full old uniform to keep and maintain, to be used in times of war. But these were older surplus uniforms, which were kept in the arsenals for years after they were needed or were from disbanded regiments. In these circumstances it is easier to understand the long clothing terms and deliveries of uniforms. The only risk was damp and fire, so correctly stored uniforms could last for a very long time.

All this would of course change during wartime, when the hard and constant wear and tear on uniforms, already rather old, would clearly not help them last for long, which was very much the case in 1808–1809.

Everything had to be shipped from Denmark and then stored in the *Norske Munderingsdepot* (Central Norwegian Uniform Arsenal) before distribution. From here they were shipped on to each regimental store or to arsenals. All the uniforms and equipment of the Nationale regiments were kept locally, in a *telthus* regimental arsenal, together with tents, knapsacks and bread-bags etc. From 1802 they would also store the two regimental 1-pdr artillery pieces with two ammunition wagons. All extra equipment and arms were kept in the fortress arsenals together with the field equipment like axes, canteens, pots, pans as well as transport wagons, transport saddles and harnesses.

A very important fact concerning the Norwegian regiments' uniforms, is that in 1769 a decision was made that, from then on, each Danish army regiment would be twinned with a Norwegian army regiment, and both were to wear the same uniforms with the same facings. This meant that each regiment in Norway should have a parent regiment in Denmark, who wore a uniform with the same regimental facings, although this was slightly modified again from 1789.

Below is the list of Danish parent regiments, followed by their adopted Norwegian regiments (some changed their names during the period or were amalgamated):

Holstenske (1785 Viborgske, disbanded in 1789) Infanteri Regiment – 1st Akershusiske Regiment (reformed in 1810)

Danske Livregiment – 2nd Akershusiske Regiment (reformed in 1810)

Falsterske Infanteri Regiment (1785: became Aalborgske, which became the 3rd Jyske in 1790) – 1st Smaalehnske Regiment (disbanded 1789)

Kongens (1808: Kronens) Regiment – 2nd Smaalehnske Regiment (disbanded 1789 and was used to form the Telemarkske Regiment in 1789)

Prins Frederiks (1806 Prins Christian Frederiks) Regiment – 1st Trondhjemske Regiment

Norske Livregiment – 2nd Trondhjemske Regiment

Bornholmske (1785: Aarhusiske, who became the 1st Jyske in 1790) – 3rd Trondhjemske Regiment (disbanded in 1789)

Oldenborgske (1785: Sjællandske who became the Kronprinsens Regiment in 1803) 1st Oplandske Regiment

Slesvigske (1785: Riberske, who became 2nd Jyske in 1790) Infanteri Regiment – 2nd Oplandske Regiment (disbanded in 1789)

Mønske (1785 who became the Oldenburgske) Regiment – 1st Bergenhusiske Regiment

Jyske (who became the Fynske Regiment in 1790) Infanteri Regiment – 2nd Bergenhusiske Regiment (disbanded in 1789)

Kronprinsens (1808 Kongens) Infanteri Regiment – 1st Westerlehnske Regiment

Dronningens Livregiment – 2nd Westerlehnske (disbanded in 1789)

This should have made logistics and the application and distribution of new uniforms and equipment much easier in Norway and as well as reusing different Danish regimental distinctions, all of which was very important due to the financial situation. Tactically, it would make it easier to form brigades, and for officers sent to Norway from Denmark lead them into action.

Theoretically the new uniform regulations were easier to apply as the reform was normally carried out by making a proof uniform, generally made in Copenhagen, which, after approval, was then sent to the Danish regiment in question. When the regiment received the proof, it was then given to the regimental tailors to apply the modifications, and then, the same uniform could then be made in Denmark and sent on to Norway to the regiment with whom they were twinned. This guaranteed that the uniforms were only made according to the king's wishes, and that except for minor details, the uniforms were the same in Denmark and Norway.

In practice this meant that Norway (or more precisely the Nationale regiments) was often at least one uniform clothing term behind Denmark, if not more, as we shall see but this was still a major improvement on the previous system, when a uniform change in Norway could take years, with several shipments back and forth of proof uniforms, to agree the correct one.

The most important uniform change and issues in Norway between 1795–1810 that we know of began with the Reform of 1789 (same uniform as in Denmark, but first generally issued in Norway *c*. 1795), with some changes in style. Norway generally followed the same reforms as Denmark, but normally three, sometimes six years behind, so the Norwegian Nationale regiments often tended to look a little old-fashioned. So, at the start of this period, the soldiers in the Nationale regiments were wearing the M1789 hat, akin to a low top hat with a wide brim. The hats were slightly altered in 1797, mainly by turning the left brim slightly up. They began receiving the M1789 coat in *c*. 1795, but they were made locally from 1797–1799, altered to the M1797 style. This was generally cut slightly shorter and the original fall down collar was turned up and stiffened so it could protect the neck better against cuts and blows. It was worn with short white breeches of the M1789 model and long black gaiters, model M1789. By 1808 the Nationale regiments had all added the new higher collar and also several regiments had cut down the length of the existing M1789/1795 coats, so they were of the same length as the new M1802 coats, the *geworbne* and NCOs had already received. This was the general uniform used by nearly all Nationale grenadiers and musketeers in Norway until at least 1810. The M1797 hats were probably used by most musketeers until 1810. The Danish army reform of 1803 meant that all regiments should have received 'hats of the new model (M1802)' as well. But this was postponed in Norway until 1805, and the 3,500 'best hats of the old model' (M1789) were to be shipped from Denmark to Norway instead. Only the *geworbne* musketeers and most of the NCOs used the M1802 hats until *c*. 1810.

As explained at the beginning of this section, there were two levels of clothing issues, one for the Nationale regiments and another for the *geworbne* (enlisted) companies; this included all the grenadier and musketeer companies of the two *geworbne* regiments. This difference was noticeable in some of their clothing issues, the most obvious being their trousers.

According to the peacetime planning, most Nationale regiments were to receive new uniforms in 1809 (Søndenfjeldske) and 1810 (Nordenfjeldske), so most of their uniforms were rather old and worn out, and were due for a change early in the campaign of 1808.

The following were the previous issue dates of the Nationale *bataljoner* in the year 1808 (the *geworbne* regiments had generally received uniforms on the same date as the NCOs):

'Red uniform coatee (*kjole*) M1789' (altered to M1799) issued between 1795 and 1799 (NCOs and drummers 1802)

Vest/waistcoat (white) issued in 1795 (NCOs and drummers 1802–1804)

Hats M1797. Issued 1801–1803 (NCOs and drummers 1802–1804). The colour of the hat band, cords and button were to correspond to the regimental button colour, as did the NCO's epaulette.

Bukser M1789/short breeches issued 1803 (NCOs and drummers 1805)

Trausser M1791 (long white gaiter trousers) issued 1808 (they appear to have been primarily issued to the sharpshooters)

Uldne bukser/woollen winter trouser (like a pair of grey long-johns) 1808

Gamascher (long black gaiters) issued in 1801 (NCOs and drummers 1806)

Sko (shoes and stockings) issued in 1803 and 1808) and *vanter* (gloves), issued in 1808

Some of the new blue gaiter trousers reached Norway, but very few, and only for the *geworbne* regiments. The Nationale regiments were expected to pay for them themselves, and as there was a general unwillingness to pay extra in the local company districts, few (if any) companies had done this before 1808. After 1808 it was impossible to get any through the blockade, and with the high price of indigo dye, this made it almost impossible and far too expensive to equip all the army with blue trousers; in fact they appear to have been rare in Norway. The men who still had them (mainly the *geworbne* and artillery) continued to wear them until they wore out. Also *capots*, also called *caput-kjoler*, which were long grey overcoats M1788 had been planned to be issued generally, but here Norway, after some discussion, had been allowed to produce them locally. They had first been able to get the cloth at favourable prices in 1808, so when the war began, they had begun a small production run of same but no more 3,000–5,000 were made between 1807–1811 and these mainly used as 'sentry coats', maybe 20–30 to a field division. In 1808–1809 there was no less than 93,000 metres of light grey cloth which lay ready, but unused in the *Munderingsdepot* (Central Uniform Arsenal) in Norway, and this was from 1810 used instead to produce new grey uniforms for the sharpshooters.

Norwegian Line Infantry Uniforms (III), 1810–1814

THE NORWEGIAN LINE INFANTRY: UNIFORMS

> Facing page
> Plate 6. Norwegian Line Infantry Uniforms III, 1810–1814
>
> The soldiers are mainly shown wearing the M1808 coat, white cloth trousers and short black gaiters. Most wear the M1808 shako and have white cloth breeches worn with short black gaiters. The *geworbne* regiments have grey breeches and short black gaiters.
>
> 1. An officer, Westerlehnske Infanteri Regiment *c.* 1811
> 2. A musketeer, 1st Trondhjemske Nationale Infanteri Regiment
> 3. A *jæger*, Søndenfjeldske Geworbne Infanteri Regiment
> 4. A sergeant of musketeers *c.* 1813, Nordenfjeldske Geworbne Infanteri Regiment
> 5. A musketeer, 1st Trondhjemske Nationale Infanteri Regiment wearing the short Norwegian *ydertrøje* (short spencer-style overcoat), also called a *kaputtrøje* or *patruljetrøje*. It was officially issued in Norway from October 1810, but had been in existence since 1808 and already used by the light units.
> 6. A sapper of the Oplandske Geworbne Infanteri Regiment
> 7. A drum major of the 2nd Trondhjemske Nationale Infanteri Regiment *c.* 1812
> 8. An officer of the Bergenhusiske Nationale Infanteri Regiment 1814
> 9. A drummer of the Telemarkske Nationale Infanteri Regiment *c.* 1813. The drum's rims are painted red, designating the reign of Fredrik VI
> 10. A so-called *fribataljon* (levy) battalion musketeer, wearing the standard *fribataljon* uniform made from simple homespun grey cloth (*vadmel*). The musketeers were normally only issued with a simple calfskin cap with a light, greyish-coloured woollen plume.

According to *Kongelig Resolution* 19 July 1808 Norway was allowed to produce their own supply of M1808 trousers, but in white cloth as they had a large supply, available to be delivered to the cloth magazines in Norway. Also, in the future shirts were permitted to be made in Norway, in both checked and striped civilian cloth, as this material was also available in large quantities in Norway.

In 1807–1808 Denmark had prepared, or at least was preparing, the following items for shipment directly to Norway, or made ready to be produced locally in Norway:

12,000 mainly red uniform coats M1808, with white waistcoats (only received during 1809–1810). A supply of M1808 shakos was postponed until 1809–1810 'as they take too much space in supply ships and uniform coats, weapons supplies etc. have priority'.

40,000 pairs of trousers, to be produced in both white and grey cloth (for light units) together with short black cloth gaiters. This was soon changed to mainly locally produced items in Norway, white trousers for the infantry, and grey trousers only for the light Infantry.

40,000 shirts (also now to be made in Norway instead in different available cloth colours; included striped cloth)

20,000 pair of shoes; further production of these was started in Norway. The shoes were hobnailed and there was not a left and right shoe as they were all the same shape, and were to be worn alternately on each foot to ensure even wear and tear. Many of those produced in 1808–1809 were made by captured Swedish soldiers, many of whom being former shoemakers.

40,000 pairs of socks (again, production of these was also started in Norway)

10,000 white cross belts M1808, with bayonet frog attached. The new shoulder belts sent to Norway were probably the new economy model with a combined cartridge box and bayonet scabbard on the same shoulder strap, as can be seen on Ljunggren's picture where the Norwegian soldiers only have a shoulder belt. Large numbers were later shipped to Norway, where limited production also started.

51,000 pairs of grey woollen gloves

93,000 metres of light grey cloth originally intended for making M1788 *capots* (greatcoats), was stored in the *Munderingsdepot* (uniform arsenal), in Norway. Instead the decision was made from 1808 to use this cloth to make new

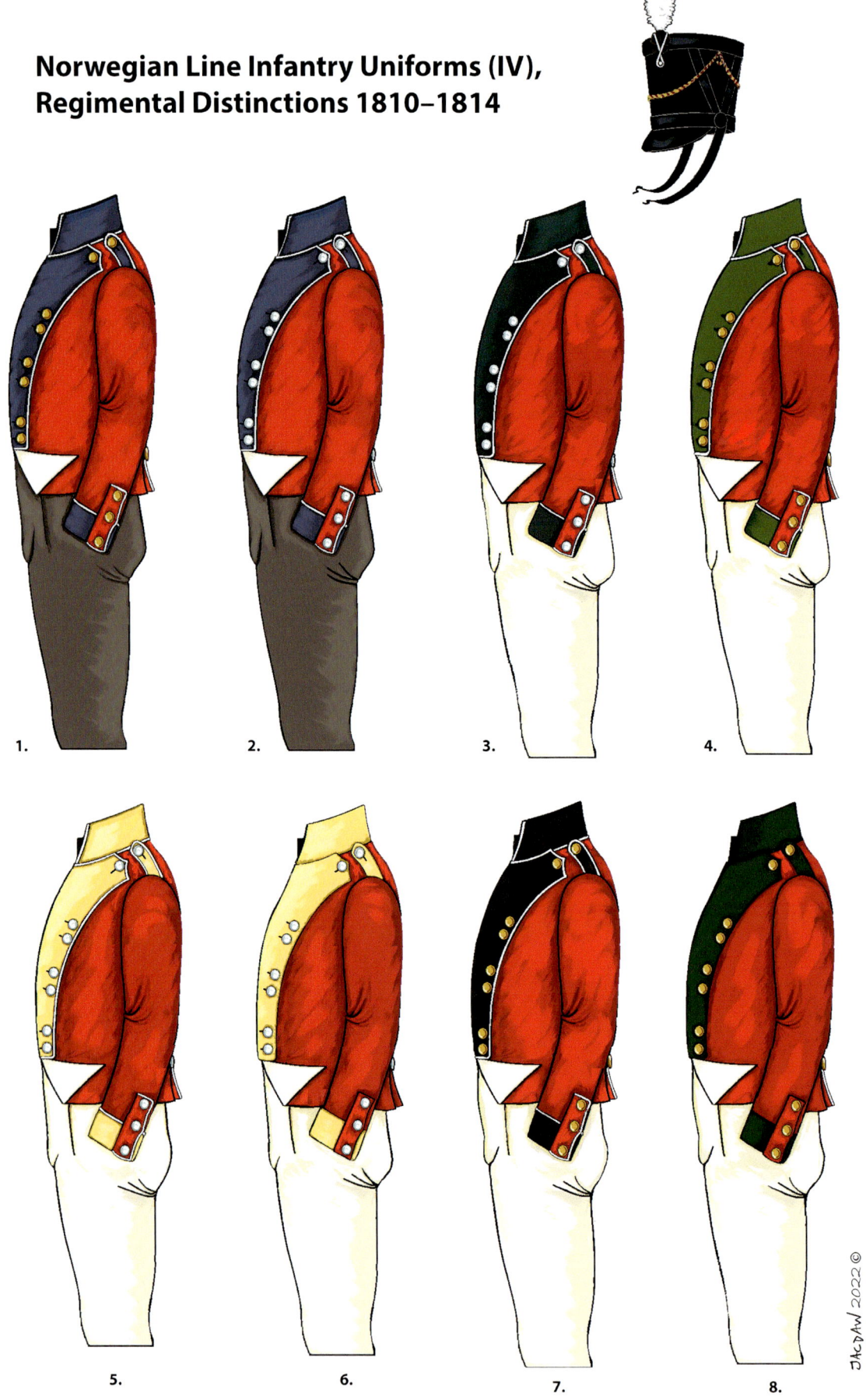

Norwegian Line Infantry Uniforms (IV), Regimental Distinctions 1810–1814

> Facing page
>
> Plate 7. Norwegian Line Infantry Uniforms IV, Regimental Distinctions 1810–1814
>
> These are the regiments retained after the reforms of 1810. They are shown wearing the M1808 coat, white cloth trousers and short black gaiters. Inset: the M1808 shako. Only the two *geworbne* (enlisted) regiments are known to have received the new grey trousers.
>
> Søndenfjeldske Geworbne Infanteri Regiment
> Nordenfjeldske Geworbne Infanteri Regiment
> Oplandske Geworbne Infanteri Regiment
> Telemarkske Infanteri Regiment
> 1st Trondhjemske Infanteri Regiment
> 2nd Trondhjemske Infanteri Regiment
> Bergenhusiske Infanteri Regiment
> Westerlehnske Infanteri Regiment
>
> The facing colours are based on those found in Möller, *Fuldstændige Tabeller over alle den Kongelige Danske og Norske Armee tilhörende, regimenters, corpers, bataillonors, borgervæbningers og frivillige etc, corpers Corpser Uniform*, Kiöbenhavn 1810. The colour of the hat band, cords and button corresponded to the regimental button colour, as did the colour of the NCO's epaulette.

grey uniforms for the reorganised light infantry. Norway already had already begun producing and distributing short spencer-like overcoats, called *kaputtrøler* or *ydertrøjer* from more readily available local homespun cloth, called *vadmel*. This style of short overcoat was mainly at first issued to the light units, but by 1813–1814 they were being used by all.

But all this materiel only first began arriving in 1809 due to the blockade, so most of the battles of 1808–1809 were fought with the men wearing mainly old worn and torn uniforms. But Denmark did everything it could, against all odds, to remedy the situation and overcome the tight Anglo-Swedish blockade.

Starting slowly from 1808 and working fully by 1810 the Norwegians began producing their own clothing, including the production of light grey M1810 uniform coats and short overcoats called *kaputtrøjer* (short, spencer-style overcoats using many different coloured cloths including light grey, dark grey, light and dark brown). As well as trousers (mainly white), shirts, shoes, and socks, were now all being produced, so as to make Norway better prepared and nearly self-sufficient, regarding uniforms, in the future.

Uniforms of the *Geworbne* Musketeers and Their Grenadiers

The *geworbne* musketeers and their grenadiers had same uniform clothing terms as Danish regiments, so by 1806 they had received the new M1803 *kraprød* (madder red) uniform, which was shorter, with smaller buttons and the turnbacks were different, and at the same time they generally received the M1802 hat. The long tight M1791 white gaiter trousers *trausser* were normally worn, as were the new blue M1802 gaiter trousers.

The special uniform of the grenadiers was, apart from the newer uniform models, used by the *geworbne* the same as the Nationale grenadiers. In 1803 the new reforms for the dressing of hair took effect both in Denmark and Norway which abolished long hair and queues, leaving all hair cut short (officers followed from 1806), although the practice may have lingered on for a while in Norway, principally in the grenadiers.

Uniforms of the Nationale Musketeers and General Uniform Details

Starting with their headgear, they began the period with the M1789 hat which resembled a low crowned top hat with a wide brim, a hat band, black cockade, loop and button and white plume. This was replaced by the M1797 hat issued in 1801–1803 (for the NCOs and *tambourer* in 1802–1804). This hat had a black cockade and white hat band and loop with a white button for the regiments with pewter buttons and a yellow hat band and loop and a yellow button for the those with brass buttons. A white plume was worn by the musketeers. As previously mentioned, the Norwegian uniform had the same cut as that of the Danish army but often one, in a few cases two clothing terms behind. Originally, they wore a *kraprød* M1789 coat which was replaced with the more familiar *kraprød* M1795 coatee (*kjole*). It was issued to the men in 1795, but NCOs and *tambourer* had received another set of same model uniform in 1802. It was cut shorter than the previous coat and the collar was stiffened and turned upright to protect the soldier's necks from cuts as well as the elements. This was the uniform used by nearly all the Nationale grenadiers and musketeers in Norway until at least 1810. A white shirt and waistcoat were worn under the coat. The soldier's throat and neck were protected by a black neck stock, probably made from stiffened cloth or horsehair.

The men still wore white breeches with knee-length black woollen gaiters (*lange gamasker*), issued in 1801, followed by the NCOs and *tambourer* in 1806, and white cloth knee-length M1789 breeches (*bukser*) issued 1803, followed by the NCOs and *tambourer* in 1805. These were worn until late in 1808, possibly longer in some companies.

The long, tight M1791 white gaiter trousers (*trausser*) were officially allowed from 1798, for Nationale sharpshooters and grenadiers in Norway, for a term of three years, but at the cost to the regiment according to *Kongelig Resolution* 13 April 1798. So because of the cost, not all regiments (if any) actually chose to buy them. The inventory of the *Norske Munderingsdepot* (Central Norwegian Uniform Arsenal) made on 15 March 1808 does not show any trousers in stock, but again as they were regimental property, they may only be traced in the Nationale regimental inventories. Some Nationale regiments may also have bought the new blue M1802 trousers, but again very few if any, besides the two *geworbne* regiments due to the cost.

As has already been mentioned, the Nationale regiments never really received the M1802 uniforms and hats.

A new uniform coatee, the M1803, which was shorter, with smaller buttons and different turnbacks, was mainly worn in the *geworbne* regiments and generally by the NCOs. At the same time, they were supposed to receive the M1802 hat, but as there were only limited supplies only the *geworbne* regiments and the NCOs received them at this time. Also, long hair and queues were abolished, leaving all hair cut short.

Uniforms of the *Geworbne Grenaderer*, from 1804 called *Tjenestegørende Grenaderer*

The grenadiers raised by the Nationale regiments, first called *geworbne* grenadiers, but from 1804 called *tjenestegørende grenaderer*, wore the same uniforms as their parent regiment, just adding the different extra marks of their trade. These were a brass tube-shaped match case worn on front of the cross belt, and often a larger grenadiers' model ammunition pouch with an *infanteri sabel* M1756 as a sidearm. They were also the only infantry allowed to wear moustaches.

The grenadiers in Norway wore the black leather Russian-inspired *Potemkin*-style M1789 grenadier cap, with a brass plate with a white caterpillar plume over it from ear to ear. It had a tall white, blue-tipped feather at the left side and a brass grenade on the back of the cap. Originally the hat had two wide cloth tails or *flyers* in the regimental facing colour laced white or yellow with a white or yellow tassel according to the button colour, worn crossed over the top of the hat on parade but allowed to hang down when on campaign. But in 1797, a regulation of 21 April, states that 'On the new hats (grenadier), these (*flyers*) shall change into red (generally), as on those with green facings, the colour fades too quickly'. That red was to be adopted as standard can be seen from the fact that the two first regiments to change had yellow facings. Also, it is apparent, based on different sources, that the original *flyers*, were replaced on all hats by a red patch with white lining and tassel, somewhat like that, latter worn on the Danish M1803 bearskin. From the *Munderingsdepot* inventory of 13 March 1808 we learn that there were at this date only two types of grenadier caps available; one common model for NCOs (silver piping and tassels) and one common model for grenadiers (white piping and tassel). This common model was painted by the Norwegian artist J. C. Dahl on the parade ground of Engen, and the central guardhouse of Bergen in 1810, clearly showing a red, white lined patch on top of the grenadier hats in Norway. These hats were worn until the grenadier companies were disbanded in 1810. In 1806 it had been planned that M1803 bearskins were to be issued to the Norwegian grenadiers from 1808, as had already been done in Denmark, but because of the war of 1807–1809 this was at first postponed and ultimately never happened. But new fatigue caps, made of grey cloth with regimental coloured turn ups were made and sent to Norway 1808. In Norway these fatigue caps, were generally called 'grey hats'. As many of the old M1789 grenadier caps had by 1808–1809 been worn out, some of these 'grey hats' were issued instead. The Bergenhusiske og Westerlehnske grenadiers took the front brass plate and rear bomb off the old grenadier caps, and had them sewn on the front and back of their 'grey hats', as replacement grenadier caps. It is not known if other grenadier companies followed suit wearing 'grey hats'/fatigue caps, but it is quite likely, especially when the number of grenadiers were significantly expanded during 1808–1809. In 1810 the grenadier companies were disbanded so the M1803 bearskins were in any case no longer needed.

The long, tight, white M1791 gaiter trousers were officially allowed from 1798, for National Sharpshooters and Grenadiers in Norway, for a term of three years, but at the cost of the regiment according to *Kongelig Resolution* 1 April 1798. So, because of the cost, not all regiments actually chose to buy them.

Uniforms of the Regimental *Skarpskyttere*

The *skarpskyttere* (sharpshooters) were basically dressed the same as the musketeers, and grenadiers of their regiment, but there were a few differences. Firstly, the white feather on their hat had a green tip. They were probably the only Nationale troops to wear the white gaiter trousers (*lærredsbukser*) and they also carried an M1796 infantry sabre. The long tight M1791 white gaiter trousers (*trausser*) were officially permitted from 1798, for 'Nationale regimental sharpshooters and grenadiers in Norway, for a term of three years, but at the cost of the regiment according to *Kongelig Resolution* 13 April 1798'. So because of the cost, not all regiments chose to buy them. Some Nationale regiments may also have bought the new blue M1802 trousers, for their sharpshooters, but again, probably few (if any), beside the two *geworbne* regiments did so, again because of the cost.

Uniforms of the Musicians (*Tambourer* and *Hornblæsere*)
Norway had no special tradition for military music. The only music was primarily the various beats of drums. All *geworbne* and Nationale musketeer companies had two *tambourer* (drummers). The *geworbne* grenadier companies had two *tambourer* also a *piber* (fifer) attached. Drums were brass in the *geworbne* companies, but a mixture of both brass and older wooden drums in the Nationale. Each battalion had a *trommekorporal* (drum corporal), and each regiment had a *tambourmajor* (drum major) to train, drill and command the drummers when they were gathered together as a band. Each regiment had also a *hornblæser* (hornist), trained in using a crescent shaped horn *halvmånehorn* (half-moon), which were used to control the amalgamated *skarpskytte* platoons. Unlike Denmark, Norway did not have any traditions for using hired bandsmen, called *hoboister*.

Uniforms of the Regimental *Tømmermænd*
Each regiment had two *tømmermænd* (carpenters/sappers) attached to each of the musketeer companies and also the grenadier companies. In 1792 it was decided that the sappers should have entrenching tools, called *skansetøj*, to clear the way or build entrenchments for the regimental artillery. Half of the regimental sappers would each carry two spades, a quarter should each carry a wide pickaxe, while the last quarter would carry an axe. The regimental sappers wore same hats and uniforms as the musketeers and grenadiers augmented with long dark brown or black leather aprons. Originally, they had been also equipped with fascine knives carried in sheaths on their belts, but they now carried small saws instead. These saws, which had a pistol style handle were carried in sheaths on waist belts like a sword. The metalwork of the sheaths would be in the regimental button colour. According to a list made by Søndenfjeldskeke Geworbne Infanteri Regiment in 1809, all 16 of their regimental sappers had apparently been concentrated into the four existing *geworbne grenader* companies, and all the sappers wore leather aprons, and carried the small hand saws and axes, but all the equipment was by then worn or needed repairing or replacing. Regimental sappers were the only soldiers allowed full beards, as a mark of their profession.

Uniforms of the Regimental Artillerymen
The regimental gunners were dressed the same as the rest of the men of their regiment, but they were armed as artillerymen with an *infanteri sabel* M1756 for personal defence. They did not carry muskets, but they had all the other equipment necessary to serve their guns.

Uniforms of the Landeværn
As they were mainly a reserve of older men not always fit for service, or former soldiers, the Landeværn did not have a specific uniform like in Denmark, but were issued the best of the previous outdated, surplus or reformed uniforms of the line regiments to which they were attached.

Uniforms of the Officers
The officers wore long-tailed uniform coats, with lapels, in the special *ponceau* (poppy red) colour allowed officers in a better-quality cloth. They wore at first black bicorn hats with a black cockade and with the button, loop and tassels in button colour, topped by a white plume. This was replaced, first with the black M1804 officer's hat, with a black cockade, hat band, and the button and loop in the regimental button colour. Long single gold and red cords and flounders looped over the second facing button, on the right side, and a white plume was worn on the left top of the hat. This was later replaced with the M1806 officers' hat, which were taller and slimmer, had a slightly different brim, with longer cords formed into three loops wound around the hat. The white plume was not to be taller than the height of the hat. These two models were worn until 1809 when they began to be replaced with the M1808 shako. Most of the officers had the new shakos made privately. The officers' model was made of leather without the 'V' strengtheners on the sides. They wore officers' white or blue *pantalongs* (pantaloons) with short Hessian officer's boots. They were also allowed to wear a red officers' overcoat M1788/98 *surtout* with a cape. From 1802, they used M1801 epaulettes and wore an M1795 red and yellow waist sash; until 1804 this was worn under the coat, thereafter it was always worn over the coat. All officers carried on their side arm, the special insignia of a regular officer a *porte épée* in red and gold silk.

Uniforms of the Officers of Grenadier Companies
They wore the same basic uniform and equipment as the other officers of their regiment. The officers of grenadier companies had tall white feathers in their hats until at least 1808, but there is evidence that this changed in 1809, were one contemporary self-portrait shows that by this date, they had begun using new M1808, shakos with a short, rounded feather with a blue top. They were also allowed to wear a red officer's *surtout*, with cape, which was a frequent occurrence during the fighting of 1808–1809. The same self-portrait of a grenadier officer shows his red officers' *surtout,* the facing colour only shown as a square patch

Norwegian Line Infantry Uniforms (V), Grenadier Equipment 1800–1810

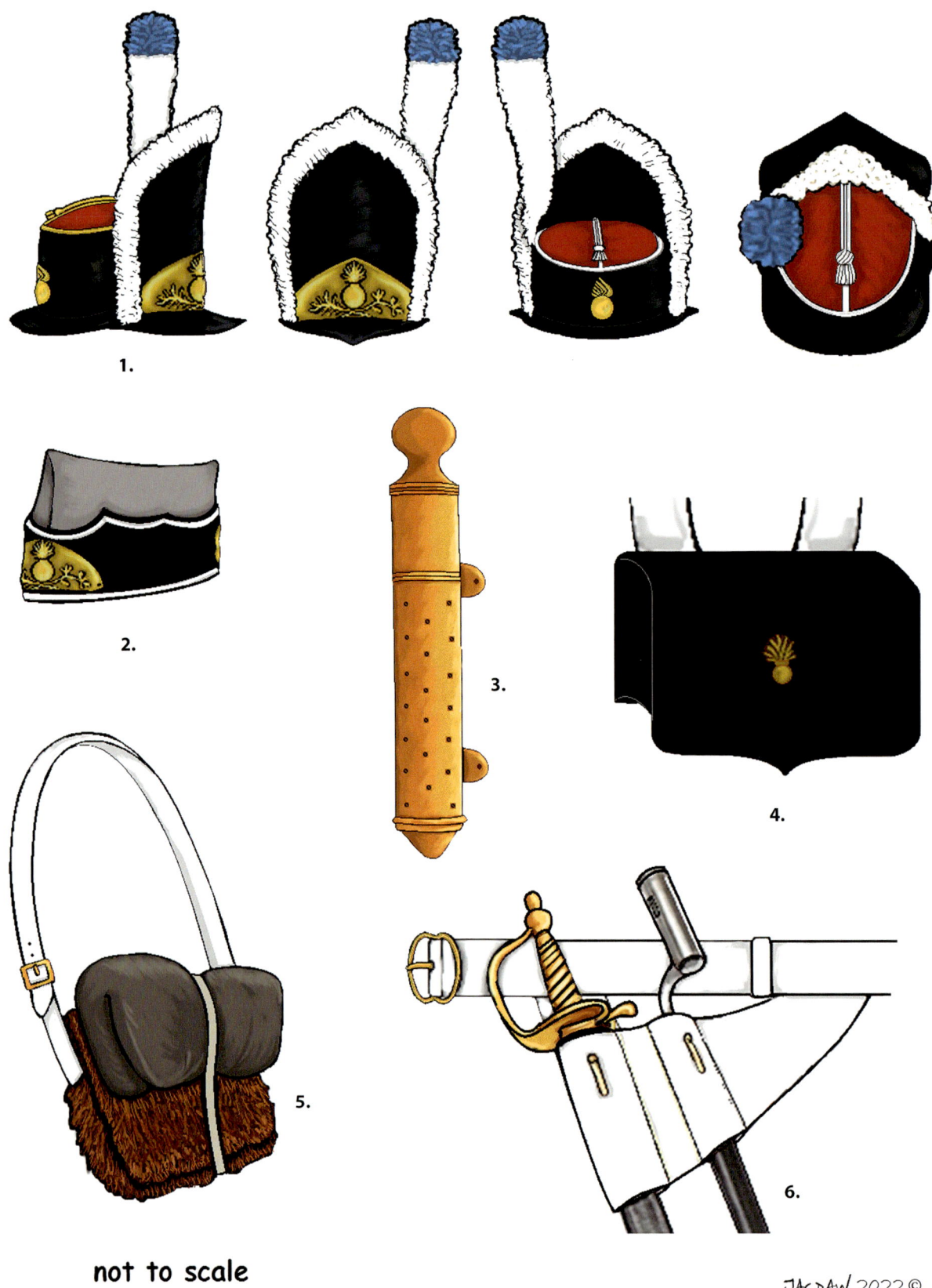

not to scale

THE NORWEGIAN LINE INFANTRY: UNIFORMS

> Facing page
>
> ## Plate 8. Norwegian Line Infantry Uniforms V, 1800–1810; Grenadier Equipment Details
>
> 1. Grenadier caps M1797, from left to right. Side view (regiment with yellow buttons), front view, rear view (regiment with white buttons), and a top view (NCO of regiment with white buttons, in silver). Originally this hat had two wide cloth *flyers* in the facing colour and was piped with the button colour on the top of the hat. But a regulation dated 21 April 1797 states that 'on the new hats, this [*flyer*] shall change into red (generally), as on those with green facings, the colour fades too quickly'. That this is to be a general order can be deduced from the fact that the two first regiments to change had yellow facings. This model is referred to as the M1797 grenadier hat. None have survived, so this is a reconstruction. These *flyers* were replaced by a red top flap like the one later used on the M1803 grenadier bearskins. That only the M1797 hat was used in Norway is confirmed, as there was only one standard model in stock in the arsenals. A number of pictures painted by J. C. Dahl in 1810 of the Bergenhusiske or Westerlehnske grenadiers, show a red top patch, not flyers, and this is the basis for the reconstruction.
> 2. Grenadier fatigue cap with grenadier cap plate with a grenade mounted on it, a stop-gap solution to replace worn out caps. This one is in the colours of the Bergenhusiske or Westerlehnske Nationale regiments who were recorded as doing this, other units probably did the same.
> 3. A grenadier match case (*lunteskjuler*) now just an ornament of their status
> 4. A cartridge box with a brass grenade on it
> 5. Old model knapsack with coat or blanket attached. Norway had been using a calfskin *ransel* (knapsack), with one sling, since at least 1749. It was made of black, brown or red calfskin.
> 6. A grenadier belt with *infanteri sabel* M1756 and bayonet

with two buttons on the front of the collar. The coat had no less than 20 buttons down the front!

Uniforms of the Officers of *Skarpskytte* Detachments

They wore the same basic uniform as the other officers of their regiment. The officers of the detached *skarpskytte* platoons had a green plume tipped white. They may also have carried whistles, suspended by a green ribbon or cord from one of their right-hand lapel buttons. They were also allowed to wear the red M1788/98 officer's *surtout* with cape, but it is possible that they may have worn grey overcoats.

Uniforms of the NCOs, and Equipment

NCOs' uniforms followed the same evolution as in Denmark, and they generally received uniforms with the same terms as in Denmark and of the same model as the ordinary soldiers, but of slightly better quality. NCOs wore the special NCO M1789 epaulette in button-coloured lace sewn on their right shoulder. They had nothing on their left shoulder. At this time Norwegian NCOs still carried a pole arm (*gewehr*)[2] as his badge of rank as well as his personal weapon. There were two principal models, the most common being the M1725 *korsgevær for underofficerer* NCO halberd supplemented with the M1769 *korsgevær for underofficer* (NCOs' spontoon), today generally known as a *lilje* (lily), after the shape of the blade. This last model was probably the more common in the two *geworbne* regiments. The total length for both weapons including the blade was generally two metres, but some found in Norway are longer (2.30 m). This may be those carried by *sergenter*, so they could be seen more clearly when in line formation, and also to denoting their higher rank. Following the military reform of 1802 regarding conscription in Denmark, efforts were made to differentiate the NCO ranks more clearly, but it is not clear if this reform was applied in Norway.

---

2   *Gewehr* originally had nothing to do with a firearm; it simply means 'a weapon'. The original German/Prussian word *kurzgewehr*, means 'a short weapon' and 1700–1800 this was a short polearm used by both officers and NCOs, normally a half-pike, spontoon, halberd or partisan in English. In the early 1700s Denmark/Norway copied rather a lot from Prussia/Germany, including the word or term *kurzgewehr*, and this was a natural word, used in the mainly German-speaking enlisted army. But from 1772 there was an awakening of the Danish nation and now Danish would be the only language to be used in the Danish/Norwegian army. So, most of the German command and military phrases were changed to Danish to better represent the new Danish/Norwegian national army. One word which was translated was the word *kurzgewehr*. But to translate it literally had no meaning in Danish. *Kortgevær*, or a musket was also called a *gevær*, and a sidearm was termed a *sidegevær*. It was decided to create a much more expressive word, in Danish, *Korsgevær* which means a polearm with a cross-formed blade. *Korsgevær*, besides the original *kurzgewehr*, were the only two words used for this type of weapon from around 1772, in both Denmark and Norway, until the Kongelige Resolution of 13 September 1805, when the use of *korsgeværer* was to be discontinued. The modern term *kortgevær* is an incorrect modern translation.

As already noted NCOs began receiving firearms from *c.* 1809–1810. The did not have a shoulder strap on left shoulder as they did not carry a crossbelt and cartridge box. When they were rearmed with firearms from *c.* 1809–1810 they were also given a shoulder strap on left shoulder, called a 'dragon' in the facing colour piped with button-coloured metallic thread. All NCOs carried an M1756 *infanteri sabel* with a yellow and red wool sword knot. From 1806 *kommandersergenter* (staff sergeants) were allowed a silver sword knot, as a sign of their status. They were also allowed to carry a small brass M1753 flute container for paper and pen etc.

Arms

The men in the Nationale musketeer and grenadier companies were equipped with a musket, mostly the M1774, which was probably the most numerous model used in Norway.[3] Nearly all Nationale infantry used this simple and sturdy musket at the beginning of the war. But as more recruits, reserves and Landeværn were called up, several older models had to be used as well, often not in the *best condition.*

The Norwegian NCOs should, according to a Royal Resolution dated 13 September 1805, have been issued with the *skarpskyttegevær M1789* (sharpshooter muskets*)*, to replace the halberds and partisans, which was planned to be introduced in Southern Norway during 1808, and in Northern Norway during 1809. But in 1808 all available *skarpskyttegevær M1789* had already been issued in Denmark, which is apparent from a reply from Frederik VI in response to a letter from the *Aggershus* arsenal, regarding a further supply of *skarpskyttegevær M1789*, stating that non could be shipped to Norway. So, while most regiments continued to use the old halberds and partisans, some NCOs probably received ordinary M1774 muskets. Only from 1810 did they begin receiving *skarpskyttegevær 1789*, when they became available from the disbanded regimental *skarpskyttere* in Norway. The *sergenter* and *corporaler* carried an M1756 infantry sabre with a thin yellow woollen sword knot stitched with red thread.

Field Equipment

Norway had been using *ransel* (calfskin knapsacks) with one sling since at least 1749,[4] made of black, brown or red calfskin. In 1798, an off-white bread-bag with one black sling was to be issued both in Denmark and in Norway. Since *c.* 1750 Norway had been issued the old water canteen M1751,[5] made of copper with a layer of tin inside, and from 1800 was the canteen used primarily in Norway. It was issued on the basis of one canteen for each two soldiers, who were supposed to share it and take turns carrying it. Although a rather old design, it was very well liked in Norway, although it was not practical to carry water in when on the march as it leaked from the lid, but was very useful to fetch water during rest and in camp. It was also very practical used as a makeshift cooking pot for boiling water, bread soup, porridge or other food. The Danish one-man M1808 canteen were never used in Norway. During 1811–1814, the Norwegian infantry even began receiving large numbers of a new and improved model of same copper two-man canteen, the M1810. Both models were kept in Norwegian service officially until 1855, but then stayed in storage in the arsenal until at least 1900.[6] When in the field the infantry received one camp axe and one copper cooking pot, which were introduced into Denmark and Norway around 1740, complete with a pan lid, for every four soldiers. But the cooking pots were slow to arrive and not in sufficient numbers, so in some companies eight soldiers were forced to share one cooking pot until they received enough.

The Reforms of 1810

In 1810–1813, the whole of the Norwegian army was modernised and reorganised, mainly through the planning and effort of the new overall commander General Prince Frederik of Hessen which resulted in a reduction of the line regiments, and the formation of new *skarpskytte* sharpshooter battalions. This led to some of the former regiments being broken up and the men redistributed among the remaining or newly formed regiments. In 1810 all the grenadier companies were disbanded, and all the company sharpshooters were abolished, but new *jæger* companies were formed to replace them. The two enlisted *tjenestegørende grenader* companies that existed in each

---

3   In 1837 there remained no less than 17,827 of the M1774 muskets in Norwegian stores, the most numerous musket model found in Norway between 1801 and 1814. For the use of Landeværn, town militias and reserve formations there were also 7,464 of the M1765 musket and other older models in stock. There was a small supply (827) of captured Swedish muskets from the 1808–1809 and 1814 campaigns in stock. They even had in stock 232 muskets of the English model. Source: *Fortegnelse over Antal og Beskaffenhed af de vigtigste i samtlige norske Landarsenaler havende militaire Fornødenheder ved Aarets Udgang*, 1837. After the official inventory of Norwegian weapons made in 1837, for the use of the Norwegian government.

4   According to *Kongelig Resolution* 14 marts (March) 1749.

5   *Interims felttjeneste reglement*. Issued for use of the infantry in 1788. *Regulativ for Bagagevognes og øvrige Feltreqvisiters antal ved den Norske Armee*, issued 23 August 1812.

6   In 1837 nearly 16,000 copper canteens M1749 and M1810 were still in use. Only around 1,600 of the Danish old-style large two-man metal canteens were found in the arsenals, and it is not known if this last model was used much, if at all. Source: *Fortegnelse over Antal og Beskaffenhed af de vigtigste i samtlige norske Landarsenaler havende militaire Fornødenheder ved Aarets Udgang*, 1837.

of the national infantry regiments were abolished and, in each regiment, one of these companies was converted into a new *geworben livkompani* (enlisted life company), which, in effect directly replaced the former grenadiers and the other into an enlisted *geworbne jæger* (enlisted *jæger*) company. Two of the line regiments were converted into light infantry (see the *skarpskyttere* regiments) and the number of *geworbne* enlisted regiments was raised to three. From 1810 to 1814 the infantry regiments had the following peacetime organisation:

The **Søndenfjeldskeke Geworbne Infanteri Regiment** (garrison: Halden)
1st Geworbne Infanteri Bataljon (one *jæger* and four musketeer companies)
2nd Geworbne Infanteri Bataljon (one jæger and four musketeer companies)
1st Nationale Bataljon (one *jæger* and five musketeer companies)

2nd Nationale Bataljon (one *jæger* and five musketeer companies)

The **Nordenfjeldske/ke Geworbne Infanteri Regiment** (garrison: Frederikstad)
1st Geworbne Infanteri Bataljon (one *jæger* and four musketeer companies)
2nd Geworbne Infanteri Bataljon (one *jæger* and four musketeer companies)
1st Nationale Bataljon (one *jæger* and five musketeer companies)
2nd Nationale Bataljon (one *jæger* and five musketeer companies)

The **Oplandske Geworbne Infanteri Regiment** (garrison: Oslo)
1st Geworbne Infanteri Bataljon (one *jæger* and four musketeer companies)
2nd Geworbne Infanteri Bataljon (one *jæger* and four musketeer companies)
1st Nationale Bataljon (one *jæger* and five musketeer companies)
2nd Nationale Bataljon (one *jæger* and five musketeer companies)

The **Telemarkske Nationale Infanteri Regiment** (garrison: Stavern)
One *geworbent livkompani* and one *geworbent jægerkompani*
1st Nationale Bataljon (one *jæger* and five musketeer companies)
2nd Nationale Bataljon (one *jæger* and five musketeer companies)

3rd Nationale Bataljon (one *jæger* and five musketeer companies)

The **Westerlehnske Nationale Infanteri Regiment** (garrison: Kristiansand)
One *geworbent* Livkompani and one *geworbent* Jægerkompani
1st Nationale Bataljon (one *jæger* and five musketeer companies)
2nd Nationale Bataljon (one *jæger* and five musketeer companies)
3rd Nationale Bataljon (one *jæger* and five musketeer companies)

The **Bergenhusiske Nationale Infanteri Regiment** (garrison: Bergen)
One *geworbent livkompani* and one *geworbent jægerkompani*
Bergenske Nationale Bataljon (one *jæger* and five musketeer companies)
Sognske Nationale Bataljon (one *jæger* and five musketeer companies)
Nordfjordske Nationale Bataljon (one *jæger* and five musketeer companies)

The **1st Trondhjemske Nationale Infanteri Regiment** (garrison: Trondhjem)
One *geworbent livkompani* and one *geworbent jægerkompani*
1st Nationale Bataljon (one *jæger* and five musketeer companies)
2nd Nationale Bataljon (one *jæger* and five musketeer companies)
1st Nordenfjeldske/ke Skiløber Bataljon (three Ski Kompagnier)
2nd Nordenfjeldske/ke Skiløber Bataljon (one *jæger* and five musketeer companies)

The **2nd Trondhjemske Nationale Infanteri Regiment** (garrison: Trondhjem)
One *geworbentlivkompani* and one *geworbent jægerkompani*
Trondhjemske Skarpskytte Bataljon (one *jæger* and five sharpshooter companies)
1st Nationale Bataljon (one *jæger* and five musketeer companies)
2nd Nationale Bataljon (one *jæger* and five musketeer companies)

As mentioned previously, the regiment did not exist as a tactical unit during mobilisation, and this was not changed by the reforms from 1810 onwards. Instead, the whole structure was enlarged and evened out. As before, an extensive reorganisation of the peacetime organisation was carried out at the transition to war. Field battalions were formed from each peacetime company forming a new field company each with 75 soldiers, chosen from the youngest, fittest and preferably unmarried soldiers. They were then merged by two companies, into what were called divisions. The field battalions were to consist of five divisions – a *jæger* division and four *musketeere* divisions. A field battalion would theoretically, field the following strength: a battalion commander, generally a colonel, a major, a battalion adjutant, an artillery officer, a battalion surgeon, four company surgeons, a *tambourmajor* (battalion drummer, drum major), an artificer, a provost marshal, five captains (one in each company), five *premiereløjtnanter* (first lieutenants), one in each company, five *sekondløjtnanter* (second lieutenants), one in each company, 50 NCOs, 10 of whom were trained in light infantry drill for the *jæger* company, 12 drummers and three *hornblæsere*, 150 *regimentsjægere*, 600 *musketeere* and theoretically five *tømmermænd* (sappers), giving a total of 842 men.

Upon mobilisation, all regiments – *geworbne* as well as Nationale – were to form up to two field battalions, each of 750 men, and a depot, also called a depot battalion, of 500 men. The depot battalion received 20 officers, 30 NCOs and four drummers from the regiment. Beside this there would be a Landeværn battalion connected with the depot battalion. They were originally intended as reserve units, with quarters centred on the major fortresses or large cities. The purpose was, as planned, was for the field battalions to be able to pick up reserve soldiers from here. This was not the case during the campaign in 1814, see below. Again, they were formed into brigade-sized all-arms combat groups, led directly by the brigade commander, as in 1808–1809.

Following the Reform of 1810

By 1814 there were now three regular *geworbne* (enlisted) regiments, each of four battalions, of which two were enlisted or regular troops and one was of national or conscripts. There were six Nationale regiments, which each had three battalions, and two companies extra of *geworbne* soldiers.

In 1812–1814, in face of the overwhelming odds against the defence of their country, especially the growing number of soldiers in the Swedish army, Norway needed more men, to defend itself against an invasion. So, a new reserve of soldiers had to be found and embodied to increase the strength of the Norwegian Army. Before 1812 all soldiers who had performed their eight-year active period of service were placed in the Landeværn as a reserve, which in time of war could, if needed, again be called in for further service. But this was not enough for the needs of the army, by 1812–1813. The previous method of enlistment used a certain district numbered a certain number of men enabled a not insignificant part of the eligible youths in some populous districts either avoiding service or only being drafted at a relatively late age. This was because the service quotes had not been changed to match the growing population. To rectify this, after a plan laid forward by Prince Frederik of Hesse; it was decided by a Royal decree in January 1812 to incorporate a large portion of the young men who had not served and put them into 13 new, so-called *fribataljoner* (levy) battalions, conscripted in the Søndenfjeldske (Southern Division). In the Nordenfjeldske (Northern Division), this increase in manpower was found instead among, the service free men, who had previously been termed as *virkelige reserver*/real reserves and here all the men down to 18 years of age, could then be conscripted. As enough officers to man the *fribataljoner* battalions, could not be found, each of the *geworbne* and Nationale companies in the Søndenfjeldske, assigned two additional NCOs, were to be employed to command the *fribataljoner* battalions, when they were mobilised. The free battalions were recruited by personnel surpluses from both infantry and cavalry companies. They were trained as infantry in the autumn of 1813, partly to strengthen the line troops,

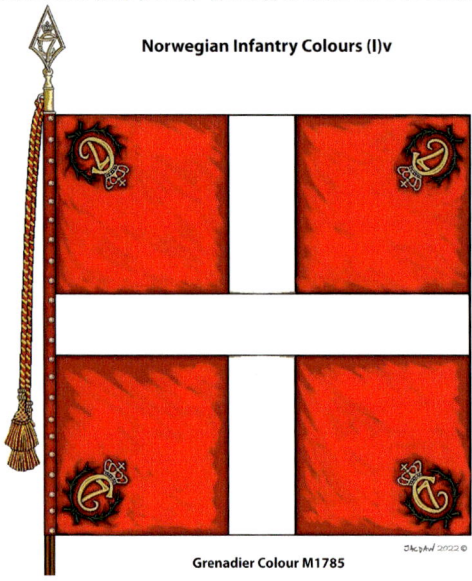

Plate 9. Norwegian Infantry Colours I, Grenadier Colour

Norwegian *grenaderfane* M1785. It was the same as the Danish model. This was in theory the equivalent of a colonel's colour or *livfane* in Denmark, but this was not so in Norway where they became the symbol of the five *geworbne grenader bataljoner*, seven after 1808–1809, which were formed in wartime and used as the backbone for most fighting in 1808–1809. They were each subdivided into two 'divisions', and each had a colour that they carried into battle. These colours were probably the most common in active service until 1810 when the grenadiers were reformed. Dimensions: width 112 cm × height 112 cm. There were 15 of these colours, two for each battalion plus a spare.

Table 2. Norwegian Infantry Regiments After 1810			
Regimental Name	Facings, Piping & shoulder straps	Button Colour	Particularities
Søndenfjeldskeke Geworbne Infanteri Regiment	Dark blue/ white	Brass	They were classed as an enlisted regiment as they had more enlisted men than conscripts than in the other regiments
Nordenfjeldske/ke Geworbne Infanteri Regiment	Dark blue/ white	White metal	
Oplandske Geworbne Infanteri Regiment	Dark green/ white	White metal	Became an enlisted or *geworbne* regiment from 1810
Telemarkske Nationale Infanteri Regiment	Grass green/ white	Brass	
1st Trondhjemske Nationale Infanteri Regiment	Straw yellow/ white	White metal	
2nd Trondhjemske Nationale Infanteri Regiment	Straw Yellow	White metal	
Vesterlenske / Westerlehnske Nationale Infanteri Regiment	Green	Brass	
Bergenhusiske Nationale Infanteri Regiment	Black	Brass, pewter in 1813	

partly to form their own independent battalions, which would form reserve brigades. The *fribataljoner* battalions constituted a significant increase in the number of privates, compared to the army of 1808. But because there was a lack of officers, weapons and uniforms, most were *fribataljoner* battalions only on paper. Christian Frederik therefore decided in the autumn of 1813, that the *fribataljoner* battalion soldiers should not operate as battalions, but instead strengthen the field battalions, by attaching 50 levies to each division so that the field battalions, now had a theoretical force of 1,000 men, and this was mostly carried out during the mobilisation in 1814, but not completed in some field battalions.

Originally it had been intended that the depot battalions should maintain the strength of the field battalions, but during the mobilisation in 1814, their personnel had already been absorbed by the field battalions, and as both the *depot* and *landeværn* battalions were used as fortress garrisons, and some also served in the field with the field battalions. So, instead two *rekrut bataljoner* (recruit battalions) were formed from the remaining soldiers from the levy battalions. So all replacements for the field battalions were then intended to come from just the two recruit battalions for the whole *Søndenfjeldske*.

This gave the following theoretical strength in 1814:

23 *feltbataljoner* with 460 officers, 1,150 NCOs, 4,612 *geworbne* and 12,638 Nationale soldiers

Three *geworbne depot bataljoner* with 60 officers, 90 NCOs and 1,500 soldiers

Five Nationale *depot bataljoner* with 40 officers, 100 NCOs and 2,500 soldiers

Three *geworbne depot bataljoner* with 600 Landeværn

Three Nationale *depot bataljoner* with 900 Landeværn

13 *fribataljoner* with 325 NCOs and 9,750 soldiers (they were all absorbed into the field battalions)

Two *rekrut bataljoner* with 1,300 replacement recruits

Following these reforms, basic tactics were also changed. Norway had followed the same infantry tactical instructions as in Denmark (infantry fighting primarily in three ranks, *jægere* and light infantry, in two ranks and open order). But more often than not fighting in two ranks and open order was used by the line infantry, largely because of the broken nature of the terrain. This was also allowed by the 1788/1801 tactical instructions when operating in such close terrain. By adding more *jægere,* fighting in open order became more common, which was better suited to the broken hilly and forested nature of the Norwegian terrain. This led, after some discussion of the lessons learned, to the following letter from Frederik VI to Prince Frederik of Hessen 1 May 1813:

As various regiments have been asked for their experience and opinion if they think the three rank or two rank formation best suited for the fighting in Norway, the result is a general order that in the future, all regiments must form their companies/divisions in two ranks and that the reserve is generally formed by the third division under the new regulations. The drill is in this way made easier, and during the manoeuvring in battle, this is in Norway to great advantage.

This change in tactics was officially ordered in Norway by a *Kongelig Resolution* of 6 May 1813, which ordered that the use of the three-rank formations was abolished, and all fighting would from now onwards be in two ranks for all units. The normal battalion fighting formations were, as in 1807–1809, two divisions, formed in two ranks, supported by a second line, formed by another two divisions, also formed in two ranks. All fighting was in linear formations, never in column.

The Uniforms 1810–1814 (see Table 2)

In 1810–1813, the whole Norwegian army was, as noted, modernised and reorganised and this also had an effect on uniforms and uniform supplies. Two regiments, the 1st and 2nd *Akershusiske* Nationale regiments were disbanded, but reformed as a new *skarpskytte* regiment. Also, the Oplandske Nationale Regiment was reformed as Oplandske Geworbne Regiment. At the same time all the remaining regiments were reorganised with a more modern organisation and their uniforms were also modernised.

This led to the distribution of a new style or model of uniforms (system 1808), and also to some change in facing colours and other unit distinctions. When the Oplandske Geworbne Regiment was formed, they received quite a large number of new *kraprøde* (madder red M1808) uniform coatees. The regiment's previous facing colour had been the older standard green colour used for several years in both Denmark and Norway. This was a fine grass green colour, but it faded rather quickly into a much paler shade which over the years had led to much criticism from the regiments. So the new uniforms had a different dark green facing colour, the same colour as their new colours (*fanen*).[7]

Because of a general shortage of brass, the second battalion of the Bergenhusiske Nationale infanteri Regiment, received new red uniforms in 1813, but with white buttons instead of the correct brass buttons.

As more and more of the Norwegian army were reformed as *skarpskytte* they took to wearing grey uniforms. *fribataljoner* (levy battalions) were also clad in grey, and the widespread wearing by all troops, including the red-clad infantry, of grey *ydertrøjer* or *kaputtrøjer* short overcoats, led to the following comment from the Austrian diplomat, General von Steigentesch in July 1814:

As all has now been called out, is everybody from the highest *Hofmarskalk* (Lord Great Chamberlain) to the lowest shepherd, dressed in a kind of uniform, which bears the colour of the country, the grey colour of its Rocky Mountains.[8]

Uniform Supplies 1810–1814

In 1808 new uniforms and shakos were introduced in Denmark and a great effort had been made to produce and ship uniforms corresponding to this reform through the blockade to Norway. But the M1808 uniform coatees were for a different more practical reason shipped first, with trousers later or produced locally in Norway. But this uniform coat was cut quite differently than the previous uniform coats, the coat was now much shorter, set higher up the chest, and the fall fronted trousers had as a consequence, a higher waist, but shorter trouser legs and they needed to use the new short black gaiters M1808 as well. These new uniform coats were after delivery in Norway met with the complaints that 'These uniforms are too small for our soldiers' (letter from Christian August to Frederik VI). But this was all a misunderstanding. Being used to the rather long M1789/1795 coats, which were used with short M1789 breeches with a low waist, and as they kept on using the older model breeches, and not the new M1808 long trousers which had a higher waist, there would be a rather large gap at the stomach. The trouble was that the new coats had been delivered ahead of the new trousers, and so did not fit well with the older breeches then in use. This was only really resolved after the end of the hostilities of 1809.

A painting by the Norwegian artist J. C. Dahl of the parade ground of Engen in 1810 gives us an insight into the real situation in Norway. It shows the men probably wearing new uniforms, but still with the old hats, at the beginning of 1810. It also depicts a hat being worn by a red clad (grenadier?) officer and also a green light infantry soldier from a Lærdalske light infantry company with the old hat, while an officer, also from Lærdalske wears the new M1808 shako. It also shows three grenadiers from the Tjenestegørende Bergenhusiske Grenaderer still wearing the M1789 grenadier caps. This was probably the situation during 1810, but strong efforts were made by the new overall commander General Prince Frederik of Hessen to rectify this, and dress everybody in the new M1808 uniform, including the M1808 shako.

But from 1810, everything was ready, and all line infantry from then on received the new *kraprøde* M1808 uniform coatee, which, as explained earlier, was much shorter, and it also had a slightly higher stiff collar, with a higher waist, and the turnbacks were slightly different. At the same time the production of the special Norwegian model of the trousers M1808, in white, which had a higher

---

7 This was a stronger colour than the previously used, but over the years both the remaining uniforms facings and also the remaining colours have all turned dark blue!

8 Regarding the use of grey *overtrøjer* and *overbukser* in general, see *Norsk Våpenhistorisk Årbok 2014 Indføringen av grå uniform i Norge i 1814*, A. H. Hauge, O. J. Moen, K. E. Strøm.

waist 'reaching to just below the heart', to conform with the new uniform coat. New short black straight-cut gaiters were worn with the new M1808 white trousers. While the *geworbne* may have received the original M1808 blue trousers at first, later they received the same trousers in grey cloth. All Nationale troops seem to have only received the Norwegian-produced white M1808 trousers from 1810. From 1813–1814, only the Norwegian-made white M1808 trousers were supplied to all line infantry in Norway; none were shipped from Denmark.

This uniform system, in many ways radically different to those before, was the first Danish uniform system which tried first of all to give the body of the individual soldier more freedom of movement, especially the waist and thighs. It was a new way of thinking regarding uniforms. This was in worked closely with the new idea of freer movement of soldiers, especially using light infantry tactics. At the same time the soldiers were drilled with more gymnastics so to get the stiffness, caused by hard manual labour out of the body, and also learning to move easier on the battlefield, and understand the necessary movements of a soldier. Also the higher collar should have been able protect the neck against sword cuts. The Danish pattern shako M1808 had also started to be delivered from Denmark, and was also slowly beginning to be produced in Norway. The M1808 shako was now to be the standard headdress for all arms. This was also designed to protect the head from the worst effects of cuts and blows. The M1808 shako slowly began to replace the old hats, both M1789 and M1798 models which were then still in use, but the hats had to wear out first during training or worn by the Landeværn and only a few of the front-line troops appear to have received shakos shortly before the start of the war in 1814.

As an aside and before moving on, there has for several years been a myth, dating back to the Norwegian artists A. Bloch and A. Hauge (amongst others), who used the Swedish artist Carl Johan Ljunggen as a source – they all show the M1808 shako with four leather side chevrons, which is wrong, it had only two. This is wrong, and this is because Carl Johan Ljunggren did not make the original eye-witness drawings (In fact none of his later drawings were actually painted by him between 1813 and 1814). They were all painted by the Swedish hussar officer and later renowned painter Hjalmar Mörner and later just copied by Ljunggren. For some unknown reason Mörner got the M1808 shako wrong on all three of his original sketches regarding Danish/Norwegian soldiers (plus some other minor details). As Ljunggren just copied them meticulously, and all who followed did just the same, without checking their facts. So, only the standard M1808 shako with just two leather side chevrons was used in Norway.

Here are the details of what each Nationale soldier was supposed to receive, according to regulations from 1810:

Plate 10. Norwegian Infantry Colours II, Søndenfjeldske and Nordenfjeldske Geworbne Regiments

Top: Søndenfjeldske Geworbne Infanteri Regiment. Four blue colours were made especially for this regiment between 1785 and 1789. They were blue with red flames in each corner, the Dannebrog and the C7 cypher (ref. FMU007608, ref. FMU007655, ref. FMU007719 and ref. FMU007720). Dimensions: width 109 cm × height 113 cm.

Bottom: Nordenfjeldske Geworbne Infanteri Regiment. Four new colours were made between 1785 and 1789 for this regiment. They were blue with white flames, the Dannebrog and the C7 cypher (ref. FMU002384, ref. FMU007710, ref. FMU007718 and ref. FMU007721). Dimensions: width 109 cm × height 113 cm.

- One M1808 uniform coat (issued from Denmark)

- One M1808 shako (issued from Denmark, but also very soon produced in Norway)

- One pair of white loose summer M1808 trousers (made and issued in Norway)

- One pair of white M1808 field trousers (made and issued in Norway)

- One pair of short M1808 gaiters (most were made and issued in Norway)

- One pair of shoes (most were made and issued in Norway)

- One pair of stockings (issued mostly from Denmark)

- And one black neck stock. (most made and issued in Norway)

But at the same time it was stipulated that the stocks of old coats, knee length breeches and long gaiters of the pre-1803 model were still to be worn during training until they wore out. In the *geworbne* regiments the stocks of older white M1791 and blue M1803 fall-fronted gaiter trousers also had to be worn out before new trousers would be issued.

In the Danish army from 1810, all soldiers were ordered in the future to wear grey trousers in the field. But as Norway was already producing the white M1808 pattern locally in large numbers for the line infantry, and had also started to produce some trousers in grey for the new *skarpskytte* light units, this never happened in Norway.

As has already been mentioned, the Norwegian army was never generally issued with the M1788 greatcoats, only some few made and supplied for each company as sentry coats, and the troops suffered heavily in the winters of 1807–1808 and 1808–1809 because of this. Also a number of heavy red cloth *vagtkapper* sentry cloaks were made locally and partly distributed, also for those on sentry duty, but they were too heavy for any other duties. To compensate for this, they were eventually issued with the Norwegian invented and produced *ydertrøje or kaputtrøje* a short, spencer-style overcoat. In Norway these were officially allowed from October 1810,[9] but had been made locally

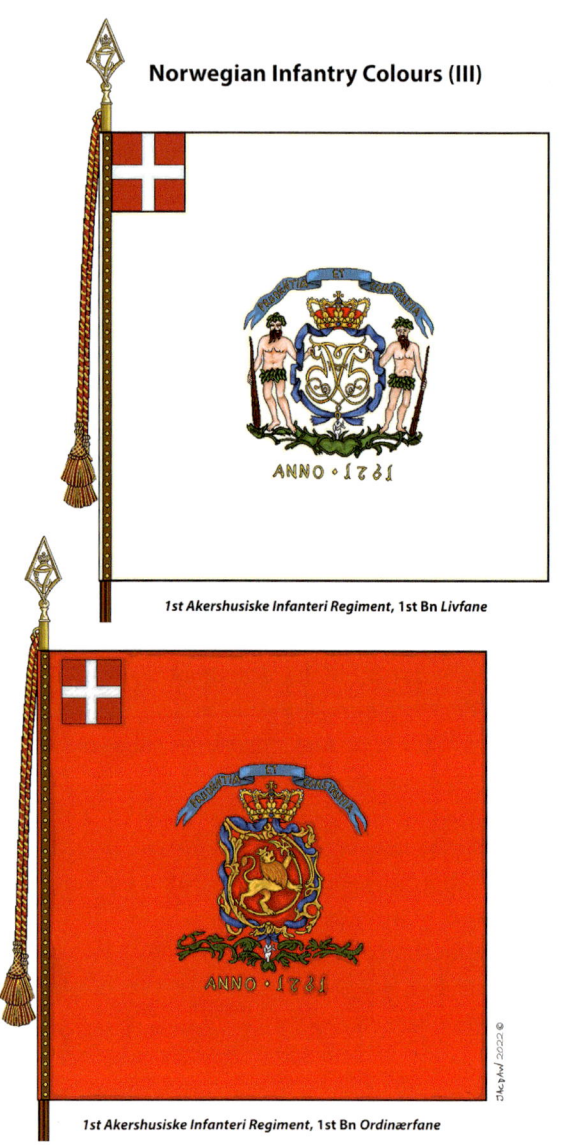

1st Akershusiske Infanteri Regiment, 1st Bn *Livfane*

1st Akershusiske Infanteri Regiment, 1st Bn *Ordinærfane*

Plate 11. Norwegian Infantry Colours III, 1st Akershusiske Regiment Livfane

Top: First battalion, Akershusiske Infanteri Regiment. A white M1761 *livfane* with mirror-imaged cypher C5. Ref. FMU002442. Dimensions unknown.

Bottom: First battalion, Akershusiske Infanteri Regiment. A red M1761 *ordinærfane* with the Norwegian Lion placed in the centre. Ref. FMU002408. Dimensions: width 145 cm × height 140 cm.

Note that the central motifs on the original colours are heavily oxidised and discoloured, so some errors of colouring and details may have crept in.

Author's reconstructions, with some reservations: the red *fane* was heavily modified after 1814 and the *livfane* was drawn based on an old black and white photograph. The position of the elephant is particularly intriguing.

---

9 According to *Kongelig Resolution* 10 October 1810. It was also approved to be 'with a cape over the shoulders'. Also 'Grey overalls with buttons down the seams', were approved on the same date. But they were probably already being manufactured and used locally

from 1807/1808, and were mainly used in 1808–1809 by the light units. They were made of locally produced *vadmel* homespun cloth. This short overcoat was to be grey, have 12 buttons and to be only waist/thigh length, but from 1810 to have an elbow length cape. They could be found in a wide range of colours. Inventories and eyewitnesses describe them as being different shades of grey, but brown and off-white are also mentioned. From Norwegian experience, this model was far more practical to move about in and better to wear for general duties. In 1810 51,000 pairs of grey gloves were also sent to Norway.

Following an Order of 18 July 1812 a new list of clothing terms was prescribed for all serving units:

> Every two years they would receive one uniform coatee, one field cap and one shako/hat feather
>
> Every three years they would receive one waistcoat and one pair of gloves (the NCO model was made of leather)
>
> Every four years they would receive one grey *ydertrøje*/short overcoat and a shako

In 1812–1813, the new reforms for officer and NCO insignia were applied, and new pointed cuffs were to be introduced in Norway, as in Denmark, replacing the previous system of epaulettes and the sash. The rank was denoted by chevrons of piping for the NCOs and chevrons of piping and rosettes above the now pointed cuffs for the officers.

The officers and NCOs had to modify their uniforms by the end of the year as this was now an integral part of their rank insignia. The soldiers continued to wear their M1808 coatees with the standard square cuffs and cuff flaps, and this never changed before after war's end 1814.

According to some later sources, the cords on new shako changed to white for musketeers, probably as red and yellow were the colour of the Danish kingdom and so under the new government they were ordered to be changed for the campaign of 1814. But this is clearly a myth, based on a misunderstanding which probably stems from Mörner's lack of detail, and Andreas Bloch's copy of the same, but we not have found any specific orders for this, and absolutely no real sources for this. Also some latter reconstructions show yellow cockades, but this was first used after 1815. Red and yellow cords were used to the end of the war.

On 10 June 1814 the new king, Christian Fredrik of Norway, declared that hereafter the entire army was to have

in Norway from *c.* 1807, probably made after a model first made in Trondheim. When they were officially approved in 1810, it was also permitted to have a separate cape. An original picture *c.* 1814, from Bergen (Dreier), clearly shows a short grey overcoat, *kaputtrøje*, with a cape, used during sentry duty.

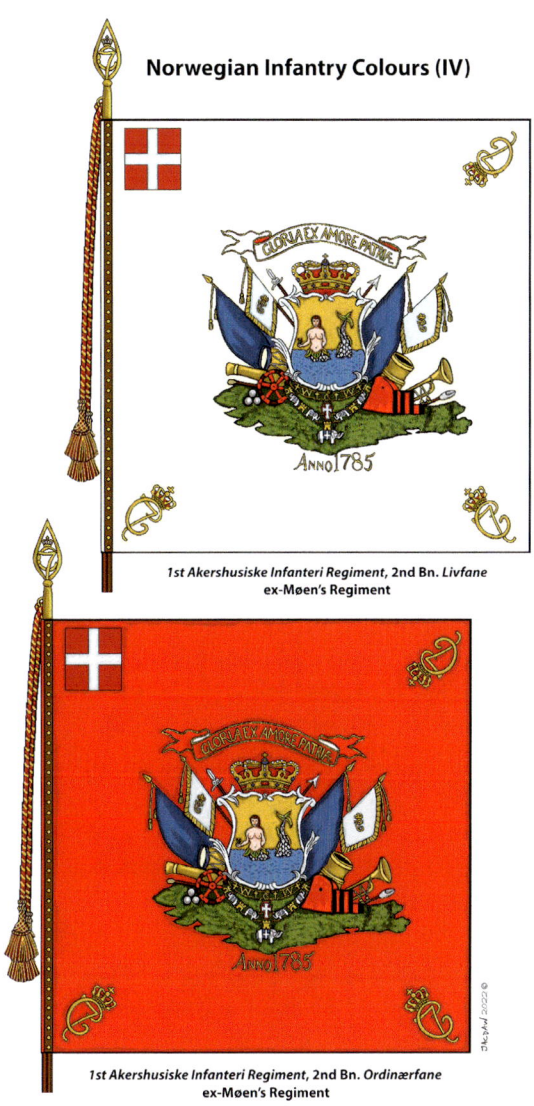

Norwegian Infantry Colours (IV)

1st Akershusiske Infanteri Regiment, 2nd Bn. Livfane ex-Møen's Regiment

1st Akershusiske Infanteri Regiment, 2nd Bn. Ordinærfane ex-Møen's Regiment

Plate 12. Norwegian Infantry Colours IV, 1st Akershusiske Regiment Ordinærfane

Top: First battalion, Akershusiske Infanteri Regiment, second battalion *livfane*, ex-Møen's Infanteri Regiment. Ref. FMU2360. Dimensions: width 125 cm × height 125 cm.

Bottom: First battalion, Akershusiske Infanteri Regiment, second battalion *ordinærfane*, ex-Møen's infantry regiment. Ref. FMU2340. Dimensions, width 125cm × height 126cm.

Author's reconstructions. Note that the central motifs on the original colours are heavily oxidised and discoloured, so some errors of colouring and details may have crept in. The field of the blue flags may not be exact and they appear to have some wavy lines on them.

grey uniforms. Regimental insignia were as before, but there were no facings, just one row of buttons. But as this was only to be introduced according to the normal clothing terms, this was not done before the end of the war. In reality, only two military units appear to have applied the new regulations before the end of the war, the new king's general staff, and the Norwegian Corps of Cadets. This order had its origin in the fact, that the new Norwegian kingdom was to receive a large quantity of grey cloth ordered from Great Britain, paid for and ready to be shipped. But pressure from Sweden forced the British government to block the order until the end of the war. Even after the enforced Swedish alliance, the line infantry regiments clung to their old red uniforms, although they finally received new grey ones made of the English cloth from 1818, and it is recorded that the last regiment to own red uniforms continued to wear them until 1864 for training.

Uniforms of the *Geworbne* Musketeers and their *Regimentsjægere*

They had same uniform terms as Danish Regiments, so they had by 1809–1810 begun to receive the new *kraprød* M1808 coatee, which was shorter, had a slightly higher stiff collar, with a higher waist, and the turnbacks were slightly different, and they had also received the new M1808 trousers which had a higher waist. The new M1808 trousers may at first have been the original blue model from Denmark, but by 1810–1814 had changed to grey M1810, also from Denmark. This is confirmed by a couple of contemporary drawings, both from 1814, of Nordenfjeldske/ke and Søndenfjeldske/ke. They may also at some point have received white M1808 trousers, made locally in Norway. They all had short black M1808 gaiters. They also received the new M1808 shako, with leather reinforcement, yellow and red cords, and a white plume for musketeers and green cords and plume for *regimentsjægere*. All had black cockades. Musketeers had white belts, while the *regimentsjægere* had black.

Uniforms of the Geworbne Liv Companie

This company had basically same uniform terms as the *geworbne*, and the same uniforms and equipment as ordinary Nationale musketeers, but as sign of their status as the first company of the regiment, the men were allowed to have an *infanteri sabel* M1756 sidearm. Also (at least in full dress and based on contemporary documents, confirmed by contemporary paintings by J. C. Dahl and J. F. L. Dreir) they were allowed to wear a tall white feather on their shakos.

Uniforms of the Geworbne Jæger Companie

Basically the same uniform terms as the *geworbne*, and had same uniforms and equipment as ordinary Nationale *regimentsjægere*, but as a sign of their status (at least in full dress) they were allowed to wear a tall green plume on their shako (based on documents confirmed by contemporary paintings by J. C. Dahl and J. F. L. Dreir)

Uniforms of the Nationale Musketeers and General Uniform Details for the Nationale

Around 1809–1811 this unit had begun to receive the new *kraprød* (madder red) M1808 uniform. They had also received the new M1808 white trousers which had a higher waist. All of the Nationale infantry regiments had white trousers in 1814, except the attached *fribataljon* soldiers, who mostly had locally made grey ones. They had all received short black M1808 gaiters, but most of those were the older long-model gaiters cut down in length. They also received the new M1808 shako with leather reinforcements. These had yellow and red cords with a white feather for musketeers. All had black cockades. Musketeers had white belts, normally (but not always) with the bayonet scabbard attached, and so wore no waist belt.

Uniforms of the *Regimentsjægere*

They had basically the same uniform terms as the Nationale, and the same basic uniform. They also received the new M1808 shako, with leather reinforcements, green cords and feather plume. All had black belts and black cockades.

Uniforms of the Musicians (*Tamboure, Hornblæsere* and *Hoboister*)

These had adopted the same uniforms of their parent regiments, including the M1808 shako. From 1810 all *geworbne* and Nationale musketeer companies had two *tamboure* (drummers) and a *piber* (fifer). The drums were the brass M1753 model in the *geworbne* companies, but still a mixture of both brass and wooden drums in the Nationale companies. The fifers' flutes were made of wood and were carried when not in use in a small brass M1753 flute container suspended with cords, probably red and yellow. Also, each *regimentsjæger* company should from then onwards each have three *hornblæsere* (hornists). This caused some problems as Norway had few men able to play a horn properly. As with weapons and uniforms, both models of brass horns (*waldhorns* and *halvmanehorns*) were in such short supply that in 1811, those *regiments jæger* hornists who had not received a proper horn were allowed to buy and use the traditional Norwegian wooden *lur* until the correct horns could be supplied from Denmark, where 230 had been ordered for shipment to Norway.[10]

---

10 Contrary to common belief, the traditional Viking-age *lur* was not always a bronze, curved horn (a rare ceremonial instrument), but was more commonly a straight horn made out of birch wood and was around one metre long. In 1800 this type of *lur* was still in use by Norwegian farmers and dairy maids in the mountains and forests for signalling and calling their beasts in from their pastures. It is still practised to this day, and it has a particularly melodious note.

THE NORWEGIAN LINE INFANTRY: UNIFORMS

Plate 13. Norwegian Infantry Colours V, 2nd Akershusiske Regiment

These colours were made in 1777.

Top: Second battalion, Akershusiske Infantry Regiment, *ordinærfane*. Ref. AM080032. Dimensions: width 135 cm x height 114 cm.

Bottom: Second battalion, Akershusiske Infantry Regiment, *ordinærfane*. Ref. FMU3089. Dimensions: width 121 cm × height 129 cm. There was also a white *livfane*, dated 1783 with the same motifs as this model, which was also carried. Ref. FMU4361.

These colours continued to be carried until they were disbanded, but in 1788 the second battalion also received some even older 1763 colours, ex-Danske Livregiment.

The central motifs on the original colours are heavily oxidised and discoloured, so some errors of colouring and details may have crept in. Author's reconstruction.

As already noted, unlike Denmark, Norway did not have any traditions of attached or hired musicians, called *hoboister* (bandsmen) but this was changed by a letter from the King (Frederik as already noted) to the Norwegian general staff dated 1 November 1811, where he allowed each regiment in Norway to hire six *hoboister* each. But if they wanted to hire more, they would have to pay out of their own pockets. So few if any regiments hired more than the six allowed. Instead, the ordinary drummers, fifers and horn blowers, when needed, were formed into a regimental band. The *hoboister* normally played different brass instruments. The *tamboure*, *piber* and *hornblæsere* wore the uniform of their parent company, together with swallows nests on the shoulders of their uniform coat, which from 1812 became slightly simpler, made of ordinary cloth only. Also, those having the rank of NCOs adopted the new cloth lace chevrons for the NCOs, and *dragoner* with white wool piping.

The *hoboister* had ordinary regimental uniforms, but were as a special insignia, allowed a white, blue-tipped plume. When the ordinary drummers, fifers and horn blowers, were part of the regimental band, they may have adopted the blue-tipped plume. The *trommekorporal* and *tambourmajor* adopted the new NCO distinctions from 1812/1813, and also a longer white, blue-tipped plume.

Uniforms of the Regimental *Tømmermænd* (Sappers)

The sappers had adopted the same uniforms of their parent regiments, including the M1808 model shako with a white feather. They retained their right to wear full beards. The *regimentsjægere*, *geworbne jæger* and *liv companie* companies did not have sappers attached.

Uniforms of the Regimental Artillerymen

The regimental gunners were dressed the same as the rest of the men of their regiment, but they were only armed as artillerymen with an *infanteri sabel* M1756 for personal defence. The attached artillery drivers and wagon train drivers, including those of the regimental baggage train, had previously been issued old uniforms, and long boots, but were by 1814 issued a simple grey uniform coat with grey collar and cuffs. Also, most were issued blue cavalry overalls, surplus from the dragoons. For headwear they received simple *kabuds* caps made of cloth, but from 1810 made of calfskin.

Uniforms of the Soldiers of the *Fribataljon*

They had a simple grey *vadmel* homespun uniform coatee, with a red collar and cuffs. It had one row of buttons at front and a pair of simple long wide trousers (overalls), also made of homespun cloth. They would be issued a pair of shoes as well. For headwear, they received simple *kabuds* caps, which were made of calfskin, like those worn by the *skiløber* with (if possible) a grey plume, which was probably made of wool, so the colour was a greyish off white. When absorbed into the line regiments, some received uniforms from their new regiment. This was done in Oplandske Geworbne Regiment, and possibly also in Søndenfjeldskeke Geworbne Infanteri Regiment. The two regiments from Trondheim did not have any levies, so did not equip any, but clothed their reserves in normal regimental uniforms (according to a letter from General Prince Frederik of Hessen 22 December 1811 to the King and his answer on the 11 January 1812 and *Kongelig Resolution* 8 November 1812).

Uniforms of the Landeværn

As a reserve of mainly older and not always so fit for service former soldiers, the Landeværn did not have a specific uniform as in Denmark, but received the best of the outdated, surplus or redundant uniforms of the line regiments to which they were attached.

Uniforms of the NCOs

The NCO uniforms followed the same changes as in Denmark, and they generally received uniforms with the same terms as in Denmark. Before the NCOs were issued with firearms, from *c.* 1809–1810, the NCOs did not have a shoulder strap, on left shoulder, as they did not carry a cartridge box, but they did have a button-coloured lace epaulette denoting their status, M1789, sewn onto their right shoulder (*sergenter* had a button-coloured epaulette M1778, on both shoulders). When they were re-equipped with firearms from *c.* 1809–1810 they were also given a shoulder strap on the left shoulder called a *dragon*, in the facing colour piped with button-coloured metallic thread. In August 1812 the new reforms of officer and NCO insignia were put in place and new pointed cuffs were to be introduced for the NCOs in Norway, replacing the previous system of epaulettes and *dragons*. The rank was instead denoted by cloth lace chevrons for the NCOs and *dragoner* with white wool piping. But as there were some problems delivering the correct cloth lace from Denmark, they were only ready by the beginning of 1813.

Uniforms of the Officers

The officers were still allowed to wear long-tailed uniform coats with lapels in the special *ponceau* (poppy red) colour allowed for officers until 1812, when they were allowed to have them in *kraprød* (madder red0. Most had done that by 1814, so as not to stand out as a target. Although first allowed blue trousers, then white, most had adopted grey trousers by 1813/1814. Although officers were still allowed to wear short hussar boots, in November 1813 the King accepted a request for black cloth for officers' gaiters. This may have been worn by some officers in 1814. Many of the officers had the shakos made privately and were still using them. They were generally entirely made of leather without the V strengtheners on the sides. They were also still allowed to wear red M1788/98 officers' *surtout*, with a cape, but as this often made them stand out as a target, several began adopting privately acquired coats in grey or short grey Norwegian *kort overkjole* or *kaputtrøje*, a short spencer-style overcoat, with cape, as also worn by most of the soldiers. But as late as 1814 some officers were still wearing them in red. In August 1812, the new reforms to officer and NCO insignia were put in place and new pointed cuffs were to be introduced in Norway as in Denmark, replacing the previous system of epaulettes and the waist sash. Rank was denoted by chevrons of piping for the NCOs and chevrons of piping and rosettes above the now pointed cuffs for the officers.

The officers and NCOs had to modify their uniforms by the beginning of 1813; they were an integral part of their rank insignia. The *porte épée*, in red and gold silk was still allowed and carried.

Uniforms of the Officers of the Geworbne Liv Companie

The officers of Geworbne Liv Companie had long white plumes for parades.

Arms and Equipment

The men in the *geworbne* and Nationale musketeer companies were equipped with a musket, mostly the M1774, which was probably the most common model used in Norway. Nearly all Nationale soldiers used this simple sturdy musket. By 1814, most were rather worn, and the locks especially gave some trouble and they often had to be repaired frequently. Another important musket was the *skarpskyttegevær* M1789, from 1810 used by the NCOs. In total Norway only received only 581 of this musket model.[11]

Also, some Nationale soldiers had to use the older M1769 and even the outdated M1745, but most of those older models were by 1808 mostly repaired and turned over to the Landeværn and from 1812, to the levy soldiers. The *Regimentsjægere* should have been issued with rifles, first the older models already found in small numbers in Norway (M1785 and M1791). From late 1810 both the *geworbne* and Nationale *jæger* companies began receiving rifles, mainly the M1791/1803 and M1803 *jæger* rifles. To go with the rifles from 1810 they were also issued with converted M1791 *hirschfängers* as a sword bayonet, used by the new *jæger* companies. In 1811 or thereabouts some M1807 rifles with the new *Khyls* lock also made their way to Norway. We know this because a surviving model exists in Norway. The rifle has 'OR J.C. I 55' stamped on the rear of the barrel. This probably refers to the Oplandske Geworbne Infanteri Regiment (OR) that was raised on 1 July 1810.

---

11 *Fortegnelse over Antal og Beskaffenhed af de vigtigste i samtlige norske Landarsenaler havende militaire Fornødenheder ved Aarets Udgang*, 1837.

Within that regiment there was a regular *geworbne bataljon* with a *jæger* company (J.C.) and the rifle could have belonged to *jæger* no 55. (55) in the first battalion.

But not all the *jægere* received rifles, especially some of those coming from the second field battalion. A known example is the 2nd *jæger division* from the Bergenhusiske Nationale Infanteri Regiment who reported that they had 98 rifles and 62 *skarpskyttegeværer* in 1814. A couple of other Nationale *jæger* companies probably had same mix of rifles and shortened muskets.

The NCOs, drummers, fifers, hornists and regimental artillerymen carried the M1756 *infanteri sabel* on a waist belt. From 1810, most Nationale musketeers received the pouch, and a bayonet scabbard attached. The infantry officers carried the officers' sabre M1789, either the official model or a privately made variant. The sword knot and tassel *porte épée* was made of red and gold silk. It was carried in a black leather scabbard with brass fittings suspended from a black leather waist belt on two slings. It had a buckle of two lion's heads and an 'S' clasp. At the start of the period some officers may still have used the old sword belt with a rectangular brass buckle. Soldiers carried the *ransel* calfskin knapsacks; most having been converted with two white leather straps for the musketeers and black for the *Regimentsjægere*. These were far more practical. They were also issued off-white *sejldugs brødpose* (bread-bags), worn on a black sling, but not all troops received them, namely the levies, some reserves and the Landeværn. In 1814 several soldiers were seen without bread-bags, but with loaves, flatbreads, salted meat and even sides of dried fish tied to their backpacks.

A contemporary picture by Hjalmar Mörner, later copied by C. J. Ljunggren, shows soldiers without bread-bags. Canteens were as described earlier. A camp axe and one copper cooking pot with a pan lid for each four soldiers were carried by the company baggage horses. Just after the end of the war in October 1814, the *Norske Commisaiats Collegion* (the Norwegian Defence Department), made a final report, where they concluded that they had during the war been able to issue nearly all the weapons, uniforms and equipment needed during and after the war. But they added 'this is only possible in the future, if the soldiers stop their bad habits of throwing lots of useful equipment away, without reason'.

5

Norwegian Infantry Colours

In the years 1761, 1775 and 1778 new stands of infantry colours were ordered and made, in both Norway and Denmark. At this time all the regiments had two battalions and each regiment received two colours, one white *livfane* ('life colour') and one regimental *ordinærfane* ('ordinary colour') for the first battalion and two regimental *ordinærfanen* for the second battalion. At this time both battalions of a regiment always fought together, so they had only needed one rallying point, therefore only one colour per battalion was issued for active service. But due to the influence of General Hutt and his modern tactical ideas, Prince Carl von Hessen, who was now the overall commander of the army, prepared a series of major tactical reforms for the army between 1785 and 1789. As all regiments in Denmark were made up of mainly enlisted soldiers at the time, in the first and second battalions, this was seen as necessary. From there on each battalion would be able to be divided into two units of two companies, called a 'division'. Also new drill and regimental organisation were put in place.

From 1785 all Danish colours were to be standardised, and the white *livfane* was to be no longer issued (with a few exceptions), and all *ordinærfane* should now be in the regimental colour and with the arms of either their province or the arms of Denmark for royal regiments and be painted on silk, no longer embroidered.

After this change in Denmark, it was decided that from 1788–1789 the Norwegian army should also be reorganised and learn the new drills. In 1789 the Norwegian army was reorganised into ten regiments of foot (there were two *geworbne* and eight Nationale regiments, some with up to four battalions each).

This also meant that all newly formed battalions in Norway were to carry two colours (generally four to a regiment plus one grenadier colour). But most regiments in Norway had already received two new colours of the old model, made between 1766 and 1787, and at some considerable cost as the Nationale recruits in Norway were in peacetime only exercised 12 days a year in company drill, and only every fourth year were they formed into the battalions of their parent regiment, in order to be exercised for 16 days in regimental drill. Furthermore, in times of war, only one field battalion was, according to the new reform, to be formed by each Nationale regiment (together with its two attached *geworbne* grenadier companies, who formed separate battalions) and they were the only battalions expected to carry any colours into battle. All other colours were, in times of war, placed in the arsenals, to be taken out again only for peacetime drills. So it was decided that only the new Norwegian Nationale regiments would receive the now surplus Danish colours (mostly issued in Denmark during the years 1766–1785). This was in the common Danish/Norwegian interest of economy and to lighten the financial burden on the Norwegian regiments in general.

The two enlisted *geworbne* regiments would each form two field battalions in war, and they would each receive four new Norwegian M1787 colours, made after the Danish 1785 model (two for each battalion) and a further M1785 colour for their two *geworbne* grenadier companies.

Each Nationale regiment would form only one field battalion each, and further two grenadier companies, and the field battalion would normally carry the original Norwegian colours issued in 1761, 1775 and 1778 in the field, and only in a very few cases were any Danish Colours carried in the field. Their two combined *geworbne* grenadier companies carried one M1785 grenadier colour. The rest of the regiment formed a combined depot/reserve/Landeværn battalion, which in theory carried the two Danish colours, but all surplus colours were normally stored in the arsenals.

Most of the Norwegian colours issued between 1766 and 1785 bore the arms of Norway, the golden crowned lion holding the axe of Saint Olaf on a red shield, surrounded with different trophy of arms or other symbols.

Notes: The Swedes looted a number of different arsenals where some of the colours were stored, and they then claimed to have won them in action, for example at Fredericksten.

References marked FMU are preserved in the collection of the Norwegian Army Museum (Forsvarsmuseet).

References marked AM are preserved in the collection of the Swedish Army Museum (Armémuseum).

References marked HAO are preserved in the collection of the Danish Army Museum, (Krigsmuseet).

NORWEGIAN INFANTRY COLOURS

Plate 14. Opplandske Nationale Infanteri Regiment pre-1810

These colours are ex–2nd Battalion, Opplandske Nationale Infanteri Regiment, which had been disbanded

Top: Opplandske Nationale Infanteri Regiment, 1st Battalion. One white M1781 *livfane* with the arms of Norway, Dannebrog and 'CR'. Ref. AM080031. Dimensions unconfirmed, but probably the same as below.

Bottom: Opplandske Nationale Infanteri Regiment, 1st Battalion. One blue M1781 *ordinærfane* with the arms of Norway, Dannebrog and 'CR'. Ref. FMU002020. Dimensions width 115 cm × height 117 cm.

Note: These illustrations are based on the original 1773 approbation drawings, so some errors of colouring and details may have crept in. Author's reconstructions.

The Grenadier Colours, *Grenaderfane* M1785

Although for simplicity the term *geworbne* is used here, for most of our period not all the grenadiers from the Nationale regiments were referred to as *geworbne*, but called *tjenestegørende grenadiers* (active serving grenadiers), or Nationale *grenaderer*, although this latter was probably not an official term. Until 1807 there were only five grenadier battalions (one *geworbne* and four Nationale). But beginning in 1808 and completed in early 1809, two more grenadier battalions were formed giving a new total of seven battalions (two *geworbne* and five Nationale). Note also that the grenadier colours were abolished after 1810, and they were no longer used after this point but stored in arsenals. There was a total of 15 M1785 grenadier colours in Norway, 14 actually carried by the grenadier battalions, and one held in reserve.

The influence of the army reform of 1788/1789 regarding colours meant that the Norwegian army was also reformed along the same lines as in Denmark, but with some regional differences. This meant that some regiments were disbanded, and their battalions and companies were transferred into new regiments or into the existing ones. Their colours followed the men from the disbanded regiments into the new regiments. The two *geworbne* regiments received new sets of colours in 1788, after the Danish M1785 model (but made specifically for Norway, bearing the Norwegian Lion).

The following is the outcome of the reform, which was how things stayed until 1810:

The Søndenfjeldske Geworbne Infanteri Regiment succeeded the 1st Smaalehnske Infanteri Regiment

Strength: enlisted musketeer companies and two *geworbne* grenadier companies; later two Nationale battalions with each six companies.

They had the following colours:

Two *Grenaderfane* M1785

Four blue colours which were made specifically for this regiment in *c.* 1785/89.[1] They were blue with red flames, the Dannebrog and the CVII cypher (references FMU007608, FMU007655, FMU007719 and FMU007720). They were carried by the two field battalions.

---

1 Skaars' explanation is that 1st Smaalehnske had no usable colours. As the regiments from 1788 should have four musketeer colours and one grenadier colour 1st Smaalehnske received four. 1st Akershusiske received two colours from Oldenburgske (really Møenske) regiment, one white and one red.

Two older green CVI colours, probably the older colours of the regiment, not used after receiving the four new ones (ref. FMU006078 and ref. FMU007650 – see * note below), but relegated to the reserve battalions

There were also two colours which had originally belonged to the Jyske Infanteri Regiment (probably not used for long and purloined in 1814 by the Swedes)[2]

* After the change in the regulations for infantry colours in 1785 and 1787 a number of older, now surplus colours from the Danish regiments were sent to the Norwegian infantry regiments in 1788:

Det Oldenburgske Infanteri Regiment (ex-Møenske), two colours were sent to the 1st Akershusiske Infanteri Regiment

Danske Livregiment til Fods, two colours were sent to the 2nd Akershusiske Infanteri Regiment

Siælandske Infanteri Regiment (ex-Oldenburgske), two colours were sent to the 1st Oplandske Infanteri Regiment

Riibske Infanteri Regiment (ex-Slesvigske), two colours were sent to the 2nd Oplandske Infanteri Regiment

Aalborgske Infanteri Regiment (ex Falsterske), two of their old colours were sent to the 1st Westerlehnske Infanteri Regiment

Det Fyenske Infanteri Regiment (ex-Sjællandske), two colours were sent to the 2nd Westerlehnske Infanteri Regiment

Det Holstenske Infanteri Regiment (ex-Lollandske), two colours were sent to the 1st Bergenhusiske Infanteri Regiment

Kronprinsens Regiment, two colours were sent to the 2nd Bergenhusiske Infanteri Regiment

Norske Livregiment til Fods, two colours were sent to the 1st Smaalehnske Infanteri Regiment

Norwegian Infantry Colours (VII)

Oplandske Geworbne Nationale Infanteri Regiment M1810, 1st and 2nd Battalions

Plate 15. Norwegian Colours VII

Oplandske Geworbne Infanteri Regiment 1810

When this regiment became the Oplandske Geworbne Infanteri Regiment in 1810 it received a stand of eight new green colours bearing the cypher of Frederik VI. When Norway was invaded and annexed by Sweden in 1814 the colours were all heavily modified. The flames, the Dannebrog and the cyphers of Frederik VI were removed and the cypher of Carl XIII of Sweden was added to the top and bottom of the fly. All eight of these colours have been preserved, references FMU2022, FMU2036, FMU2351, FMU7545, FMU7628, FMU7707, FMU13485 and FMU7745. They have all been modified. Dimensions: width 130 cm × height 110 cm.

Note: The preserved colours today appear to be blue due to discolouration; the original green has faded to blue. Author's reconstruction.

---

2   They were rather new and finely made colours, not cheap or of low quality in any way.

Jyske Infanteri Regiment, two colours were sent to the 1st Smaalehnske Infanteri Regiment

Kongens Regiment til Fods, two colours were sent to the 2nd Smaalehnske Infanteri Regiment

Prins Fredericks Infanteri Regiment, two colours were sent to the 1st Trondhjemske Infanteri Regiment

Aarhusiske Regiment (ex-Bornholmske), two colours were sent to the 2nd Trondhjemske Infanteri Regiment

Det Viborgske Infanteri Regiment (ex-Holstenske), only one of their (green) colours was sent to the 3rd Trondhjemske Infanteri Regiment

The Nordenfjeldske Geworbne Infanteri Regiment, which was formed from the 2nd Oplandske Infanteri Regiment

Strength: 1st and 2nd Nationale battalions and two *geworbne* grenadier companies

They had the following colours:

Two *grenader fane* M1785

Four colours which were specially made around 1785/89 for this regiment. They were blue with white flames, the Dannebrog and the CVII cypher (ref. FMU002384, ref. FMU007710, ref. FMU007718 and ref. FMU007721).

There were also two other colours, probably never used, from the Riibske Infanteri Regiment (ex-Slesvigske) (ref. FMU002451 and unknown) but relegated to the reserve battalions.

The 1st Akershusiske Infanteri Regiment

Strength: 1st and 2nd Nationale battalions and two *geworbne* grenadier companies

They had the following colours:

One *grenader fane* M1785

For the first, or field, battalion, one white M1761 colour with mirror imaged CVII cypher (ref. FMU002442) and one red M1761 colour bearing a Norwegian lion (ref. FMU002408)

For the second battalion, one white colour came from the Oldenburgske Infanteri Regiment (ex-Møenske Infanteri Regiment) (ref. FMU002360) and one red colour also from the Oldenburgske Infanteri Regiment (ex-Møenske Infanteri Regiment)(ref. FMU002340)

The 2nd Akershusiske Infanteri Regiment

Strength: 1st and 2nd Nationale battalions and two *geworbne* grenadier companies

They had the following colours:

One *grenader fane* M1785

For the first (field) battalion, one white M1783 colour with the Norwegian Lion over seven mountains (ref. FMU 004361) and one red M1777 colour with the Norwegian Lion over seven mountains (ref. FMU 003089)

For the second battalion, one white colour from the Danske Livregiment til Fods (Swedish Army Museum ref. AM080029) and one yellow colour from the Danske Livregiment til Fods (ref. FMU002450)

The Oplandske Infanteri Regiment formed from 1st Oplandske Infanteri Regiment[3]

Strength: 1st and 2nd Nationale battalions and two *geworbne* grenadier companies

It had the following colours:

One *grenader fane* M1785

For the first (field) battalion, one white M1781 colour with the arms of Norway, the Dannebrog and a CR cypher (lost) and one blue M1781 colour with the arms of Norway, the Dannebrog and CR cypher (ref. FMU002020)[4]

---

[3] Amongst the drawings of colours taken (stolen!) by the Swedish army in 1814, there is one of a fragment of a colour with the mirror image of a CVII cypher and underneath the arms of Jutland. This is probably one of the colours they found in Frederiksten Arsenal after the surrender. Probably it was never carried, and it was in tatters but still useful as a trophy.

[4] There is no clear information which colours Oplandske took over in 1789, but as the 2nd Oplandske was taken over by the new Nordenfjeldske in same year, and apparently they received a complete set of colours for the new regiment in 1785/89, they would

The second battalion had one white M1781 colour Sjælandske Regiment (ex-Oldenburgske Regiment) (ref. FMU000048). It had a white field with a small Dannebrog in the top quarter by the staff, in the centre the crowned arms of Holstein (or two bars *gules*) within the chains of the Order of the Dannebrog and Order of the Elephant surrounded by a trophy of arms on a green grass island, in each of the other angles the crowned monogram of CVII. Under the shield, the title DET OLDENBORGSKE REGIMENT TIL FODS written on a pale red ribbon. And one green M1781 colour of the Sjællandske Regiment (ex-Oldenburgske Regiment), ref. FMU007612). It had the same motifs as the preceding colour. Embroidered, not painted.

The Telemarkske Infanteri Regiment was created in 1789 with a battalion from the 2nd Smaalehnske and a battalion from the 1st Westerlehnske Regiments together with two *geworbne* grenadier companies

Strength: 1st and 2nd Nationale battalions and two *geworbne* grenadier companies

They had the following colours:

One *grenader fane* M1785

For the first (field) battalion, one white M1781 colour with the arms of Norway, the Dannebrog and the CVII cypher and the motto *Følg mig Nordmænd, Strid med mod, vid at seier Koster blod*, which translates as 'Follow me Norwegians, fight with courage, you know that victory costs blood' (ref. FMU007465). Also one red M1781 colour with the same motifs as the preceding colour (ref. FMU007433).

For the second battalion, one white colour, the *livfane*, originally made for the Kongens Regiment til Fods which bore the combined arms of Denmark (ref. FMU2017) and one blue colour, the regimental colour, originally made for the Kongens Regiment til Fods which bore the combined arms of Denmark (ref. FMU002451)

Telemarkske Nationale Infanteri Regiment,
1st Bn *Ordinærfane*, ex-2nd Smålenske Infanteri Regiment

Plate 16. Norwegian Colours VIII

Telemarkske Infanteri Regiment

This regiment carried an M1781 colour from the reformed ex-2nd Battalion Smaalehnske Infanteri Regiment, Reference FMU007433. Width 127 cm × height 122 cm. There was a white (*liv*) colour (ref. FMU007465) bearing exactly the same inscription and motifs.

Author's reconstruction.

The Westerlehnske Infanteri Regiment formed partly from the 1st and the former 2nd Westerlehnske Infanteri Regiments.5

Strength: 1st, 2nd and 3rd Nationale battalions and two *geworbne* grenadier companies.

They had the following colours:

One M1785 *grenader fane*

For the first or field battalion, two colours, one white and one yellow from the ex-2nd Westerlehnske Regiment (ref. FMU00 7746, ref. FMU00116). These colours have a peculiarity, insofar the arms and supporters have been cut out from some older colours and been stitched onto new sheets.

---

have had no need for more colours. It is therefore logical to think that Oplandske then received the two M1781 colours from the 2nd Oplandske which seems to be more likely.

5   Probably this regiment only used the former Danish colours 1789–1814, and not specific Norwegian models.

For the second battalion, one white colour (ex-Dronningens Livregiment, ref. HAO7746) and one grey/blue (ex-Dronningens Livregiment, ref. HAO7546). They also had the following colours: one white colour Aalborgske Infanteri Regiment (ex-Falsterske Infanteri Regiment, ref. FMU005979), one red colour Aalborgske Infanteri Regiment (ex-Falsterske Infanteri Regiment, ref. FMU005969), one white colour Fyenske Infanteri Regiment (ex-Sjællandske Infanteri Regiment, reference missing) and one yellow colour Fynske Infanteri Regiment (ex-Sjællandske Infanteri Regiment, ref. FMU007613). The Bergenhusiske Infanteri Regiment

Strength: 1st, 2nd, 3rd and 4th Nationale battalions and two *geworbne* grenadier companies.

They had the following colour:

One *grenader fane* M1785

For the first (field) battalion, one white M1773 colour with a Norwegian Lion standing over seven mountains (FMU 21582) and one red M1773 colour with a Norwegian Lion over seven mountains (ref. FMU 21583, ref. FMU007520).6

The second battalion had one white colour from the Holstenske Infanteri Regiment (ex-Lollandske Infanteri Regiment) (ref. FMU007521)

The 1st Trondhjemske Infanteri Regiment

Strength: 1st, 2nd and 3rd Nationale battalions, one skiløber battalion and two geworbne grenadier companies.

They had the following colours:

One M1785 *grenader fane*

For the first (field) battalion, one white M1773 colour bearing a crowned mirror image CVII cypher surrounded by a blue ribbon with the Order of the Elephant, and one yellow M1775 ex-Søndenfjedske colour with the arms of Norway (ref. FMU013471)

---

6 One of those colours should have been white, so there is some doubt to which regiment FMU007520 actually belonged to. Possibly the correct white colour (*livfane*) is missing?

The second battalion had one white M1768 colour from the Prins Frederiks Regiment (ref. FMU013474), and M1768 colour from the Prins Frederiks Regiment (FMU013476).7

The 2nd Trondhjemske Infanteri Regiment

Strength: 1st, 2nd and 3rd Nationale battalions and two *geworbne* grenadier companies.

They had the following colours:

One Dannebrog *grenader fane* M1785

For the first (field) battalion, one white colour with blue flames with the arms of Norway and the motto HILD KRIGER MELLEM KLIPPER FØDE OG FÆGT PAA SEYER ELLER DØD ('Hail to the warrior, born between the mountains, fight victoriously or die') (ref. FMU 013473). Also one blue colour with white flames with the same motto and motifs as the preceding colour (ref. FMU02353). Both

---

7 The two colours sent to 1st Trondhjemske from Prins Frederiks Geworbne Regiment, had, according to normal logic, the wrong motif for colours belonging to a Prince's regiment (normally his mirror imaged monogram or the arms of a Prince of Denmark). They clearly carried the common arms of a lesser island, which was totally unthinkable in those times (used in common, for Fyen, Falster and Bornholm). But research into the archives of the Prins Frederiks Geworbne Regiment (later to become Prins Christian Frederiks Regiment), gave the following reason for this abnormality. Formally this regiment had been named Lollandske Geworbne Regiment (1735–1753), and in 1748 had asked for a new set of colours with 'some special mark or arm of the island of Laaland', but this did not happen for a number of reasons. Instead the new colours sent had the full arms of Denmark in a blue band (as had the old ones) until the reign of Christian VII. In 1753 they changed the name to Prins Frederiks Geworbne Regiment and the newborn little brother of the future King Christian VII was made the formal commander. But the regiment apparently could not let go of the idea that it should not bear the ordinary arms of Denmark, and still wanted a special regional distinction. Apparently the real commander of the regiment, General von Grambow, persuaded the young prince to accept the idea of not having his special arms as a prince on the new colours, so when Christian became king in 1766, his little brother quickly asked for new colours of a special design agreed with von Grambow. But the King took his time, and only in 1769 were the designs allowed as a special favour to his brother. Apparently the Prince paid for them himself, but in reality, although a set of splendid colours, they carried only the common arms of a lesser island upon them. Prince Frederik started a new tradition when first he, then later his son Prince Christian Frederik, hammered special nails with their monograms and year of issue into their regimental colours.

Plate 17. Norwegian Colours IX

Westerlehnske Nationale Infanteri Regiment

Top: M1773 white *livfane*, ex-2nd Battalion of the Westerlehnske Regiment, ref. FMU7746. Dimensions: width 148 cm × height 157 cm.

Bottom: M1773 Yellow *ordinærfane* ex second battalion of the Westerlehnske Regiment ref. FMU116. Dimensions: width 145 cm × height 145 cm.

These colours are noteworthy as the arms and supporters have been cut from older colours and stitched onto new sheets, a practice not unknown in Norway.

Author's reconstructions.

were ex-Nordenfjeldske Geworbne Infanteri Regiment colours received in 1788.

The second battalion had one white colour made with arms of Denmark and the Dannebrog, cut out from an older colour (1732 perhaps), sewn onto a white silk cloth. Today only the cut-out arms of Denmark remain (under reference FMU013468), and one green colour M1777, from the Viborgske Infanteri Regiment (ex-Holstenske Infanteri Regiment) (ref. FMU013475). The white M1777 colour remained in Denmark, where it is preserved in Krigsmuseet under ref. 142 (087).

The Army Reform of 1810

These reforms of 1810–1813 modified the Norwegian Army in preparation for a major war with Sweden. All the grenadier companies were disbanded as were some line regiments. The light infantry was heavily increased and some of the disbanded regiments were converted into light infantry, so they did not carry colours. All the regiments had a new organisation; each now had four battalions, but only two field battalions, so in theory they needed eight colours. Only one regiment received a new set of colours (Oplandske) for all their battalions. It is possible that a few second battalions may have carried old Danish colours, but all the evidence points to the work done to reassign the older Norwegian colours between regiments, so that nearly all field battalions, at least in 1814, had Norwegian colours. But information is scarce, and in several cases, one cannot be sure which colours were really carried between 1810 and 1814. All the surplus colours were put into store; probably they were mainly the Danish colours together with the oldest Norwegian colours (a number of these were taken by the Swedes in 1814 as easy trophies from the fortress of Frederiksten, but only after the fighting had ceased).

The Søndenfjeldske Geworbne Infanteri Regiment

Strength: 1st and 2nd *geworbne* battalions and the 1st and 2nd Nationale battalions

The Nordenfjeldske Geworbne Infanteri Regiment

Strength: 1st and 2nd *geworbne* battalions and the 1st and 2nd Nationale battalions

The Oplandske Geworbne Infanteri Regiment

Strength: 1st and 2nd *geworbne* battalions and the 1st and 2nd Nationale battalions

They received a set of eight new M1811 colours. These had a dark green field with a small Dannebrog in the top hoist by the staff, gold crowned FVI monograms in green laurels on the outer angles, with the Norwegian arms of a gold lion on a red field within a large gold star. Probably all the Geworbne battalions at least had them and the Nationale battalions expected to receive the same, in different colours, but the armistice of 1814 changed that (refs FMU002022, FMU002036, FMU002351, FMU007545, FMU007628, FMU007707, FMU007745 and FMU013485). These colours now have a bluish hue due to fading, which has created some confusion over the years.

The Akershusiske Skarpskytte Regiment

They returned all their colours to store, as sharpshooter regiments did not carry colours, as did the 2nd Akershusiske Infanteri Regiment, which had also been reformed.

The Telemarkske Infanteri Regiment

Strength: 1st, 2nd and 3rd Nationale battalions[8]

The Westerlehnske Infanteri Regiment

Strength: 1st, 2nd and 3rd Nationale battalions[9]

The Bergenhusiske Infanteri Regiment

Strength: 1st, 2nd and 3rd Nationale battalions[10]

The 1st Trondhjemske Infanteri Regiment

Strength: 1st and 2nd Nationale battalions and the 1st and 2nd *skiløber* battalions[11]

The 2nd Trondhjemske Infanteri Regiment

Strength: One light battalion and the 1st and 2nd Nationale battalions.[12]

Norwegian Infantry Colours (X)

Bergenhusiske Infanteri Regiment, 1st Bn Livfane

Bergenhusiske Infanteri Regiment, 1st Bn Ordinærfane

Plate 18. Norwegian Colours X

Bergenhusiske Infanteri Regiment

Top: The 1st Battalion had an M1773 white *livfane*, ref. FMU21582.

Bottom: The 1st Battalion also had an M1773 red *ordinærfane*, ref. FMU21583, there may have been another red colour, but this is not confirmed.

Notes: The central motifs on the original colours are heavily oxidised and discoloured, so some errors of colouring and details may have crept in. For clarity, the motifs are shown a little larger than the originals. Author's reconstructions.

---

8 The Liv Companie and 1st Jæger Company were *geworbne*.
9 The Liv Companie and 1st Jæger Company were *geworbne*.
10 The Liv Companie and 1st Jæger Company were *geworbne*.
11 The *skiløber* battalions did not carry colours, so all surplus colours were put into store. As in the other regiments the Liv Companie and one *jæger* company were geworbne.
12 The light battalion did not carry any colours, so all surplus colours were put into store.

Then there is also the question of to what extent the colours were actually carried during the war and which units did so. For example, in 1808 the whole of Staffeldt's brigade was ordered to leave their colours in storage, as he wanted the whole brigade to be trained as light infantry. However, as some Norwegian colours were supposedly captured in the field as late as 1814, it is reasonable to assume that the colonels and brigade commanders decided otherwise, as colours were still useful as a rallying point and for morale.

> Facing page
>
> Plate 19. Norwegian Colours XI
>
> Bergenhuiske Infanteri Regiment
>
> From 1788 this battalion carried an old colour of the Holstenske Infanteri Regiment which in turn had carried the colours of the disbanded Lollandske Infanteri Regiment from 1785. The red is described as *lakersrød* ('salmon' red).
>
> The flag shown here is of the 2nd Battalion, ref. FMU7521. Dimensions: width 125 cm × height 119 cm. Although described as the belonging to the 1st Battalion, this *livfane* appears to have belonged to the 2nd. The red *ordinærfane* was left in Denmark, but it has not survived.
>
> Note: The central motifs on the original colours are heavily oxidised and discoloured, so some errors of colouring and details may have crept in. Author's reconstruction.

> Plate 20. Norwegian Colours XII
>
> Trondhjemske Infanteri Regiment
>
> Top: The first battalion had an M1773 white *livfane*, ref. FMU13470. Note that Trondhjemske is spelled Thrundhiems.
>
> Bottom: In 1788 they received a yellow M1775 *ordinærfane*, ex-Søndersfeldske Infanteri Regiment, who had just received a stand of new colours. Battalion unknown. Ref. FMU13471. Dimensions: width 126 cm × height 116 cm.
>
> Author's reconstructions.

> Plate 21. Norwegian Colours XIII
>
> Trondhjemske Infanteri Regiment
>
> These were the ex-M1780 colours of the Nordenfjeldske Infanteri Regiment.
>
> Top: The 1st Battalion had a white M1779 *livfane* with blue flames and the arms of Norway. Motto: HILD KRIGER MELLEM KLIPPER FØDE OG FÆGT PAA SEYER ELLER DØD. Ref. FMU013473. Dimensions: width 122cm × height 127 cm.
>
> Bottom: A blue M1779 *ordinærfane* with white flames and the arms of Norway. Motto: HILD KRIGER MELLEM KLIPPER FØDE OG FÆGT PAA SEYER ELLER DØD. Ref. FMU002353. Dimensions: width 125cm × height 125 cm.
>
> Author's reconstructions.

NORWEGIAN INFANTRY COLOURS

Norwegian Infantry Colours (XI)

Bergenhusiske Infanteri Regiment,
ex-Lollandske Infanteri Regiment, 2nd Bn

Norwegian Infantry Colours (XII)

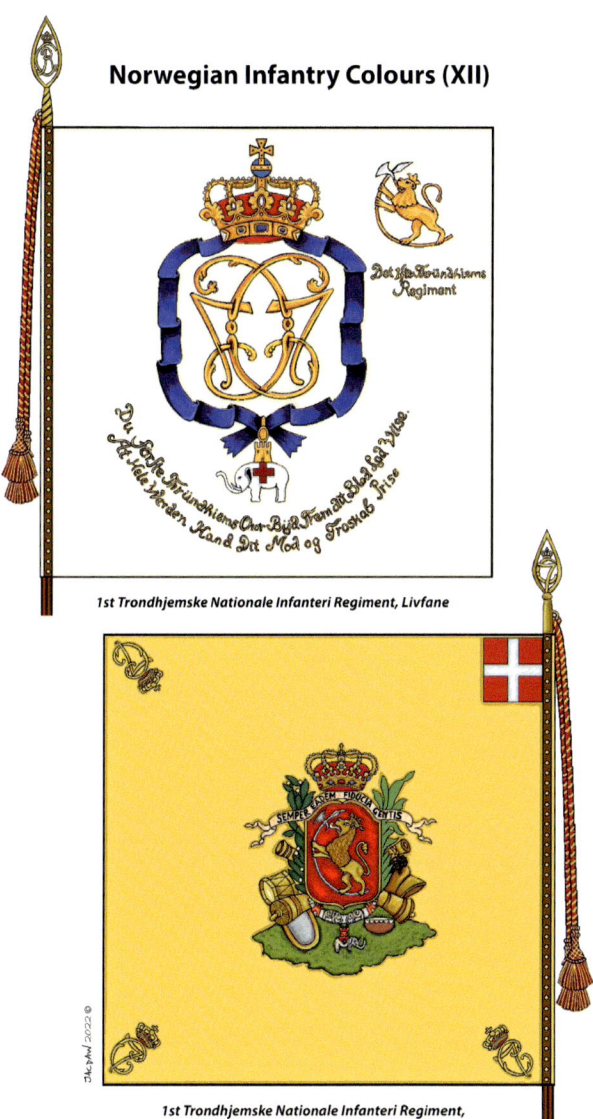

1st Trondhjemske Nationale Infanteri Regiment, Livfane

1st Trondhjemske Nationale Infanteri Regiment,
Ordinærfane ex-M1775 Søndenfjeldske Infanteri Regiment

Norwegian Infantry Colours (XIII)

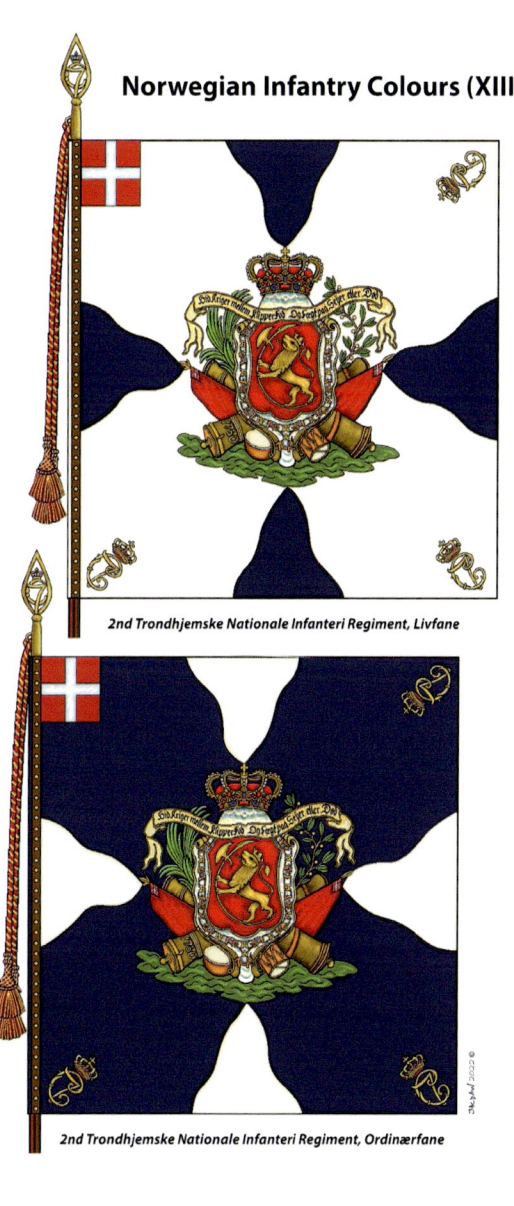

2nd Trondhjemske Nationale Infanteri Regiment, Livfane

2nd Trondhjemske Nationale Infanteri Regiment, Ordinærfane

6

The Norwegian *Jægere*, Light Infantry and Ski Troops

Origins and Organisation

Throughout the history of Norway, light infantry had always been used on an unofficial basis. They were first formally organised into two small ski battalions in 1774, one attached to Trondhjemske Infanteri Regiment and the other to the Oplandske Infanteri Regiment. In 1788 the Norwegian *jæger* unit, Norske Geworbne Jæger Corps was created. It was formed from a reorganisation/renaming of the Holstenske Geworbne Jæger Corps with a cadre from the Slesvigske Jæger Corps, and it was merged with several locally raised Norwegian light units. They became the most prestigious regiment in Norway.

They worked first as three independent formations until 31 July 1801, when a major reorganisation took place. The light infantry branch of the Norwegian army was reorganised and enlarged. The light infantry was now concentrated into the Norske Jæger Corps together with Søndenfjeldske Skiløber Bataljon.[1] The Nordenfjeldske Skiløber Bataljon[2] was still part of the Trondhjemske Infanteri Regiment. A new light infantry company the Lærdalske Lette Infanteri Companie was raised, and they were attached to the Bergenhusiske Infanteri Regiment.[3]

The Norske Jæger Corps

From 1801 this was a three-battalion regiment, with the following battalions:

> The Norske Geworbne Jæger Corps who had four *geworbne jæger* companies

Peacetime strength: 13 officers, 57 NCOs, nine *hornblæsere,* 240 *jægere* and 240 *jægere* on furlough

The Norske Lette Infanteri Bataljon (who had six Nationale territorial light companies)[4]

Wartime strength: 13 officers, 30 NCOs, 13 *hornblæsere* and 600 *lette infanterister*

The Søndenfjeldske Skiløber Bataljon (with three Nationale territorial ski companies)

Wartime strength: 13 officers, 15 NCOs, six *hornblæsere*, 300 *skiløbere* and 150 Landeværn

The main task of the new *jæger*, *lette* and *skiløbere*, was reconnaissance, to protect the front and flanks of the army and disrupt the enemy doing the same job. In battle, their main function was to disrupt the good order of the enemy linear formations. With a skirmish line 50–100 paces in front of their own lines, the enemy would be forced to start firing so early that they did not achieve maximum effect of their firepower. The intention was to drain the enemy firepower and win control before they entered the effective killing zone. But light infantry was never to fight it all out, so if the enemy kept on advancing in strength, the light troops would withdraw so as to avoid being overrun. They would then protect the flanks of their own infantry, and if the enemy was repulsed, they would pursue them vigorously. The light troops used horns or whistles because their calls were the only thing that could be heard effectively, used when changing formation in the field. They started to apply the tactical skirmish system of spacing the men out in pairs, with one firing while one loaded, so they were able to keep up an effective non-stop fire whilst presenting dispersed front, lowering casualties. Although this system

---

1 First raised in 1747, originally composed of three companies, based in Hofske, Elverumske and Åmotske. They were from 1810, attached to the Akershusiske Skarpskytte Regiment.
2 First raised in 1747, originally composed of three companies, based in Holtålske, Snåsenske and Meråkerske. They were attached to 1st Trondhjemske Regiment.
3 *Leirdalske Kompanies Historie fra 1801–1817 Af Kaptajn H. J. Barstad*, 1901.
4 They were a former line infantry battalion, the Ullensagerske Nationale Bataljon but now trained as light infantry.

was applied in other armies, the Norwegians applied it with a rigour not always found elsewhere, much to the discomfort of the Swedish army. This was an early example of modern skirmish tactics which heightened effectiveness whilst lowering casualties. They were deployed in platoons or 'chains'. A *jæger* 'chain' was a line of *jægere* – working in pairs – one behind the other, with each pair approximately 10 paces apart. Such formations were usually sent out about 50 metres in front of the musketeer battalions, to disrupt the enemy advance, enticing them to open fire too early. The tactic was implemented and perfected by the well-known Major General Johannes von Ewald.

The men of the *skiløber* companies were trained and organised as light infantry soldiers and were mainly employed on reconnaissance and patrol duties. In the winter snows however, ski-trained troops had greater mobility and could in some respects function as light cavalry in winter.

When on skis they generally deployed in two lines, the first was the firing line, the second the support line, ready to fill any gaps, with the officers and hornists behind them. They were highly respected by the Swedes who frequently suffered from these *kommandos* (or as they were called then, partisans). In summer they reverted to normal *jæger* tactics. The Nordenfjeldske and Søndenfjeldske *skiløber* battalions throughout the period described here (*1790–1814*), were formed as two battalions, but with only three ski companies each.

Field Strengths 1808–1809:

Norske Geworbne Jæger Corps. In 1808, 16 officers and 546 *jægere*; in 1809, 16 officers and 736 *jægere*.

Norske Lette Infanteri Bataljon. In 1808, 13 officers and 643 *lette;* in 1809, 12 officers and 843 *lette*.

Søndenfjeldske Skiløber Bataljon. In 1808, nine officers and 321 *lette*; in 1809, nine officers and 471 *skiløbere*.

Lærdalske Lette Infanteri Companie. In 1808, three officers and 107 *lette*; in 1809, three officers and 107 *lette*.

During the war of 1808–1809 the light troops performed well. The Norske Geworbne Jæger Corps, nicknamed Staffeldt's Green *Jægere*, had successfully fought in many actions, but they were of course, disciplined enlisted soldiers with many years of training behind them. Of the other light troops, the newly formed Lærdalske Lette Infanteri Companie, had excelled with their speed, boldness and almost furious desire to attack.

The New Organisation of the Norwegian Light Infantry 1810–1814

In 1810 a complete reorganisation of the Norwegian army was implemented, and this included the light infantry. The light infantry was drastically reformed and enlarged. The combat during 1808–1809 had shown that Norway was a perfect country for light infantry and light infantry tactics. So, the number of light infantry companies was raised from just 17 in 1807 to nearly 82 (this includes those formed and attached to ordinary line battalions). In 1810 the Norske Jæger Corps were reformed into a three-battalion regimental sized formation, with the Norske Jæger Corps with four *geworbne* companies, the Walderske Skarpskytte Bataljon which had five *skarpskytte* companies and a *jæger* company and the former Bergenhusiske Skarpskytte Bataljon with six *skarpskytte* companies and a *jæger* company (the famous Lærdalske Jæger Companie).[5]

The light infantry was reorganised into the following battalions/companies:

Det Norske Jæger Corps:

Norske Geworbne Jæger Corps: 1st, 2nd, 3rd and 4th *geworbne jæger* companies

Walderske Skarpskytte Bataljon. One *jæger* and five *skarpskytte* companies

Bergenhusiske Skarpskytte Bataljon. One *jæger*[6] and five *skarpskytte* companies

Akershusiske Skarpskytte Regiment (also known as the Akershusisken Legion)

---

5   The independent light company, the Lærdalske Lette Companie 1801–1810 was raised in 1801 under the title Leirdalske Skiløbercompanie at Leirdal, officially the fourth company of Sogns line battalion of the Bergenhusiske Infanteri Bataljon but in reality, were an extra independent ski company attached to the Bergenhusiske Nationale Infanteri Regiment. But the following year, it was decided to reform it as a light company instead. The company fought with distinction, but also had a reputation for being somewhat reckless. It was often used for patrolling and made some successful raids and long rang patrolling behind enemy lines. On one of those raids, they allegedly killed a couple of prisoners, not being able to bring them back, and this also gave them the reputation of some cruelness. Although not a true ski company, it is recorded that they did on occasions use snowshoes, but it is not recorded if they also may have used skis on occasion as well.

6   The *jæger* company was originally known as the Leirdalske Lette Infanteri Companie. In 1810, they received new green uniforms M1808, and for the first time M1802 hats, direct from Denmark. They were dressed wholly in grey in 1814.

THE DANISH ARMY OF THE NAPOLEONIC WARS VOLUME 3

The *Norske Geworbne Jægerkorps* (Norwegian Enlisted *Jæger* Corps)

THE NORWEGIAN JÆGERE, LIGHT INFANTRY AND SKI TROOPS

> Facing page
>
> Plate 22. The Norske Geworbne Jæger Corps (Norwegian Enlisted Jæger Corps)
>
> Top row:
>
> 1. *Jæger c.* 1802–1807. The men wore the M1798 uniform until 1808, but the officers and NCOs were issued a new M1802 uniform in 1806, but the differences were minor.
> 2. Officer *c.* 1806–1809. The officer's coat tails and turnbacks, not visible here, were white.
> 3. *Jæger c.*1808
> 4. *Hornblæser c.* 1808
> 5. Officer 1810–1812. Officers and NCOs would have changed their cuffs in 1812 and removed their epaulettes and waist sash when the new rank distinctions were adopted.
>
> Bottom row:
>
> 6. & 7. A *jæger* 1810 (front and rear views). Note the loose ball purse (*kuglepug*) issued in 1810. From 1790 they used a special combined knapsack and extra ammunition pouch, called a *skydetaske* (*jaeger* bag), made of leather with a cover of badger skin. Between 1802 and 1806 it was converted into an ordinary knapsack with a thinner strap.
> 8. *Hornblæser c.* 1810–1812.
> 9. An officer in M1789 overcoat (*surtout*) 1810–1812
> 10. A *jæger* in the M1810 *kort ydertrøje* (short overcoat) used as winter dress worn with grey overalls with bone buttons. On the march a cape could be added.

1st Nationale Skarpskytte Bataljon.[7] One *jæger* and five *skarpskytte* companies

2nd Nationale Skarpskytte Bataljon. One *jæger* and five *skarpskytte* companies

3rd Nationale Skarpskytte Bataljon. One *jæger* and five *skarpskytte* companies

Søndenfjeldske Skiløperbataljon (three Nationale companies)

One *geworbent livkompani* and a *geworbent jæger* company[8]

Also, the light cavalry unit Akershusiske Ridende Jæger Corps was officially part of this regiment.

Besides these, three further light units were attached to the two Trondheim infantry regiments:

1st Trondhjemske Nationale Infanteri Regiment:
1st Nordenfjeldske Skiløber Bataljon (three Nationale companies); 2nd Nordenfjeldske Skiløber Bataljon[9] of one *jæger* and five Nationale ski companies.

2nd Trondhjemske Nationale Infanteri Regiment:
Trondhjemske Nationale Skarpskytte Bataljon, one *jæger* and five *skarpskytte* companies.[10]

---

7 This was the former Norske Lette Infanteri Bataljon. For a short while they may have continued to use their old green uniforms, but rather quickly changed into the new grey uniform M1810 *c.* 1811.

8 They were in peace to be garrison troops at Kongsvinger fortress, and in the field, to act as Guards of the Headquarter, not field units. They were dressed in green uniforms from Norske Jæger Corps.

9 There has been some doubt regarding whether this battalion ever received *skiløber* uniforms. But a newly discovered letter from Major General von Bang, commander of 1st Trondhjemske Nationale Infanteri Regiment, makes it clear that the battalion had in fact in store, a complete set of new green uniforms for all, and that they even had some extras, which he suggests could have been used by Røråske Frivillige Jæger corps. Source: Norsk Våpenhistorisk Årbok 2008 *Uniformer ved Skiløperbataljonerne 1747–1826* Trond Bækkevold.

10 We know very little about this unit, but it was both formed, organised and probably also equipped/dressed as a *skarpskytte* battalion, in grey uniforms in 1813–1814. But there is no official information about uniforms, and most secondary information suggests that they wore their old red uniforms. See later.

Norwegian Light Infantry (*Norske Lette Infanten*)

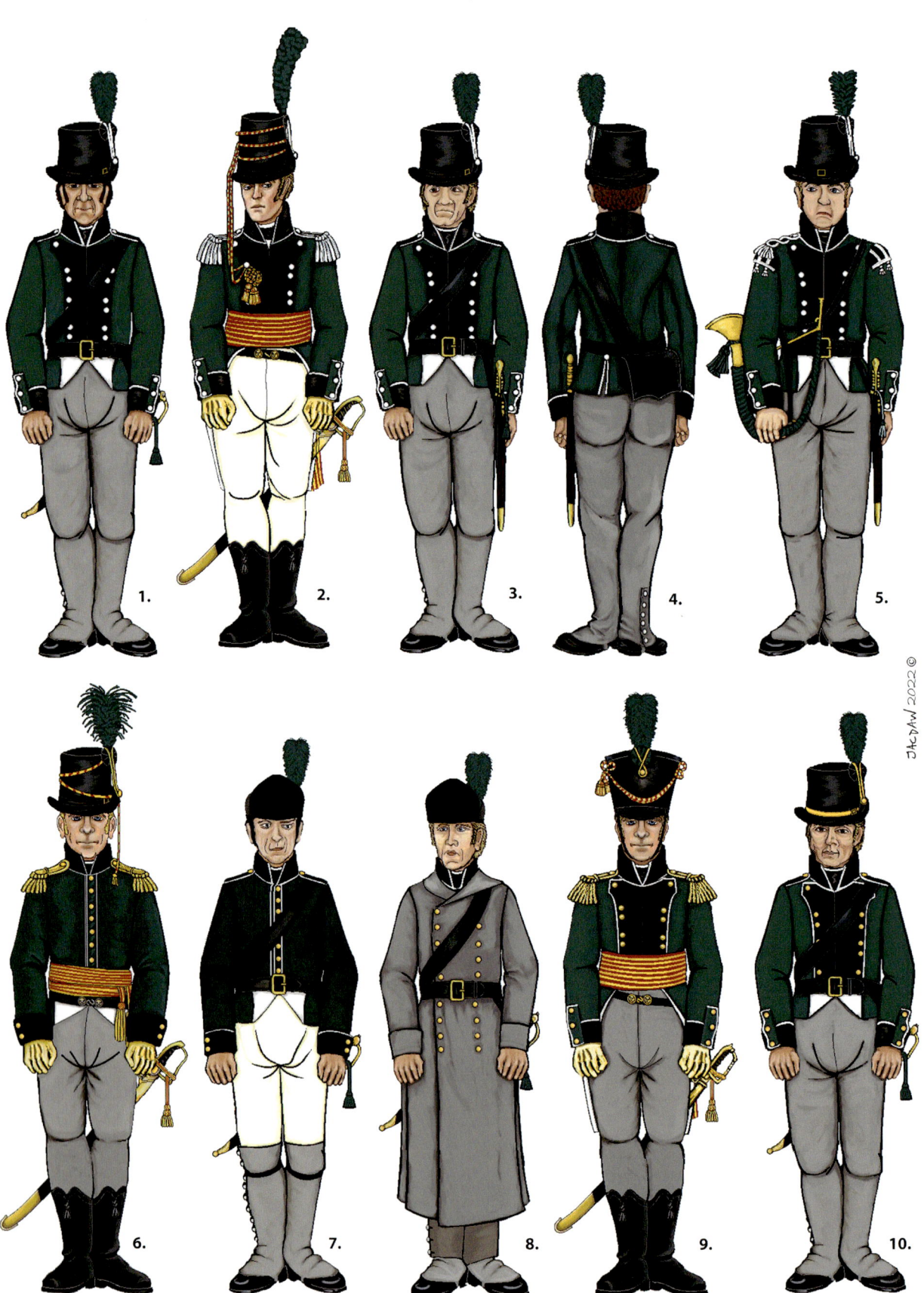

THE NORWEGIAN JÆGERE, LIGHT INFANTRY AND SKI TROOPS

> Facing page
>
> Plate 23. Norske Lette Infanteri (Norwegian Light Infantry)
>
> Top row:
>
> 1. Light infantryman Norske Lette Infanteri Bataljon, *c.* 1806; note that he carries an M1756 sabre as a sidearm.
> 2. An officer of the Norske Lette Infanteri Bataljon, *c.* 1808
> 3. Light infantryman, Norske Lette Infanteri Bataljon (front view) *c.*1808
> 4. Light infantryman, Norske Lette Infanteri Bataljon (rear view) *c.* 1808
> 5. *Hornblæser c.* 1807 of the Norske Lette Bataljon
>
> Bottom row: Lærdalske Lette Infanteri Companie
>
> 1. Officer Lærdalske Lette Infanteri Companie, *c.* 1802–1810. The officers wore a coatee.
> 2. Light infantryman, Lærdalske Lette Infanteri Companie, wearing the *skiløber* uniform 1792
> 3. Light infantryman, Lærdalske Lette Infanteri Companie wearing the *skiløber* uniform 1792, grey overalls (*warbukser*) and long overcoats M1798, which, although they should have been returned in 1803 were used in the winter of1808–1809, the only unit to use the overcoat M1792.
> 4. From June 1810 the officers of the Lærdalske Lette Infanteri Companie received new green uniform coats, possibly M1803 light infantry coats, with lapels, and all with white lining and grey trousers, sent from Denmark along with privately acquired shakos.
> 5. In June 1810 the men received M1803 hats, not shakos, and what appear to be M1808 uniform coatees, M1808 grey light infantry trousers and short black gaiters.

The *skarpskytte* battalions formed field battalions by calling up trained soldiers who were on furlough, and formed them into one *jæger*, and four *skarpskytte* companies each of 120 soldiers (the theoretical organisation was 12 officers, 42 NCOs, 12 *hornblæsere* and 600 soldiers). The Bergenhusiske Skarpskytte Bataljon had one extra company formed as a depot. The Akershusiske Skarpskytte Regiment and Walderske Skarpskytte Battalion had reserves available from the levy battalions, while their Landeværn were employed separately.

The Akershusiske Skarpskytte Regiment had a special role and a special organisation. When mobilised it was to send its two Geworbne companies to the headquarters, and the three Nationale (peacetime) battalions were to form up as quickly as possible and march out as an *avant-garde* for the three brigades planned to be sent up to defend the border, as dictated by the defence plan of 1813. The reason behind this was that these battalions had their conscription districts along the border. The regiment was to earmark 750 men from each battalion who, upon mobilisation were to immediately report for duty. The battalions thus received the same number of soldiers as the regular field battalions and were organised like them. But they had been trained together so everybody knew each other, and they were also all better trained in light infantry tactics, so each company were able to fight as independent formations, if needed.

Field strength in 1814:

Norske Geworbne Jæger Corps: 16 officers, 24 NCOs, 8 *hornblæsere* and 520 *jægere*

Walderske Skarpskytte Bataljon: 13 officers, 30 NCOs, 12 *hornblæsere*, 600 *skarpskytte* and 300 Landeværn

Bergenhusiske Skarpskytte Bataljon: 13 officers, 30 NCOs, 12 *hornblæsere*, 600 *skarpskytte and* 350 Landeværn. Also, a depot company with two officers, five NCOs, two *hornblæsere* and 100 *skarpskytter*.

Akershusiske Skarpskytte Regiment: 2,450 *skarpskytte* 300 depot company/levies, and 900 Landeværn.

Søndenfjeldske Skiløberbataljon: nine officers, five NCOs, seven *hornblæsere*, 600 *skiløbere* and 150 Landeværn.

Nordenfjeldske Skiløperbataljon: nine officers, five NCOs, seven *hornblæsere*, 300 *skiløbere* and 150 Landeværn.

The Walderske Skarpskytte Regiment had some levies attached as reserves, and the Søndenfjeldske Skiløperbataljon had a full *fribataljon* (Østerdalske Fribataljon) added, which was used to bring the battalion up to double strength. By 1814 the Søndenfjeldske Skiløberbataljon had trained enough levies so it could double its companies to 200 soldiers (they had no depot or battalion artillery).

All the new *skarpskytte* units organised from 1810 received new light grey uniforms 1810–1813 (the last early in 1814) including the Søndenfjeldske Skiløber Bataljon. They began receiving the M1808 shako from late 1809 and they all had them by 1813. Regarding their weapons, only the *jæger* companies received rifles, all ordinary sharpshooters had to make do with ordinary muskets, as Denmark were unable to supply rifles in the large numbers needed (more than 2,000 new rifles would have been needed to arm them all).

Another major reform was that from this point, Norway would in the future make and provide nearly all types of uniforms and most kit, except their weapons, for all soldiers in Norway. This change had been prepared, for some time and had started slowly in 1807–1808, but was fully underway by 1810–1811.[11]

The *skarpskyttere* or light infantry again used the same uniforms and rank insignias as in the Danish army but with dark green facings and green cockades. Barely distinguishable from the *jægere* except for their armament, most were armed with various models of muskets as rifles were in short supply.

The *Jæger* and Light Infantry Uniforms 1790–1810

In many ways, although Norway followed Danish styles, the Norwegian uniforms, especially those of the *jægere*, lights and in particular the ski units were always a little bit different to those worn in Denmark. Several reasons were responsible for this, but the mostly it was the economy, the climate, the difficulty in receiving supplies from Denmark and their traditions.

Norway was normally allowed different terms for the supply of uniforms and would sometimes be allowed to produce them in local materials. Also, any changes made in Denmark would only be implemented three to six years later in Norway, again mainly because of the special organisation and service, of the Nationale soldiers and a tight local economy in Norway.

Norway had the following clothing terms for 1790–1810:

> Norske Geworbne Jæger Corps. This was a *geworbne* (enlisted) unit, so as the only Norwegian light unit it had Danish clothing terms (six-year cloth terms).
>
> NCOs, *hornblæsere* and *jægere*. M1803 uniform coat and waistcoats: three years for each (two in six years, should change in 1804 and 1808).

White summer/parade and grey M1791 field trousers *traussers* (gaiter trousers): two years.

Hats (NCOs had silver cords on their hats): two years, so they would have worn M1802 hats in 1808).

Officers: two-year terms, but they were expected to buy their own uniforms.

The following were Nationale (conscripted) troops, so had longer terms:

> Den Norske Lette Bataljon, Lærdalske Lette Companie and *skiløbere*.

Officers: two-year terms, but they were expected to buy their own uniforms.

NCOs had the same as NCOs of the *jægere*, but the hat was replaced every three years (so probably had M1802 hats by 1808).

Hornblæsere: uniform coat and waistcoat vest: six years

Short white M1789 breeches *bukser*: three years (they may have received long white and grey M1791 *traussers* (gaiter trousers) from *c*. 1803).

Long black gaiters M1789: four years.

Hats M1798 (NCOs had silver cords on their hats): eight years.

Lette and *skiløbere*

Uniform coat and waistcoat vest: 12 years

Short white M1789 *bukser* (breeches): six years

(The *lette* may have received long white and grey M1791 *traussers* from *c*. 1808)

Long black gaiters M1789: eight years

Lette hats M1798: 12 years

Skiløbere casket M1788: 12 years

Skiløbere wahrbukser: 24 years

---
11 See the line infantry section.

And so even if they had long peace time clothing terms, nearly all the Nationales and *skiløbere* needed new uniforms in 1808–1809.

Norske Geworbne Jæger Corps Uniforms, 1801–1814
In 1801, the corps were wearing the M1789 hat with a black hat band, a green side plume, black cockade and a white loop with a pewter button. They wore a 1798 pattern uniform, which consisted of a dark green coatee with black collar, cuffs and narrow lapels, green cuff flaps (three buttons) and large white front turnbacks. Their shoulder straps were black, piped with a thin silver lining. The buttons were pewter or white metal. They had a white waistcoat and white gaiter trousers M1791 for parades, and grey M1791 trousers for service, and their shoes were black. This uniform should have been replaced around 1804 with a new M1803 uniform, but as they had rather large stocks of older uniforms, for peace service, these were probably first issued 1806–1807 and so they used the M1803 model until *c*. 1810. This had a rigid vertical collar, slightly different lapels and was shorter, but the rest was basically the same. By 1807 the white gaiter trousers had been replaced generally with a pair of grey trousers which they kept until 1814 at least, but by then they had been modified and were now worn with low black gaiters. From *c*. 1804, all soldiers were required to cut their hair short.

From 1806–1807 they wore the M1803 hats, but appear to have started replacing them with M1808 shakos around 1809–1810. They had a green plume, cords, a dark green cockade and a white loop and pewter button.

Although it had been planned that M1788 *capots* (greatcoats), should have been worn in Norway, the Norwegians had wanted to produce the *capots* themselves, but production began slowly and in small numbers in 1808. Instead they apparently wore the green M1785 sleeveless cloak with cape (the same form as the old cavalry cloaks), and also the woollen belly belt M1788, worn in cold winter weather. First, in 1808–1809, they may have received a few *capots* M1788 to use as sentry coats, but then in 1808 they quickly began receiving the new short Norwegian overcoats, in grey, called a *kaput-trøjer* or *ydertrøjer,* made from local homespun cloth, called *vadmel*. It was normally light or dark grey. From 1808–1809 they began receiving new green M1808 coatees and grey M1808 light infantry trousers, short gaiters M1808 and ordinary shakos M1808, with a green cockade, cords and feather. According to plans, they should have changed to a whole new grey uniform from 1810. But they reported back that they had large stocks of useful green coatees, both M1808, and also very large stocks of older green coatees, easy to convert to same model. They were then allowed to keep on using their green M1808 coatees, even in 1814, and they never changed into grey.

Norske Geworbne Jæger Corps Artillery Detachment/Gunners
The Norske Geworbne Jæger Corps had two 1-pdr M1766 *amusettes*, attached to the battalion and served by the *jægere* from *c*. 1789. The *geworbne* light artillerymen had the same uniform as the rest of the *geworbne jægere*, but they carried only *hirschfängers* as a sidearm, as well as the necessary equipment to serve their guns. The *geworbne* light artillerymen had the same uniform as the rest of the *geworbne jægere*, but with only *hirschfängers* as sidearms, and of course the equipment required to serve their guns. It is possible that the guns' woodwork was painted grey and iron fittings black, so as to better fit in with their light infantry support role.

Norske Geworbne Jæger Corps *Hornblæser* Uniform
The *hornblæsere* wore the same uniform as the NCOs, and they followed the same evolutions. On their shoulders they had black swallows' nests with white lace edging, bars and three tassels and a silver NCO epaulette on their left shoulder, and their shoes were black. By 1813–1814 the swallows' nests had probably lost their tassels.

As a sidearm they carried a *hirschfänger* on a black leather belt. Their instrument was a *halvmåne* (crescent horn), which was carried by the corps *halvmåneblæser* (staff hornist) whose horn normally had one more preset note than the rest), while each company had officially two *halvmåneblæsere*. But, normally, only one had a *halvmåne*, while the other had a *waldhorn* (French horn). So the *ritmester*, on the right of the company, was followed by a *halvmåne*, while the *løjtnant*, on the left of the company, was followed by a *waldhorn*. This enabled everybody to hear where the horn signals came from, even in the heat of battle.

Norske Geworbne Jæger Corps NCOs
They wore basically the same uniform as the *jægere* to start with, including the M1789 hat with a green plume, black cockade and a silver loop and pewter button and it had green cords, flounders and tassels. The cockade became green on the new shakos in 1809–1810, but they had generally newer model uniforms, and already from 1804 they had begun to receive the new M1802 uniforms, in a slightly better quality, with NCO distinctions (NCOs had one epaulette with button-colour fringes and lining on facing colour backing on their right shoulder from 1803, sergeants had the same epaulette, but on both shoulders). Also from 1809–1810, they began receiving new green M1808 *jæger* uniforms in NCO quality and with NCO insignia, and possibly the M1808 NCO shakos, with the new green cockade, green cords and also a feather. They never adopted the grey M1810 uniforms.

In 1812 the uniforms were modified with the new rank insignia with pointed cuffs. They carried the same arms as the

The Norwegian Sharpshooters (*Norske Skarspkyttere*), 1810–1815

THE NORWEGIAN JÆGERE, LIGHT INFANTRY AND SKI TROOPS

> Facing page
>
> Plate 24. Norske Skarpskyttere (Norwegian Sharpshooters) 1810–1815
>
> Top row:
>
> 1. Officer, Akershusiske Skarpskytte Regiment c. 1811–1814. The officers and NCOs would have changed their cuffs in 1812 and removed their epaulettes and waist sash when the new rank distinctions were adopted in 1812. This officer has made his uniform with a darker coloured better-quality cloth bought in Denmark.
>
> 2. *Jæger*, Akershusiske Skarpskytte Regiment c. 1813–1814. The *geworbne* and three ordinary *jæger* companies of the regiment were armed with rifles, but the remaining sharpshooters had muskets sent from Denmark, mainly of recent models.
>
> 3. Officer, Walderske Skarpskytte Bataljon c. 1814
>
> 4. Sharpshooter Walderske Skarpskytte Bataljon c. 1814. A contemporary drawing made by the Swedish officer Hjalmar Mörner in the summer of 1814 confirms that the Walderske Skarpskytte Bataljon only carried a cartridge box on a bandoleer with the bayonet attached. No waist belt was worn.
>
> 5. *Hornblæser*, Akershusiske Skarpskytte Regiment c. 1811.
>
> Bottom row:
>
> 6. Officer, Bergenhusiske Skarpskytte Bataljon c. 1811.
>
> 7. Sharpshooter, Bergenhusiske Skarpskytte Bataljon c.1812. Although they received the new uniform, they only had hats and they continued to use white belting as they had not yet received the newer black models. They only received their shakos and black belts in July 1813.
>
> 8. Officer, Bergenhusiske Skarpskytte Bataljon c. 1812. Officers and NCOs would have changed their cuffs in 1812 and removed their epaulettes and waist sashes when the new rank distinctions were adopted in 1812.
>
> 9. Sharpshooter, Akershusiske Skarpskytte Regiment c. 1811–1814, wearing the M1808/1810 short overcoat with grey overalls
>
> 10. *Hornblæser*, 1812–1814, Bergenhusiske Skarpskytte Bataljon, showing the new rank distinctions.

jægere. It is possible that they, like the NCOs of the Norske Lette Bataljon and Leirdalske Lette Infanteri Companie, wore *porte épées* in green and white wool (see later).

Norske Geworbne Jæger Corps Officers

Until 1805 the officers wore a black M1790 bicorn hat with a green plume, black cockade and a silver loop and button. From 1801, they were also allowed to wear hats in the field. They wore the officers' M1800 uniform, a dark green, long tailed coat with black velvet collar, cuffs and lapels, green cuff flaps (three buttons), with white lining and long white turnbacks. The buttons were silvered pewter.

They wore a white waistcoat and white and grey breeches. Their footwear was a pair of black hussar boots. From 1802 hey had silver epaulettes M1801 and a red and yellow waist sash M1795, worn under the coat until 1803, then over their coat, covering the sword belt. An official order specified that 'All officers' sword belts are to be worn just below the waist sash, normally covered by the sash'.

This was replaced first with the M1802 officers' coat in around 1804. This new uniform had a higher collar and waist, and slightly shorter tails and lapels. There was also a new M1804 officers' hat, soon replaced for most with the M1806 officers' hat, which were taller, slimmer and had more elaborate cords. Hat bands were black. With this uniform they also received a pair of grey light infantry M1800 *pantalongs* (pantaloons) for service dress. They kept the white pair for full dress. In 1809 they started to wear M1808 officers' uniform coats, and M1808 officers' shakos with red and gold cords, and the new green cockade. From 1806 a new model sword belt was introduced. In same year, all officers had to cut their hair short. When the new grey uniforms were proposed in 1810 the officers of Norske Geworbne Jæger Corps (the foremost unit in Norway as far as we know), rejected this uniform, and instead they were allowed to wear out the green (1808–1810 model) uniform first, a uniform they probably only first received in 1810–1811. The complete unit was, according to the clothing terms, to change after 1814, so few officers, even those who from 1812 were allowed to buy a uniform at their own expense, probably never did. From 1812 the uniforms were modified with the new rank insignia with pointed cuffs and the officers were to cease wearing the waist sash and epaulettes. In winter the officers wore an officer's *surtout* M1788–98, a grey overcoat with a low standing collar which had a black square patch either side at the front with two silvered buttons. It could be worn with or without a short, detachable cape.

Arms and Equipment, Norske Geworbne Jæger Corps

Before 1807 Norway did not have many rifles, including some made locally in 1711–1755. But when the Norske Geworbne Jæger Corps was formed in 1788 the men received some Danish-made M1785 rifles. In 1790 they received 200 shortened muskets for training. In 1793 they returned 392 spare rifles to the arsenal of Frederikstad, probably because they had received a number of new M1791 rifles. In 1796, when they moved to new barracks in Christiania (Oslo), the made a list of their arms: 720 *rifles* (M1785 and M1791) and 572 *karabiner*, probably shortened M1774 muskets used for training purposes. The Norwegian *jæger* corps apparently began receiving new Danish M1803 *jæger* rifles (around 500) from late August 1807, but it is not clear whether those received may have been transferred to arm the new *Regimentsjægere* (regimental *jægere*) from 1810. As a sidearm they had received the *hirschfänger* M1791. In 1806, those used by the rifle armed *jægere* were rebuilt into the M1791/1803, with a bayonet attachment.[3] It was stressed that all firing should be done without it attached and it was only to be attached at the last possible moment, mainly against sudden cavalry attacks. Against a retreating and broken enemy 'the rifle shall be slung over their back, the hirschfänger drawn and with it in the hand, prisoners taken, and all others struck down'.

As equipment, they had a black leather cartridge box on a black leather bandoleer. They carried the standard *jæger* black leather waist belt with a brass belt buckle, (rectangular belt plate with Danish arms for NCOs), on the left the standard priming flask M1787, with a powder measurer as a stopper. This was used throughout the period. From *c.* 1809–1810 they were the first unit in Norway to receive 794 *kugle-poser* ball bags, made at the workshop at Aggershus, which when received were worn hanging from a strap at the right of the waist belt. On the right they carried the *hirschfänger*.

The Norwegian *jæger* corps had a special model combined backpack and ammunition pouch, called a *skydetaske* (*jæger* bag), made of leather with a cover made of badger skin. This was carried on a strap across the body at the left hip. The *jæger* corps carried theirs until 1818, but by then they were described as very worn-out, crimped and stiff.

The Norske Geworbne Jæger Corps may have been the only Norwegian unit which carried the old white metal two-man Danish model canteen, brought with the corps from Denmark in 1788. They had standard Danish *sejldugs brødposer* (white sailcloth) bread-bags with black slings.

The officers were armed with an M1789 sabre, or a variation of same, carried first on a black M1790 sword belt with a square golden plate with the arms of Denmark in silver, and a black leather M1806 belt, with two lion's head buckles with an 'S' clasp in 1807, both had two slings.

Uniforms of the 2nd Battalion of the Norske Jæger Corps, the Norske Lette Bataljon

The Norske Lette Bataljon (light infantry battalion) entered the war in 1808, wearing the M1789 hat with a green side plume, black cockade and a white loop and a pewter button. They wore the light infantry M1798 uniform, which consisted of a dark green coatee with black collar, cuffs and lapels, green cuff flaps (three buttons) and white front turnbacks. The collar, cuffs and cuff flaps were piped white, but not the lapels. Their shoulder straps were black, piped white. The buttons were pewter or white metal. The coatee had a rigid stand up collar and it grew shorter by 1808, but the rest was basically the same. At first, they did not receive the grey light infantry trousers, but kept their M1789 breeches, with long black gaiters, but were allowed the same white and grey gaiter trousers M1791, as worn by the *jæger* corps in July 1802 and they were adopted at next change. Their shoes were black. Their bandoleer and waist belt were also made of black leather from 1802. They kept this uniform until around 1810, when they were reorganised into the new Akershusiske Skarpskytte Regiment as its 1st (Ullensagerske) Battalion, and adopted grey uniforms M1810 (see later). They did not at first acquire any overcoats, but then began to receive the new more practical and economic Norwegian-made short overcoat (called both an *ydertrøje*, *kaputtrøje* or *patruljetrøje*), made in grey woollen homespun cloth from 1809. They were only officially issued from October 1810, but were in use by the light units much earlier. As they had received their uniform coats in 1802, and they had a term of 12 years, they were according to normal peacetime terms only due for a change *c.* 1814. But plans were drawn up for a premature change to the M1808 uniform in 1809–1810, but this apparently did not go ahead. Instead, in 1810 they were renamed the 1st Bataljon Akershusiske Skarpskytte Corps and were one of the first Norwegian units to change into new grey M1810 uniforms, and the M1808 shako in 1811. They probably retained their M1756 infantry sabre.

Norske Lette Bataljon Artillery Detachment/Artillery Gunners

According to the plans of 27 February 1802, they retained their two 1-pdr *amusettes*. They, as in all infantry battalions of the Norwegian army except the two ski battalions, had attached artillery for close support. This was also the rule after the 1810 reforms, where all Nationale *skarpskytte bataljoner* could keep theirs as well. The light artillerymen wore the same uniform as the rest of the light infantrymen, but were armed only with infantry sabres together with the necessary equipment to serve their guns. It is probable that their guns were painted grey for the woodwork and black for the iron.

Norske Lette Bataljon *Hornblæsere*
The *hornblæsere* wore the same uniform as the NCOs but with black swallows' nests with white lace edging, bars and tassels (three) and a silver NCO epaulette on their left shoulder. They had a white waistcoat and white gaiter trousers, and their shoes were black. They kept this uniform, slightly modified, until 1810. They used a *halvmaane* (crescent horn) or a *waldhorn* (French horn). See above for the use of different types of horns under Norske Geworbne Jæger Corps *Hornblæser* Uniform.

Norske Lette Bataljon NCOs
The NCOs wore basically the same uniform as the light infantry soldiers at first, including the M1789 hat with a green plume, black cockade and a silver loop and pewter button, and had green cords, flounders and tassels. But generally they wore newer model uniforms, and already from 1806 they began received the new M1802 uniforms of a better quality, with NCO distinctions. Also from 1809, they began receiving new green M1808 *jæger* coats in NCO quality, and with distinctions. We do not know if they received the new M1808 shakos in 1809–1810. They carried the same arms as the light infantry soldiers. Probably, as the NCOs of Leirdalske Lette Infanteri Companie, they wore *porte épée*s in green and white wool.

Norske Lette Bataljon Officers
The light infantry officers wore the officers' M1800 uniform, a dark green, long tailed coat with black velvet collar, cuffs and lapels, green cuff flaps (three buttons), all except the lapels piped white, their pockets were piped white, and it had also long white turnbacks. The buttons were silvered pewter.

They had a white waistcoat and white and grey breeches. Their footwear was a pair of black hussar-style boots. From 1802 they had M1801 silver epaulettes and a red and gold waist sash, worn under the coat until 1803, then over it.

This was first replaced with the M1802 officers' coat around 1804. This new uniform had a coat had a higher collar and waist, slightly shorter tails and lapels. Also the new M1804 officers' hat was mostly replaced with the M1806 officers' hat, which were taller, slimmer and had more elaborate cords, as soon as it was possible. Hat bands were black. With this uniform they also received a pair of grey light infantry M1800 *pantalongs* (pantaloons) for service dress and they kept the white pair for full dress. In 1809 they started to wear M1808 officers' uniform coats, and M1808 officers' shakos, with red and gold cords, and probably the new green cockade. From 1806 a new model sword belt was introduced. Also in same year, all officers were required to cut their hair short. The light infantry officers, like the *jæger* officers, wore the officer's *surtout* M1788/98, which was a grey overcoat, with a low standing collar, and at the front, a square patch in black, with white lining, and two silvered buttons. It could be worn with a short detachable cape. They were for winter and foul weather, but were regularly worn on the march, and also in combat.

The Laerdalske Lette Infanteri Companie
This unit was formed in 1801 at Leirdale as the fourth company of Sogn's line battalion of the Bergenhusiske Nationale Infanteri Regiment. Originally called the Leirdalske Skiløber Companie, it was renamed in 1802 as the Lærdalske Lette Infanteri Companie. From 1563, the farmers in Lærdal had been exempt from military service due to the heavy duties of maintaining roads and transport in Lærdal and over Filefjell. When in 1801 the King wanted to also enlist the men of Lærdal in the army, following the new system of recruitment, there was a revolt, which had to be put down by military force; the leader, Anders Olsen Lysne, was convicted and later executed. Several other ringleaders received long prison sentences. But in 1808 King Frederik VI pardoned those who were still in prison due to the company's excellent record in combat.

This legendary company fought throughout the wars of 1808–1809 and 1814. In 1811 the company was led by a Danish officer, *Ritmester* Wilhelm Jürgensen. In the spring of 1808, the company marched as the avant-garde from Lærdal to Hedmark to camp at Elverum and took part in the Battle of Trangen and the Battle of Jerpse. They were much used for patrolling and 'partisan overfald' raids. On one of those raids they allegedly killed a couple of Swedish prisoners, not being able to bring them back, and this gave them the reputation of cruelty and ruthlessness. They continued to raid and skirmish with Swedish troops on the frontier up until 1814 when they fought the Swedish invaders on the border at Østfold. They won probably the greatest number of Dannebrogs for such a small company, both officers and men, many of whom were later commissioned as officers in the army.

Uniforms of the Lærdalske Lette Infanteri Companie
When the company was raised in 1801, it was to receive M1793 ski uniforms and ski equipment, but the following year it was reformed as a light company instead. The men were to turn in their (grey) winter overcoats and overalls M1793 (see later), but retain the rest of the M1793 uniforms until the next issue (1814). The company never functioned as an ordinary ski unit, but as a light unit.

In 1804–1805 new equipment was received from Copenhagen including a short green M1793 coatees (called a vest/waistcoat) with a black standing collar and square cuffs, one row of yellow buttons and a double line of white piping, down the front of the coat, at each side of the opening, so when buttoned, it appeared as three lines. Short sleeveless white waistcoats were worn, a black leather M1793 *cachett* (cap) with a green plume, white breeches, with grey (possibly later changed into black) long gaiters and black shoes. Black leather belts and an infantry sabre.

In 1808, when the company left for the front, the men received grey light infantry overalls (M1793 overalls), called *wahrbukser* for winter wear, with bone buttons down the outside leg. They had a calfskin *ransel* (knapsack), and a sailcloth bread-bag. Every second soldier carried a copper canteen, which two men shared.

According to a list of materiel losses written on 23 August 1808, they clearly had been able to also retain their long grey winter overcoats, or *capot kjoler,* as the company noted 24 of them as 'lost during the previous campaign'. In December 1808, they noted that all their green coatees and all their grey light infantry overalls were worn out.

In 1809 they all received a pair of new white trousers M1808, shoes and undergarments, all made in Norway. On 23 June 1810 they received new green uniform coats, possibly M1808 coats with lapels, as a painting by J. C. Dahl from this year, shows them in what looks like this pattern of coat. By 1810 they also had apparently received M1802 hats with green feathers.

Hornblæsere Uniform

Hornblæsere used *halvmånehorn*, crescent-shaped horns. They wore the same uniform as the soldiers but with black swallows' nests with simple yellow lace edging. They did not have NCO status in the ski battalions, or the Lærdalske Lette Infanteri Companie either, until *c.* 1810.

NCOs

Basically NCOs wore the same M1793 uniform as the soldiers to start with, including the M1793 *cachett* felt cap with leather outer lining, worn with a green feather. The NCOs had probably received M1803 light infantry hats, by 1808, with black cockade and a silver loop and pewter button and green cords, and tassels. It also had a tall green feather. The abovementioned list of materiel losses written on 23 August 1808, state the loss of 'one NCO hat with feather and NCO cords'. Generally, they had newer uniforms, of a slightly better quality, worn with the NCO insignia of their rank in yellow lace. The NCOs of the Lærdalske Lette Infanteri Companie wore *porte épées* in green and white wool, again according to the list from 23 August 1808.

Officers' Uniforms

The officers had same model short green coatee as the soldiers, but in better quality cloth, and worn with all officers' insignia. Sometime before 1808 the officers had received the M1803 light infantry hats.

In October 1809 the officers received cloth to make new M1808 uniforms, and possibly they also adopted the new M1808 officers' shakos, as these can be seen in a contemporary painting by J. C. Dahl in 1810.

Arms and Equipment of the Light Infantry

The principal musket used by the Norske Lette Bataljon and Lærdalske Lette Companie was the ordinary M1774 infantry musket, with a bayonet, but a few older models were probably also used. The Norske Lette Bataljon, as with the Lærdalske Lette Companie, had a standard black leather waist belt with a rectangular open brass buckle belt. On the left they carried a bayonet scabbard, and both carried the M1756 *infanteri sabel,* in a black leather scabbard. Finally they carried a black leather cartridge box on a black leather bandoleer at the left hip.

For their personal belongings they had the older model infantry knapsack, in calfskin with just one black carrying strap, slung like a satchel. They also had an off-white bread-bag on a black leather strap and the same old model two-man canteen as used in Norway, which two soldiers took turns to carry. The hornists carried an infantry sabre on a black leather waist belt.

The officers were armed with a model 1789 officers' sabre on a black leather M1806 belt with lions' heads and an 'S' clasp.

On 27 February 1802 the Norske Lette Bataljon received two 1-pdr *amusettes* and they kept them after 1810, when they were reorganised as 1st Bataljon, Akershusiske Nationale Skarpskytte Corps.

The New Grey-Uniformed *Skarpskyttere* 1810–1814

After the lessons learned during 1808–1809, it was decided to totally reform the whole Norwegian army, and for the light infantry this started with a set of official uniform drawings approved by a *Kongelig Resolution* (royal resolution) dated 25 May 1810. The coloured drawings sent from Denmark showed both officers' and soldiers' uniforms, as uniforms were to be made locally, and officers also had to get their own uniforms tailored locally. The new organisation was further made official by a *Kongelig Resolution* dated 1 July 1810, whereby the light infantry especially was both enlarged and reorganised. But as mentioned earlier, the new light infantry, the *skarpskytte bataljoner* (sharpshooter battalions), were from then on to be all uniformed in new grey uniforms. But because of shortages of the correct (dark) grey dye prescribed in Norway, and the presence of a large supply of light grey uniform cloth, originally intended for long grey overcoats, another *Kongelig Resolution* dated 16 December 1810 authorised that all light *skarpskytte bataljoner* and ski battalions uniforms were to be produced locally, in *middelgråt* (light grey). Officers were allowed to buy the correct dark grey uniform cloth for their uniforms from Denmark. So at the beginning of 1811, uniform production started in Norway, but there would be some delay before all units could be fully equipped with the new uniforms.

But some local circumstance dictated that a few were allowed to keep their older green uniforms, including the Norske Geworbne Jæger Corps, and two *geworbne skarpskytte* companies of the 1st Nordenfjeldske Skiløber Bataljon. Also the 2nd Nordenfjeldske Skiløber Bataljon were still wearing their green uniforms until after 1814 (for the two last mentioned, see under the ski battalions). Belts were to be black, and packs and field equipment, were to be standard issue.

Uniforms of the Akershusiske Nationale Skarpskytte Regiment

The Akershusiske Skarpskytte Regiment was the first unit in 1811–1812 issued with the approved, slightly modified sharpshooters' M1810 uniform, which consisted of a single-breasted light grey coatee with a high square green collar, cuffs and shoulder straps all piped white. There was a double line of green piping down the front of the coat at each side of the opening, so when buttoned, it appeared as three lines. It had one row of 10 pewter buttons and the front turnbacks were green. It had an opening at back with green lining and two pewter buttons. They wore a pair of fall-fronted grey breeches and short black gaiters (pewter buttons). Their headwear was a black shako with a green cockade with a white loop and pewter button, green cords and plume. Prince Frederik of Hessen wanted the Akershusiske Skarpskytte Regiment be fully equipped with rifles, because of their intended use as a front-line unit. This can be seen in a letter from Prince Frederik of Hessen, at Christiania on 24 March 1810, to King Frederik VI: 'May I ask for my new Skarpskytte regiments. That you would send up 2,000 rifles; we have only 1,200 here, and they are earmarked for the use of the regimental jæger companies.' The King agreed, but although Denmark made a huge effort to make and send more rifles to Norway, this was not enough, and the Akershusiske Skarpskytte Regiment's arms and equipment were unchanged, only the *jæger* companies receiving rifles.

The Geworben Liv Companie and Geworben Jæger Companie

In 1811 both received green *jæger* coatees, grey trousers worn with black gaiters (from the surplus stock from the Norske Geworbne Jæger Corps) and the M1808 shako with green cords and feathers. The Geworbne Liv Companie had black belts, an infantry sabre M1756 as a sidearm, musket and bayonet. The Geworbene Jæger Companie had black belts, a *hirschfänger* as a sidearm and a rifle with equipment. There exists an 1813 list of cloth, arms and equipment, which states they were to receive grey uniforms, so this is possibly the uniform they both received in 1814.

Landeværn and *Fribataljon* of the Akershusiske Skarpskytte Regiment

The regiment first wore a mixture of green uniforms from the Norske Lette Bataljon, and old red uniforms from the Søndenfjeldske and Nordenfjeldske infantry regiments. In 1813 the 100 active Landeværn received grey coatees and trousers. To this were added a shako and green plumes. They also received black bandoleers and waist belts. As they also received leather protection to the *hirschfänger* bayonet attachment, and in 1814 two bags for loose rifle balls, they must have been attached to the regiment's *jæger* companies. Later they received bread-bags, backpacks and short overcoats.

Regimentsjægere, the Akershusiske Skarpskytte Regiment

They wore same basic uniform as the sharpshooters, adding black belts, a sidearm (*infanteri sabel* or *hirschfänger*), rifle and the necessary equipment for the same.

Artillery Gunners, the Akershusiske Skarpskytte Regiment

Their uniform was the same as the *skarpskytter*, only adding the equipment needed to serve their guns. They did not have firearms, only an infantry sabre for personal protection.

Hornblæsere, the Akershusiske Skarpskytte Regiment

The *hornblæser* uniform was the same as the *skarpskytter*. Their headwear was a black shako with a green cockade with a yellow loop and brass button, green NCO cords and plume. On their shoulders they had green swallows' nests with white lace edging and bars. Until 1812–1813 they wore M1789 NCO epaulettes, as they ranked with NCOs, but after that the uniforms were modified, the epaulettes discontinued, and replaced with the new chevron rank insignia worn on pointed cuffs.

They may have worn NCO model *porte épée*s in green and white wool.

NCOs, the Akershusiske Skarpskytte Regiment

The NCOs wore the same uniform as the sharpshooters, but with a silver/white epaulette on their left shoulder. Their headgear was a black shako with a green cockade with a yellow loop and brass button, green NCO cords and plume. In 1812–1813 the uniforms were modified, the epaulettes discontinued, and replaced, with the new chevron rank insignia M1812, worn on pointed cuffs.

Officers of the Akershusiske Skarpskytte Regiment

Their new uniform consisted of a single-breasted light grey tailed coat with square green collar and cuffs all piped white. There was a line of green piping down the front of the coat, on the pockets (three buttons) and on the green turnbacks on the tails, and 10 silvered buttons. On their shoulders they bore silver epaulettes. They wore a pair of fall-fronted grey breeches and black Hessian boots. Their headgear was a black officers shako M1808, with a green cockade and a white loop and silvered button, gold/yellow and red cords and a green feather. In 1812–1813 the uniforms were modified with the new M1812 rank insignia with buttons and chevrons, worn over pointed cuffs, and officers were to cease wearing the waist sash and epaulettes M1801. They carried an officer's M1789 sabre or variant, with a gold and red *porte épée*, carried on a black leather M1806 belt with a lion's head clasp.

The Walderske Skarpskytte Bataljon

The battalion received their new grey uniforms rather late. It was not until shortly after 27 September 1813, they changed from the remaining old worn red uniforms into grey. Before that they had just 1810 grey uniforms. Later they received 12 uniforms for *sergenter*, 18 uniforms for *corporaler*, 12 uniforms for *constabler*, one uniform for the staff *hornblæser*, 12 uniforms for other *hornblæsere* and 522 uniforms for *skarpskyttere*. In total this amounted to 757 grey uniforms. According to the approved uniform pattern, the new uniform for the Walderske Skarpskytte Bataljon would consist of a single-breasted light grey M1810 coatee with green collar, square cuffs and shoulder straps all piped white. There was double line of green piping down the front of the coat, at each side of the opening, so when buttoned, it appeared as three lines. It had one row of 10 brass buttons and the front turnbacks were green. At the rear there was an opening with green lining, and two brass buttons. They wore a pair of fall-fronted grey breeches and short black gaiters (wooden buttons). Their headgear was a black M1808 shako with a green cockade with a yellow loop and brass button, green cords and feather. They received black bandoleers and waist belt. An eyewitness painting by the Swedish hussar lieutenant Hjalmar Mørner in 1814 shows them as part of the brigade of Colonel von Hegermann, north of Kongsvinger. It shows the new light grey uniform of the Walderske Skarpskytte Bataljon. However this is a simpler uniform than that approved. His shako is without cords and plume. His coatee has no piping on both sides of the buttons and just one white bandoleer (which may be a mistake by Mörner; it was probably black), and no waist belt. This shows us that as they received their uniforms so late and, in some haste, their uniforms were probably simplified, and there is no information about how, other than that the regiment's *jæger* company received a black bandoleer and waist belt.

Regimentsjægere, the Walderske Skarpskytte Bataljon
They wore same basic uniform as the sharpshooters, but with a black belt and bandoleer; theoretically they had a *hirschfänger* but probably an infantry sabre M1756 instead, rifle and the necessary accoutrements.

Hornblæsere, the Walderske Skarpskytte Bataljon
The *hornblæsere* wore the same uniform as the sharpshooters. They wore a black shako with a green cockade with a yellow loop and brass button, green NCO cords and plume. On their shoulders they had green swallows nests with yellow lace edging and bars. Until 1812–1813 they wore M1789 NCO epaulettes, as they ranked with NCOs. But after that, the uniforms were modified, the epaulettes abolished, and replaced with the new chevron rank insignia worn on pointed cuffs. They may have worn NCO *porte épée*s in green and white wool. Their arms and equipment were unchanged.

NCOs, Walderske Skarpskytte Bataljon
They wore the same uniform as the sharpshooters. Their headgear was a black shako with a green cockade with a yellow loop and brass button, green NCO cords and plume. They had a gold/yellow epaulette on their left shoulder. In 1812–1813 the uniforms were modified with the new rank insignia M1812, with pointed cuffs, and the NCOs were to cease wearing their epaulette.

Officers, Walderske Skarpskytte Bataljon
Their new uniform consisted of a single-breasted tailed light grey coat, with square green collar and cuffs all piped white. There was a line of green piping down the front of the coat, on the pockets and green turnbacks on the tails and one row of 10 golden buttons, at the front. On their shoulders they had gold epaulettes. They wore a pair of fall-fronted grey breeches and black Hessian boots. Their headwear was an officer's black M1808 shako, with a green cockade, a gold loop and gold button, gold/yellow and red cords and a short green feather. In 1812 the uniforms were modified with the new rank insignia, with pointed cuffs, and the officers were to cease wearing the waist sash and epaulettes. They carried an officers M1789 sabre, or variant, with a gold and red *porte épée*, carried on a black leather M1806 belt with a lion's head clasp.

Landeværn, Walderske Skarpskytte Bataljon
On 14 July 1813 they received 300 repaired old red coatees and 305 old waistcoats. They later received grey light infantry trousers and short black gaiters.

The Bergenhusiske Skarpskytte Bataljon
When the battalion was first formed in 1810, it wore the old red uniforms with the black facings of the Bergenhusiske Infanteri Regiment M1798. The men did receive new M1803 hats, maybe adding new green plumes.

In December 1810 new light grey uniforms were to be sent by ship from Christiania to Bergen, but due to the bad weather and the blockade, the shipment was delayed. Only on the 30 May 1811 were 500 complete uniforms, 500 pairs of grey trousers and 500 *kaputtrøjer* (grey coats) actually delivered (not enough for all, so the Lærdalske Jæger Companie, which was to be their new *jæger* company, only received their grey uniforms in January 1814). At same time the Bergenhusiske also received new M1803 light infantry hats, and they all still wore white infantry model belts and were armed with old M1774 muskets. In 1810 they only had three crescent horns available, but very few soldiers were proficient in playing them. So probably drums and maybe *lurs* were used until at least late 1811. By late 1811 the battalion had trained 11 hornists and by 1813 there were 14 hornists and a staff hornist, all equipped with crescent horns.

In July 1813 they finally received 42 NCO shakos, 709 ordinary *jæger* shakos, 751 new model white trousers (for summer use) and new black cross belts and waist belts. They also received 25 *skarpskyttegeværer* (for NCOs), 500 new muskets (M1791?) and 107 *hirschfängere* with bayonet attachment (for the *Lærdalske Jæger Companie*). The *profossen* (provost NCO) received a black plume for his shako, as a special mark of his rank and position. In September they received green plumes for all shakos.

This new uniform for the *Bergenhusiske Skarpskytte Bataljon* consisted of a single-breasted light grey M1810 coatee with green collar, square cuffs and shoulder straps. There was a double line of green piping down the front of the coat, at each side of the opening, so when buttoned it appeared as three lines. There was one row of 10 brass buttons and the front turnbacks were green. They wore a pair of fall-fronted grey breeches and short black gaiters. Their headwear was a black shako with a green cockade with a yellow loop and brass button, green cords and plum *c.* 1812. In 1814 Prince Christian Frederik inspected the battalion and praised it for being 'Probably the best equipped unit I had previously seen, with fine and plentiful uniforms and equipment, including new overcoats.'

Leirdalske Lette/Jæger Infanteri Companie

In June 1810 the *jægere* received complete new green light infantry uniforms with black facings and white lining and white waistcoats. They had already received grey trousers and short black gaiters. Shortly afterwards they received light infantry hats M1803. The same year they became part of the Bergenhusiske Skarpskytte Bataljon, as the Lærdalske Jæger Kompani, and wore the uniform of their regiment (see above). In 1812 they again all received a pair of new white trousers, shoes and small clothes, all made in Norway. In September 1813 the whole company received green plumes for the shakos already issued. At the same time, they all exchanged their old M1774 muskets for rifles and new rifle equipment. In January 1814 they received complete new grey uniforms with the same facings as the Bergenhusiske Skarpskytte Bataljon. The *hornblæsere* used the previous *halvmåne* horns. They wore the grey M1810 uniform when they went to war in 1814.

Artillerymen of the Bergenhusiske Skarpskytte Bataljon

Like all other battalions it received two 1-pdr *amusettes* and an ammunition/supply train, which was served by the battalion. Their uniform was the same as the *skarpskyttere*, just adding the equipment needed to serve their guns. They did not have firearms, only an infantry sabre. Their artillery pieces may have been former horse artillery *amusettes*, painted grey and with black ironwork.

Hornblæsere of the Bergenhusiske Skarpskytte Bataljon

The *hornblæsere* wore the same uniform as the *skarpskyttere*. They had a black shako with a green cockade with a yellow loop and brass button, green NCO cords and plume. On their shoulders they had green swallows' nests with yellow lace edging and bars. In 1812 the uniforms were modified with the new rank distinctions, with pointed cuffs. They may also have worn *porte épées* in green and white wool as NCOs. Their arms and equipment were unchanged.

NCOs of the Bergenhusiske Skarpskytte Bataljon

The NCOs also wore the same uniform as the sharpshooters, with a black M1808 shako with a green cockade with a yellow loop and brass button, green NCO cords and plume. They had a gold/yellow epaulette on their left shoulder. In 1812/1813 their uniforms were modified with the new rank insignia on the pointed cuffs and the NCOs were to remove their epaulette.

Officers of the Bergenhusiske Skarpskytte Bataljon

The officers' new uniform consisted of a single-breasted tailed light grey coat with square green collar and cuffs. There was a line of green piping down the front of the coat, on the pockets and it had green turnbacks on the tails and one row of 10 gilded buttons at the front. On their shoulders they had gold epaulettes. They wore a pair of fall-fronted grey breeches and black Hessian boots. On their heads they wore an officer's black shako with a green cockade with a gold loop and silvered button, yellow and red cords and plume *c.* 1812.

In 1812 the uniforms were modified with the new rank insignia with pointed cuffs and the officers were to cease wearing the waist sash and epaulettes. They carried an officers model 1789 sabre, or variant, with a gold and red *porte épée*, carried on a black leather M1806 belt with a lion's head clasp.

The Trondhjemske Skarpskytte Bataljon

We know very little about this unit. All that is known for sure is that it was planned in the 1810 reform to begin training in light infantry tactics, and that the officers and

THE DANISH ARMY OF THE NAPOLEONIC WARS VOLUME 3

Norwegian Ski Troops (*skiløber*)
1790–1814

THE NORWEGIAN JÆGERE, LIGHT INFANTRY AND SKI TROOPS

Facing page

Plate 25. Norwegian Ski Troops (*Skiløber*) 1790–1814

Top row, left to right:

1. Ski trooper wearing the 1789 summer uniform. Both the Søndenfjeldske Skiløber Bataljon and Nordenfjeldske Skiløber Bataljon wore this uniform up to end of 1809, with only small variations.

2. A *halvmaneblaesere* in winter uniform with sky blue overalls and grey woollen gloves, standard winter issue for all

3. An officer *c*. 1808 wearing the M1792/98 uniform with the M1802 epaulettes. The NCOs received a similar uniform on the same date. Both the Søndenfjeldske Skiløber Bataljon and the Nordenfjeldske Skiløber Bataljon wore this uniform up to end of 1809.

4. A ski trooper of the Nordenfjeldske Skiløber Bataljon wearing their old M1774 red hussar-style coats with black fur. These coats were eventually shortened to the size of a pelisse.

Bottom row, left to right:

5. The Nordenfjeldske Skiløber Bataljon actually used new M1793 uniforms received in 1809 from Denmark, together with M1808 shakos, until *c*. 1812. In 1814 these uniforms were given to the newly formed 2nd Nordenfjeldske Skiløber Bataljon in 1814, used by this battalion between 1814 and 1815.

6. A *skiløber* of the 1st Nordenfjeldske Skiløber Bataljon in 1814 wearing the Trondhjemske Skiløber uniform M1808, based on a contemporary drawing made by the Swedish officer Hjalmar Mörner in the summer of 1814. Also an original *hornblaeser* uniform conserved in the Universitsmuseet Trondhjem. Note the green trousers, yellow buttons and the white fold-down cuffs.

7. Officer, 1st Søndenfjeldske Skiløber Bataljon, wearing the new grey uniform in 1814. The officers received better quality cloth from Denmark, of a darker grey colour, to tailor their M1810 *skiløber* officer's uniforms. Following the Resolution of 4 December 1811 they were allowed to retain them, just changing facing colours. They were also allowed to retain the M1810 officer's pouch and bandoleer that they had already adopted.

8. A *skiløber* of the 1st Søndenfjeldske Skiløber Bataljon wearing the new grey uniform they adopted from the Akershusiske Skarpskytte Regiment in 1814.

NCOs received whistles. Apparently, it also began training some hornists. But we do not know if it ever received any new uniforms. It had apparently been planned that the battalion would also receive new grey M1810 uniforms and probably also be dressed as a *skarpskytte* battalion, but we have no evidence that this happened before war ended in 1814. Instead it may have been planned that the men should receive green uniforms, but again this is not confirmed, and probably they used their old red uniforms until the end of 1814. In 1814 they had, as far as we know, a strength of around 380 *skarpskytter,* formed into a field battalion, with three divisions.

Arms and Equipment, *Skarpskyttere* 1810–1814

Although there had been plans, and also a general wish, to arm more men with rifles, this was simply not possible, both because of the blockade, and the sheer number of rifles the Danish weapons factory were able to produce. So most of the new *skarpskytte* soldiers, used standard infantry muskets, but efforts were made so that they would be the first to receive the new M1791 and M1794 muskets arriving from Denmark, which were thereafter reserved mainly for their use.

Most of the new regimental *jæger* companies were issued with the Danish M1803 *jæger* rifle, but some instead received the new modern M1807 rifle, with the new inside lock. It had been the intention that all of Akershusiske Nationale Skarpskytte Regiment should be issued with rifles, but insufficient numbers reached Norway to equip more than their attached *jæger* companies. Norway only received around 1,500 of these modern rifles, although Denmark went to great lengths to supply them. From a preserved rifle M1807 we learn that the regimental *jæger* company of the first battalion of the Akershusiske Skarpskytte Regiment was equipped with this rifle. The other two regimental *jæger* companies had M1803 rifles. The *skarpskytte* should, according to the plans, have carried a standard black leather waist belt with a rectangular open brass buckle belt, and on the right side carry a bayonet and an M1756 *infanteri sabel* in a black leather scabbard. They carried a black leather cartridge box on a black leather cross belt, but not all were lucky enough to receive a sidearm or a waist belt. One known example is where an eyewitness clearly notes of a trooper in the Walderske Skarpskytte Bataljon, that he did not have a waist belt and bore no sidearms. He carried just a black leather cartridge box with a black bayonet scabbard attached on a black leather cross belt.

The *skarpskytte jæger* companies carried the standard M1787 *krudthorn* (priming flask) and from 1813 a shot bag for loose ammunition, found on the waist belt (they were allowed to have two more in of these in reserve, in their cartridge box). A *Kongelig Resolution* made in October 1813 ordered that the *kugle-poser* (ball bag), should, be used by all *Regimentsjægere* (those of the *skarpskytte* too) in Norway. They carried as a sidearm, either a *hirschfänger* or maybe in some cases M1756 infantry sabres, as did other regimental *jægere*. The *hornblæsere* carried either a *hirschfänger* or more likely an M1756 infantry sabre on a black leather waist belt. NCOs in most cases carried the M1789 *skarpskyttegevær* and an M1756 infantry sabre, while the officers were armed with a M1789 officers' sabre, or variation of it, on a black leather M1806 belt with lions' heads and an 'S' clasp.

For their personal belongings, the *skarpskyttere* at first had the older model infantry backpacks in different colours of calfskin, with just one carrying strap, slung like a satchel. But most were converted to two shoulder straps from 1810, which was much more practical. Some may have received the Danish M1808 backpack to be used by light units from 1810, but most probably they continued to use the older converted packs. Each sharpshooter should have had an off-white *sejldugs brødpose* (bread-bag), worn on a black sling. They were, as before, issued the old copper water canteen M1751, issued one canteen to each two soldiers, who were supposed to share it and take turns carrying it. Although rather old, it was very well liked in Norway. But in 1813–1814, the Norwegian infantry began receiving large numbers of a new and improved model of the same copper two-man canteen, the M1810. It was taller and had a greater volume and rather well made. A number of camp axes, and one old model copper cooking pot, with a pan lid for each four soldiers, were carried by the company train horses.

The Ski Troops of the *Skiløber* Battalions 1789–1809

Throughout the whole of this period the two ski battalions, the Søndenfjeldske and the Nordenfjeldske Skiløber Bataljon were each organised as three light *ski* companies. During the fighting in 1808–1809, which took place mainly during winter season, with lots of snow, both the *skiløber* battalions showed their worth on several occasions. The soldiers of the ski battalions were trained and organised as light infantry soldiers and were mainly employed on reconnaissance and patrol duties, whether there was snow or no snow. In the winter snows however, ski-trained troops had greater mobility and could, and in some respects did, function as a kind of light cavalry.

They were highly respected by the Swedes who frequently suffered from these partisans, and were never so effective using ski units themselves. In summer they served as ordinary light infantry, and reverted to standard *jæger* tactics. Sometime before the 1814 campaign some changes were made. The Søndenfjeldske Bataljon was doubled in size, that is, reinforced by doubling the ranks and adding levies, but without doubling the number of officers. Until 1810 both the Søndenfjeldske and the Nordenfjeldske *skiløber* battalions wore the same basic uniform, M1789; only officers and NCOs adopting the new M1793 uniform. In late 1809 Nordenfjeldske received new green uniforms M1793/1798, from Denmark, but also a new model green uniform, tailored in Trondheim during 1808–1811.

Although not described here, different line infantry, *skarpskyttere*, as well as some volunteer companies also used skis or snowshoes on occasion during the winter.

Uniforms (*Skiløbere*) 1789–1810

The history of their uniforms is rather confusing when seen by a modern historian. Firstly even when official new regulations for uniforms were published, they were not always implemented at once, or sometimes only the officers and NCOs made the changes. But this was again a result of the fact that the *skiløbere*, as the Nationale, did not do much real service in times of peace. In Norway, they only exercised 12 days a year, in company drill. Only every fourth year, they had to form into their parent *skiløber* battalion, in order to be exercised for 16 days on battalion manoeuvres. By 1790 both the Søndenfjeldske and Nordenfjeldske ski battalions had received completely new M1789 *skiløber* uniforms (but only Søndenfjeldske, as far as we know, received the new grey M1789 greatcoat). All this points to the fact that both battalions had plentiful stocks of older, but still fine, nearly unused uniforms, as they had only been used for the rather short yearly training, and the drilling of new *skiløbere*.

The new M1789 uniforms were therefore mainly kept packed down in the company *telthuse* (arsenals). In 1793 a complete new green summer uniform, with light grey overalls (*wahrbukser*) and long light grey overcoat as a winter uniform, for both battalions, according to normal clothing terms, should both have been issued with both in 1802/1803, but this did not happen. Both battalions had, as noted, a rather large number of older, mainly M1774 uniforms, still usable, and together with other usable older kit, were in fact, used for training.

So in the end, the hornists and ordinary soldiers only received the planned new M1793 undergarments of white *bukser* (breeches), grey *skisokker* (gaiters), shirts, socks etc. while the issue of the rest of the new M1793 uniform, of short green jackets, with black collar and cuffs, new grey overcoats and new grey *warbukser* (overalls) was allowed to be postponed until 1808–1809, probably agreed by all involved, as this did ease the finances of the two battalions involved. But new black leather bandoleers and new black waist belts had been approved in 1790 When the old white belts were to be replaced, (according to the *Norsk Våpenhistorisk Årbok 2008, Uniformer ved Skiløperbataljonerne 1747–1826,* Trond Bækkevold), they were in fact issued to the Nordenfjeldske Skiløber Bataljon in 1795 and Søndenfjeldske Skiløber Bataljon in 1799. Also in 1798 the officers received the new M1793 green uniform, as did the NCOs in 1802/1803, but the hornists and ordinary soldiers of both battalions kept on using the older, mainly M1774 uniforms, for their peacetime drill, and the new M1789 uniforms were kept firmly stored in the local arsenals and not used much. But then suddenly and unexpectedly, the war broke out in 1807. So from late 1807, and the beginning of 1808, both the Søndenfjeldske and the Nordenfjeldske ski battalions began to be issued with the M1789 uniforms.

This uniform had the following elements. Firstly the M1789 regulation (summer) pattern uniform which consisted of a double-breasted (nine buttons each side), medium blue/grey blue coat (the same colour cloth as that used for Danish hussar uniforms), which reached down to the thighs. It had a specially designed yellow collar with a brass button on each side, so it could be folded up in cold weather. It had a yellow split and apparently pointed cuffs, (one button) for summer wear. For headwear the men received the M1789 *cachet/kaskett*, a low, mitre-shaped cap made of felt with an outer lining of leather. On the raised front there was a simple stamped brass Norwegian lion.

For winter wear they had a pair of medium blue overalls M1789 (called *wahrbukser*) with bone buttons. down the outside leg (they were always to be worn, when on skis), and they should both also had received the M1789 light grey greatcoats (*capot kjoler*), with a yellow collar (two buttons) and yellow square cuffs for use in winter and cold weather. However only the Søndenfjeldske Skiløber Bataljon did in fact receive this overcoat. The Nordenfjeldske Skiløber Bataljon instead kept using the old red M1774 hussar-style fur coats, but probably in a more practical shortened version (as seen on a contemporary picture painted by J. F. L Dreier *c*. 1810). From *c*. 1809–1810, probably both battalions began receiving short jacket style overcoats called *ydertrøjer, kaputtrøje* or *patruljetrøje*, as an alternative overcoat. They had also grey leather reinforced wool gloves in winter.

Hornblæser
The hornists wore the standard M1789 uniform coat until 1809–1810. The *hornblæsere*'s swallow's nest was probably a standard 1789 model, yellow with simple white tape border and vertical stripes, but from the 1801 cloth terms, we know it were simple cloth lace, without knots, but exact details are unknown. They also wore the summer white *bukser* (short breeches) M1793, with grey gaiters and blue winter overalls M1789. Hornists in ski battalions were not considered NCOs, as those in *jæger* and light battalions were, and this was first introduced around 1810.

NCOs
The NCOs of the Nordenfjeldske Skiløber Bataljon began receiving the M1793 regulation pattern uniform in 1796, while the NCOs of the Søndenfjeldske Skiløber Bataljon first received their M1793 uniform in 1798, long before the soldiers and hornists. There is some doubt if they received the full uniforms at first, but by 1802 they were wearing them in full. They added yellow/gold lace NCO epaulettes on their right shoulder. The new uniform M1793 was a single-breasted green coatee, officially called a *Vest* (waistcoat), which had a black collar and cuffs, with a double line of white piping down the front of the coat at each side of the opening, so when buttoned, it appeared as three vertical lines. It had no piping on the collar or cuffs. It had brass buttons and white turn-ups at the front. They had light grey M1793 trousers worn with long grey gaiters which reached over the knee. It is possible that they also wore the new M1793 *cachet/kaskett* (low cap) made of felt with an outer lining of leather. This bore no shield at front, but did have a dark green plume at the left side. Some may also have worn new M1802 hats by 1808–1809. By 1808, they had received grey light infantry gaiter trousers, grey overalls and grey NCO overcoats. They may have worn NCO *porte épée*s in green and white wool.

Officers
The officers of the Nordenfjeldske Skiløber Bataljon also received the M1793 coatees long before the soldiers, in 1796. The officers of the Søndenfjeldske Skiløber Bataljon received their coatees in 1798. Officers of *skiløber bataljoner* all wore short coatees as a special distinction, not the normal long-tailed officer's coats. Their coatees had two false pockets piped white. In 1803 they received gold epaulettes M1801. The officers wore hats instead of the cap and from around 1805 the new officers M1804 hats (later also the M1806) with gold and red cords and a green plume or long feather. By 1808 they had received grey summer gaiter trousers, grey winter overalls and grey officers' overcoats. They carried an officers' M1775 *skiløber sabel*, modified after 1788, or the officers' M1789 sabre, with a gold and red *porte épée*, carried from about 1807 on a black leather M1806 belt with a lion's head clasp.

Arms and Equipment
The *skiløbere* had for many years used a growing variety of rifles, mainly the M1755 *skiløber* rifle, but some that were as old as M1711. In 1794 they had the following weapons. The Søndenfjeldske Skiløberbattaljon: 171 different old model rifles, 150 new shortened muskets and 200 old *ekcerser geværer* (training muskets), and their sidearms

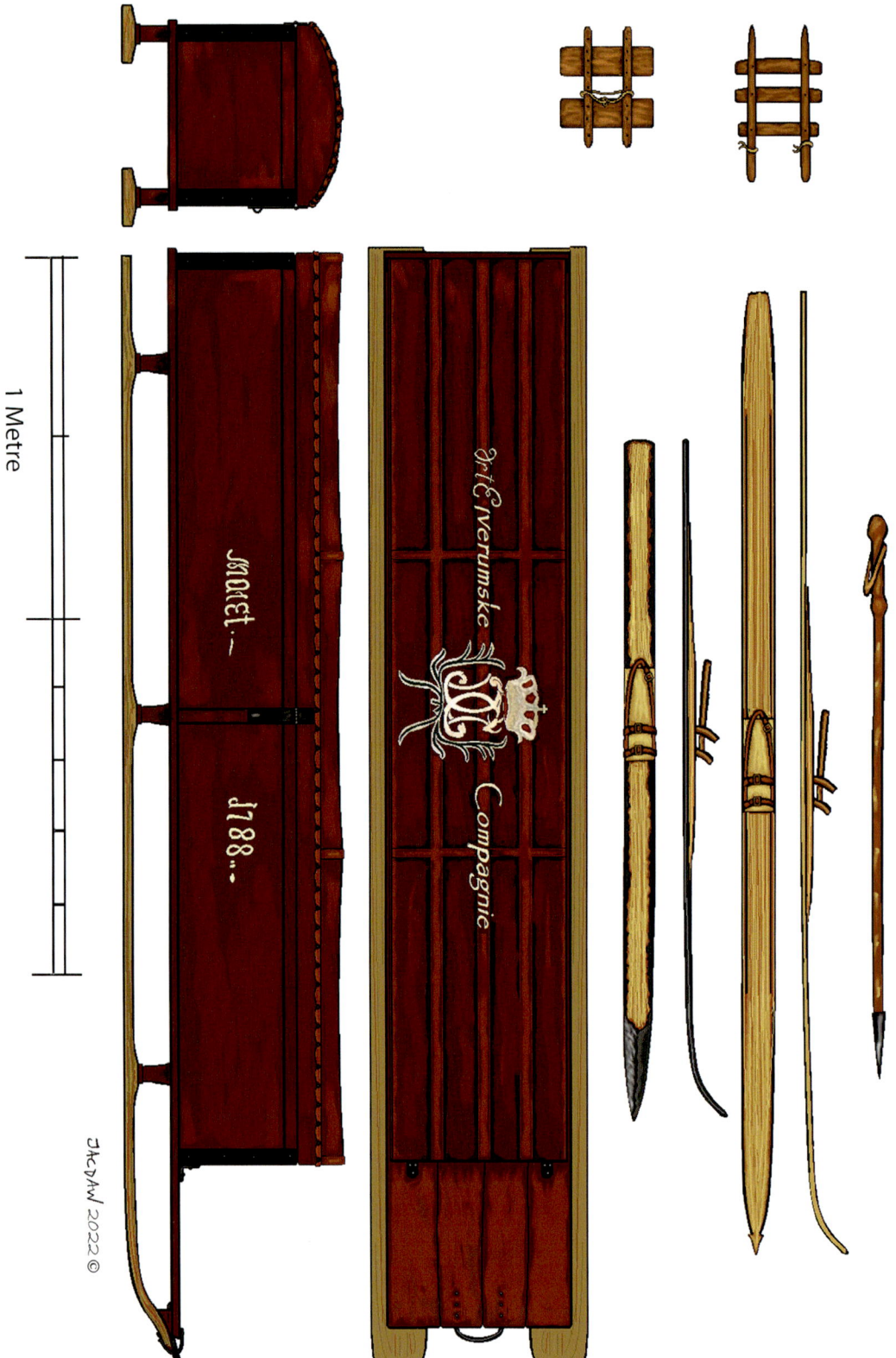

Norwegian Ski Troops (*skiløber*) 1790–1814, Equipment and Skis

THE NORWEGIAN JÆGERE, LIGHT INFANTRY AND SKI TROOPS

> Facing page
>
> Plate 26. Norwegian Ski Troops (*Skiløber*) Equipment and Skis
>
> Top to bottom:
>
> • Steel-shod ski stick; the skiers, only carried one and used it with their right hand. They also used it in battle as a rest for their rifles.
>
> • The long ski (*langski*)was for sliding andwas worn on left foot
>
> • The short ski (*andor*) was covered in skin for pushing and was worn on the right foot. At the same time more modern skis were being made at Telemark, with both skis the same length which resembled modern skis, but with an upturned tip and shovel at both ends with a camber in the centre. To what extent they were employed is not well documented, but so far as is known at least two companies of the Nordenfjeldske Skiløber Bataljon used them.
>
> • M1788 ammunition sledge. This was a wooden box based on the older standard box of the ammunition caissons and mounted on a ski frame. In was made of wooden panels with metal angles and the lid was a wooden frame covered with thick canvas and painted. Originally it was probably painted red with blackened ironwork, as in the regimental wagon train. Here it is shown as reddish brown, its actual state, but the red was probably a little brighter when it was first made. It could be pulled by one or two horses in tandem. A platoon of 10 men were detailed to carry ammunition, provisions and extra kit (kettles, hand axes, overcoats and probably a tent or two) and on occasion it could also be used to evacuate the wounded.
>
> • Two models of contemporary snowshoes (*truger*), sometimes also used by ordinary infantry soldiers

were 321 *skiløber sabel* M1774/98. Before the outbreak of war in 1808 they received new rifles, probably the M1785 and M1791 rifles, with M1787 *krudthorn* (priming flasks), from surplus stocks from the Norwegian Jæger Corps. The Nordenfjeldske Skiløberbattaljon had 170 different older model rifles, mainly M1755, 300 old *ekcerser geværer* (shortened muskets) and their sidearms were 321 *skiløber sabel* M1774/98. All ski soldiers had a gun cover, to protect the firearm during transport, and also a separate protective cover for the lock when not in use. They all had a flask of oil to protect their firearms. In 1774 the *skiløbere* were the first soldiers to receive a small copper oil flask to protect their weapons from rust. It was kept in the ammunition pouch, together with other tools and rags, and they also had a *fængnål* (pricker) to clean the touchhole. All also had a special *skinsæk* (skin sack) M1774 knapsack, worn with two straps. Ski soldiers were the first soldiers to receive backpacks, in 1774, with two straps, so as to carry them on the back. It was the view that the normal backpack, with just one carrying strap, was a hindrance while skiing, as it moved about uncontrolled. So the ski soldiers were the only soldiers, until 1808/1810 at least, to use a backpack with two carrying straps. The *skinsæk* M1774 was made of brownish/yellow hairless skin, with three lock straps, and the inside was divided into two compartments.

The ski soldier's sidearm was a weapon specially designed for the ski units in 1774. It was an infantry-type sabre, based on the M1756 infantry sabre. It was updated in 1798: the hilt was made slimmer, the side guards were removed to avoid getting in the way when skiing, and the weapon was strengthened and the blade made longer. The ski soldiers' sabre was known as *skiløber sabel* M1774/98. All but one of the surviving samples are marked as belonging to companies of the Nordenfjeldske Siløber Bataljon. Blade length 58.5 cm, width of blade 3.8 cm, weight 0.88 kg, length: 74.2 cm.[12]

Some of the officers carried the *skiløber sabel* M1775/88, modified after 1788 as used in Norway, and others used more modern M1789 officers' sabres.

Special Equipment Including the Skis

The Søndenfjeldske ski battalions used skis of the Østerdal type. These were skis of uneven length. They were traditional in the districts where the companies were recruited, and it would have been difficult for the men to use another type of ski.

The Østerdal ski differs from others in several ways, the most obvious difference is the length, and special characteristics. The long ski (*langski*) was made for sliding and had a length of a little over three metres. The short ski was called an *andor*, and was no more than two metres long with fur on the underside, either seal or reindeer, and a steel tip. It was used to kick off and for scaling hills. The *andor* at least had military markings, usually the soldier's number.

In the Nordenfjeldske ski battalion two of the three companies used a different type of ski called *snåsa* skis, where both skis where of equal length and had an upward pointing tip at both ends. When the new regulations came in 1804, they allowed for two similar-sized skis without the fur backing; probably they were *snåsa* skis.

---

12 Source: Kay S. Nielsen, *Danske blankvåben*.

Normally the skiiers used only one ski stick, made of wood with an iron spike and a leather thong. The stick could double as a musket rest for even more accurate shooting. The skis and stick were generally of varnished wood or painted white. Each soldier normally had a new pair and an old pair of skis. They also had two pairs of *skisko* (skiing shoes) to use when on skis.

Snowshoes
The snowshoes (*truger*) of the period were rectangular, usually of two wooden runners and two to three traversal slats in mortises like a ladder. They had leather laces. There were a number of variants, as most appear to be rather rustic and locally made. There was also a round wooden version for the horses.

Transport
Each company had several ski sledges of type M1788 drawn by one or two horses in tandem, used for ammunition, provisions and extra kit (kettles, hand axes, overcoats, etc.) for 10 men of the company. According to the inventory made in 1837, the Norwegian army had 192 ammunition and supply sledges available. It is not fully clear if all were in stock in 1800–1814, or some were made later (source: the official inventory list of all Norwegian weapons after a complete inventory made in 1837). Legend has it they were also used for transporting wounded and dead, if needed. Empty, a ski sledge weighed 27 kg. Two types are known, and each company was supposed to have 10 open sledges and four equipped with chests. Three of these are still preserved in Norwegian museums, and they are painted dark red with black ironwork. Two of them are marked Åmotske Compagnie and the Elverumske Compagnie with the year 1788 painted on both of them in white paint.

In Norway most off-road transport, especially when the ground was not covered by snow, was done using small sturdy pack horses, with a special transport saddle called a *kløvsaddel*. This permitted different sacks, bundles, barrels and all kinds of equipment to be carried. Several companies, including the ski companies, had special transport cases or chests, made especially for different equipment. The Elverumske Skiløber Companie had several of this type of these transport chests, and it was easy to hang one on each side of the *kløvsaddel*. Ordinary infantry, and the artillery, also used this kind of transport.

The New Grey and Green Uniforms 1809–1814
In 1812 the Søndenfjeldske Skiløber Bataljon was issued with a uniform identical to the Akershusiske Skarpskytte Regiment/Akershusiske Skarpskytte Regiment, even though in 1810 it had been planned that they should receive their own distinctive uniforms, the new grey M1810 *skiløber* uniform, with black facings. But instead they adopted the same modified light grey M1810 *skarpskytte* uniform as used by the Akershusiske Skarpskytte Regiment which was a single-breasted light grey coatee with a square green collar, cuffs and shoulder straps, all piped white. There was a double line of green piping down the front of the coat, at each side of the opening, so when buttoned, it appeared as three lines. It had one row of 10 white metal buttons and the front turnbacks were green. They wore a pair of fall-fronted grey breeches and short black gaiters with wooden buttons. They had a black M1808 shako with a green cockade, a white loop and white metal button. It had a low green plume and green cords.

Uniforms of the Attached Østerdalske Fribataljon
They used their ordinary grey levy uniforms, with red collar and cuffs and grey trousers, both in homespun cloth. They wore a black *cachette/kaskette*, a low cap made of calfskin. They had black belts and they used the older rifles and older shortened muskets, surplus from Søndenfjeldske Skiløber Bataljon.

Hornblæsere, Søndenfjeldske Skiløber Bataljon
Their uniform was the same as that of the *skiløbere*. Hornists did not have the status of NCOs in the ski battalions, but apparently this was changed in 1810. Their headgear was a black shako with a green cockade, with a white loop and metal button, green NCO cords and feather. On their shoulders they had green swallows' nests with white lace edging and bars. They may also have adopted NCO *porte épées* in green and white wool. As NCOs they wore silver lace M1789 NCO epaulettes until 1812 or 1813. After 1813 their uniforms were modified; their epaulettes were abolished and replaced with the new chevron rank distinctions worn on pointed cuffs. They probably had NCO *porte épées* in green and white wool.

NCOs of the Søndenfjeldske Skiløber Bataljon
They wore the same uniform as the *skiløbere*, but with a silver/white epaulette on their right shoulder. Their headwear was a black shako with a green cockade, a white loop and metal button, green NCO cords and plume. In 1812–1813 the uniforms were modified. The epaulettes were discontinued, and replaced with the new chevron rank distinctions M1812, worn on pointed cuffs. They may have continued to wear NCOs *porte épées* in green and white wool.

Officers of the Søndenfjeldske Skiløber Bataljon
Their new uniform consisted of a single-breasted light grey short coat, like the *skiløbere* with square green collar and cuffs, all piped white. They also had a double line of green piping down the front of the coat, at each side of the opening, so when buttoned, it appeared as three lines. It had 10 silvered buttons. At the back were two false, white-lined pockets, and four silvered buttons at the opening at the back. On their shoulders they wore silver epaulettes.

They wore a pair of fall-fronted grey breeches and short black Hessian boots. Their headwear was a black officer's shako with a green cockade, with a silver loop and silvered button, gold/yellow and red cords and a green plume. The uniforms were modified in 1812 with the new rank distinctions of buttons and chevrons, worn over pointed cuffs, and the officers were to cease wearing their waist sash and epaulettes. From 4 December 1811 they were allowed to wear short grey officers' coatees M1810 and also the black M1810 officers' cross belt and pouch with a badge inscribed FRVI. They were to change the facing colours from the original black, to green piped white, although it is not stated as such in the resolution. They normally carried an officer's M1789 sabre, or variant, with a gold and red *porte épée*, carried on a black leather M1806 belt with a lion's head clasp. In winter they had grey overalls and probably the new grey officers overcoat M1810.

New Green Uniforms for the Nordenfjeldske Skiløber Bataljon 1808–1814

According to the plans, in 1809/1810 all soldiers and NCOs of the Nordenfjeldske Skiløber Bataljon should finally have begun receiving the new short green coatee M1793, called a *vest* (waistcoat), probably with some M1808 modifications, like on the collar. Until then the Nordenfjeldske Skiløber Bataljon had used the M1789 light blue summer and same model winter uniform. They had also kept on using the old red M1774 fur coats, but were shortened to same size as the grey *kaputtrøjer*. Also old red and yellow fatigue caps had been used. But, from the end of 1809 they finally began receiving the new M1793 coatee and new light grey M1793 *wahrbukser* (overalls) and possibly also some grey M1793 overcoats, shipped from Denmark.

But because of the isolated and in many respects independent command of the Northern Division, production of uniforms had already begun in Trondheim in 1808. Previously they had been allowed to tailor many of their own uniforms, and had in 1808–1811, on their own initiative been tailoring new green *skiløber* uniforms, which we will call the Trondhjemske *skiløber* uniform M1808, for the future use of the Nordenfjeldske Skiløber Bataljon. Trondheim had several open trade routes to Archangelsk until 1812, and also later through Russian-occupied Finland, and so it was possible to buy rifles, gunpowder, flints, grain and general supplies, and also cloth; in particular, green Russian army cloth. Apparently, the production of Trondhjemske *skiløber* uniform M1808 was stopped in 1811.

In 1809 Trondheim began to receive shakos M1808 with green cords and a short green feather from Denmark. So the Nordenfjeldske Skiløber Bataljon as far as is known, first wore the green M1793 coatees, which they began receiving late in 1809. It had a standing collar, black facings piped white and brass buttons, worn with shakos. They were then expected to change into new grey M1810 uniforms. But on the 31 July 1811 they had asked for, but were not permitted to change into, the grey M1810 uniforms, as according to the normal clothing replacement terms, this would be done in 1812/1813. The record states clearly that the request was refused 'as they already have new green uniforms, ready for issue in 1812/1813'. So except for the officers who had received cloth to make themselves new grey M1810 full dress uniforms if they wanted to, the Nordenfjeldske Skiløber Bataljon did not wear any grey uniforms before 1822. This 'new green uniform' was clearly the Trondhjemske *skiløber* uniform M1808. This is confirmed by a contemporary eyewitness painting, made in 1814.

During the 1814 campaign the Nordenfjeldske Skiløber Bataljon, part of *Oberstløjtnant* von Rodes' brigade was protecting the left flank of the main army, between Elverum and Vang, centred on Løten, in Hedmark. A contemporary painting by the Swedish hussar officer and painter Hjalmar Mørner, probably drawn shortly after the ceasefire of 14 August 1814, clearly shows what appears to be soldiers from both von Rodes and the brigade of Colonel von Hegermann, operating in the vicinity of Kongsvinger. It shows the red uniforms, worn with grey trousers, of the Nordenfjeldske Geworbne Regiment, the grey uniform of the Walderske Skarpskytte Bataljon, and most interestingly what can be identified as two *skiløbere* from Nordenfjeldske Skiløber Bataljon wearing the uniform they allegedly received in 1812. And they both clearly wear the Trondhjemske *skiløber* uniform M1808.

Both soldiers wear green M1808-style coatees, with a black collar and lapels, piped white, with yellow buttons and white frontal turn ups. Both have white square cuffs. This last detail may simply be to differentiate them from the Røråsk Bjærg Jæger Corps. Both soldiers also wear a pair of tight green trousers and short black gaiters. One is armed with a rifle and has black belts and a brown *skinsæk* (backpack). Besides this contemporary information, both an officer's and a *hornblæser* uniform (M1808) are preserved, belonging to the Trondhjemske *skiløber*. They confirm the details known of the Trondhjemske *skiløber* uniform. It has been suggested that these two uniforms could be 1812 uniforms of the Trondhjemske Frivillige Jæger Corps, but this is not certain, and they should be seen as variations of *skiløber* uniform M1808 produced in Trondheim between 1808 and 1811. After 1817–1822 they were probably used by some members of Trondhjemske Frivillige Jæger Corps, of which the *hornblæsere*, as is suggested by the uniform, had previously served, in the Nordenfjelske Skiløber Bataljon.

Hornblæsere of the Nordenfjeldske Skiløber Bataljon

Their uniform was the same as the *skiløbere*. Hornists did not have a status as NCOs in the ski battalions, but this apparently changed around 1810. Their headwear was a black shako M1808, with a green cockade, a yellow loop and brass button, green NCO cords and plume. On their shoulders they had black swallows nests with yellow lace edging and bars. Until 1812–1813 they probably wore M1789 NCO epaulettes, to indicate their new status as NCOs, but after that date the uniforms were modified, the epaulettes discontinued, and replaced with the new chevron rank distinctions worn on pointed cuffs. An original *hornblæser* green coatee is conserved in the Vitenskapsmuseet, Trondheim. It bears all the known elements of the Trondhjemske *skiløber* uniform M1808.

What is interesting is that it is sewn in exactly the same style as an early M1808 coatee from the Nordenfjeldske Geworbne Regiment (FMU.004528–1). The early models had squarer front lapels than the later model, and an example can also be found on the preserved Trondhjemske *skiløber* uniform M1808. This points to fact that it was made after an early M1808 proof copy of the uniform. It is made of standard slightly coarse cloth, typical of soldiers', hornists' and NCOs' uniforms. It has black shoulder rolls with thin yellow piping and five stripes across them. The collar has been modified for wear after 1817 and it has pointed black and white lined cuffs, which again may be a latter addition, but could also be the new cuff of an NCO from 1812–1813. It is not unlikely that NCOs and officers adopted pointed cuffs, and in a different colour to that of the ordinary ski soldiers. There are several indications that the correct buttons and lace for the new distinctions took its time to reach all of Norway, and that Trondheim, received them last of all. Possibly the hornists just had the pointed cuffs, and no chevrons. They may also have worn NCO *porte épées* in green and white wool.

NCOs of the Nordenfjeldske Skiløber Bataljon
The NCOs wore the same green uniforms as the *skiløbere*, but with a gold laced epaulette on their right shoulder. Their headgear was a black shako with a green cockade with a yellow loop and brass button, green NCO cords and feather. In 1812–1813 the uniforms were modified, the epaulettes abolished and replaced with the new M1812 chevron rank distinctions, worn on pointed cuffs. There are indications that the correct buttons and lace for the new distinctions took their time to reach all of Norway, and that Trondheim received last of all. So perhaps NCOs, at least for a time, just had the pointed cuffs, and no chevrons before 1813–1814. They probably kept wearing their NCO *porte épées* in green and white wool.

Officers of the Nordenfjeldske Skiløber Bataljon
The officers as far as we know wore the M1793 coatee, with added changes, until *c*. 1812. On 22 September 1810 the officers received cloth to make themselves grey M1810 full dress uniforms.

This new officers' uniform consisted of a short, dark, single-breasted grey coatee, with brass buttons, a square standing black collar and cuffs, all piped white, and short tails. There was a double line of green piping down the front of the coat at each side of the opening, so when buttoned, it appeared as three lines. It had 10 gold buttons, four gilt buttons on the back, at the opening, and two false pockets piped green. It had green frontal turnbacks. On their shoulders they had gold M1801 epaulettes. They wore a pair of fall-fronted grey breeches and short black Hessian boots. Their headgear was a black officer's shako with a green cockade, a gold loop and gilt button. It had gold and red cords and a short round green plume. Like the officers of the Søndenfjeldske they were probably allowed to carry the black M1810 officers' cross belt with pouch, with a gilt FRVI badge, as permitted for the officers from the Søndenfjeldske Skiløber Bataljon. But for service in the field, we have an example of a preserved officer's coat, made after the same model as the Trondhjemske *skiløber* uniform M1808, which clearly indicates that it was this is uniform that the officers wore in 1814. It is made of fine green cloth, with a black velvet collar, facings and pointed cuffs, with white lining. It has 14 gilt buttons at the front and two gilt buttons on each cuff. It also has two horizontal false pockets at the back, a feature only found on officers' uniforms, and four gilt buttons at the rear opening. It had white late-style more pointed M1808 frontal turn-ups and white cloth lining. The cuffs are pointed, as used by only officers and NCOs until around 1818–1820 in Norway.

In 1812 the uniforms were modified with the new rank distinctions with pointed cuffs and the officers ceased wearing the waist sash and epaulettes. There are several indications that the correct buttons and lace for the new distinctions took time to reach all of Norway, and that as with many other items, Trondheim received it last. This was probably the field uniform worn by officers in 1814 with either the original green or new grey trousers M1810 with short black boots and shako. They probably also wore the black M1810 officer's cross belt with pouch. They carried an officer's M1789 sabre, or a variant of same, with a gold and red *porte épée*, carried on a black leather M1806 belt with a lion's head clasp.

The 2nd Nordenfjeldske Skiløber Bataljon
This unit was officially raised in 1810 and it was also attached to the 1st Trondhjemske Nationale Regiment, and at first, they were dressed and armed as a musketeer battalion as this was their original role. But correspondence dated 1814 from the commander of 1st Trondhjemske Nationale Regiment, Major General C. G. von Bang, clearly states that both the 1st and 2nd Nordenfjeldske Skiløber Bataljoner 'have enough green uniforms available, of two [different] models, to equip them both, and even enough to supply some to the Det Kongelige Frivillige Røroiskebjerg Corps.' He also clearly states that although they have a full supply

of new grey uniforms, they 'have at this moment no use for them, before next uniform term'.

Since 1808, Trondheim had been making their own ski uniforms, apparently with cloth bought from Russian merchants. So they had both produced their own model Trondhjemske *skiløber* uniform M1808, and also received large stocks of the *skiløber* uniform M1793/98 from Denmark from 1809 to 1813. In 1814 the 2nd Nordenfjeldske Skiløber Bataljon probably wore a mixture of green *skiløber* uniform M1793/98, and maybe also some the green Trondhjemske *skiløber* uniform M1808 (probably by a number of complete companies). Headwear was probably the old black *cachette/kaskette* caps. They should have received short light grey woollen overcoats, but when Christian Frederik inspected them on 13 February 1814 he stated that 'They all looked as fine soldiers, but their equipment was rather varied, with different types of uniforms and several model overcoats, in different colours and also old worn muskets. All this I ordered to be solved quickly'. In 1814 there were, as far as is known, around 380 *skiløbere*, formed into a field battalion of three divisions.

Arms and Equipment
Due to the blockade of Norway it was extremely difficult to obtain new more serviceable firearms, so the different *skiløber bataljoner* had to use a variety of different weapons. The Søndenfjeldske Skiløber Bataljon began receiving surplus rifles from the Norske Geworbne Jæger Corps in 1807–1808. These included the *jæger* rifle M1785 and M1791, together with the M1787 *krudthorn* (priming flask). The M1785 and M1791 *jæger* rifles did not have a bayonet socket. In 1813–1814 the older model rifles and old shortened muskets were probably used to equip the levies adopted into the battalion (source: *Hærmuseets årbok* 1960).

Because of the remoteness of its garrison it was more difficult to get new rifles for the Søndenfjeldske Skiløber Bataljon, whose rifles and muskets were generally old and worn. But in 1809 the 2nd Nordenfjeldske Division (2nd Northern Military District), had by its own initiative been allowed to buy 400 Russian M1795/1806 rifles, imported from Archangelsk and delivered by ship with other much needed stores, to the Nordenfjelds (Northern Military District). The first were issued to the Nordenfjeldske Skiløber Bataljon and maybe to the *jæger* company (*selbuske kompanie*) of the 2nd Nordenfjeldske Skiløber Bataljon in 1814, and possibly also to others in the Northern Military District. In Norway this is called the M1808 rifle. It is possible that the original Russian sword bayonet was not used, and it was used either without a bayonet or modified to use a standard *hirschfänger* bayonet M1803.

The old rifles (M1711 and M1755) and the shortened M1774 (and other old) muskets not needed for training were also pressed into service by 2nd Nordenfjeldske Skiløber Bataljon and they had (as far as is known), ordinary bayonet attachments. The ski battalions were by now equipped in a similar way as the other *jægere* and sharpshooters. They had the black leather light infantry/*jæger* waist belts, cross belt and cartridge pouch. The M1789 powder horn was used by Søndenfjeldske Skiløber Bataljon, but not by the Nordenfjeldske Skiløber Bataljon, which first had older or substandard rifles, then Russian rifles, none of which used priming flasks. They kept on using the copper oil flasks to protect their weapons from rust, kept in the ammunition pouch, together with tools and rags. Field equipment was as before.

7

The Norwegian Cavalry

Organisation

Originally, from the early 1600s until the late eighteenth century the Norwegian cavalry arm was very large, but by the 1780 it was clear that, although still a very good force, it was necessary to reform them and reduce the numbers of men and regiments. This was decided for a number of reasons, not least the costs of maintaining them and difficulty in breeding horses suitable for cavalry that could operate in the harsh climate.

Following the short war against Sweden in 1788 where the cavalry a played a significant role, there was very briefly a plan to convert some dragoons into heavy cavalry *rytter* to face up to the Swedish heavy cavalry, but it never happened. In any case the geography of Norway did not exactly make for good cavalry country.[1]

Following the reforms of 1784, a major effort was made from 1806 onwards to modernise the Norwegian cavalry, in particular their equipment, by adopting Hungarian saddles and shabraques amongst other measures, but this was interrupted by the war, followed by the drastic reduction of the cavalry in the 1811 reforms. The cavalry had already been converted to dragoons and a mounted *jæger* (light cavalry) corps was formed. The role of the Norwegian dragoons was that of mounted infantry, while retaining (some) ability to fight as traditional cavalry.

The cavalry was rarely concentrated, but instead were distributed in penny packets of companies to the brigades and used mainly for reconnaissance and orderly work, or as guards for the artillery, and were rarely, if ever, gathered in double-company squadrons as regulated, and many men remained dismounted due to the lack of fodder for the horses. The fodder was reserved primarily for the train and the artillery draught horses. An exception was during the battle of Lier in 1814 where a company of the Akershusiske Ridende Jæger Corps successfully charged and repulsed the Swedish infantry, which shows that they were still quite capable of performing as cavalry.

In 1784 the major reform of the cavalry produced the following results:

The 1st Sødenfjeldske Dragonregiment, originally raised in 1702, became the Akershusiske Dragonregiment in 1784 and was eventually disbanded in 1811

The 2nd Sødenfjeldske Dragonregiment which had originally been raised in 1708 with seven companies became the Smaalehnske Dragonregiment in 1784, and was disbanded in 1811

The 3rd Sødenfjeldske Dragonregiment, which had originally been raised in 1749 with eight National companies now became the Oplandske Dragonregiment in 1784, and in 1811 was renamed the Søndenfjeldske Dragonregiment

The 4th Sødenfjeldske Dragonregiment, which had originally been raised as the Dragoner Nordenfjelds, was renamed the Nordenfjeldske Dragonkorps or Trondhjemske Dragonkorps in 1701. In 1711 it was renamed as the Trondhjems Dragonregiment, and in 1715 was renamed yet again as the Nordenfjeldske Dragonregiment.

---

1 During the preparations for the short war with Sweden in 1788 the M1773/78 sword was issued to Nordenfjeldske Dragonregiment to form some of the Norwegian dragoons, into *ryttere* heavy cavalry in preparation for the campaign in Sweden. But apparently the M1773/78 was not well liked, and the swords were found to be too heavy and cumbersome for use by the dragoons; they weighed three kilos, including scabbard, and they were 116.9 cm long. Furthermore the role of the *ryttere* did not adapt at all well to the Norwegian and Swedish terrain. They were then put into store (permanently). We do not know the exact numbers, but in 1837 there remained in store: '1,829 one and double-sided heavy cavalry pallasker'. Probably a 1,000 of those were the single-edged M1773/78 straight swords, the rest probably the double edged M1803 Landeværns *rytter pallask,* which were sent in some numbers to Norway in 1811–1813 to modernise the sidearms of the Norwegian dragoons, but were found to be inferior to the M1740 and M1750 swords already in use. Source: *Fortegnelse over Antal og Beskaffenhed af de vigtigste i samtlige norske Landarsenaler havende militaire Fornødenheder ved Aarets Udgang 1837* (the '1837 list' for short) and several articles in *Våbenhistorisk selskab*.

In 1783 it became the Trondhjemske Dragonregiment (again) and finally in 1811, the Trondhjems Dragonkorps. The dragoon regiments were all composed of conscripts except for the Akershusiske Dragonregiment which had one enlisted company attached in 1806–1810.

Training

A *Kongelig Resolution* on 19 December 1806 ordered that the Norske Husar Detachment (the Norwegian Hussar Detachment), was to be reformed and transferred as a Geworbne (enlisted) dragoon company into the Akershusiske Dragonregiment, and that this company would form and in the future run a central cavalry school to train both Norwegian Officers and NCOs in the newest cavalry drill, manoeuvres and tactics. The former Hussar Detachment, now the Geworbne Dragon Kompagni, was hereby recognised as the premier cavalry unit in Norway, which had been trained under the most recent (Danish) cavalry regulations. So it was logical that it was chosen to form a cavalry school where it was to train four officers and four NCOs selected from each of the four Norwegian dragoon regiments in the latest cavalry regulations, who would then use the training they had received to teach the men of their parent regiments these new regulations. This was a major step forward in modernising the Norwegian cavalry.

Also, a *Kongelig Resolution* dated 5 June 1807 stated that they would, in order to get the best enlisted personnel, be allowed to select 16 dragoons, from the Oplandske, Smaalehnske and Akershusiske dragoon regiments. The best dragoons, chosen to enlist for service in the Den Kongelige Livgarde Til Hest (Royal Horse Guards) in Copenhagen, would instead be transferred to the Geworbne company.

These dragoons should be 'The best looking, best trained and most likely to otherwise be chosen as NCOs'. Volunteers of the same qualities were also selected from the Trondhjemske Dragonregiment. If there were any places open in the Geworbne company only the most able men would be allowed to enlist. After they had performed two years' service, they would then be allowed to return to their original regiments having been promoted to an NCO rank.

In 1808 the four regiments of dragoons theoretically each had between seven to eight companies for a total strength of 3,900 cavalrymen, or roughly 950 officers and men per regiment.

The Akershusiske Dragonregiment had seven dragoon companies. From 1807 one Nationale company was transferred to the horse artillery, and a *Geworben* enlisted company was added, formed from the former 'hussar detachment' effectively becoming the elite company.

The Smaalehnske Dragonregiment had seven dragoon companies.

The Oplandske Dragonregiment had eight dragoon companies.

The Trondhjemske Dragonregiment had eight dragoon companies

The three first regiments were part of the 1st Søndenfjeldske (1st Southern Division) and the last Trondhjemske Dragonregiment was part of the 2nd Nordenfjeldske (2nd Northern Division).

A *Kongelig Resolution* dated 21 April 1811 ordered a major reform of the cavalry in Norway where they were to be reorganised into only two regiments and a separate corps. A major change of uniforms was ordered for the following:

The Trondhjemske Dragonregiment, which now only had four Nationale companies based in Skogn, Strinden, Værdal and Stjørdal. Their theoretical strength in the war of 1814, as they were not mobilised during the war was Nationale: four staff personnel, eight officers, 16 NCOs, four trumpeters, 200 *dragoner* and 120 *landeværn*.

The Søndenfjeldske Dragonregiment, which was created with the men from the disbanded Smaalehnske, Akershusiske and Oplandske dragoon regiments, had 12 Nationale companies in 1810. The companies of 50 men were based in the districts of Biri og Vardal, Midtre Hedmark, Ullensaker, Skedsmo, Østre Toten, Søndre Hedmark, Vestre Hedmark, Nordre Hedmark, Søndre Toten, Hadeland and Nannestad and were grouped into six squadrons of which three (in theory) were mounted and three on foot. From 1811 their theoretical strength was 1,729 men including officers, NCOs, trumpeters and dragoons. Their actual strength in the war of 1814 was, Nationale: 12 staff, 24 officers, 48 NCOs 12 trumpeters, 840 *dragoner* and 300 *landeværn*. There was also a depot company of two NCOs, two trumpeters and 120 *dragoner*. In 1814 most of the men served on foot because of the lack of horses, as the artillery had priority, and a general lack of horse fodder.

The following are details of the few known, active mounted dragoon companies, from the Søndenfjeldske Dragonregiment in 1814, as part of Major General von Arenfeldt's brigade:

Ullensakerske Compagnie: Major Christoffer von Ingier
Strength: one lieutenant, two *sergenter*, three *corporaler*, two trumpeters and 70 dragoons

The Norwegian Dragoons and *Ridende Jægerkorps* 1803–1814 (I)

THE NORWEGIAN CAVALRY

> Facing page
>
> Plate 27. The Norwegian Dragoons and Ridende Jæger Corps 1803–1814
>
> Uniforms
>
> 1. Oplandske Dragonregiment, officer in full dress *c.* 1805 wearing buff leather breeches
> 2. Smaalehnske Dragonregiment, trooper in full dress *c.* 1805 carrying an M1734 dragoon *pallask* and wearing buff leather breeches
> 3. Akershusiske Dragonregiment, officer in full dress *c.* 1808 wearing buff kersey breeches
> 4. Trondhjemske Dragonregiment, NCO trumpeter in full dress *c.* 1808 carrying an M1740 dragoon *pallask* and wearing buff kersey breeches
> 5. Oplandske Dragonregiment, trooper in service/campaign dress *c.* 1808 carrying an M1734 dragoon *pallask*, wearing blue cavalry overalls over buff kersey breeches.
> 6. The Trondhjemske Dragon Corps was reorganised and reamed in 1811. Picture shows a *ritmester* in service/campaign dress *c.* 1814 wearing blue cavalry overalls over buff kersey breeches. Norway had received very large stocks of the blue cavalry overalls M1797/1800, and buff kersey breeches in 1808–1811, from Denmark, and had, after the reorganisation of 1811, such large stocks remaining that all the dragoons continued to wear them up to the end of the war. They were even able to supply blue cavalry overalls to both mounted artillery and supply train drivers.
> 7. The Søndenfjeldske Dragonregiment was reorganised and renamed in 1811. Picture shows a trooper in service/campaign dress *c.* 1814 carrying an M1750 *dragonpallask*, wearing blue cavalry overalls over buff kersey breeches. These breeches were in theory supposed to be replaced with grey ones sent from Denmark in 1810, but because of the large stocks of blue cavalry overalls remaining in Norway, the Akershusiske Ridende Jæger Corps were the only cavalry unit to use grey ones, which they did from 1812.
> 8. Akershusiske Ridende Jæger Corps. *Premiereløjtnant* of the *geworbne* (enlisted) company in full dress *c.* 1814, wearing buff kersey breeches.
> 9. Akershusiske Ridende Jæger Corps, trooper in service/campaign dress *c.* 1814 carrying an M1750 *dragonpallask* and wearing the new grey M1810 cavalry overalls over buff kersey breeches. The Akershusiske Ridende Jæger Corps was the only cavalry unit to use grey overalls from 1812. Note that the red lining has been replaced by a dark grey/black lining.
> 10. Akershusiske Ridende Jæger Corps, NCO trumpeter of the *geworbne* company in full dress uniform *c.* 1814 wearing buff kersey breeches. Shown carrying a *dragonsabel* (light cavalry sabre) M1808 with a brass hilt.

Skedsmoske Compagnie: Ritmester Hans Ernest Von Sparre
Strength: a lieutenant, two *sergenter*, three corporaler, two trumpeters and 70 dragoons

A further six dragoon companies were employed as a foot battalion, in Colonel von Rodes' brigade.

The Akershusiske Ridene Jægercorps was formed in 1811 with one Geworbne (enlisted) company formed from the old hussar company which had become the Geworbne company of the *Akershusiske* dragoons, and three Nationale companies, who were raised from the dragoons of the disbanded regiments, including one other company from the Akershusiske dragoons and two companies of the ex-Smaalehnske dragoons, reorganised into three companies of 75 men. The companies were based on Trøgstad, Eidsvold/Ness and the *geworbent kompani* at Rakkestad.

In principle they were supposed to scout, and fight mounted, but if necessary, they could operate dismounted, but only 'on special occasions'. In time of war the Geworbne company would act as guides and guards for the general in command of the army.[2] The three other companies together with a battalion from Akershusiske Skarpskytte Regiment would be divided up, to serve in the first three brigades. A company of this regiment, the Eidsvoll/Nesiske company, was the only cavalry unit to carry out a mounted charge during the war at the battle of Lier in 1814.

Strength during the war of 1814: Geworbne company; two staff, four officers, five NCOs, two trumpeters and 70 *geworbne jægere,* and the three Nationale *jæger* companies had three staff personnel, nine officers, 15 NCOs, six trumpeters and 210 Nationale *jægere*.

---

2 Only in 1820 was this changed in the Danish cavalry. It is also possible that the NCOs in Norway may not have worn any shoulder straps at all during 1812–1814.

The Norwegian Dragoons and *Ridende Jægerkorps* 1803–1814 (II), Equipment

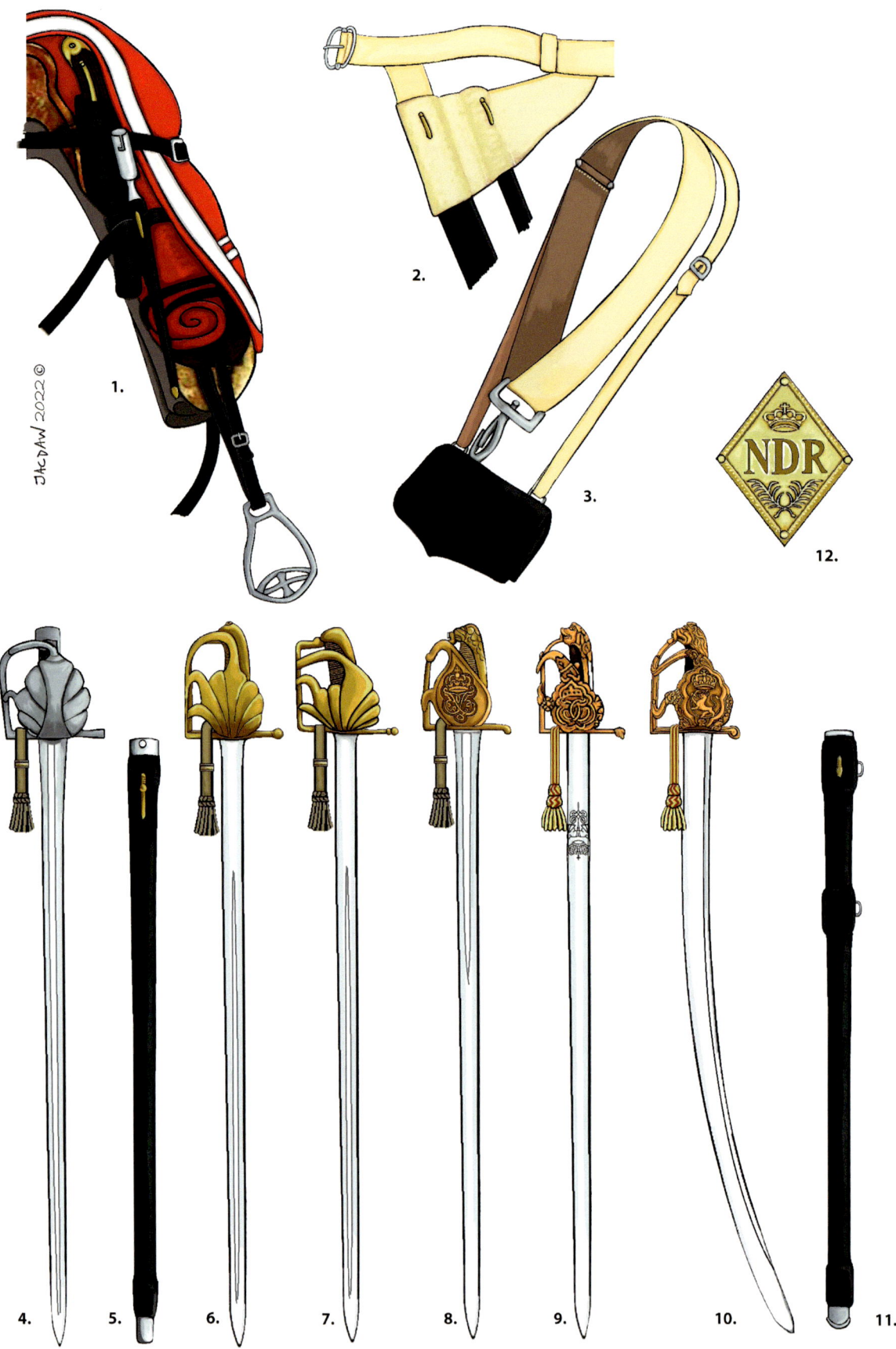

> Facing page
>
> Plate 28. The Norwegian Dragoons and Ridende Jæger Corps 1803–1814, II Equipment
>
> 1. Detail of bayonet strapped to the left pistol holster *c.* 1810
> 2. Dragoon waist belt showing frogs for *pallask* and bayonet
> 3. Dragoon musket and pouch belts
> 4. M1734 *pallask* with a steel hilt
> 5. Early scabbard with locket for the frog on the waist belt
> 6. M1740 pallask with a brass shell hilt
> 7. M1740 *pallask* with a brass shell hilt, variant
> 8. M1750 *dragonpallask* with a brass shell hilt bearing a crowned royal cypher (FV). Note the lion's head on the pommel. A more elaborate variant exists, possibly a senior NCO's model.
> 9. An officer's variant of the M1750 *dragonpallask* with an elaborate brass shell hilt bearing a crowned royal cypher; note the lion's head on the pommel.
> 10. This elaborate sabre mounted on the hilt of an old *pallask c.* 1700, is based on a model which belonged to Oberst Peter Andreas von Hiort of the Trondhjemske Dragonregiment (after an original portrait painted in 1808, and a sabre of same style conserved in the Army Museum in Oslo). This is yet another example of older weapons being upgraded or recycled. Other dragoon officers may have used variants of the M1789 officer's sabre, like *rytter* officers in Denmark.
> 11. Scabbard crudely converted with rings for suspension from a cavalry belt. Note: the remains of a locket are still visible.
> 12. Brass rhombic hat plate stamped with NDR (Norske Dragonregiment) under a crown and over a pair of crossed palm fronds.

Dragoon Uniforms

In 1801 the men were still wearing M1785 bicorns with a white loop, button and plume with their madder red M1798 lapelled coatee with the collar, cuffs and lapels in the regimental facings and a shoulder strap on the left shoulder only. Some companies continued to wear the M1798 coats until 1814. Some companies, probably the depot or reserves were still wearing the M1789 lapelled coats with other more recent items of dress as late as 1807 and later.

They continued to wear buckskin breeches and black leather M1785 cavalry boots with spurs. Their equipment was equally rather old-fashioned with large buff leather cross belts for their muskets with a smaller shoulder belt with their cartridge pouch carried over their left shoulder. They had a buff leather waist belt with a steel or white metal open buckle and frogs for their swords and bayonets.

The officers also wore a bicorn with a silver loop, button and tassels with a black cockade and a white plume. They had a long-tailed carmine red-lapelled coat with the regimental facings and silvered buttons. As a special privilege the Norwegian dragoon officers could use same type of crimson coat as that used by the Danish (and Norwegian) artillery officers throughout the period 1800–1814. They also wore a pair of buff leather breeches and short black Hessian boots, silver epaulettes and a red and yellow waist sash.

From 1806 the bicorn was gradually replaced with an M1804 hat, after a *Kongelig Resolution* dated 14 December 1804, followed by another on 11 February 1805, wherein hats are approved for all four dragoon regiments, as was a brass rhombic shield with the lettering 'NDR' under a crown, which would be issued 'according to the next term'. The hat had a white band with a white metal buckle, white loop with a white metal button, a black cockade and small white plume and red and yellow cords with tassels.

Troopers wore an M1798 model coatee which was madder red in the same cut as the infantry with white metal/pewter buttons for all regiments. Their coat had white linings and front turnbacks, a tradition of the dragoons, like Prince Frederik Ferdinand's regiment in Denmark. However, from 1806 they were now technically classed as light dragoons and were now allowed buff frontal turn-ups and lining. Their sleeveless waistcoats were white, faced red for NCOs from 1806.

According to the clothing terms to be applied from 8 January 1807, their old buckskin breeches were to be replaced with new yellow *kirsey* (kersey) cloth breeches for full dress. With these they received a pair of short black cavalry boots with spurs, and they should also have begun to be issued with a pair of fall-fronted blue M1797/1800 cavalry overalls,[3] with leather reinforcing on the inside legs, crotch and around the seat, piped red with buttons down the outside leg for ordinary service or campaign. According to an inventory of the Norske Munderingsdepot (Central Norwegian Uniform Arsenal) of 15 March 1808 they held in stock 1,499 new cavalry boots with spurs and 1,000 blue cavalry overalls, all ready to be issued.[4] Probably the Akershusiske regiment had already been issued with both kersey cloth breeches, overalls and boots. The dragoons were however still wearing yellow breeches and blue overalls in 1814. In theory these should have been changed to white *kirsey* breeches and grey overalls with dark grey lining ('for issue next term') in 1810. But this never happened; instead they were allowed to keep the buff *kirsey* breeches and blue overalls, and 'wear these out first' as they still had large new stocks of them. As far as is known, only the Akershusiske Ridende Jæger Corps ever received the grey M1810 overalls, and only the Geworbne company received the white cloth *kirsey* breeches M1810. In 1814 the Geworbne company received '25 pairs of white *kirsey* trousers'. They were probably only for parade use as they were part of Prince/King Christian Frederik's staff.

Between 1811 and 1814 the new cavalry units had (according to internal orders, letters, etc.) all been issued with new M1808 *rytter* shakos, but the dragoons kept their rhomboid hat plates and attached them to the new shakos. The new shako had a black chinstrap combined with white metal chin scales. The loop for the shako was white with a black cockade, a short white plume and yellow and red cords.

Around 1810 the dragoons began to be issued with the M1808 coatee which had a much higher waist and only one shoulder strap on the left only, as per regulations.[5] All through this period the dragoons continued to use the red woollen cavalry cloak, not the grey model.

Trumpetere (Trumpeters)

The dragoon drummers had been replaced by trumpeters in 1789. The painter Andreas Bloch suggested that the trumpeters still used the sleeve lacing of the previous century, without citing his sources, but the author has found no proof to support this. According to the clothing terms of 8 January 1807, we know that trumpeters (who were not classed as NCOs) of the Akershusiske, Trondhjemske, Oplandske and Smaalehnske dragoon regiments should have been issued with 'silver lace and six knots to place on uniform as distinction' (a swallows' nest with three knots on each shoulder). However it was decided that the trumpeters of the Geworbne company of the Akershusiske Dragonregiment which was classed as the most prestigious unit of the Norwegian cavalry, should wear an NCO's uniform to mark their status (an NCO's epaulette and a *dragon* on the left shoulder). Also, as they had been allowed to keep their *pauker* (kettledrummer) 1807–1811, he was also classed as a NCO so he did not wear swallows' nests, but NCO's distinctions instead (this was an NCO's epaulette on the right and a *Dragon* on left shoulder). But it was decided that the *pauker* (kettledrummer) of the regiment, and the trumpeters of the Geworbne company of the Akershusiske Dragonregiment, should wear an NCOs uniform to mark their status (an NCOs epaulette and a 'dragon' on the left shoulder). But in the Geworbne company of the Akershusiske Regiment, which were classed as the most prestigious unit of the Norwegian cavalry, all their trumpeters were classed as NCOs, and as such did not wear swallows' nests but NCO distinctions. Also as the Akershusiske Regiment was the first of the Norwegian dragoon regiments, they had been allowed to keep their *pauke* (kettledrummer between 1807 and 1811), and he was also classed as a NCO so did not wear swallows' nests, but NCO distinctions instead. (This was an NCO epaulette on right and a *dragon* on the left shoulder).

From 1812 the dragoon trumpeters would receive swallows' nests in plain white tape, without knots and NCO cuff distinctions.

In 1811, when the Geworbne company and part of the regiment were reorganised as the Akershusiske Ridene Jæger corps, an official letter of 24 August 1811 allowed the former *pauker* of the Akershusiske dragoons, to be kept, but now as part of the staff of the Geworbne company of the Ridene Jæger Corps. His uniform was to be that of an NCO. Both of the preserved copper kettledrums are stamped with the Norwegian coat of arms and both of the covers have also been conserved (Norwegian Army Museum).

---

3   Royal approval of the 6 September and written to the Norwegian cavalry on 10 September 1811. It was generally stated that Norwegian dragoons were in the future to have same belts and sword scabbards as the Danish cavalry (*ryttere* and dragoons), and that the bayonet frog, which until then was worn beside the sidearm on the waist belt, was now to be worn 'the same way as its worn by the Sjællandske Rytter Regiment', strapped to the left pistol holster.

4   *Indkomne sager nr. 7, Artilleri Corpset 6 April 1793*. According to the 1837 list there were 1,870 of the M1740 and M1750 *dragonpallasker* remaining in stock.

5   In a letter from the Danish *General Commerce Collegium* (Danish War Department) to the *Norske Commerce Collegium* (the Norwegian War Department) dated 10 September 1811, reply to a question from the Søndenfjeldske Dragonregiment, which asked what they should do as they had received from Denmark new Danish model sabre belts with straps, but all their scabbards were of the old model, to be carried on a waist belt. They (and also Trondhjemske Dragon Corps) were told to convert all the old scabbards to the Danish standard, and from then on, place the bayonet scabbard at the right front of saddle, strapped under the left corner of the *valdrap*.

NCOs

The dragoon NCOs used the same rank distinctions as in the Danish army (see Volume 2). This included the cords which were thicker, double tressed, than those of the men. From 1812 the officers and NCOs adopted the new cuffs and rank insignia, but the privates continued to use the earlier square cuff style with the cuff flap. Evidence suggests that Norwegian NCOs had no shoulder belts and consequently no shoulder straps.

Officers

The officers' M1804 hats were the same model as the troopers including the rhomboid brass plate, but of better quality with a silver loop and button, a white plume and gold and red cords, flounders and tassels. They also adopted the more modern officer's hat M1806. At first, they had the M1798 long tailed *karmoisin røde* (carmine red coats) for full dress, but probably poppy red (ponceau) coats also for service dress, both having the regimental facings and silvered buttons. Some probably had tailored M1803 coats. The officers were allowed buff turnbacks on their tailed coats. They also wore sleeveless waistcoats, originally buff yellow but then white from 1806. The officers wore a pair of buff yellow leather breeches and short black Hessian-type boots and on service or campaign they could wear blue cavalry overalls with white Hungarian style lacing and white piping down the outside leg.

In 1812 the officers were allowed to wear, when not on duty, a single-breasted red undress coat with a collar and cuffs in the regimental facings with false pockets piped buff, short tails and rear buff turnbacks. It had a single row of silvered buttons down the front, the size and number of buttons varied as there were apparently no clear rules regarding the number of buttons for officers coats after 1810, as several known examples have a rather large number of buttons (up to 22), which was apparently quite a common fancy and one of the few accepted deviations from regulations.[6] They carried both the officers' versions of the *dragonpallask* (broadsword), and officers M1789 Sabre (or variants), all worn with the gold and red sword knot (*porte épée*) carried on first a M1790 black leather belt with square belt buckle, with the arms of Denmark, and later a black leather M1806 belt with a lion's head clasp.

The Regimental Facings

Akershusiske Dragonregiment. 1784, disbanded 1811. They had white facings with white lining and flat white metal buttons.

Smaalehnske Dragonregiment. 1784, disbanded 1811. They originally had yellow facings, but changed to blue facings piped white with white lining and flat white metal buttons *c.* 1809.

Oplandske Dragonregiment. 1784–1811. Became the Søndenfjeldske Dragonregiment from 1811–1814. They originally had blue facings, but changed to *strågul* (straw yellow) facings with buff lining and flat white metal buttons in 1809.

Trondhjemske Dragonregiment. 1784–1811, became Trondhjemske Dragonregiment in 1811–1814. They originally had green facings piped white with white lining and flat white metal buttons. From 1811 the piping and lining was changed to straw yellow.

Arms and Equipment

The dragoons carried a *dragonpallask*, two pistols (several models were used, but generally the M1772), a dragoon musket *dragongevær* M1767 and a bayonet as they were still classed as mounted infantry. Originally the bayonet was carried on a frog on their waist belt with their sword. On 10 September 1811 all dragoons were ordered to carry their bayonet scabbard strapped to the left-hand pistol holster and not on their waist belt.[7]

The different regiments were armed with different swords, according to availability of supplies:

> The *dragonpallask* M1734 had an iron shell hilt with a thumb ring and a leather grip. These were carried by the Oplandske Dragonregiment and the Smaalehnske Dragonregiment.
>
> The *dragonpallask* M1740 had a brass shell hilt with a thumb ring. The grip was bound with brass wire. This was mostly used by the Trondhjemske Dragonregiment, together with some M1750 *dragonpallask*. There were a number of variants of the form of the shell.
>
> The *dragonpallask* M1750 had a brass shell hilt bearing the mirror cypher of *FV*. The pommel had a lion's head, the grip was bound with brass wire, and it had a thumb ring. This model was carried by the Akershusiske Dragonregiment, later Søndenfjeldske Dragonregiment. According to records, 703 of this model were

---

6　According to the information in *Kongens Klæder* by Karsten Skjold Petersen, pp.281 and 284, the Akershusiske Dragonregiment and the Smaalehnske Dragonregiment returned their yellow waist and cross belts to the arsenal. The best of them would be reused for 'new black belts and waist belts' (the exact source is not stated).

7　*Detalje Over De fornødne Feldt Requisitter for et marcherende dragon regiment af den Norske Armee,* issued *1791. Regulativ for Bagagevognes og øvrige Feltreqvisiters antal ved den Norske Armee.* Issued on the 23 August 1812.

The Norwegian Dragoons and *Ridende Jægerkorps* 1803–1814 (III), Housings and Shabraques

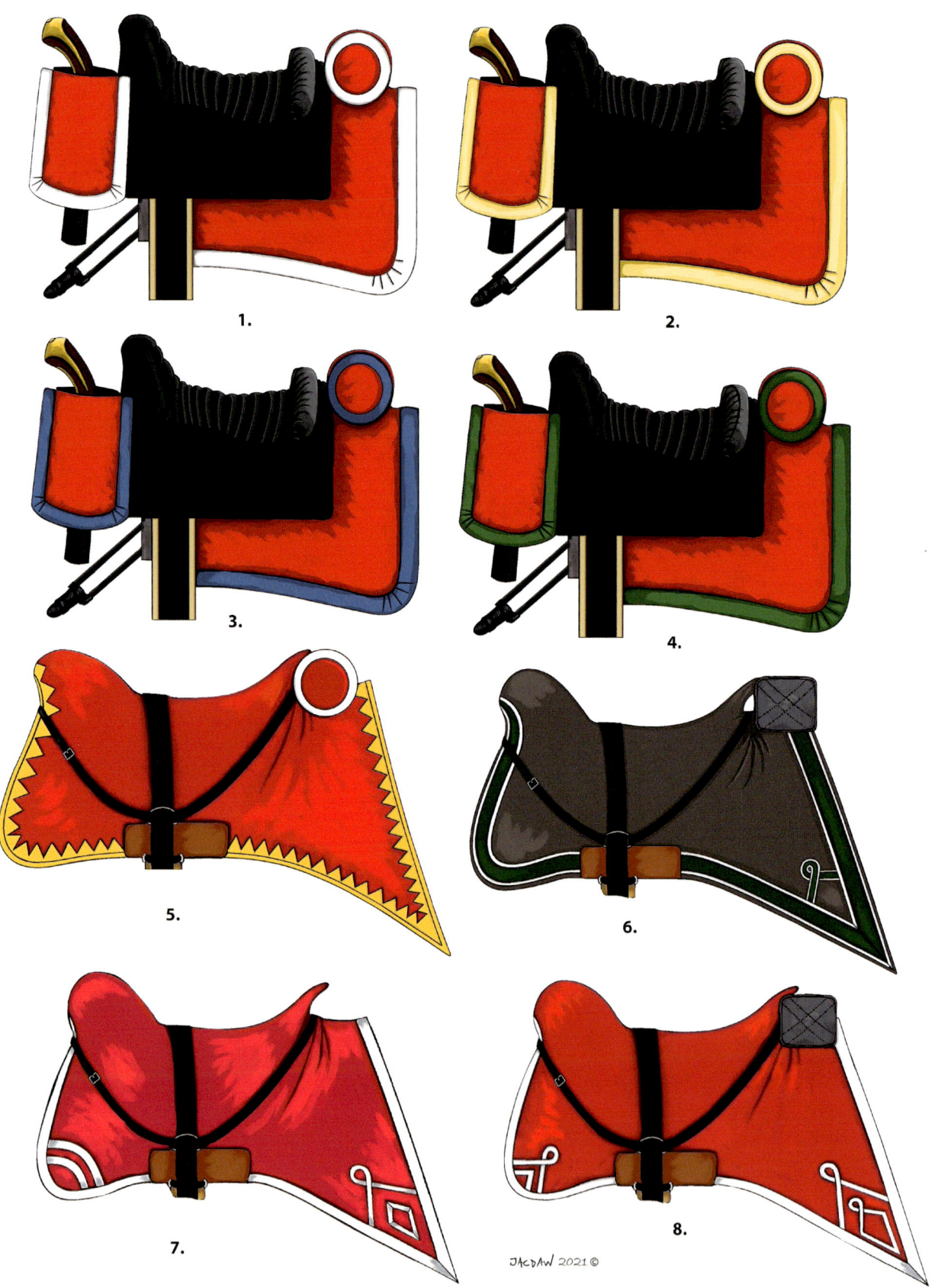

THE NORWEGIAN CAVALRY

Facing page

Plate 29. The Norwegian Dragoons and Ridende Jæger Corps III, Housings and Shabraques

1. Akershusiske Dragonregiment. This is the old-style solid tree saddle and housings, *skaberak* 1785–1810, showing the muzzle boot for the musket on the far side. Note the round valise behind the saddle.

2. Oplandske Dragonregiment. This is the old-style solid tree saddle and housings, *skaberak* 1785–1810, showing the muzzle boot for the musket on the far side. Note the round valise behind the saddle.

3. Smaalehnske Dragonregiment. This is the old-style solid tree saddle and housings, *skaberak* 1785–1810, showing the muzzle boot for the musket on the far side. Note the round valise behind the saddle.

4. Trondhjemske Dragonregiment. This is the old-style solid tree saddle and housings, *skaberak* 1785–1810, showing the muzzle boot for the musket on the far side. Note the round valise behind the saddle. Saddles shown as black leather, but dark brown leather is also possible.

5. The little information we have of saddlecloths used in Norway concerns the *valdrapper* (shabraques) used by the Hussar detachment until 1806, which was the same model as those used by rest of the regiment in Denmark/Holstein. In 1806 the detachment was reformed into a *geworbne* dragoon company, but they were allowed to keep their former Hussar *valdrapper*, but the blue wolf tooth and white lining were to be replaced with a yellow wolf tooth border. The result was this rather unique *valdrap*, which was still used by the first company of the Akershusiske Ridende Jæger Corps up to *c.* 1826.

6. Author's reconstruction of the *valdrap* of the Akershusiske Ridende Jæger Corps. There are no contemporary illustrations of what it really looked like, and the only information is that 'The former dragoons will turn in their red *valdrapper*, and receive new grey ones', another that they 'were to be grey with green lining'. This was the model presumably used by the other companies, inspired by the shabraques of the Danish Ridende Jæger Corps.

7. Dragoon officer's shabraque, ordered in 1807, used with the new Hungarian saddle but only delivered and used by all dragoon officers from *c.* 1810. All lace was silver.

8. Dragoon trooper's shabraque, ordered in 1807, used with the new Hungarian saddle but only delivered and used by all dragoons from *c.* 1810. During the major reforms of the Norwegian cavalry in 1811 it was recorded that the former Akershusiske and Smaalehnske dragoon regiments both had 'Hungarian saddles and *valdrapper* in red and white'. The new-style trooper's valise is shown attached behind the saddle.

shipped to Norway in 1793.[8] There were several variants of the form the shell took; some were rather plain and others more elaborate, possibly some were dragoon models and others were for the NCOs or officers.

But Prince Frederik of Hessen's army reform of 1811 wanted to modernise these rather old-style sidearms: 'The Norwegian dragoons are still using *pallasker* from the reign of King Frederik V, and still wear them in old-style waist belts. In general, first I wish to modernise the Akershusiske Dragoner with more modern side arms, so that the other cavalry can act accordingly with them in due time.' (letter from Prince Frederik of Hessen, in Christiania, 24 March 1810, to King Frederik VI).

Originally the *pallask* scabbards were of dark brown leather; later they were blackened, with steel chape and lip with a brass stud for the frog. In 1811 it was ordered that the scabbards be converted to the standard Danish cavalry model with two suspension rings, this was carried out forthwith, but somewhat crudely in many cases.[9]

Their waist belts were the old buff/yellow M1777 model, with a simple oval brass buckle and a frog for the *pallask* and a frog for the bayonet. These were officially in use until 1811, but were probably still in service as late as 1814 (possibly whitened by then).[10] Their cartridge

---

8 In 1837 nearly 16,000 copper canteens were still in use. Only perhaps 1,600 of the Danish old-style large metal canteens were found in the arsenals, and it is not known if this last model was ever used much, if at all.

9 According to the information in *Kongens Klæder*, Karsten Skjold Petersen, p.284, the Akershusiske Dragonregiment and the Smaalehnske Dragonregiment had 'Hungarian saddles and *valdrapper*' (exact source is not stated, but this is most likely).

10 *Våbenhistorisk Tidsskrift Bind* 34. No. 8. 2001. *Forbindelsen til Norge næsten afbrudt* by Erik Troldhuus. It has a copy of an original list of weapons shipped to Akershuus arsenal, Norway from 23 December 1807, and up until 1808, p.281. Akerhuus arsenal was the main arsenal of all the regiments of the Søndenfjeldske (Southern Division). This means that the request from the arsenal and shipment from Denmark concerned those weapons 'needed, but out of stock' or 'new equipment needed, not in stock'.

Norwegian Kettledrummer, *Akershusiske Dragonregiment* c. 1808

> Facing page
>
> Plate 30. Norwegian Kettle Drummer, Akershusiske Dragonregiment *c.* 1808
>
> This was the only official kettledrummer in Norway. In 1811, when the Akershusiske Dragonregiment was reorganised into the Akershusiske Ridene Jaeger Corps, the kettledrum player was maintained but now as part of the staff of the *geworbne* company, and he adopted the new grey uniform M1810 with NCO distinctions. The banners (*paukefane*) originally belonged to the 1st Søndenfjeldske Dragonregiment and were made of red silk with gold embroidery and silver fringes, made in 1740. According to tradition the drums had been taken from the Swedes in 1677. They received new banners in 1740. The motto on the scroll is DEO ET POPULO, the official motto of King Christian VII of Denmark, and underneath, ANNO 1740. They are preserved in the collection of the Army Museum in Oslo, under the reference FMU71. Dimensions unknown, but they were probably 60 cm wide × 110 cm long.
>
> Author's reconstruction. Some details are missing as certain motifs have degraded and are now simply some last pieces of thread, and it was not possible to identify them correctly so they have not been drawn. There appears to have been a motif or cypher in the lower corners, again not clearly identifiable.

pouch (*patrontaske gehæng*) and musket bandoleer (*karabingehæng*) were of the old yellow leather model used before 1798. The standard Danish M1798/1808 cross belt in whitened leather slowly replaced the older model from 1810. As field kit, they also carried the M1751 copper canteen lined with tin for fetching water, cooking and transporting their rations, one canteen for two men, taking turns to carry it, on the saddle.[11] From 1812 like the infantry they began to receive a new taller much more practical M1810, with a lid, so popular that it was still in use in 1855 in Norway and still in the arsenal stores as late as 1900.

The officers carried a more elegant model of the *pallask*, similar to the M1750, but engraved with either a crowned royal double mirror cypher of either Christian VII or Frederik IV, or with the Norwegian Lion holding the axe of St Olaf. Sometimes older, high-quality blades could be mounted on these hilts, and from 1800 several officers mounted new more modern sabre blades on these hilts. A sabre mounted on the hilt of a *pallask* can be seen on a fine portrait of *Oberst* Peter Andreas von Hiort, commander of the Trondhjemske Dragonregiment, and also two such side arms are preserved (one in Denmark and one in Norway). This was clearly a common way for a dragoon officer to modernise or upgrade his sword into a sabre whilst keeping the distinctive hilt. Also other types of privately acquired officer's sabres were being worn.

It is not clear if the officer's M1808 silver bandoleer with cartridge pouch was officially permitted for the officers in Norway, but this is likely, as they had the same status as light dragoon officers in Denmark from 1811.

---

11 *Hærens Blankvåben på Napoleonskrigens tid*, Niels M. Saxtorp: Våbenhistoriske Årbøger 1974. *Correspondance protocol I årene 1811–1812 nr. 2674 af 21. Maj 1811*: 'It was permitted to ship dragoon sabres (M1808) to the Akershusiske Ridene Jægercorps, 100 at a time and 600 in total.'

Horse Furniture

In the *Kongelig Resolution* of 2 August 1790, regarding the *Munderingsoversigt*, it is noted that all four dragoon regiments had the mid-eighteenth century-style *Bomsadler* (solid-tree saddles), and 'shabraques with loose holster covers', which both had a replacement term of 24 years. They had been issued in 1782 from another list, so were, according to the established terms, due for replacement in *c.* 1806–1807.

The shabraques had rounded corners and separate pistol covers, but apparently no flounces, and were bordered with a broad woollen galloon in the facing colour according to the clothing terms of August 1790.

The valises were of the old round red cloth valises as used in Denmark, all bordered in the facing colour for the troop, and in silver for the officers and fringes for the superior officers (see illustrations). Theoretically they should have been issued with the new Hungarian saddle and shabraques (*valdrapper*) in 1807 according to a resolution of 8 January 1807, which corresponds with the clothing terms described in 1790. So they should have received them between 1808 and 1810 at the latest. It can be seen on a list from the *Norske Munderingsdepot* (Central Norwegian Uniform Arsenal), dated 15 March 1808, that they had in stock ready for another delivery to the dragoons a total of 460 saddles. These were clearly of the new Hungarian model and with *valdrapper*.

The Akershusiske and Smaalehnske dragoon regiments were both recorded as having received the Hungarian-style shabraques in 1811. They were probably red with white lace like the Danish dragoons a button-coloured border. The date when these shabraques were adopted is not known, but is at least as early as 1808–1809 for some of them if not earlier. The valises were to be of the grey cloth square model with black straps, although some probably still had the older model. The officers probably changed their saddle cloth earlier, in 1807 to 1808.

The Norwegian Hussars / Det Norske Husardetasjement

In 1796, one enlisted hussar detachment/company with three officers, six NCOs, two trumpeters and 60 hussars, with 71 horses, were sent to Norway's main city Christiania (Oslo). Only 35 of the hussars were enlisted in Denmark, the rest were to be enlisted in Norway; later even more would be enlisted in Norway.

The company first served as a kind of guard and police detachment in and around the main city of Christiania attached to the headquarters of the Viceroy´s staff. In 1806–1807 the unit was reorganised as an extra *geworbne* dragoon company of the Akershusiske Dragonregiment. In 1808 this company was now composed of four officers, nine NCOs, two trumpeters and 50 dragoons with 59 horses. Also, it was considered a kind of elite company and reckoned to be 'the first cavalry unit of the Norwegian army' and was responsible also for the training, at a special cavalry school, of selected dragoon officers and NCOs for all the Norwegian cavalry. They also served as 'guides' for the general staff in the field.

Only one contemporary and rather naïve illustration of them, rather faded and damaged, exists in Norway. They are shown wearing their original hussar uniforms.

Hussar Uniform

According to the contemporary illustration referred to above, their uniforms was virtually the same as the Danish model worn by their parent regiment, so in 1801 this consisted of a cylindrical black felt hussar *shactelhue* (mirliton) of the Prussian style with a false wing which was decorated with white lace. On left side it had a white plume over a black cockade. The mirliton had white cords and flounders for the troopers. The mirliton appears to have been rather soft and of crude manufacture.

The hussars wore a light blue cloth dolman which had five rows of white metal buttons with white tassels attached to them with white braids between the buttons and white lace on all the borders and on the seams on the back of the dolman, although the exact form is unknown. It had a red collar with white lace trim and red pointed cuffs piped white with white trefoils.

Their crimson red pelisse had black fur trim, four or five rows of buttons, two on each side, with white braiding and loops and a white lace border around the black fur and white trefoils, and all the buttons were made of white metal. It was supposed to be worn slung down the rider's back like a cloak, but in fact they wore them slung over their shoulder like any other hussar in Europe. In this way it gave a little protection to the bridle arm. Around their waist they wore a barrel sash of red wool with white barrels, cords and tassels.

They wore a pair of pale yellow, fall-fronted buckskin leather breeches and had black leather Hungarian boots with white lace and tassels. They carried a leather sabretache, the face covered in light blue cloth with red wolf's teeth piped and bordered in white lace; embroidered in the centre in white thread was the crowned royal cipher CVII, and the bonnet of the crown was red. Buff leather gloves were worn with small gauntlet cuffs, not always shown on contemporary pictures.

Horse harness was in black leather Hungarian-style including the half-moon ornament hanging from the throat strap. They had a red Hungarian-style shabraque with medium blue wolf's teeth piped white, and a white outer lace border (*Kongelig Resolution* 19 December 1806). See Volume 2 for a complete description of their uniforms.

In February 1806 the former hussar detachment was reorganised as an extra *geworbne* dragoon company of the Akershusiske Dragonregiment. They received new dragoon uniforms, but they kept their original belts, equipment and weapons. They were also allowed to continue to use their old *Husar valdrapper* (saddle cloths) but would 'change the colour of the wolf tooth edging, from blue into yellow' (*Kongelig Resolution* 19 December 1806). It is not mentioned if they kept their sabretaches, but they were probably somewhat worn by now and logically they were due to be withdrawn from service.

One particular detail of note is that they were the only cavalry in Norway who were allowed to wear moustaches as hussars, and as no order to stop this is to be found, they probably kept on wearing them. In December 1808 there was an official order to ship '100 dragoon sabres' (hussar sabre M1792) from Denmark to Norway, and it was probably for use by this company to replace its old and worn M1776 hussar sabres.

Mounted *Jæger* (*Ridende Jæger*) Uniform

These mounted *jægere* were dressed similarly to the sharpshooters and were armed as light dragoons. Their uniforms were similar to those of the Akershusiske Skarpskytte Regiment, the only difference being the extra cavalry equipment. They received their grey uniforms in 1812, but it was decided that they should wear out their dragoon uniforms first, so they were first issued with them in 1813.

They wore a black M1808 *rytter* shako (without rhombic plate). The new shako had a black chinstrap, combined with white metal chin scales. It had a green cockade with a pewter button in the centre, with a white loop and a pewter button. A short green plume and green cords (NCOs had thicker cords). Their uniform consisted of a medium grey single-breasted jacket lined white with green collar and square cuffs and grey cuff flaps all piped white. The front of the coatee was piped in green on either side of the row of pewter buttons and the frontal turn ups were green. Their shoulder strap was green piped white. They were issued with white waistcoats. They had a pair of fall-front straw yellow *kirsey* breeches for full dress, and pair of medium grey fall-front overalls with dark grey galloon and pewter buttons down the outside leg for service wear (*Kongelig Resolution* 21 April 1811). In 1814 '25 [pairs] of white Kersey trousers', were delivered to the *geworbne* company. These were probably for the formal parade and sentry use only, as they were part of Prince/King Christian Frederik's headquarters staff. For foul-weather wear they wore a grey cape. They also had a pair of buff gauntlets and short black hussar-style boots with spurs.

The Uniform of the Trumpeters and the Kettledrummer
The trumpeters wore the same uniform as the men, but with green swallows' nests laced with white tape. They also had a 'staff trumpeter' who wore sergeant's distinctions. Their equipment consisted of a black leather waist belt with a rectangular brass plate buckle and a black leather bandoleer. The kettledrummer wore the uniform of an NCO.

Uniform of the NCOS
The NCOs had the same uniform as the mounted *jægere*, but their black shako had thicker green NCOs cords and a slightly larger plume. The uniforms from 1812 were with the new chevron rank insignia M1812, worn on pointed cuffs.

Officers' Uniform
Their uniform consisted of a single-breasted tailed light grey coat with square green collar and cuffs, all piped white. There was a line of white piping down the front of the coat, on the pockets (three buttons) and on the green turnbacks on the tails and ten silvered buttons. On their shoulders they had silver epaulettes. They wore a pair of fall-fronted yellow breeches, or grey overalls, and black Hessian boots. Their headgear was the M1808 *rytter* officers' black shako, with a black chinstrap, combined with silvered metal chin scales, and worn with a green cockade with a white loop and silvered button, gold/yellow and red cords and a green feather. They wore the new M1812 rank insignia, with buttons and chevrons, worn over pointed cuffs. They carried an officer's M1789 sabre, or variant, with a gold and red *porte épée*, carried on a black leather M1806 belt with a lion's head clasp.

Arms and Equipment
Their shabraques (*valdrap*) were grey, with green edging, possibly with white piping on the green and rectangular grey valises (*mantel sacks*). An exception was the first *geworbne* company who continued to use their former hussar model shabraques (*valdrapper*), had a term of between 16 and 24 years and also the former hussar harness decorated with cowrie shells, the last detail probably only used for the more formal parade and sentry use, as they were part of Christian Frederik's personal headquarters staff. They continued to use both up to around 1825.

The Akershusiske Ridende Jæger Corps were armed differently to the other cavalry regiments. The first or *geworbne* company used the hussar carbine M1795, and the rest of the mounted *jægere* were intended to be armed with same after 1811. As far as is known, around 299 M1795 hussar carbines were shipped for their use 1812–1813. They were the only Norwegian cavalry unit ever to receive carbines and no one in Norway (dragoons included) ever received cavalry rifles. The mounted *jægere* were issued with separate ramrods from 1813, to use with the hussar carbine M1795.

The former hussar detachment (*geworbne* dragoon company) from 1811 became the *geworbne* mounted *jæger* company and continued to carry their original M1792 hussar sabre. As many of the mounted *jægere* had previously served as dragoons, at first, they continued to carry their *dragonpallask* (straight swords or broadswords), and some were apparently still carrying them during the campaign of 1814. They also keep on carrying a pair of long M1772 pistols.

According to Niels Saxtorph it was formally decided in 1811 to equip the Norwegian mounted *jægere* with the new brass-hilted *dragon sabel* M1808, and when they were ready, to ship 100 sabres at a time to Norway (600 total, so some may also have been intended for use by some of the dragoons). But because of the tight British blockade of the Norwegian harbours only a few got through before the end of 1813, when all shipping was again blockaded from April/May 1814. At most probably only 200–300 reached Norway. The arms of the officers are not specified, but they were probably a pair of better-quality privately acquired pistols and one of the several different officer's hussar light cavalry sabres available.

8

The Norwegian Dragoon Guidons

In 1784 the Norwegian cavalry was reformed, but this meant that not only did they change their unit names and in some cases their uniforms, but also their guidons, generally with older models which had originally belonged to other regiments.

The cavalry, who were all dragoons by this time, were still carrying guidons. Some of these guidons were already quite old and had already been passed on from one regiment to another over the years. The fact that they were quite old was not a major problem as they were rarely if ever taken into the field and were only brought out for parades and reviews. These older guidons were swallow-tailed and were quite complex. The cloth was always silk damask.[1] Thanks to the research of Erik Aagaard and Jørgen K. Larsen we now have a much clearer picture of what they looked like.

The Akershusiske Dragonregiment

Originally this regiment was called the 1st Søndenfjeldske Dragonregiment and was renamed the Akershusiske Dragonregiment in 1784. By 1806 it was composed of one *geworbne* company (the former hussar detachment) and seven Nationale companies. In 1811 it became the Akershusiske Ridende Jæger Corps.

In 1702 the dragoon regiment had been given new guidons for its eight companies. Three of these guidons are now in the Army Museum in Stockholm. They were purloined from the storehouse in Fredrikstad by the Swedish during their occupation of 1814 as easy trophies of war. These guidons were made of thin yellow silk and painted with silver and gold.

In 1738 the regiment received a red guidon from the disbanded Danish Østre Skjællandske Dragonregiment which guidon still exists (ref FMU47). It has the embroidered crowned arms of Sjælland (or three lions *passant azure langued gules*, nine hearts *gules*) in the centre of the guidon placed vertically with lions as supporters over a trophy of arms, and below the arms and trophy there was a bird in flight and a scroll with a motto. The mottos for these two guidons are unknown. On the tails of the guidon there were the crowned cyphers of the king, Christian VI, a double intertwined CVI in silver thread. They were also given one white and two blue guidons which had previously belonged to the 2nd Søndenfjeldske Dragonregiment via Paulsen's enlisted dragoon regiment, which had been converted into an infantry regiment. It is not known which standards these were. They probably also had one unofficial standard of the former hussars (ref. FMU000050). They had one white and three red guidons (a red one is preserved, ref. FMU000047).

The Smaalehnske Dragonregiment

This regiment was originally called the 2nd Søndenfjeldske Dragonregiment and was renamed the Smaalehnske Dragonregiment in 1784. It was composed of seven Nationale companies, and had one white and three red standards.[2]

These dragoon companies were first assembled as a regiment in 1689 with six enlisted and four Nationale companies. The enlisted companies had white guidons and the national companies white guidons with a salamander on them.

In 1708 the regiment had seven companies and were given seven new blue and white guidons with a motive and motto. The colonel's guidon no longer exists. It was completely white with a standing lion holding a pair of scales in his front paws. The 2nd company had a dog striking down a deer, the 3rd company's motif is unknown, the 4th company had a salamander surrounded by flames, the 5th company a sun, the 6th company an image of 'Fortuna', but this standard no longer exists, and the 7th company had an elephant and insects.

The regiment was expanded after 1715 and a further three guidons of this type were made. Some of these went together with their company to Paulsen's enlisted regiment that was later converted into an infantry regiment. One was white with a wild man fighting with a dragon that is supposed to have been Paulsen's colonel's guidon, one

---

1 Damask is a reversible figured fabric of silk with a pattern formed by weaving which became particularly popular for cavalry standards during the early baroque period. Damasks are woven with one warp yarn and one weft yarn, usually with the pattern in warp-faced satin weave and the ground in weft-faced or sateen weave.

2 One white guidon is preserved, ref. FMU006094, as is one red one, ref. FMU6092.

THE NORWEGIAN DRAGOON GUIDONS

Plate 31. Norwegian Dragoon Guidons I, Smaalehnske Dragonregiment

These guidons were originally made in 1731 for the Østre Sjællands Dragonregiment (one white and three red ones). The two guidons were used from 1784 by the Smaalehnske Dragonregiment until the regiment was disbanded 1811. In 1784 the two other red guidons of the Østre Sjællands Dragonregiment (but with different mottos) were given to the Akershusiske Dragonregiment, and carried until 1811, after which they followed their troopers into the newly formed Søndenfjeldske Dragonregiment.

Top: White *liv* guidon with the motto JEG ER VEIVISEREN ('I lead the way') embroidered in gold thread on a light blue or silver scroll, obverse and reverse identical. Ref. FMU.006094. Dimensions, width 85 cm × height 80 cm.

Bottom: Red squadron guidon with the motto FRIMODIGHED OG STYRKE ('Bold and Strong') embroidered in silver on a gold scroll; obverse and reverse identical. Ref. FMU006092. Dimensions, width 85 cm × height 85 cm.

Note: the cloth used for these guidons was damask, a fabric made of woven silk. These were not the only guidons used by this regiment. Author's reconstructions.

had a hunter shooting a bear and one depicted David and Goliath. These three guidons were later transferred to the Nordenfjeldske Dragonregiment.

In 1731 the regiment was given two guidons, one white and one red from the disbanded Danish Østre Sjællandske Dragonregiment. The white guidon had embroidered in the centre the crowned arms of Sjælland (or three lions *passant azure langued gules*, nine hearts *gules*) placed vertically with lions as supporters over a trophy of arms, below the arms and trophy there was a 12-pointed star and a scroll with the motto JEG ER VEIVISEREN ('I lead the way'). On the tails of the guidon there were the crowned cyphers of the King, Christian VI, a double intertwined CVI in silver thread, ref. FMU6094. The red guidon had the same decor, but with an elephant and the motto FRIMODIGHET OG STYRKE ('Boldness and Strength'). The guidons had silver fringes, cords and knots. The original silver finial, a spear head, was inscribed '1739 2nd Søndefjeldske Dragonregiment C VI'. The regiment was finally disbanded in 1811.

The Oplandske Dragonregiment

The regiment was originally raised as the 3rd Søndefjeldske Dragonregiment in 1749 with eight Nationale companies, and was renamed the Oplandske Dragonregiment in 1784.

It was given four guidons in 1749, one colonel's guidon made of white damask with the crowned Danish-Norwegian coat of arms with supporters and a collar of the Order of the Elephant and a collar of the Order of the Dannebrog. In each angle of the staff there was a gold crowned lion of Norway. Over the arms there was a blue scroll with the motto PRUDENTIA ET CONSTANTIA in gold lettering. The guidon had gold and silver fringes, gold cords and knots. The finial was a simple spear head. The three red damask squadron guidons which bore a vertical crowned cypher of King Frederik V in gold thread surrounded by a collar of the Order of the Elephant only, in each angle of the staff a gold crowned lion of Norway. Over the arms there was a blue scroll, also with the motto PRUDENTIA ET CONSTANTIA in gold lettering. The guidon had gold and silver fringes, gold cords and knots. The finial was a simple spear head. The regiment also had two red and yellow company quarter flags.

In 1784 the regiment had one white and three red standards. One white (ref. FMU004816) and three red standards (Refs FMU004813, FMU004817 and FMU004827) have also been preserved.

The regiment was finally disbanded with the reorganisation in 1811 and their guidons were probably reissued to the new Søndefjeldske Dragonregiment in 1811.

The Trondhjemske Dragonregiment

The regiment was originally raised as the Nordenfjeldske Dragonregiment with eight Nationale companies, and was renamed the Trondhjemske Dragonregiment in 1784. Originally, they had three standards which had come from Paulsen's enlisted regiment. One was white with a wild man fighting with a dragon that is supposed to have been Paulsen's colonel's standard, one with a hunter who is shooting a bear and one with David and Goliath. These three guidons were later transferred to Nordenfjeldske Dragonregiment. In 1733 the regiment was given four guidons from the disbanded Danish Vestre Sjællandske Dragonregiment.

There was one white guidon (ref. FMU13994) and three red guidons, all with the crowned coat of arms of Sjælland in the centre of the fly and the crowned cypher of a double CVII in gold thread with a scroll underneath with a motto. The white had the text D'ETRE FIDELLE A MON DIEU ET MON ROY ('I am Loyal to my God and King') on one side and JE M'EN FAIS MA PREMIERE LOIX ('I make this my first law') on the other. The red guidon had the text PLUS TOUT MOURIR QUE MANQUER A MON DEVOIR ('I would rather die than betray my duty', as in loyalty). The text was the same on both sides. The mottos of the other two are not known. The fringes, and probably the cords and knots as well, were gold. In 1811 all four were kept in the regimental depot and in service, but one of the red guidons needed some repairs. They had one white and three red standards. The white one and one of the red models have been preserved and still exist today (a white standard reference unknown, and a red one (ref. FMU013462).

The Cavalry Reform of 1811

In 1811 the Norwegian cavalry was also completely reformed in yet another major reorganisation. Their strength was nearly halved, and all the regiments were made lighter. A mounted *jæger* regiment was also raised.

The Trondhjemske Dragonregiment was reformed into the Trondhjemske Dragon Corps with four companies. It had one white and three red standards as before.

The Søndenfjeldske Dragonregiment

This was a new regiment created in 1810 from the companies of the disbanded dragoon regiments with 12 companies. They probably reused the guidons of the disbanded Oplandske Dragonregiment, but the exact distribution of their former standards into the new regiment is not clear.

Norwegian Dragoon Guidons (II), Trondhjemske Dragonkorps

Plate 32. Norwegian Dragoon Guidons II

Trondhjemske Dragonregiment

Their guidons were originally made in 1731, and belonged to the Vestre Sjællandske Dragonregiment. In 1784 the regiment became the Trondhjemske Dragonregiment, and in 1810 the Trondhjemske Dragon Corps.

Top: the White *liv* guidon bore the motto D'ETRE FIDELLE A MON DIEU ET MON ROY on the obverse and on the reverse JE M'EN FAIS MA PREMIERE LOIX, embroidered in gold thread on a light blue or silver scroll. The text in English reads 'To be loyal to my God and King', followed by 'I make this my first law'. The finial bears the cypher of Frederik IV. Ref. FMU.13994. Dimensions: width 83 cm × height 101 cm.

Bottom: A red squadron guidon with the motto PLUTÔT MOURIR QUE MANQUÉ A MON DEVOIR ('Die rather than betray my duty') embroidered in silver on a gold scroll, obverse and reverse identical. Ref. FMU.13462. Dimensions: width 83 cm × height 101 cm.

Note: the cloth also used for these guidons was damask. These were not the only guidons used by this regiment. Author's reconstructions.

The Akershusiske Ridende Jæger Regiment

Raised with one *geworben* company (formed from the old hussar company, which had then become a *geworbne* company) and three Nationale companies were raised from the former dragoons from the remainder of the disbanded regiments. No official standards were carried, but we know of two standards which were probably used by the *geworbne* company.

This standard is classed as unknown, but it probably originally belonged to Det Norske Husardetasjement given the similarity to the Danish hussar standards, and in all likelihood followed them to the Akershusiske Dragoncorps around 1806 when the hussar company was transferred to that regiment. It is possible that the guidons followed them to the Akershusiske Ridende Jæger Regiment in 1811. It is most unlikely that they actually carried guidons on the field of battle.

The field was white, possibly a *livfane*. On the field there was an image of an eagle flying out of a storm cloud with lightning flashes over the land in natural colours. There was a motto in gold which reads PER TALA, PER IGNES, with arms through fire on a scroll. The guidon had gold fringes and cords.

Another is a white company standard of unknown age, but clearly from Akershusiske Ridende Jæger co*rps* from before 1814 as it bears a royal crown and underneath A. R. J. C. This is probably a company standard, made for the use of the Geworbne company, when it was used as a mounted guard for the headquarters of King Christian Frederik in 1814.

9

The Norwegian Artillery

Organisation in 1803 and Deployment During the War

In Norway the artillery followed the same modernisation and reorganisation process as in Denmark, but with a number of modifications because of the geography, logistics and economy specific to Norway. The blockade during 1807–1814 made it almost impossible to supply all that was needed.

The formal organisation of the Norske Artilleri Brigade (Norwegian Artillery Brigade) was made after a *Kongelig Resolution* of 19 May 1797, followed by a more detailed plan dated 17 June 1797.[1] But the original plans were slightly reorganised for Norway, with modernised horse artillery (new short 20 calibre 3-pdr pieces), and generally heavier howitzers (long 10-pdr and 20-pdr howitzers). It was this revised organisation which was used 1800–1814.[2] New carriages were to be made for all the regular artillery after plans made by the new Norske Artilleri Konstruktions Kommision (Norwegian Artillery Construction Commission). They were to be produced locally after the 1799 Model, and this was applied to all 3-pdr gun carriages (1802–1808), while apparently only some of the 6-pdr M1766 field carriages were 'modernised'. The two 6-pdr and 12-pdr reserve companies were not modernised, but kept their original M1766 carriages.

The Norske Artilleri Brigade was organised from 1803 into the following companies:

> 10th Ridende Artilleri Companie: 8×3-pdr M1799, 2×10-pdr (short) M1789 howitzers (Christiania/Oslo)

> 11th Fod Artilleri Companie: 8×6-pdr M1766, 2 × 20-pdr M1772 howitzers (Christiania/Oslo)

> 12th Fod Artilleri Companie: 8×3-pdr M1766, 2×10-pdr (long) M1789 howitzers (Christiania/Oslo)

> 13th Fod Artilleri Companie: 8×3-pdr M1687/1759, 2×10-pdr (short) M1789 howitzers (Fredrikstad)

> 14th Fod Artilleri Companie: 8×3-pdr M1687/1759, 2×10-pdr (short) M1789 howitzers (Trondhjem)

> 15th Fod Artilleri Companie: 8×3-pdr M1766), 2×10-pdr (long) M1789 howitzers (Christiania/Oslo)

A further 6-pdr (Frederikssten) and a 12-pdr company (Aggershus) were held in reserve (unmanned) probably all mounted on the old M1766 carriages.

There was also a reserve of former pieces, used by the regimental artillery and kept in the arsenals and fortresses, of some 32 old 16 calibre 3-pdr guns and also a large supply of fortress and coast artillery, not covered here.

The Enlisted *Geworbne* (Regular) Artillery Companies

To understand the Norwegian organisation, one has to understand how guns in the period were served. The officers were all regular trained artillery officers (normally educated in Denmark), while all NCOs were enlisted, and had been trained at the Norske Artilleri Underofficers Skole (Norwegian Artillery NCO school). Each company comprised a *commandersergent* (sergeant major), a *fourer* (staff sergeant) and eight *sergenter*.

To actually serve the guns (cleaning, loading, priming, aiming and firing), the artillery had a trained class of enlisted personnel. They comprised 10 *overconstabler* (bombardiers), 50 *constabler* and two *hornblæsere*. In time of peace they maintained the guns and took care of training, while up to half of the personnel were allowed to go on furlough (termed *frimænd*) and worked in the towns. But in times of war more personnel were needed to help manoeuvre the guns (matrosses) and also keep up

---

1 The 10th Ridende Artilleri Companie (horse artillery company) had from 1789 used 1-pdr M1766 *amusette*, but from 1803 was re-equipped with light 20 cal/3-pdr M1799 pieces.

2 The list found in *Dansk Artilleri i Napoleonstiden*, by Ole L. Frantzen, pp.59–61, is wrong in several details.

the supply of ammunition and, if needed, step in to help serve the guns. These extra 'helpers' were to come from the Nationale *constabler* (national gunners) who were classed as *underconstabler* in Denmark. To crew each gun five or six regulars and seven to eight 'helpers' from the Nationale *artillerister* was necessary.

Nationale Artillery Companies
The four Nationale artillery companies had been transferred from the infantry on 1 January 1790, but they had no permanent officers attached and only a *sergent* and two *corporaler*. Each company had a strength of 100 Nationale *constabler* (gunner's assistants) trained as artillery helpers. They were like all Nationale troops, only called on to train or serve for a short period, 28 days each year. But the youngest, strongest and unmarried Nationale *artillerister* were allowed to enlist as Geworbne if needed, and in case of war, all were to be ready to serve as *underconstabler* (gunners 3rd class), and so bring the *geworbne* companies up to full war strength. Nationale companies were normally divided up to serve in different regular companies. Those not so used (mainly the older and married men, termed *Landeværn*) were used to serve in the fortress artillery. The Nationale artillery companies comprised the following:

Søndenfjeldske Nationale Artilleri Compani
Nordenfjeldske Nationale Artilleri Compani
1st Akershusiske Nationale Artilleri Compani
2nd Akershusiske Nationale Artilleri Compani

The Akershusiske Nationale Artilleri company was transferred, without officers, from Akershusiske Dragonregiment on 1 January 1807, and used to bring the 10th Ridende Artilleri company up to strength.

It had a strength of three *corporaler*, two *hornblæsere/* trumpeters and 75 Nationale *constabler* gunner's assistants, as horse artillery helpers. Note in the above, the NCO rank *corporaler*, was only used in the Nationale companies, not in the *geworbne* companies.

Fortresses, Arsenals and Coastal Batteries
There were numerous fortresses and coastal batteries, mainly served by detached regular officers, NCOs and a few gunners from the *geworbne* companies with some Nationale gunners and *Landeværn* attached as gunner's assistants in times of war.

The artillery had seven main arsenals for the fabrication of ammunition, repairs, construction and storage of equipment and stores. While all bronze pieces were cast in Denmark, most of the iron, fortress and naval guns were cast in Norway. But Norway did not have the same expertise as the Swedish iron foundries, and they had not fully mastered the casting techniques and so the haste, coupled with supply problems during the war, made this even worse, and several pieces were so badly cast in the Norwegian foundries and they were distrusted by the gunners and used with reluctance, as several simply exploded (with devastating effects on the crew) when fired. Understandably, they did not have much confidence in them.

The Use of Artillery During the Fighting in Southern Norway 1808–1809
During the fighting against the Swedish invasion of 1808–1809, parts of nearly all of the Geworbne companies took part, not at full strength but at only one third to a half strength, in the field. Probably both kept a ready reserve, but also a general lack of correct horse feed reduced the number of horses that could be made available. One exception was the 10th Ridende Artilleri Compani attached the Brigade Holst at Frederiksstad, who managed to field their full strength, as the company owned their own horses. Also on several occasions the Geworbne companies, were mixed with other companies and even on occasion with the regimental artillery. The fortress of Frederiksten managed to field an 'Improvised Field Company', with four 3-pdr M1687/1756 guns, one 20-pdr M789 heavy howitzer, two 1-pdr M1766 *amusettes* and seven 10-pdr portable mortars. They were also part of the Brigade Holst. The 14th Fod Artilleri Compani in Trondhjem also used some of its guns during 1808, and during the short invasion by Sweden from Jamtland it was a mixed battery of four 3-pdr guns and two 10-pdr portable mortars, and a separate section of two 10-pdr portable mortars was also created. The artillery did do a good job during the war, especially in the first battle of Lier on 18 April 1808, and the battles of Berby on 10 June 1808 and Prestbakken on 14 June 1808.

In 1809 General Prince Christian August gave orders that because of the lack of forage, nearly all the cavalry should turn in their horses and give the best to the regular artillery, and also that all infantry regiments should leave their 1-pdr M1766 *amusettes* behind, and all their gunners and horses should also be transferred to keep the regular artillery up to strength. By this means, he managed to form the following active companies:

10th Ridende Artilleri Companie: Eight 3-pdr 20 calibre M1799, two 10-pdr (short) howitzers (Major von Haffner)

11th Fod Artilleri Companie: Four 6-pdr 22 calibre M1766 guns. (combined with *15th Fod Artilleri Companie*)

12th Fod Artilleri Companie: Eight 3-pdr 22 calibre M1766, two 10-pdr (long) howitzers (Major von Schilling)

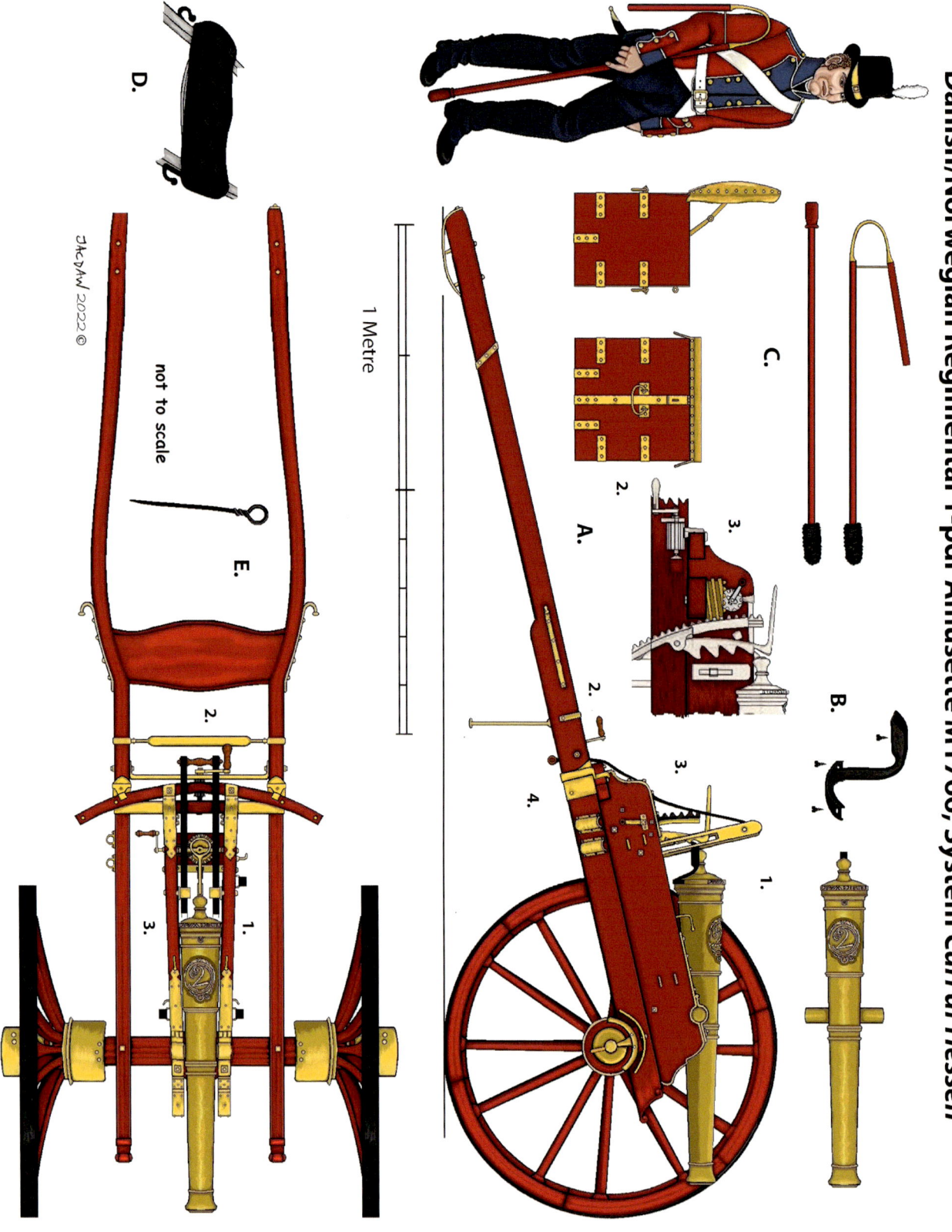

> Facing page
>
> Plate 33. Norwegian 1-pdr M1766 *Amusette*
>
> The Norwegian 1-pdr M1766 *amusette* was used principally by the infantry's regimental artillery, mainly by the regiments of the 1st Søndenfjeldske, hence shown here in red with yellow ironwork, the colour of the regimental artillery, with the exception of those used by the *geworbne jæger corps* and the *Lette Bataljon* before 1810, and later those used by the *skarpskytte bataljoner*, which apparently remained painted grey with black ironwork.
>
> A. Aiming and Traversing Mechanisms
> 1. Quick release bars
> 2. Traversing handle and gear
> 3. Levelling ratchet and crank shaft made of brass
> 4. Quick-release handle
>
> B. Tooth or wedge bracket added under the knob of the cascabel, to fit into the elevating device
>
> C. Top to bottom:
> - Crooked sponge *krumvisker*
> - The standard combined rammer and sponge *visker og ansætter*
> - Ammunition box *kantine*. Each gun had two, carried on a special saddle, one each side of the shaft horse. It was here the ready ammunition was kept, and it had two trays of 24 ready-to-fire rounds (ball or canister, sabot and powder charge).
>
> D. Padded seat used on the 1-pdr 1788 horse artillery version only. There were 16 of these available in Norway. Later they were also used by the Bergenhusiske Nationale Regiment (four pieces) and the Christiania Bys Frivillige Artilleri Corps (12 pieces). All M1788 guns were painted bluish grey with black ironwork.
>
> E. Priming pin, a pair of which were placed in holders on the insides of the cheeks of the carriage.
>
> Shown here is a regimental artilleryman of the Søndenfjeldske Geworbne Infanteri Regiment holding a *krumsætter*.
>
> Author's reconstruction.

13th Fod Artilleri Companie: A detachment only of two 3-pdr 16 calibre M1687/1759 guns.

15th Fod Artilleri Companie: Seven 3-pdr 22 calibre M1766, two 10-pdr (long) howitzers (Premierløjtnant von Anzee). The full company was one gun short, but was strengthened with four 6-pdr M1766 guns from the 11th Fod Artilleri Companie.

The combined former regimental artillery, with six 1-pdr M1766 amusettes

Two of the artillery company commanders received the Order of the Dannebrog for bravery during the fighting in 1808–1809

The Norwegian Artillery in Action Against the Swedish Invasion of 1814

The following artillery companies were active during the war:

A 3-pdr foot company with Staffeldt's brigade (Østfolden)

A 3-pdr foot company with Hegermann's brigade (in front of Akershus)

A half 3-pdr foot company with Krebs' Detachment (in front of Kongsvinger)

The second 6-pdr foot company and first 3-pdr Ridende Compani (six 3-pdr pieces and two 10-pdr howitzers) with Arenfelt's brigade (central front)

In reserve was a 3-pdr (Nationale mounted?) company

The fifth 3-pdr foot company and one Nationale 3-pdr mounted company were near Trondheim

The artillery did a good job during the fighting in 1814, particularly at the second battle of Lier and the battles of Matrand, Skotterud and Onstadsund.

The fortress artillery also fought well during the siege of Frederiksten. The Norwegians also captured a Swedish 3-pdr gun with its limber at the battle of Skotterud thanks to a Norwegian artillery sergeant called Svend Larsen.

Nationale (Kørende) Artillery Companies (Mounted Artillery) in Southern Norway 1811–1814

In 1811 there were plans for the Norwegian artillery to be strengthened and made more mobile. As Norway's extremely rugged terrain and the roads were often in a poor state of repair, moving traditional artillery was not an easy task. So now another more mobile organisation was planned and organised (at least on paper). At the same time the cavalry had shown themselves to be difficult to feed in the south and were not very useful in the difficult terrain, other than for some reconnaissance and scouting. So as a consequence, the cavalry was reduced from four dragoon regiments into just one and a half dragoon regiments and a mounted *ridende jæger regiment* (light horse regiment). The best of these troopers, now redundant, were transferred to the artillery with their surplus horses and some equipment as *kørende nationale artillerister* (mounted national artillery).

The Søndenfjeldske Kjørende Artilleri Bataljon

This battalion was organised into four *kørende* artillery companies:

1st Søndenfjeldske Nationale Kørende Artilleri Companie
2nd Søndenfjeldske Nationale Kørende Artilleri Companie
3rd Søndenfjeldske Nationale Kørende Artilleri Companie
4th Søndenfjeldske Nationale Kørende Artilleri Companie

One company was formed by two companies from the Akershusiske Dragonregiment (the first) and the remaining three from six companies from the *Smaalehnske* Dragonregiment. Each company had a theoretical strength of four officers, one sergeant, a *fourer* (staff sergeant), eight *corporaler*, 10 NCOs, four *hornblæsere*, 150 Nationale gunners and 100 'reserves'. The officers and NCOs, according to the plan, would mainly be transferred from the regular artillery, while the others would be retrained former dragoons. It is not known how many horses they were allowed to retain, but as only one company was activated, probably only a few (perhaps approximately 150).

The initial intentions, as much as can be deducted, was that the mounted national artillery should, as the Nationale *artillerister* before them be attached to the four regular 3-pdr artillery companies, as gunners assistants, but transported on horses, so as to make the companies more mobile. However, the lack of forage consequently a lack of horses, as well as a lack of training changed their plans and the horses were was reserved to pull the guns instead. So instead, plans were made to reform just one regular company into a *kørende artilleri compani* (mounted artillery company), the 13th Fod Artilleri Compani which had eight 3-pdr M1687/1759 and two 10-pdr (short) M1789 howitzers.

Turning our attention to the carriages and ordinance, Norway chose not to follow the Danish model, but formed mounted artillery, better suited to the uniqueness of the Norwegian terrain. Although information is sparse some trials were made with the 13th Fod Artilleri Companie during the years 1810–1814. The limbers were designed in Norway, and they found the best way to mount the gunners and the methods to train them were used for the whole company. It was also used to form the 1st Søndenfjeldske Nationale Kørende Artilleri Compani in the same way. In theory, both companies should have been equipped with eight 3-pdr M1687/17593 guns and two 10-pdr (short) M1789 howitzers. But none of the 10-pdr howitzers were available in Norway or could be sent from Denmark, and few 3-pdr M1687/1759 guns were available. In the end the new Søndenfjeldske Nationale Kørende Artilleri Compani apparently only received only six 3-pdr M1687/1759 pieces. This is confirmed by the '1837 list', which tells us that there were in the arsenals '20 limbers for the mounted artillery', but only '14 carriages for the mounted artillery'.

From photographs of an original model found in Norway, and what apparently is the same carriage in both a complete piece found in Norway and one in the *Krigsmuseet* (War Museum) in Denmark, the modifications were only a set of new lifting handles, so the pieces were easier to lift off the limbers. The carriage of the two 10-pdr (short) M1789

---

3   The 3-pdr 16 calibre M1687/1759 pieces had been the backbone of the Norwegian regimental and field artillery until they were replaced by the 1-pdr 22 calibre M1766 *amusette* and the 3-pdr M1766 cannon. At first the regiments were allowed to keep their old guns in their arsenals. In 1803, 16 were taken over by the field artillery, and modernised with new carriages and new aiming devices. But in 1808 plans were made to modernise the remaining guns as well. So a list of spare parts (lifting rods for 25 new *stillemaskiner* (aiming devices) were ordered from Denmark by the arsenal at Aggershus. But this was refused in a letter from the King to the Danish *Commerce Collegium* (War Department) on 3 December 1808 as they should have been able to produce them in the Norwegian workshops as there were none to spare in Denmark. Eventually they were produced in Norway, but in insufficient numbers.

howitzers of the regular company is simply described as a howitzer carriage. But all these changes took time, so they were only ready in 1813, as apparently there had been little training done by the 1st Søndenfjeldske Nationale Artilleri Compani before the beginning of 1814.

The other three Søndenfjeldske Nationale artillery companies were instead used to support the fortress artillery or transferred as *constabler* (gunners 2nd class), to the regular artillery, serving on foot. In the two companies that were actually formed the mounted gunners for each of the guns would serve as gunners assistants, and would be mounted on horses (six). By adding seats to the ammunition box on the limber for two gunners and with two more gunners mounted on the limber horses a total of four regular *constabler* and *overconstabler* could follow each piece of the company. The regulars would serve the guns themselves, while the mounted Nationale gunners 3rd class would help (lifting, pulling, pushing and supplying ammunition). The NCO acting as gun commander would also be mounted. Four gun/train drivers were also part of each gun crew, of which one or two would also act as horse holders when the guns were in action. They normally had two-wheeled ammunition carts for their munitions. In 1814 the 4th (formerly the 13th) 3-pdr foot artillery company (Kaptajn Niels Christian Von Dahm), saw active service, as did the 1st Søndenfjeldske Nationale (*kørende*) 3-pdr artillery company (Ritmester Knud von Knudsen).

Norwegian Artillery in Action against the Swedish Invasion in Southern Norway 1814

The following artillery companies were active in the south during the war in 1814:

1st (10th) horse artillery company (Kaptajn Niels Von Schiött)

2nd (11th): 1st ½ company of 6-pdr foot artillery (Kaptajn Guttom Von Rustad); 2nd ½ company of 6-pdr foot artillery (Premiereløjtnant Johan George von Bodum?)

3rd (12th): 1st ½ company of 3-pdr foot artillery (Oberstløjtnant Jacob Frederrich von Schilling?); 2nd ½ company of 3-pdr foot artillery (Premiereløjtnant Christian Von Meidall)

4th (13th) 3-pdr foot (mounted?) artillery company (Kaptajn Niels Christian Von Dahm)

5th (14th) 3-pdr foot artillery company (Kaptajn Ernest Anton Von Hinrich). In Trondheim.

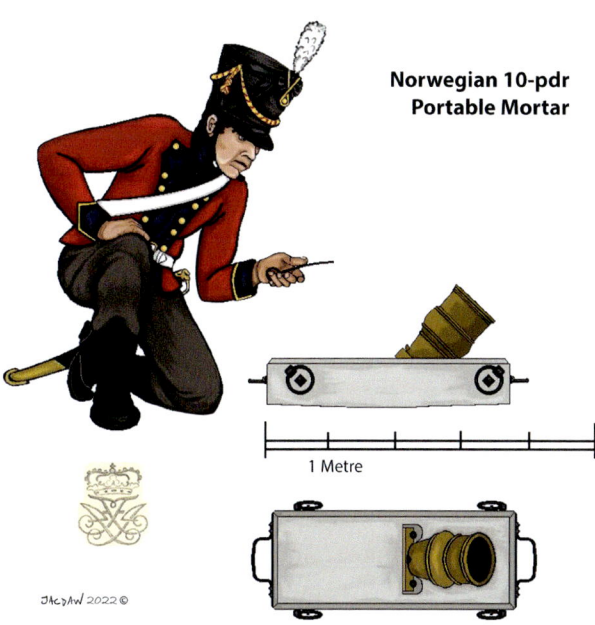

Plate 34. A Norwegian 10-pdr Portable Mortar

These two-man portable mortars were mounted on a wooden block-type bed with a fixed trajectory. They were extensively used in Norway, mainly within the Nordenfjeldske as an infantry support weapon, not for sieges. This one is painted grey showing that it belonged to the Nordenfjeldske; elsewhere the natural wood was left untreated. The Nordenfjeldske carried two on each specially made *morter vogne* (mortar sledge gun carriages) of the Trønderlavet M1809 system as a replacement for howitzers.

As most were cast under Frederik IV (1671–1730), they had his crowned monogram engraved on the chase. They were served by regimental gunners – serving as assistants as was normal in the Nordenfjeldske as they had no Nationale gunner assistants attached – and *geworbne* gunners, as shown here with a *constabel*, wearing an M1808 coatee and a pair of the new grey trousers *c.* 1813.

THE DANISH ARMY OF THE NAPOLEONIC WARS VOLUME 3

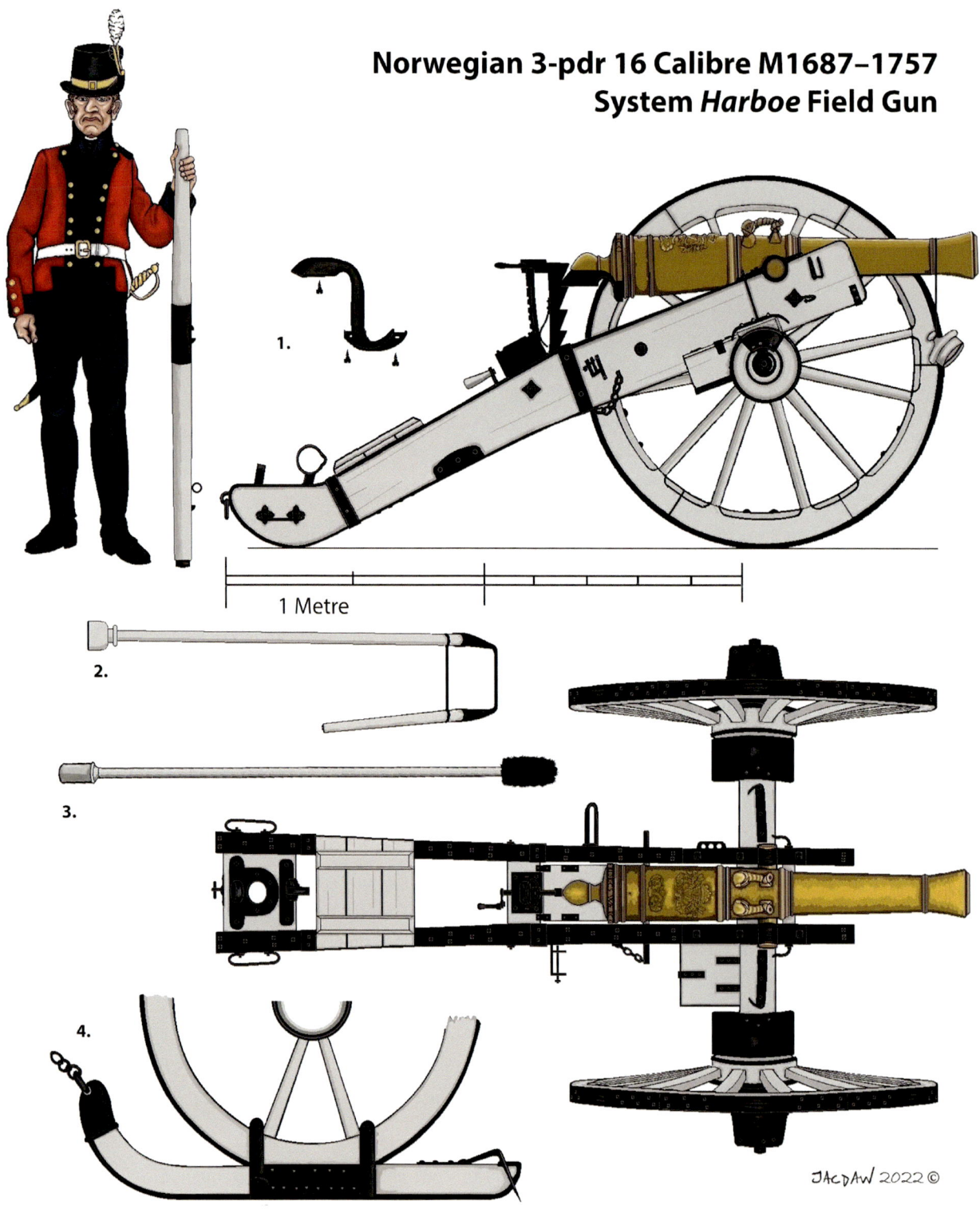

Norwegian 3-pdr 16 Calibre M1687–1757 System *Harboe* Field Gun

> Facing page
>
> Plate 35. Norwegian 3-pdr 16 calibre M1687–1757 system *Harboe* field gun
>
> The 16 calibre, 3-pdr piece. Between 1802–1806 these were remounted on the M1799 field carriage, which was slightly modified again in 1811.
>
> 1. Tooth or wedge bracket, which was added under the knob of the cascabel, to fit into the elevating device.
> 2. Crocked rammer (*krumsætter*)
> 3. Combined sponge and ramrod (*visker og ansætter*)
> 4. Special skis as used by the Søndenfjeldske in winter for their artillery carriages, limbers and wagons. They were simply bolted on, one per wheel, and chained to the carriage. Note the brake to avoid the gun sliding when firing.
>
> Shown with a Nationale artillery gunner's assistant *c.* 1808, he is wearing an old model coat (M1789/1799). He is wearing a pair of blue M1803 gaiter trousers which were also issued to the Nationale artillery from *c.* 1803 and is holding a trail spike (*løftestang*) to manoeuvre the gun, painted grey for the foot artillery. The Nationale artillerymen were attached as assistants primarily to manoeuvre the piece and fetch ammunition, and for that reason they had no cross belt and pouch. This was the most obvious difference between a regular *geworbne* gunner and a Nationale gunner. A 3-pdr gun had a crew of an NCO, four regular *geworbne* gunners and five Nationale assistants.
>
> Author's reconstruction.

6th (15th) 3-pdr foot artillery company (Premiereløjtnant Johan Carl Von Møller)

1st Søndenfjeldske Nationale (*Kørende*) Artilleri Companie (Ritmester Knud von Knudsen). It is possible that this company was broken down into two three-gun half-companies.

6-pdr reserve company (commander unknown), eight 6-pdr guns and four 20-pdr howitzers.

The following is the available information on how the artillery was distributed in 1814:

The 2nd 6-pdr foot artillery company (divided into two), and 1st 3-pdr Ridende Artilleri Companie (eight 3-pdr pieces and two 10-pdr howitzers), with Arenfelt's brigade on the central front

A 3-pdr foot artillery company with Stabel's brigade

Two 3-pdr foot artillery companies with Staffeldt's brigade (Østfolden)

A 3-pdr foot artillery company with Hegermann's brigade (in front of Akershus)

A 3-pdr foot artillery ½ company (Premiereløjtnant Christian Von Meidall) with Krebs' brigade

A 3-pdr foot artillery ½ company with Rodes' brigade

In reserve was the 1st Søndenfjeldske Nationale 3-pdr Kørende Artilleri Companie with Arenfelt's brigade

A 6-pdr reserve company was being made ready for action in Christiania

The artillery did good service during the fighting in 1814, and at the second battle of Lier, and the battles of Matrand, Skotterud and Onstadsund. At the battle of Langnes farm on 9 August 1814 the artillery was used with great effect against the three fruitless Swedish attacks. Their brigade commander Colonel Diderik von Hegermann later described how shots from the Norwegian cannons 'made it look like a wagon had rolled through the attacking columns from head to tail'.

The fortress artillery also fought well during the siege of Frederiksten. Also the Norwegians captured a Swedish 3-pdr gun with its limber and two ammunition wagons at the battle of Skotterud, officially taken by a Norwegian artillery sergeant called Svend Larsen.

The Norske Artilleri Brigade as Reorganised in 1814

After the declaration of independence in 1814 the Geworbne companies were renumbered, and the artillery was organised on a more permanent basis:

Geworbne/regular artillery companies:

1st 3-pdr Ridende Compani in Christiania/Oslo
2nd 6-pdr Fod Compani in Christiania/Oslo
3rd 3-pdr Fod Compani in Christiania/Oslo
4th 3-pdr Fod Compani in Fredrikstad
5th 3-pdr Fod Compani in Trondheim (see 'The Artillery of the 2nd Northern Division')
6th 3-pdr Fod Compani in Christiania/Oslo

There were one 6-pdr and one 12-pdr batteries held in reserve, of which the 6-pdr company was made ready for field service, but was only fit to take the field at the end of the war, and even then, only as position artillery.

Søndenfjeldske Nationale (Kørende) Artilleri Bataljon
Organised in 1811, but only one company was formed as an artillery company, while rest were spit up as gunners 3rd class, and transferred to the regular companies or to serve in the fortress artillery.

1st Søndenfjeldske Nationale *Artilleri Compani* (3-pdr)(the only company formed, as planned)

2nd Søndenfjeldske Nationale Artilleri Compani (served 1814, mainly as fortress artillery crews)

3rd Søndenfjeldske Nationale Artilleri Compani (Served 1814, mainly as fortress artillery crews)

4th Søndenfjeldske Nationale Artilleri Compani (served 1814, mainly as fortress artillery ++crews)

Regimental Artillery Used in Southern Norway 1800–1814

Although the regimental artillery in Norway, as in Denmark, was technically not part of the regular artillery organisation, it was such an important factor in the war that it is simpler to describe it here. The regimental artillery in Southern Norway had 1-pdr *amusette* light pieces. Two such pieces were allocated to each battalion, and it was the men of the regiment who served and manoeuvred them. Often, they were collected together into a brigade battery with four to eight guns. The two regimental guns were served by 30 musketeers, trained as artillerymen. The regiments converted into *skarpskytte bataljoner* in 1810 kept their regimental guns until after the end of the war in 1814. The young (19-year-old) Second Lieutenant Jens Christian von Schrøder tells us in his memoirs that he 'to my great joy was given command of the two 1-pdr *amusettes*, supporting the first field battalion of the Telemarkske Nationale Regiment.' He describes his cannons as manoeuvrable, accurate, and effective. But he admits 'their effect was probably not great, and the greatest was probably the confidence our infantrymen had in them, and the moral impression they made on the enemy when he heard that he had artillery against him.' Quoting his old friend from 1814, the future Danish Major General Rye, whom he met in Denmark in 1848, 'Our people liked them, the enemy did not, and more could not be demanded!'

The Artillery of the 2nd Nordenfjeldske

The artillery of the 2nd Nordenfjeldske (Northern Division) is described separately as it was an independent command, but also had a different organisation and was equipped differently. At the beginning of the war the 2nd Nordenfjeldske, with its main base at Trondhjem, had not yet begun to implement the new artillery reforms as fully as the 1st Søndenfjeldske had. In 1808 it was composed of the following:

14th Fod Artilleri Companie

Eight 3-pdr 16 calibre M1687/1759 cannons in newly made M1799 carriages

Two 10-pdr M1789 (short) howitzers, on former M1788 horse artillery *limon lavetter* (galloper carriages)

115 gunners, 45 *stykkuske* (gun drivers) and 90 horses

Guns and mortars used as regimental artillery etc:

Eight 3-pdr 16 calibre M1687/1759 cannons mounted on old carriages (possibly M1766)

Four 10-pdr Coehorn mortars

These were mainly served by regimental gunners from the 1st and 2nd Trondhjemske Nationale Infanteri Regiments

In reserve:

Four 1-pdr M1766 *amusettes* and 14 10-pdr Coehorn portable mortars

The commander, General George Frederick von Krogh (the elder) was used to independent command

and took the following necessary decisions. As already mentioned, the country was mountainous, hilly, and full of streams and forests with very few usable roads. For most of the year snow, ice or mud hindered the movement of the artillery, even on roads. Even if his forces were quite meagre as he could field only two infantry field battalions, the Nordenfjeldske Skiløber Bataljon, Rørros Frivillige BjergJæger Corps and a few dragoons. While the 14th Fod Artilleri Compani kept its guns in defensive positions at Røros, Innherrad and Kristianssund, von Krogh was still able to make two small diversionary attacks against the Swedish in 1808. To support those attacks, some of the gunners were detached to man some 1-pdr *amusettes* and portable 10-pdr Coehorn mortars, which were the only artillery able to be used. Furthermore, because of the rough terrain, all ammunition had to be carried by packhorses. With the forces invading Jamtland was a light mixed company of two 1-pdr guns and two 10-pdr Coehorn portable mortars. Here, the Swedish used of a couple of 6-pdr cannons in the Jærpen fortification, which stopped the attack after a fruitless artillery exchange. During the invasion into Hærjedal a detachment of two 1-pdr guns and six portable 10-pdr Coehorn mortars were used, but here the hostilities only went as far as some skirmishing.

After the lessons learned in 1808, General van Krogh created a commission to plan and produce a completely new artillery system which could travel on both on wheels and on skies and under the worst climatic conditions. It was based on an idea by his son, Captain George Frederich von Krogh (the Younger), based on the sledges used by the iron ore mine at Roerros. This system was the Trøndelag (Trondheim) artillery system M1809. During 1809–1810, the following was produced:

> Sixteen 3-pdr 16 calibre M1687/1759 cannons, on new M1809 carriages
>
> Two 10-pdr M1789 (short) howitzers, on new M1809 carriages
>
> Four 1-pdr M1766 *amusettes*, on new M1809 carriages
>
> Sixteen mortar wagons, each with one 10-pdr Coehorn portable mortar

Each gun, howitzer and mortar had or was followed by an ammunition sledge. This ammunition sledge had different-sized ammunition boxes, mounted on same type of sledge as the guns. The wheels and axle were detachable thus transforming the carriage into a real sledge.

In all, 150 carriages/wagons M1809 were produced in several workshops in and around Trondheim.

In 1811 the cavalry and artillery of the 2nd Nordenfjeldske were reorganised. This led to the reduction of the Trondheim dragoons and the surplus dragoons were reformed as gunners:

> Nordenfjeldske Artilleri Bataljon, organised in two Nationale foot artillery companies:
>
> 1st Nordenfjeldske Nationale Artilleri Companie
> 2nd Nordenfjeldske Nationale Artilleri Companie

Each company had a theoretical strength of four officers, 10 NCOs, four hornists, 150 gunners and 100 reserves. The officers and NCOs would be transferred from the artillery; the others would be trained from the former dragoons. The Nordenfjeldske Artilleri Bataljon was also allowed to keep 300 dragoon horses (150 for each company). It was merged, together with the regular 14th Fod Artilleri Companie, into two artillery companies, all equipped with the new M1809 carriages and materiel. The regular gunners served the guns, while the former dragoons provided help.

The *Nordenfjeldske Artilleri Bataljon*

For field service the battalion was merged with the regular 5th (former 14th) 3-pdr Fod Artilleri Compani (Kaptajn Ernest Anton Von Hinrich), into two artillery companies (1st and 2nd companies), all equipped with the new M1809 carriages and materiel and organised into the following:

> 1st Nordenfjeldske Artilleri Companie
> Eight 3-pdr 16 calibre M1687/1759 cannons, on new M1809 carriages
>
> Four mortar wagons each with one 10-pdr Coehorn portable mortars
>
> 2nd Nordenfjeldske Artilleri Companie
> Eight 3-pdr 16 calibre M1687/1759 cannons, on new M1809 carriages
>
> Two 10-pdr M1789 (short) howitzers, on new M1809 carriages
>
> Four mortar wagons each with one 10-pdr Coehorn portable mortars

Also, some regimental artillery was formed by the 2nd Nordenfjeldske in 1814:

> Two 1-pdr M1766 *amusettes* on new M1809 carriages

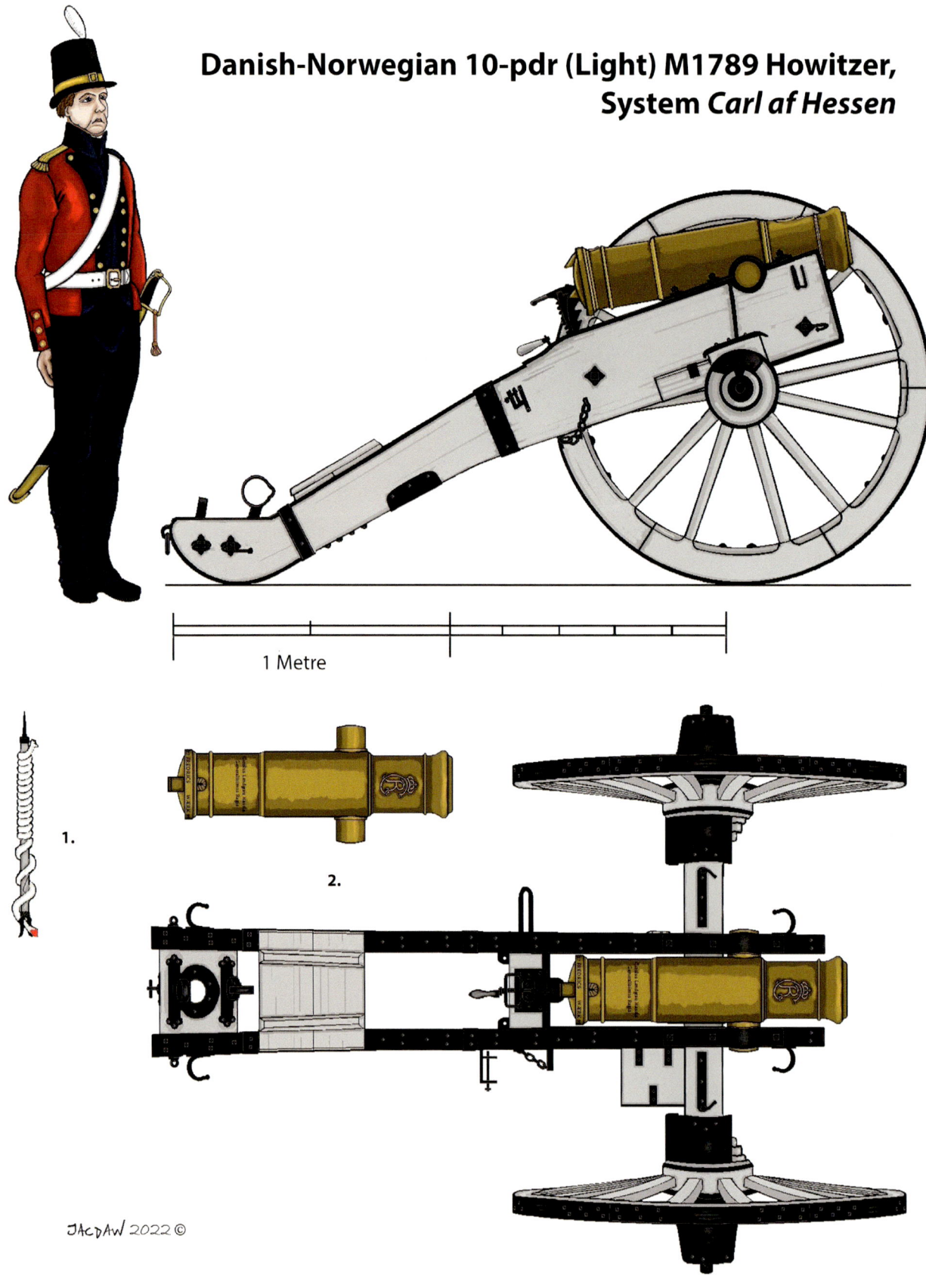

Danish-Norwegian 10-pdr (Light) M1789 Howitzer, System *Carl af Hessen*

1 Metre

> Facing page
>
> Plate 36. Danish–Norwegian 10-pdr (light) M1789 Howitzer System *Carl af Hessen*
>
> The howitzer is shown mounted on an M1799 carriage.
>
> 1. Linstock (*luntestok*)
>
> 2. Howitzer barrel. Engraved in front of the vent was *Carolus Landgrav Hassis/Generalisimus Regis* ('Prince Carl, the General commanding in Norway'). On the front of barrel there was a crowned 'CR' (Christian Rex, for King Christian VII of Denmark). Around the breech was 17 FREDRICS WÆRCK 89'.
>
> Shown with a foot artillery *geworbne overconstabel* (bombardier) c. 1808, armed with the new M1802 artilleryman's sabre.
>
> Author's reconstruction.

Four mortar wagons each with one 10-pdr Coehorn portable mortars

The Ordnance used in Norway, in Particular Those Types Specific to Norway

The Norwegian ordnance had followed Denmark but modernisation had not been so quick there as in rest of the kingdom. For a long period, rather old ordnance was used in Norway and the most modern was the Harboe M1687 system. Following the artillery reforms made in Denmark and the suggestion made by General von Huth to Prins Carl of Hessen, modernisation began in Norway in August 1774. This first modernisation concerned the regimental artillery, where the old 3-pdr 16 calibre M1687/1759 pieces were replaced with the lighter more mobile 1-pdr 22 calibre M1766 guns, the so-called *amusettes*. Between 1774 and 1790 Norway received about 75 of these. In 1788 an experimental horse artillery company was formed for the duration of the short campaign in Norway against Sweden; by 1790 this company had 16 1-pdr 22 calibre M1766 *amusette* guns and four brand new 10-pdr (short) howitzers M1789, all on *limon lavetter* (galloper carriages). But from 1802 they were re-equipped with 3-pdr 20 calibre M1798 pieces.

The 1-pdr pieces or *amusettes* were mainly employed as regimental artillery during 1800–1814, mainly by the infantry regiments of the 1st Søndenfjeldske (the 2nd Nordenfjeldske only employed five, preferring old 3-pdr pieces instead). They were manned by the infantry, two per field battalion. Also the volunteer Christiania Frivillige Ridende Artilleri Corps (volunteer horse artillery of Christiania), had 12 1-pdr 22 calibre M1766 *amusette* guns as well. Here the lightness of the gun was seen as an asset in broken and difficult terrain, but the effect of the shot was not very effective. It did have some unique features.

It was originally intended that the gunner could aim and fire the gun while still seated on the gunner's seat. The gunner could swivel and aim the barrel with a limited traverse on the gun carriage, but was capable of well-aimed shots. A handle placed at the back of the carriage which could be turned by the gunner's left hand to swivel to the left or right. From the start the barrel had a little triangular 'tooth' or wedge added to the end of the 'knob' or button of the cascable for the new elevating and traversing system on the carriage. On the right side of the carriage there was another handle, which could only be used by the right hand; this was to move the barrel up and down. This handle operated in a tandem arrangement with a vertical bow with notches. There was a little triangular tooth mounted on an iron bracket bolted underneath the cascabel button and the breech that would fit into these notches. The gun was capable of being fired whilst still harnessed to the draught horses (this must have involved a lot of training for the horses though). Limbers were not required for the *amusettes* as they were harnessed directly to the rear draught horse (two in tandem, but both controlled by the driver on the rear horse). Although they were followed by a two-horse ammunition cart, the gun team also carried two standard ammunition boxes, one each side of a *kløvsadel* (pack saddle) on the lead horse. Normally the carriages and carts used by the infantry regiments were painted red, the same colour as the red uniforms of the infantry, with metal parts painted yellow. It is probable however that the guns of the Norske Geworbne Jæger Corps and later the Norske Lette Bataljon were painted grey with black fittings. Also the guns of the *skarpskytte bataljoner*, formed 1810, had their guns painted in grey and black.

The calibre was 5 cm; length of bore 110 cm; total length of gun barrel 120 cm. The trunnions were positioned below the bore. Weight: 201 kg. The total number cast was 191.

Gun carriage: These pieces were mounted on *limon* (galloper carriages), with the horses in tandem

Norwegian 3-pdr 16 Calibre Sledge Gun, *Trønderlavet* M1809

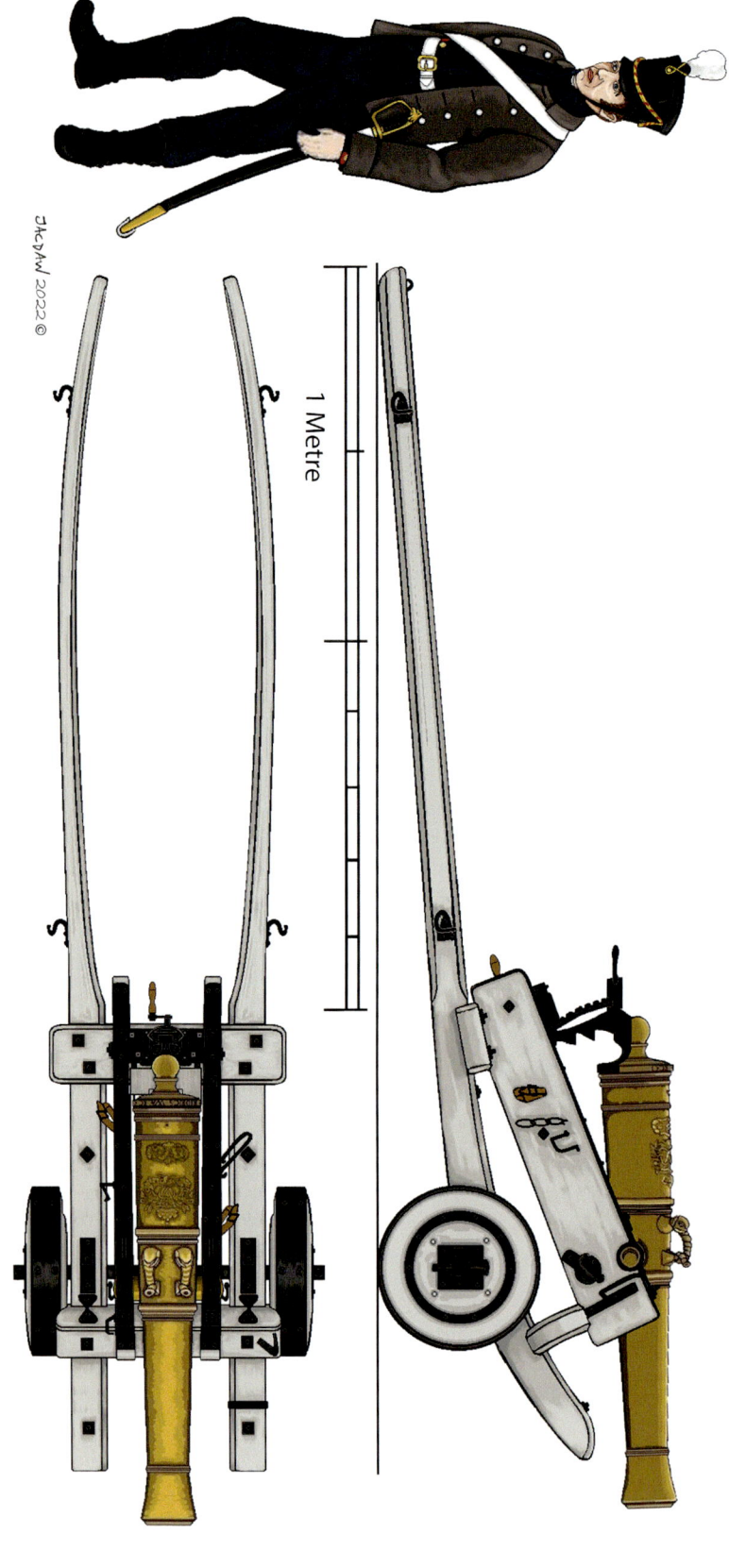

Plate 37. Norwegian 3-pdr 16 calibre sledge gun, in Trønderlavet M1809.

This was a system developed in the north of Norway to cope with the extreme climate and harsh geography of the region. It was a 3-pdr 16 calibre M1687–1757 system *Harboe* with the barrel mounted on a wheeled sledge pulled by a pair of horses in tandem. Each gun was followed by an ammunition limber also mounted on a wheeled sledge, also pulled by a pair of horses in tandem. Further reserve ammunition for each gun was carried in an ammunition wagon, again mounted on a wheeled sledge, pulled by two horses in tandem. In summer they were all wheeled and in winter just the skis were used and the wheels were stored on the ammunition sledge.

Alongside is a Geworbne *constabel* (lance corporal or gunner first class) wearing a *ydertrøje*, a short overcoat, which the artillery began receiving from 1808–1810, and he is armed with the new M1802 artillery sabre c. 1812. Author's reconstruction, made after an original plan and an example conserved in the Rustkammeret (the 'The Armoury' museum in Trondheim).

Wheel diameter 125 cm; length of gun carriage 126 cm; width of gun carriage (front) 15 cm; width of gun carriage (rear) 20 cm; length of shafts 375 cm; width of carriage including the wheels 125 cm

The ammunition wagons of the regimental artillery were the older model of two-wheel carts with the horses in tandem:

Wheel diameter 125 cm; length of ammunition box 115 cm; width of ammunition box 45 cm; height of ammunition box 45 cm; width of cart including the wheels 125 cm; total length of cart including the hay rack 375 cm

The following new equipment was also shipped to Norway between 1772 and 1789:

Eight 12-pdr M1766 guns, sixteen 6-pdr 22 calibre M1766 guns, ten 20-pdr M1772 howitzers, sixteen 6-pdr 22 calibre M1766 guns and four 3 36-pdr M1766 howitzers. All complete with their limbers.

To support this array of hardware were 193 M1766 two-wheeled ammunition carts, 83 of the M1765 four-wheeled ammunition wagons and a four-wheeled staff wagon with coffers and boxes for storing items such as maps and records. There were 12 of the M765, four-wheeled supply wagons, two four-wheeled field forges for use by artillery blacksmiths and two blacksmith's equipment wagons, a wagon for heating cannonballs and 15 two-wheeled hospital carts.

In 1789 a special light 10-pdr howitzer was accepted into use and between 1789 and 1799 some 16 howitzer barrels were cast, and according to some sources they were all shipped to Norway for use there. But this is incorrect, and in fact only six were shipped to Norway. It is true that a *Kongelig Resolution* of 15 November 1799 suggests this, but as the 10 others were already in use in Denmark, this did not happen. Only four 10-pdr (short) howitzers M1789, for the use of the new horse artillery and only an additional two were actually sent to Norway between 1788–1803. These were the 10-pdr light howitzer designated as the 10-pdr 61.3 calibre M1789 howitzer, calibre 13 cm. Weight 170 kg and total length 83 cm.

In 1803 the modernised 3-pdr horse artillery company was made up of the following.

The 10th Ridende Artilleri Companie replaced its 1-pdr M1766 *amusettes* in 1802, with the first eight 3-pdr 20 calibre M1799 guns cast in Denmark, and two 10-pdr (light) M1789 howitzers, all on new M1799 carriages, as they were considered more suitable than a light 6-pdr in the Norwegian terrain.

Two (light) 3-pdr foot artillery companies, the 13th and 14th, were formed in Norway after 1803, by using the older M1687/1759 barrel but now mounted on a new carriage, the M1799. But this took time and as late as 1808 parts for the levelling mechanism were missing and ordered to be made locally by the Danish king. In 1811 further plans were made to use the remaining 3-pdr M1687/1759 barrels for some of the new mounted companies, but only one new company was formed and this only comprising six guns. They used the M1799 limber with the small 3-pdr ammunition chest which were modified in 1806 with the addition of seats and a footrest for two gunners (the M1811 mounted limber), while the rest rode on the limber horses and former dragoon horses. Although the Danish mounted artillery normally had six-horse teams, the information points to the fact that in Norway only four-horse teams were used.

However the 2nd Nordenfjeldske used the M1687/1759 barrel, for its special (Norwegian) designed sledge and wheeled *Trøndelag* (Trondheim) artillery system M1809.

Calibre 7.6 mm; length of bore 123.2 cm; total length of gun barrel 138.6 cm; weight of barrel 198–202 kg; numbers cast: 202. There were in fact in two main models: 60 were cast in 1748 mainly for Norway and 142 cast 1757–1762 some for Norway, but 88 were for the Danish regimental artillery.

The 10-pdr portable Coehorn mortars which could be carried by two gunners by the handles at the end of the woodblock were very popular and according to the '1837 list', 81 were still held in the arsenals. In 1808 the arsenal of Aggershus asked for more to be sent to Norway, but this was refused by the Danish king in a letter of 3 December 1808, 'as none are available at the moment'.[4]

In 1772 Norway received 83 new four-wheeled wagons for artillery ammunition M1776. In 1798, to improve the turning circle of the wagon, and so the general mobility; General Huth suggested to alter the axle and give it a set of smaller (45 cm) wheels, which enabled the wheels to turn under the wagon body. This was done to all wagons in Denmark/Holstein, but it is not known if this modification was made in Norway.

They were all painted pearl grey, and this was the first occasion that this colour was used in Norway on wagons, and they were normally drawn by four horses. The Danish artillery equipment grey was called pearl grey, and in fact it was very close in shade to the English equipment grey,

---

4   Source: *the '1837 list'* and Letter from the King (Fredrik VI) to the *Danske Commerce Collegium* (War Department) 3 December 1808.

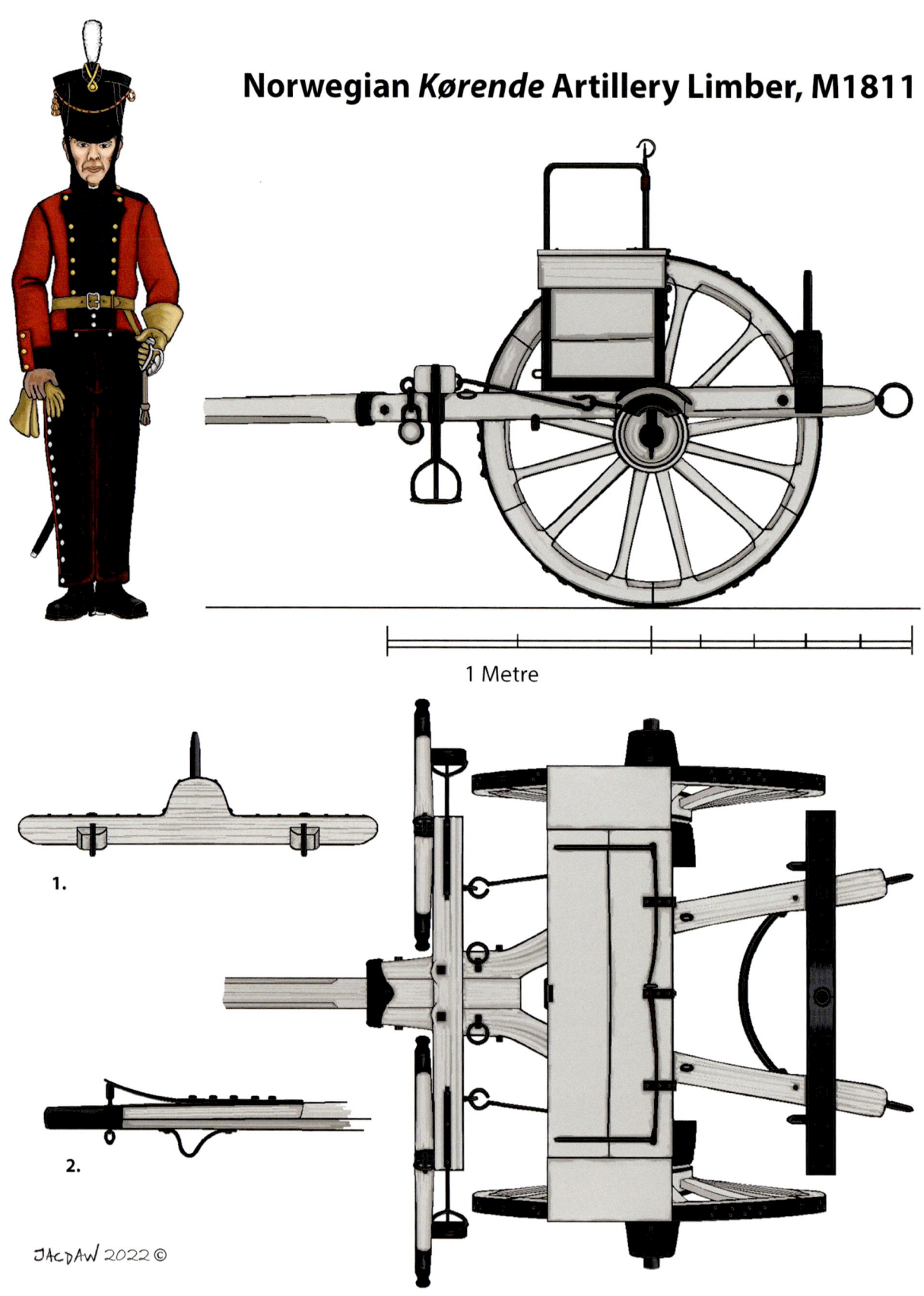

Norwegian *Kørende* Artillery Limber, M1811

> Facing page
>
> Plate 38. Norwegian *Kørende* Artillery Limber M1811
>
> These mounted artillery limbers or *kørende forestillinger* were unique to Norway and probably only 20 or so were actually built between 1811 and 1814. They were used with the 16 calibre M1687–1757 3-pdr guns and a couple with 10-pdr howitzers. They were probably sufficient for just one (full strength) regular company and one reduced company. The first company of the Søndenfjeldske Nationale Kørende Artilleri Bataljon, a six-gun company, were equipped with them.
>
> Shown with a *kørende* Nationale *constabel*, a gunner's assistant and former Norwegian dragoon wearing his old uniform coatee modified with blue facings and blue overalls, but still carrying his former dragoon *pallaske*. The men rode beside the guns and dismounted to manoeuvre them, while the guns themselves were served by *kørende geworbne* gunners.
>
> Author's reconstruction made after a model conserved in the Norwegian Army Museum (Forsvarmuseet) in Oslo.

used by the British artillery during the Napoleonic wars and later.

> The M1765 artillery ammunition wagon was used by the 12-pdr, 6-pdr, and 3-pdr foot companies
>
> The 12-pdr wagons could carry 80 ready-to-fire shells
>
> The 6-pdr wagons could carry 130 ready-to-fire shells
>
> The 3-pdr wagons could carry 210 ready-to-fire shells.

Artillery Arms and Equipment

The *geworbne* gunners first carried *Faskinkniv M1777 for konstabler,* which were used in Norway until 1807. It had a lion's head hilt. The scabbard had two pockets for two 'vent pickers'. The *geworben* gunners then received the *artilleri sabel* (artillery sabre) M1802. They were probably made by just adding new sabre blades and scabbards to the hilts of the previous sidearm. This became the standard artillery sabre for the Norwegian artillery from 1807 with a standard black scabbard.[5] As field equipment they received knapsacks, with one sling, and bread bags, two-man canteens and six-man copper cooking pots were carried on the limbers and wagons.

Saddle Cloths

Exactly when the Norwegian artillery changed saddle cloths is not known, but information suggests it was in 1807. These new shabraques were red with blue galloon around the border.

Artillery Uniforms

The uniforms of the Norwegian artillery seem to have followed their Danish counterparts a lot closer than in the rest of the Norwegian army, due to a common centralised administration of stores for the artillery corps, even though the Holstein, Danish and Norwegian artillery brigades were considered as separate units. Norway followed the same uniform changes as in Denmark in 1808, but introduced them much later, from 1810–1811. Also the clothing terms were different between the five Geworbne companies (which had basically the same terms as in Denmark), and the Nationale (territorial) companies, which had rather longer terms, as in peace time they served as a rule no more than 14 days a year. The clothing terms were those according to the 'Rules of clothing allowances' 1803–1806:[6]

> Geworbne NCOs, *overconstabler* and *hornblæsere*
> 1st year: shirt and shoes, a pair of blue trousers and a pair of white canvas *bukser* breeches
> 2nd year: one hat and one red coat
> 3rd year: one waistcoat and one pair of gloves

---

[5] The first production was made by fitting the previous M1777 hilt with a new sabre blade. When by 1808 all hilts had been used, the rest of the sabres had new cast hilts of same model (with clearer details in casting) and slightly different blades. Most found in Norway have the old hilts. One remaining sabre has the following marking: '13 C 7 = 13. Artillery Company no 7'. According to the list of all weapons available for the Norwegian army made in 1837, there were a total of 579 different models of artillery sabres in store. Source: *Fortegnelse over Antal og Beskaffenhed af de vigtigste i samtlige norske Landarsenaler havende militaire Fornødenheder ved Aarets Udgang 1837* ('Inventory list of all Norwegian weapons in 1837, for the use of the Norwegian government').

[6] *Munderingsreglement for det Kongelige Artilleri Corps 8th June 1803*. The same rules were followed by the next main uniform terms in 1806.

Norwegian Artillery Uniforms 1803–1814

THE NORWEGIAN ARTILLERY

Facing page

Plate 39. Norwegian Artillery Uniforms

Top row:

1. Foot artillery officer in hat M1804, and the specially coloured crimson officer's coat 1805
2. Foot artillery officer in shako M1808, and a standard officer's red-coloured officer's coat 1811
3. Nationale gunner/assistant in 1812, with a new shako M1808 which the men began receiving from 1810
4. Hornist, 1811, in shako M1808 and new blue *trausser* M1808, worn with short black gaiters
5. Artillery train driver (*artilleri træn kusk*) c. 1814, in the new uniform the men began receiving from 1813, with blue cavalry overalls. Artillery drivers (*stykkuske*) had basically the same uniforms as Nationale *artillerister*; before 1807 they had high boots and caps, after 1807 they had blue cavalry overalls and hats or shakos.

Bottom row - Horse Artillery, 10th Ridende Artilleri Kompani

6. Officer in parade dress with M1806 hat, crimson artillery officers' coat and yellow breeches, 1808
7. A horse artillery constabel, *c.* 1808, rear view, shown with a 'shot bag'
8. A horse artillery officer in field uniform, wearing shako M1808 and the new horse artillery officer's gold cross belt M1808, lined crimson, probably also used by Norwegian horse artillery officers c. 1811.
9. A Nationale horse artillery gunner *c.* 1814 wearing shako,
10. Horse artillery trumpeter with the new distinctions M1812, and swallows' nests in yellow tape and no fringes, *c.* 1813.

Geworbne, **constabler**
1st year: A pair of blue trousers and a pair of white canvas *bukser* breeches
2nd year: One red coat
6th year: One waistcoat and two hats

National/Territorial NCOs
1st year: Shirt and shoes

2nd year: A pair of blue trousers and a pair of white canvas *bukser* breeches

4th year: A hat

6th year: A red coat and one blue waistcoat

Nationale *constabler* and *tamboure*

6th year: A shirt, stockings and shoes. A pair of blue trousers and two pairs of white canvas *bukser*

8th year: One hat

The Geworbne (Enlisted) Regular Foot Artillery Companies
Between 1804 and 1810 the Geworbne regular foot artillery gunners wore a black hat with a yellow hat band, white plume, a black cockade, yellow loop and a brass button.

They probably had the M1802 hats, as they received new uniform items as per the Danish uniform terms.

They wore a *kraprød* (madder red) M1798, later M1802, coatee with blue cuffs with red cuff flaps, three buttons, a blue collar, blue lapels and blue frontal turnbacks and brass buttons. They had a shoulder strap on the left side only. They had a pair of fall-fronted blue gaiter trousers M1803.[7]

From 1810–1811 they had the standard M1808 shako with white cords and a short plume. They also received the new shorter M1808 *kraprød* coatee with a high dark blue collar, cuffs, and frontal turn-ups with yellow (brass) buttons and underneath, a white waistcoat. They never adopted pointed cuffs. Their blue trousers should have been changed for a white and a grey pair from 1810/1811, but it looks like most retained the old long blue ones. Most pairs were cut short to be worn with short black gaiters. The Norwegian artillery also adopted the locally made grey *overtrøjer/kaputtrøjer*, the short, spencer-like overcoats. They were equipped with a white leather waist belt with an artillery sabre, and a black pouch for priming fuses and equipment on a white leather cross belt. This was more or less the standard uniform of all artillery between 1810 and 1814.

---

7   The Norwegian artillery tried to continue using the blue trousers in the artillery, but experiments with local dyeing apparently did not succeed: in 1814 the artillery received 100 'violette pantaloons' (violet trousers). According to contemporary sources, this was not an uncommon outcome when trying to dye white cloth blue with cheap natural dyes.

The Geworbne (Regular) 10th Norske Ridende Artilleri Companie

Generally, this company had the same basic uniforms at the other regular artillery, but adding special distinctions, cavalry style equipment and arms.

They first wore M1802 hats with a brass rhombic shield stamped with 'RA'. In 1810 they began receiving the new M1808 shako, reusing the shield. They also had a grey field cap with blue border.

Otherwise they wore the same basic uniform as foot artillery, but with yellow cavalry-style breeches, blue overalls, with red lining and metal buttons, and other cavalry equipment. Initially they carried an M1796 *sabel for ridende artilleri*.[8] This was apparently supplemented with a special new variant M1809 *sabel for ridende artillery*.[9] From 1811 they began using grey overcoats (short, it is believed) to replace the old red cloaks.

Nationale *Constabler* (Gunners

As these men were Nationale conscripts, they were only considered as a reserve of manpower for the regular artillery and fortress artillery, and as such, only trained like other Nationales, for 28 days a year. There seems to have been some delay in replacing the old uniforms and equipment and most men started the war in 1808 in old and worn uniforms. As they served continuously from thereon, they also began receiving new uniforms, as the rest of the gunners did, from 1809–1810. As a rule they wore plain uniforms with simple shoulder straps. The new pointed cuffs were not worn by the *underconstabler* (gunner's assistants), but only by the officers and NCOs due to the 1812 reforms in rank insignia. They at first carried infantry sabres M1756 as sidearms, and it is possible that they kept using them throughout the war.

The (Mounted) Artillery of the Søndenfjeldske and Nordenfjeldske Kørende Artilleri Bataljon

Until the reform in 1811, they had worn old dragoon uniforms of their former regiments. They first kept their old dragoon hats from 1806–1806 with a white plume at left side, and probably a yellow loop and hat band added. From around 1812 the M1808 shako began to be issued, also with a white plume. They first converted the best remaining former dragoon uniforms, into a 'new' artillery gunner's uniform. This was an ordinary red coatee with dark blue collar, cuffs, and frontal turn-ups with yellow (brass) buttons and a white waistcoat. They all kept their former yellow cavalry trousers, and their blue cavalry overalls. This was probably the standard uniform of all the (mounted) Nationale artillery between 1811 and 1814. The new pointed cuffs were not worn by the *underconstabler* (gunners 3rd class) as they were now called, only by the officers and NCOs due to the 1812 reforms in rank insignia. The (mounted) Nationale artillery appears to have been suitably supplied with red dragoon-type cloaks well into 1814. They were armed with a variety of weapons from their former dragoon regiments.[10]

The *Artillery Stykkuske* (Train Drivers) and *Tænkuske* (Waggoneers)

Between 1800–1814 the *stykkusk* artillery train drivers wore a black cap (*casquette*) with a madder red artillery coatee which had a dark blue collar, dark blue lapels and cuffs and the buttons were brass. They also had a dark blue waistcoat, buff kersey breeches, grey stockings and high black boots. From 1812 they received blue cavalry overalls and grey fatigue caps, with a blue turn-up. They had a white leather belt with an M1756 sabre.

Tænkuske used until 1812 a red and blue cloth cap *kabuds*, worn with all kinds of older uniform, mixed with civilian clothes, buff kersey breeches, grey stockings and high black boots.

---

8 The *dragonpallask M1734* with iron hilt was according to most information the sidearm still used by Smaalehnske Dragonregiment, which provided six of their former dragoon companies for the new *Søndenfjeldske Kørende Artilleri Bataljon*. The two other dragoon companies, from the Aggerhusiske Dragonregiment had *dragonpallask M1750*, the four companies from Trondhjemske Dragonregiment, which formed the Nordenfjeldske Kørende Artilleri Bataljon, had M1740 *pallasker*. It appears that there were not enough M1802 sabres in store, so they retained their old sidearm, in their new role as mounted gunners.

9 This model was in fact a repaired *Husar sabel* M1761, with new scabbards, many new blades and at least 50 with new cast hilts (cast 1799). In total 567 were made and delivered by 1799. According to plans all three horse companies were to receive them (Norway included), but information points to that only the Geworbne gunners and drivers in Norway received 96 sabres, while none were provided for any Nationales who were intended to be part of the company in wartime. These sabres are probably counted among the 125 old hussar sabres mentioned in the '1837 list', of which probably 90 were the M1796 sabre, while 35 were probably *Hussar sabel* M1776/92 from the former *Hussar detachment*/Geworbne dragoon company ('1837 list'). Probably the Nationales were issued with either the M1791 *hirschfänger*, formerly used by the Norwegian horse artillery, or kept their former *dragonpallask* as a sidearm. Two preserved sabres have original markings for the horse artillery company: No. 28 and No. 116, which may show that the full number of sabres available by 1814 was probably around 125, but probably mixed with the M1809 horse artillery sabre.

10 In 1809–1810 a total of 150 new M1809 *sabel for ridende artilleri* were made by using new M1792 blades and new cast hilts M1802. This sabre is also found in collections in Norway, and maybe 75 were shipped to Norway, intended for use by the Nationale companies of the horse artillery. They (because of the similar hilts), were probably counted between the 579 different models of artillery sabres, in the '1837 list'.

From 1812 they wore a black levy calfskin *casquette*, a single-breasted red coat with a dark blue collar with a yellow K on the left and a yellow A on the left, and dark blue cuffs and front turnbacks. The cuff flaps were red, and the buttons were brass. They also had a pair of dark blue cavalry overalls with black leather inserts and pewter buttons down the outside leg and black boots. They had a white leather belt with an M1756 sabre. From 1813–1814, they were also issued a black cap (*casquette*) with a double-breasted grey coatee with a fall-down collar, a short grey waistcoat and a pair of dark blue cavalry overalls. It is possible that this uniform was only worn by the *trainkuske* (waggoners) of the infantry regiments.

Musicians

There is very little information available on the musicians' uniforms. Originally they had drums, but they were replaced in Denmark with horns from around 1803, and some years later in Norway. The new *hornblæsere* uniform would have had dark blue swallows' nests with yellow lace and probably an epaulette as the artillery hornists held the rank of an NCO (see illustration). The hornists were first issued with crescent shaped horns (*halvmånehorn*), but these appear to have been replaced later with the lighter French horns (*waldhorns*). In 1808, the horns were wrapped with blue bindings and had a black leather straps in Denmark and Norway probably followed suit. When allowed, regimental bands and *hoboister* in 1811, some of the first so hired were apparently gunners (*hornblæsere*) on furlough.

NCOs

They wore the same uniform as the gunners and followed the same uniform changes, but with epaulettes denoting their rank. The rank insignia was as for the Danish artillery. All regular gunners carried a kind of distinction on their right shoulder, as sign of their specialist status.

Sergent (sergeant): Two flat gold epaulettes with short fringes (M1778)

Overconstable (bombardier). A flat gold epaulette with short fringes (M1778)

Nationale *underofficer* (bombardier). A gold looped lace band with fringes at the end (NCO distinction M1789)

Constable (lance corporal/gunner 1st class). A thin double gold cord, with a fringe on the end. In Denmark the *constabler* lost their distinctions in 1804, but it appears they continued in use in Norway until 1812. From 1812/1813 they received the new cuff rank insignia with chevrons on top of the cuffs

Commandersergent (sergeant major): three yellow lace chevrons on the pointed sleeve

Sergent (sergeant): two yellow lace chevrons and a brass button on the pointed sleeve

Underofficer/bombarder (NCO): two yellow lace chevrons on the pointed sleeve

Overconstabel (gunner 1st class): one yellow lace chevron and a brass button at the pointed sleeve

Constabel (gunner 2nd class): one yellow lace chevron on the pointed sleeve

In Denmark the junior NCOs initially carried a M1777 *Faskinkniv for Overkonstabler*, and it was used in Norway until 1807. It had a gilt helm-shaped pommel. The scabbard had two pockets for two vent pickers. Sergeants had the *Kårde or artilleriets underofficerer* M1777 (small-sword for NCOs M1777). The *Artilleri sabel for underofficerer* M1802/M1802 sabre was specially made for the artillery NCOs in 1804 to 1806. This was a variation of the M1802 sabre; numbers made are not known, but in 1868 there still remained 154 in the arsenals in Denmark, so there were not fewer than that made. It is not clear how many of this model were actually issued in Norway, but some must have been, probably and mainly to the sergeants.

Officers

The Norwegian artillery officers were allowed the special crimson coat colour and blue *pantalongs*, worn with short black officer's boots. They wore M1802 or the M1801 epaulettes, with a standard waist sash and port épée. They were allowed new white and grey trousers from 1810. They may have retained the previously issued blue trousers for a while, but they very quickly favoured the new grey trousers. They began to receive the new *kraprød* M1808 officer's coats from 1812, but most did their best to also retain their crimson coats. The officers started to receive M1808 shakos in 1810. It had a black cockade, a yellow loop and a brass button, and had gold and red cords. The new rank insignia with pointed cuffs, with buttons and chevrons, were adopted by the officers from 1812.

Part II

10

The Danish Landeværn and Kystmilitsen

Uniform Generalities

At this time lapelled coats were seen as the mark of a professional soldier, while single-breasted uniforms were in general only used by the *Landeværn*, volunteers, town militias and other non-regular soldiers.

Where the militias had lapels, it generally indicated that they were seen as more important, more exposed, therefore more likely to find themselves on the battlefield, like those of Bornholm, who were in reality permanently on the front line.

Therefore when a volunteer unit was allowed to have lapels, this showed that their status had risen, and they were seen as more professional, more engaged in the war than the others, or in some cases had a royal patron. In other units it was only the officers and NCOs who were permitted lapels, again theoretically to differentiate their more professional status and probably some former military service.

Another generality was that shoulder straps were rarely authorised for the militia before 1807. In the units which still wore hats, the officers tended to use bicorns of different shapes and models as well as hats until 1804–1806 when round hats became the norm.

It is also to be noted that many of these units had colours while others only had fanions, sometimes only to mark the headquarters, sometimes with a fanion per company, and a very few had a fanion big enough to be classed as a colour. Surprisingly a number of these have survived. These were nearly always privately designed and paid for by the members of the unit. Where known they are noted here.

The Landeværn (in the German-Speaking Parts Called *Landwehr*) 1801–1808

The Landeværn were first raised rather hastily during the short war with Great Britain in 1801, mainly as a volunteer force, raised through the initiative of locals. But it was not fully operational and only partly uniformed and armed. Only a few company-sized formations existed, and although a uniform was allowed, most wore either converted civilian clothes or non-standard uniforms. As the regular army was slowly being reformed, especially from 1803, a much more modern centralised and functional system was organised. On 8 June 1803, the new 'organisational plan' for the Landeværn was made official. One of these new measures was the creation of a reserve of trained soldiers, now officially called the Landeværn entirely made up of former conscripts, between 26 and 32 years of age, having done either eight years' service as Nationale soldiers before 1802 or six years' service as conscripts after the new system from 1802. But as the first class of conscripts were first called up in 1803, they had to finish their previous service engagements first. Here it appears among other things that the company establishment would as a starting point now only be 120 Landeværns*mænd*. But there were simply not enough former soldiers available to start equipping and training the planned Landeværn at all before 1806, even the reduced-strength companies, and those raised in a hurry in 1807 could, as a consequence, not muster more than 100 soldiers a company at best. They were intended only for local defence, coastal defence and to garrison some important fortresses, supported by regular forces. Uniforms were from 1803 to be made centrally by the *Militære Uld manufaktur* (the Military Cloth Factory), but distributed locally at the first gathering of the *Landeværn*. Arms were also to be stored centrally, and would first be distributed 'when needed'. Also, in the same year, a large order for new arms was placed with the arms factories, to be delivered during 1803–1814.

The first mustering of the Landeværn was on Zeeland in 1806, were they all received uniforms, made by the Danish *Militære Uld Manufaktur* (hat coat and gaiter trousers), but since then had not been able to train in larger formations than a company, and even this very rarely. Nor were they very well led either. Their officers were local landowners, former officers, often old or young inexperienced gentlemen having done a short term in the officers' school, and nothing else. But in 1807 the totally unexpected war caught everyone by surprise, and nothing was ready, and there was simply not enough time to get everything in order. In 1807 they were poorly armed, with few muskets, and many of these muskets were old models in poor condition. Also they suddenly found themselves in a role for which they were never intended, and were nearly cut off from any help from regular forces. They really stood no chance against a

THE DANISH ARMY OF THE NAPOLEONIC WARS VOLUME 3

Danish *Landvaern* and Coastal Militia

1.
2. not to scale

> Facing page:
>
> Plate 40. Landeværn and Coastal Militia
>
> Top, left to right:
>
> • Landeværn officer *c.* 1801. The bicorn was not worn after 1804, because a *Kongelig Resolution* of March 1803 ordered that from 1804 'all officers' including all Landeværn officers were to wear hats.
>
> • Landeværn officer *c.* 1805
>
> • Landeværn NCO *c.* 1807
>
> • Landeværn drummer *c.* 1807 with an M1753 brass drum, although many would have had old painted wooden drums. as most of the brass drums were stored in the Copenhagen arsenal.
>
> Bottom, from left to right:
>
> • Landeværn private showing one variation of the civilian undergarments. Inset illustrates an example of the Danish red bonnet.
>
> • Landeværn private showing another variation of the civilian undergarments; his hat is probably a civilian hat militarised into an M1802 hat, which was taller and slimmer.
>
> • *Befalingsmænd*/officer of Kystmilitsen (coastal militia) *c.* 1809. His sash and M1801 epaulettes denote an ex-regular officer, while the *befalingsmænd* (ordinary officers) wore a different uniform.
>
> • A better dressed Kystmilitsen man *c.* 1809. Most had only civilian clothes with just the special *Kystmilitscockade*, which was red with a white cross badge on the hat. Some men were only armed with a pike and some were issued with old muskets, carbines or even civilian fowling pieces.
>
> Weapons:
>
> 1. M1801 *Kystmilitspike*
>
> 2. Boarding pike, supplied by the navy *c.* 1800
>
> Note that all of the epaulettes in the militia were sewn directly onto the uniform, so no belts could pass under the NCO's fringed epaulette. Until 1806 most NCOs of the Landeværn still carried halberds.

well prepared fully trained veteran British army. Although some bravery and stubbornness were shown in the fighting in 1807, the results were overall disappointing, and this lack of success led to their disbandment. In October 1807 these short-lived Landeværn were turned over to the line regiments for training and in 1808 they were formed into the third and fourth *Annekterede* (reserve) battalions of the line regiments instead.

Organisation

Each battalion was supposed to consist of four companies, and each one was supposed to have consisted of three officers, 12 NCOs and 150 men, so each battalion was only about 400–500 strong in at first, and only expected to reach full strength of 600 from 1808. Again, and theoretically, the youngest were supposed to be aged from 27 to 32 years old and the eldest were aged from 33 to 38 years old. They were then supposed to be formed into regiments of several battalions (in reality this was the same as the army brigades under the command of a major general).

As already stated, these were official units and they came directly under the control of the regular army. These regiments were:

The Nordre Sjællandske Landeværns Regiment. Ten battalions, raised in 1801, disbanded in 1808.

The Sønrdre Sjællandske Landeværns Regiment. Nine battalions, raised in 1801, disbanded in 1808.

The Fynske Landeværns Regiment. Eight battalions, raised in 1801, disbanded in 1808.

The Nordre Jyske Landeværns Regiment. Three battalions, raised in 1801, disbanded in 1808.

The 1st Østre Jyske Landeværns Regiment. Five battalions, raised in 1801, disbanded in 1808.

The 2nd Østre Jyske Landeværns Regiment. Four battalions, raised in 1801, disbanded in 1808.

The Vestre Jyske Landeværns Regiment. Four battalions, raised in 1801, disbanded in 1808.

The Slesvigske Landeværns Regiment. One battalion, raised in 1802, disbanded in 1808.

The Holstenske Landeværns Regiment. One battalion, raised in 1802, disbanded in 1808.

There were also the following smaller formations:

The Samsøe Landeværn. An all-arms formation, raised in 1801, disbanded in 1808.

The Langelandske Landeværns Bataljon raised in 1801, disbanded in 1808.

The Helgolands Landeværn, raised in 1805, disbanded in 1807.

A number of fortress artillery companies were raised, by concentrating all former artillery soldiers into one company in one of the regiment's battalions:

The Nordre Sjællandske Landeværn Regiment with two artillery companies serving in the fortress of Kronborg

The Sønrdre Sjællandske Landeværn Regiment with four artillery companies serving in Copenhagen

The Slesvigske Landeværn Regiment with four artillery companies serving in different fortresses and batteries

The Holstenske Landeværn Regiment with four artillery companies serving in different fortresses and batteries

A further two companies were formed in Jutland.

Although not formally organised in peacetime, the regiments were also expected, when active to raise Landeværns dragoon formations out of former cavalrymen, if possible. During the fighting on Zeeland at least 300 such Landeværn dragoons were formed, and some were also raised in Schleswig and Holstein, and maybe in Jutland in 1807–1808.

Some of these units were ineffectually engaged during the battle of Koege on the 29 August 1807 between British troops commanded by Major General Wellesley covering the siege of Copenhagen and the Danish militia raised on Zeeland (*Sjælland*). It ended in a British victory, but it was also known as the *Træskoslaget* or 'Battle of the Clogs', since a later account said that most of the Danish Landeværn threw away their heavy wooden clogs when they were fleeing. But this is a myth. This name, as far as can be ascertained, was thought up later by local gossiping and scornful comments, mainly by the womenfolk shortly after the battle. The name was then used by the more radical parts of different political parties who expressed anti-military feelings, and who were strongly against commemorating the 100th anniversary of the battle in 1907. A smaller number of the Landeværn did wear clogs and not shoes, but they were clearly not thrown away in such numbers that nobody noticed it until 100 years later.

Uniforms

Uniforms had been first approved in 1801, but although colours and general style formed the basis of the uniforms, which were to be made by the *Militære Uld Manufaktur*, and followed the style of the army's M1802 uniforms. The uniform coat and white gaiter trousers were distributed locally at the first mustering of the *Landeværn*. Belts and bread bags were also distributed to some battalions. They wore a black felt hat, and a contemporary illustration shows it to be somewhat dilapidated and with larger brims with a green plume with a white loop and hat band. The hat could probably be replaced with a *topplue*, the traditional tasselled red woollen cap, if enough hats were not available. Some civilian hats were also pressed into service in 1807.

From around 1806 they were issued with a single-breasted red coatee with sky blue cuffs and collar piped white. The cuffs were closed with two buttons hidden by the turned back cuffs, and generally the coatee was of a generous cut, as it was expected to be worn over a civilian waistcoat, smock or shirt. Coats had white piping on either side of the row of buttons.

Most of the men were issued with a pair of fall-fronted white gaiter trousers, but in general they were not issued shoes, and the men had to provide them themselves, so some during the fighting in 1807, they cut off the gaiter trousers at the knees, so that they could wear long stockings and civilian Hessian boots or long stockings and wooden clogs. Some few wore their own work breeches generally of a dark woollen or unbleached linen cloth.

As footwear was not provided, the men had to provide their own, but the problem was that outside of Copenhagen very few people either wore or even possessed shoes. In the countryside many still went barefoot or wore wooden clogs. For many years to come, training soldiers from an agricultural background to wear boots or shoes remained a problem, as many suffered from foot sores or open wounds on their feet because they were quite simply not used to wearing boots or shoes as many went bare foot in civilian life. The majority of soldiers unfit for duty were usually due to foot problems. But it is a myth that the majority of the Landeværn wore wooden clogs. A very detailed eyewitness account made the day after the battle[1] of the Landeværns*mænd* who were captured, describes them as:

---
1 *Rejsen til Kioge i månederne August og September 1807*, F. C. Agre.

Their uniforms, had probably, when issued, with green plumes, red coatees and long white trousers, looked grand, except for their long hair, long striped civilian waistcoats and different civilian footwear (clogs are not mentioned as such), but all are now worn, dirty and discoloured (to be expected after a battle) including the trousers, which some have cut off, at the knees.

This last must be those who had worn footwear other than shoes. But this source mentions only civilian footwear, and nothing about either clogs or bare feet. Also in his description of the battlefield the same source mentions nothing about discarded footwear, but only uniform coatees, hats and arms. He also reported that 'some were without uniforms, as they had tried to hide to avoid capture'.

Their equipment was made of black leather, a cartridge box on a bandoleer, a belt with a bayonet frog and a canvas knapsack/bread bag on a black shoulder strap. It is possible that the belts were not always black, and some could have been brown leather from older recycled equipment. They were not issued with canteens, so they tended to bring their own, and contemporary illustrations show them to be large and round.

Landeværn Officers' Uniforms

From 1801 the officers were allowed a single-breasted, long-tailed coat M1795, in the special poppy red colour of *ponceau*, lined white with a medium blue collar and cuffs piped white, white turnbacks, white metal buttons, white breeches, black Hessian boots with tassels, an old-fashioned bicorn with gold tassels, a black cockade with a silver loop and a green plume. The coat had silver epaulettes (see illustration). In 1804 the officers were ordered to replace their bicorn with a round hat which had a white hat band, mixed gold and red cords and tassels and a black cockade with a silver loop. From 1806 several changed to the new officers' hat M1806, taller and with longer and more elaborate cords than before.

The officers carried a sabre, models unknown, and they wore the red and yellow waist sash as they were now considered part of the regular army. The above-mentioned eyewitness describes the captured officer's uniforms:

> The officers' uniforms, maybe splendid at parades, looked, especially the white trousers and waistcoats, dirty after service in the field (and battle). Coats were worn both short (M1801) and long over the stomach (M1806). One has long skirts (M1801), and one has short skirts (M1806). Some wore short boots, other long ones. Hats, both low (M1804) and high (M1806), and plumes were either low (M1804), or long (M1806), and in different shades of green.

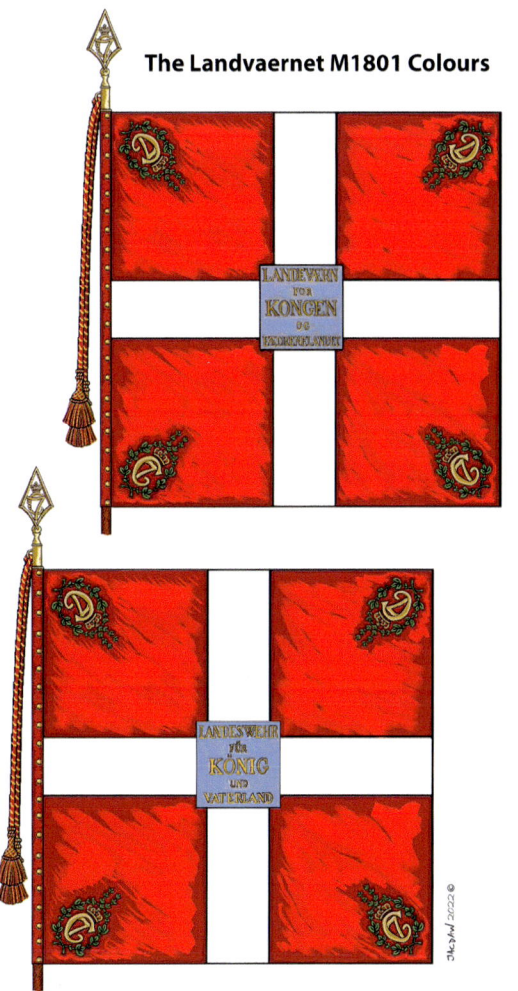

Plate 41. The *Landeværnet* M1801 Colours

Top: the *Landeværnet* M1801 colours had the Dannebrog overall with a light blue coloured cartouche in the centre with gold text. This is the Danish version. The obverse and reverse were identical. Several of these colours are preserved in the Tøjhusmuseet under the reference Fa275.

Bottom: the *Landeværnet* M1801 colours had the Dannebrog overall with a light blue cartouche in the centre with gold text, this is the German version for the *Landeværnet* units from Schleswig and Holstein, the German-speaking part of Denmark. The obverse and reverse were identical. It is preserved in the Tøjhusmuseet under the reference Fa297. These were recycled in 1808 and used by the newly formed 3rd and 4th battalions of the line regiments with the central panel removed.

This plate has already been shown in Volume 1, but in a different context.

Landeværn NCOs' Uniforms
The NCOs had an epaulette on their left shoulder only, but otherwise they were dressed and equipped as the men.

Landeværn Drummers' Uniforms
The drummers wore the same uniform as the men, but with simple swallows' nests of white tape sewn directly onto the uniform. There was a shortage of drums, so they used the standard brass drum M1753 only when available. The older wooden drums had either no arms at all painted on them, or had local or royal arms painted with natural colours. Until they were needed all drums were to be stored in the main arsenals, so the Zeeland Landeværn in 1807 probably did not receive many of theirs, but had to make do with locally sourced drums. In 1801 many town militias had, in a patriotic spirit, bought or received new M1753 drums for their companies, also a number of 'fire drums were gladly turned over to the Landeværn together with their arms so they did not have to use them against the British themselves; patriotic, but not foolhardy'.

These are the arms known to have been issued in 1801.

The Nordre Sjællandske Landeværns Regiment: M1774 muskets (repaired and most with a new stock)

The Søndre Sjællandske Landeværns Regiment: M1774 muskets (repaired and most with a new stock)

The Fynske Landeværns Regiment: M1765 dragoon muskets (repaired and hook removed)

The 1st Østre Jyske Landeværns Regiment: M1801 Landeværns muskets

The 2nd Østre Jyske Landeværns Regiment: M1801 Landeværns muskets

The Vestre Jyske Landeværns Regiment: M1801 Landeværns muskets

The Slesvigske Landeværns Regiment: A mixture of M1791 and 1794 muskets

The Holstenske Landeværns Regiment: A mixture of M1791 and 1794 muskets

The state had provided repaired older muskets or muskets made up from spare parts left over from the production of new muskets (often a combination of parts from several different models).

The problem was that when muskets were distributed from 1801, there were no regional arsenals so generally they had been badly stored in local depots where there was no one to repair or keep them maintained in working order. They became rusty and many were damaged. Therefore it was decided in future that all arms were to be returned to the arsenals to be cleaned and repaired (on Zeeland and the isles, this meant to Copenhagen).

They should 'in case of war, be hurriedly distributed again' but as the attack in 1807 came as a surprise until the very last moment, only a handful of wagon loads of weapons (2,634 M1774 muskets), and two regimental M1766 3-pdr guns managed to leave Copenhagen before the British closed the ring. This left the Landeværn to use whatever weapon they could find, from the arsenal of Korsøer, local stocks, and including all the muskets from most of the town militias on Zeeland, this gave them 3,000 more muskets, but these were often of older models, often worn out and not all in good working order. All soldiers in fact received a musket, so the idea that they were mostly armed with pikes, spears, straightened pitchforks and scythes is a modern myth.

Colours
These are the units were later reformed and became the 3rd and 4th battalions of the line infantry regiments, and originally they had simple national flags (Dannebrogsfane) which had the usual red field with a white cross, and although the details for some of them are unknown, most had a either a white or medium blue-coloured rectangle stitched in the centre of the cross with the inscription Landeværn FOR KONGEN OG FAEDRENELANDET ('Land Guard for King and Country') in gold lettering shaded black. The obverse and reverse were identical.

In general these squares of cloth bearing the inscriptions were removed when the Landeværn were transformed into reserve battalions.

The inscription was in written in German for the colours carried by the troops from the German-speaking regions of Holstein, Schleswig and probably Oldenburg, so it read *Landeswher Für König Und Vaterland*. These colours were first issued in 1801.

Most if not all of the colours bore a gold crowned royal monogram of Christian VII in each corner surrounded by green laurels but unfortunately, we do not know which regiments had them. There appear to have been a number of variations in the design of the cyphers used.

In 1808 when they were disbanded all the men fit for active duty were used to form the two reserve battalions, the 3rd and 4th battalions, for each of the line infantry regiments. They were then re-equipped and dressed in the uniforms of their new parent regiments. How long this took is not clear, but some of these new battalions were ready for field service by 1812.

The Landeværn Artillery 1807

As previously stated only three of the 3-pdr regimental guns, supposed to be used by the Landeværn actually left Copenhagen before the British siege closed in. They found another seven old 3-pdr guns which were stored in different places in Zeeland, but some of those had an older and smaller calibre, which created trouble with the ammunition supply. They distributed one gun to each infantry battalion, but there were not enough to go round (a couple of the late arrivals did not receive any at all). They also found three old 6-pdr guns and they apparently were formed into a makeshift artillery battery. Artillery carts were also lacking and some of the guns had to make do with civilian wagons for their ammunition. Most of the guns were apparently short 3-pdrs and 6-pdr guns of the old M1687/1757 *Harboe* system. They had been transferred to the *Landeværnet*, town militias, citizen guards, and local coastal defences after 1801. (A few had been used to fire salutes on private estates).

The men serving the guns were former gunners and former artillery officers or NCOs. They wore the standard Landeværn uniform, although some officers wore official artillery uniforms in 1807, and the gunners may have had white belts, and white plumes instead of green. They bore only swords as side arms. Several of these former gunners were formed into special Landeværns artillery companies, to help serve guns in fortresses and coast batteries. On Zeeland, the 8th Battalion Nordre Sjællandske Landeværns Regiment was raised as an artillery battalion, serving guns at the fortress of *Kronborg*. The 6th Battalion Søndre Sjællandske Landeværns Regiment were also formed as an artillery battalion and served in Copenhagen during the siege. There were a number of other artillery battalions in Schleswig, Holstein and Jutland.

The End of the Landeværn

In 1808 when the Landeværn were disbanded, all the men still fit for active duty were used to form the two reserve battalions, the 3rd and 4th battalions, for each of the line infantry regiments. They were then re-equipped and dressed in the uniforms of their new parent regiments, how long this took is not clear, but some of these new battalions were ready for field service by 1812. The Prins Frederik Ferdinands Dragon regiment was formed from the former Landeværns cavalry on Zeeland. Of those who had served in the Landeværns artillery, two Nationale *artilleri bataljoner* were formed: one battalion as the Danske Bataljon (eight companies were formed around Zeeland and two in Jutland) and the Holstenske Bataljon (six companies formed in Schleswig and Holstein).

Samsøe Landeværn, from 1808 the Samsøe Land Milits

They were raised as formal a part of the Landeværn in 1801 and were disbanded in 1814. They were not really a normal militia, but more of a 'legion' as it contained infantry, artillery and cavalry. In fact their organisation was closer to that on Bornholm as this was also an island, so this probably influenced the need for an all-arms militia as they were fairly isolated. The organisation was as follows. Their strength between 1807 and 1814 was, for an infantry company, four officers, eight NCOs, three drummers, a musician (hornist) 128 musketeers and 30 rifle-armed *jaegere*. The *rytter* squadron had two officers, five NCOs, a trumpeter, 42 *ryttere* armed with *dragongeværer* (dragoon muskets), (old) *pallasker* (broadswords) and (old) pistols. The mobile battery (all the officers and NCOs were regular artillery gunners and wore the uniforms of the artillery corps. The 96 *feltartillerister* (field gunners) and 28 *kuske* (artillery drivers) were *Samsøe* personnel. The company served eight 3-pdr guns and two 10-pdr howitzers. According to T. Thaulow's *Samsø i krigsårene 1801–14,* published in Samsoe in 1934, their coastal militia had 179 front rank pikemen (armed with spears or navy pikes) and 291 second rank shot armed with a wide variety of old muskets.

Uniforms of the Infantry

The infantry uniforms bore some close resemblance to those authorised for the Bornholmske National Infanteri in 1799, and as they previously had only been obliged to serve in the navy, the blue colour fitted in fine.

The infantry other ranks wore round hats with a black cockade and a green plume, and a single-breasted dark blue coat with white collar and cuffs with yellow metal buttons. Their fall-fronted trousers were, from 1801 to 1808, blue for the infantry and gunners. In 1809 they were replaced with grey trousers. They had black belts like the *Landeværn*. They were all armed with an old bayonet musket. Some 30 men were classed as *Jaegere* and they had a white feather with a green top on their hats and they carried a rifle with a sword as a sidearm.

In 1811 a new uniform was proposed which had white lace on the front. It was finally accepted but with modifications as the lace was not authorised, but the rest was accepted. Their hats were replaced with the shako M1810, but with a blue plume and cords. The colour of their uniform remained unchanged, but their fall-fronted dark grey trousers were confirmed, worn with short black gaiters. The new uniform also had pointed cuffs (1811–1812). The *jaegere* had the same uniform, but with green cords and plume.

Uniforms of the Officers
The officers wore lacquered round hats, a single-breasted, tailed dark blue coat with white collar and cuffs with yellow metal buttons and blue breeches. 'Møllers liste 1810', confirms the blue in 1810 for the officers. All other details are unknown. Some probably acquired officer's shakos privately after 1808.

Uniforms of the Cavalry
The cavalry *landrytter* wore a hat with a white plume, and it had the brass *rytterskilte* (rhombic) shield of the heavy cavalry. This probably that meant that they also had 'RR' as lettering on the shield, but this is speculation as none have survived. They wore a dark blue coat with a white collar and cuffs, and *Møllers liste 1810* shows yellow piping. The buttons were brass, and their breeches were yellow. They had until c1809 a pair of fall-fronted yellow trousers, but they were also allowed grey trousers from 1810, and officers and probably the *ryttere* as well apparently kept on wearing their yellow breeches, at least for church parades and official assemblies. They had a brown leather shoulder and waist belt of the older *rytter* model (probably wider than the contemporary style). The details of their horse furniture are unknown.

Uniforms of the Artillery
The field artillery (*feltartillerist*) of the mobile battery c. 1810 had a hat with a white plume. They wore a dark blue coat with a red collar and cuffs piped white, with white lining. They may have kept on using their old dark blue trousers until they wore out. They also kept using the old brown leather cross belts and carried a sword on their waist belts.

The coastal artillery (*kystartillerist*) wore the same uniform as the field artillery, but without the white piping. Boots were probably only used by a few gunners; the rest would have worn shoes.

They received an M1801 Landeværns colour, with probably the text Landeværn *for Samsøe* written on the blue patch.

The Local Defence Force of the Islands of Langelanske and Ærøe
The Langelanske Infanteri Bataljon was first raised in 1801–1803 as part of the Landeværn. In 1808, following the siege of Copenhagen, it was reorganised like the rest of the former Landeværn, and finally disbanded in 1816. It was composed of a battalion of five companies, formed by the former local Landeværns battalion in the same strength and organisation as the 3rd and 4th battalions formed from the Landeværn for the regular regiments, with four musketeer companies; a former independent Landeværns company on the Island of Ærøe was classed as a *jaeger* company. The battalion was only used for local defence.

Uniforms
Until 1808, all had received standard Landeværn uniforms. From 1808, they received new dark blue facings to their coatees. It had a red collar with dark blue patches piped white. The lapels and the round cuffs were dark blue piped white, while the cuffs had red cuffs flaps piped white and it had white metal buttons. They kept on using their long white trousers. The musketeers received new shakos with red and yellow cords and white plumes and also white waist and cross belts. They had black leather cartridge pouches.

The (*jaeger*) company on the Island of Ærøe kept their old black leather waist and cross belt from the Landeværn. At first they had hats with a green plume, but later they may have received shakos. They were armed with muskets instead of rifles.

The Local Defence Force of the Island of Helgoland
Only in November 1805 was a formal Landeværn formed for the defence of the island of Helgoland, the *Landwehr-Verordnung für Helgoland*. This stated:

> That all residents of Helgoland, with the exception of the official councilors who are not officers, are required to serve in the Landeværn between 20 and 60 years of age. Everyone should be trained, but when two companies with 240 men, 20 NCOs and four drummers are formed, the older men will join the reserve. Neither officers nor men receive salary or food or pieces of equipment; they have to provide their own uniforms in brown cloth (the everyday dress of the island), with red collars and lapels added; the Landwehr should only serve on the island and in no case be deployed elsewhere. Firearms, side arms and black belts will be provided, by the king.

It is not clear if they received hats with green feathers. To strengthen the Landeværn, an enlisted detachment from the Altonariske Jaegergrenader Companie were sent to the island with an officer, a sergeant, two corporals, a *hornblæsere* and 24 *jaegergrenaderer*. But in September 1807 after a short fight the island was captured by an overwhelming British invasion force. Helgoland then became an important centre of British commercial smuggling of contraband goods to Hamburg and intrigues against Napoleon. The Treaty of Kiel (14 January 1814) forced Denmark to cede Helgoland to George III of the United Kingdom.

The Coastal Militia (Kystmilitsen)
They were raised in 1801 at the same time as the Landeværn, and technically were supposed to support them if needed, as the Landeværn, were to support them also, when needed. They were disbanded much later, in 1814.

They were not actually soldiers, but militia of a sort recruited from the coastal population, including fishermen and farmers as well as local craftsmen, not eligible for conscription, and normally without former military training. The rank and file were called *kystbevogtere* which translates literally into coast guard. Until 1808 they had no official uniforms (except NCOs and officers from 1803). From 1808 the men had an official uniform and although this uniform had a distinct naval look, in fact they had no boats! Although little has been written about them it has become obvious from recent research that they were far more active than previously thought, guarding the coast, helping Danish shipping, keeping a watchful eye on British ships, and doing their best to prevent raids, and their service is still much underestimated. All did their bit in assisting the regular forces. There were numerous skirmishes with British ships (or privateers in their service) from 1808 to 1814. The Kystmilitsen were also instrumental in keeping open the 'bread route' to Norway, from Northern Jutland.

Uniforms

Although officially raised from 1801, first in 1803 some rules for uniforms were introduced, but only for officers, and they were probably not widely adopted. With the outbreak of war in 1807, things began to be taken more seriously, and in 1808 some more official uniform rules were approved. The ordinary coastal militia soldiers generally only wore the common woollen cockade, red with a white cross which was made and distributed to all the coastal militia men. Ordinary coastal militiamen wore this together with their civilian clothes, but if some had the means and wished to do so, they were also allowed to make themselves a uniform (coat or jacket) in blue cloth with one row of buttons and white collar and cuffs. A contemporary illustration shows a *kystmilits mand* in 1807 wearing a short red jacket tailless jacket, what appears to be buff leather breeches, white stockings and clogs and he has a low crowned black civilian hat. Uniforms were finally ordered, and some were even distributed. In January 1809 the clothing depot in Copenhagen was to provide 'A short Blue coat, with white collar and cuffs, a pair of blue Navy trousers, an old hat with a white plume and a pair of shoes'. This was for the 72 gunners of the coastal militia helping to serve the various different coastal batteries. This is the only known record of centrally distributed uniforms. The uniforms were obviously had a naval influence.

The ordinary coastal militia soldiers were armed with a sword or cutlass and either a boarding pike in the front rank or an old musket, a carbine or even a fowling piece in the second rank.

Officers' Uniforms

The commanding officer (*overbefalingsmand*) wore a blue uniform with a white collar, cuffs and long tails with white turnbacks. To this he added two citizen militia epaulettes, with three knots, and a yellow and green *port épée*, and as a citizen militia officer he did not wear a sash. This was the only officer allowed a bicorn hat, with gold cord and white plume. If he was also an *amtmand* (county official), which he often was, he was allowed to wear his red uniform as well.

Former regular officers (on their pension or out of regular service), serving as a *befalingsmand* (officer) in the Kystmilitsen (coastal militia), were allowed a uniform like those worn by Landeværn officers, with one row of buttons, in blue with white collar, cuffs and long tails with white turnbacks. As stated in the regulations, 'They may wear the officers model epaulettes also a sword knot and waist sash in golden yellow and red'. He wore a hat with the brim turned up on one side with a white plume held in place by a woollen red cockade with a white cross together with gold and red cords.

The other *befalingsmænd* were respected locals, landowners, nobility, ship captains and so forth, and wore a uniform in same colours, but with two rows of buttons in a more civilian-style. To this they wore the same epaulettes, and *port épée* as citizen militia officer but no sash. Their hat had a broad gold band and white plume, held by a woollen red cockade with a white cross.

Underbefalingsmænd (NCOs) had just one citizen militia epaulette, and a simple white/green *port épée*. Their hat had a gold band and white plume (later it apparently acquired a blue tip). Like the rest of the unit they also wore a woollen red cockade with a white cross.

In 1812 the epaulettes were to be removed from all coats and instead a system of lace on the collar and cuffs used instead. The officers were armed with a sabre, often of naval origin carried on a black belt and frog. The belt had both the old square buckle and the new lion's heads clasps. Some may have brought private pistols along.

11

The Danish Volunteer *Jægere*

The Kongens Livjæger Corps

This corps was initially raised in March 1801 as a supplementary 'citizens' guard' including a regimental staff and eight musicians, and only disbanded in 1870. It was the first official corps of volunteer *jægere*.

Originally they were only two companies strong, but in 1802 they were raised to four companies of 100 men each plus the officers. In 1802 they were raised to 120 men per company and were again augmented in 1809 to 135 men. They were all were recruited from the middle class citizens of Copenhagen. This unit fought during the siege of Copenhagen in 1807.

In December 1807 the Kongens Livjæger Corps was reclassified as a 'regular' unit. On 4 December 1807 the King decided that:

> As this corps on several occasions have done well, shown resolve and order, mainly during the siege of Copenhagen, have shown bravery and the will to fight as true soldiers for king and motherland and covered themselves in glory, for this I will now give a reward, but also as an encouragement for the future, by from now on this corps will now rank as a regular formation, and it will keep its rank in line, from this date on, outranking any following formed regular formation which may be raised. Also all officers (and NCOs) shall rank in line with regular officers.

The officers and NCOs where allowed to adopt the same epaulettes, sword knot and waist sash as regular officers. They were also allowed to adopt the same cockade (black) as regular soldiers, in lieu of the former green cockade, but it is not known if they did so.

Uniforms of the Kongens Livjæger Corps

Their first uniform consisted of a black hat with a green side plume and cords, cockade with a gold loop and a green double-breasted coatee with black lining, collar and cuffs and gold buttons. They wore grey breeches with green Hungarian knots and black boots. The men had a black leather ventral cartridge box.

Originally the officers appear to have had the early wide-brimmed round-topped jæger hat with both brims turned up with a green horsehair or feather *raupe* or caterpillar over the top fore and aft and a white cockade, this was worn until *c.* 1806.

In 1806/07 the uniform changed and they now had a tall *czapska*-type hat which had a black leather hexagonal crown, body, peak and ear and neck flaps and it had a green turban, green ball tuft, cockade, cords and flounders. This was later replaced with a shako.

They wore a short coatee in dark green cloth with upturned front corners. The collar, half lapels with nine small brass buttons grouped in threes, pointed cuffs, lengthwise, lining and upturned corners were black and the buttons were pewter. The coatee had six rows of black braiding beneath the half lapels.

They wore grey breeches with a black Hungarian knots and black Hungarian boots. They were equipped with a black leather cartridge box on a shoulder belt[1] and waist belt with a brass buckle, a powder horn and a *hirschfänger* M1801/03. From *c.* 1803, they were converted with a 'bayonet stud' with a green knot and a rifle.[2] The men were permitted to wear beards if they so wished. They all wore a black cravat with what appears to be a braided leather cord hanging down the front.

NCOs' Uniforms of the Kongens Livjæger Corps

The NCOs had a green cockade under the ball tuft, white cords and a gold epaulette on the right shoulder and black shoulder strap piped gold on the left. Their boots had tassels and their sabre knot was white.

The officers then adopted the *czapska*, they had gold cords and flounders and a green cockade, silver buttons on his jacket, gold epaulettes, a crimson red and golden yellow waist sash and knot, on the left a black leather cartridge box and shoulder belt from which hung a powder horn, green

---

1 This did not have a wooden block inside, but had room for three 'ball bags', spare flints, and a set of tools for the maintenance of their musket.

2 The Kongens Livjæger Corps was equipped first with the M1791 rifle without bayonet attachment, then with M1803 with bayonet attachment. The same models of rifles were used by most volunteer *jægere* also. Some had bought own rifles also.

body and cords with metal fittings. From 1801 the officers had a simple black cross belt with a simple black pouch but officially from 1810 they were allowed a special sealskin-covered pouch, it probably also had royal monogram of the new king Frederik VI like all other light infantry officers.

They had grey breeches with elaborate black Hungarian knots and Hessian boots, a sabre in a black scabbard with brass fittings and a red and gold sabre knot. They carried rifles and pistols.

Hornblæsere Uniforms of the Kongens Livjæger Corps

Each company had two crescent hornblowers *halvmåneblæsere*. From 1806 they were allowed black 'swallows' nests' with yellow lining and three yellow tassels. The Corps also employed eight French horn-blowers *waldhorn blæsere*, as musicians. The corps also had a choir and used to sing specially composed songs, both on the march and in camp and even in battle.

According to the uniform regulations of November 1806, it was specified that there were two types of 'swallows' nests' allowed. One model was for the ordinary *halvmåne blæsere* (crescent horn-blowers) who had swallows' nests with yellow knots and lace on a black ground. But the *waldhornblæserer* (French horn-blowers) had gold knots and lace, on a black ground. As musicians they also played several other types of brass instruments.

Officers' Uniforms of the Kongens Livjæger Corps

Several sources state that as the Kongens Livjæger Corps had a special status from its formation in 1801, it was allowed a lot of regular distinctions rather early. But these were first official after a number of royally approved drawings from 1806. So regarding epaulettes, until 1806 they wore the older 'militia' model 1801, with epaulettes with tassels. In 1806 they agreed to 'serve outside of Copenhagen, on all of Zeeland if needed'. As a consequence they asked to adopt new uniforms and epaulettes, and they were allowed to 'wear epaulettes of same model as the *Landeværnet*' (the standard army model 1801) as well. The is confirmed by the approved drawings. Also the standard army *port épée* is confirmed by the approved drawing. From 1807, with effect from 1808, they were also allowed to wear the regular army red and yellow model waist sash and sword knot. Several of Johannes Senn's drawings show these waist sashes worn as early as the siege of 1807.

In full dress the officers had gold edging on their *czapska*, a gold-braided green dolman with black collar, small square lapels with gold buttons and buttonhole lace, front turn-ups and pointed cuffs laced gold, green breeches and gold Hungarian knots on a black base. All the leatherwork was black piped gold. The shoulder belt had a gold shield with the royal arms, and boots had gold lace and tassels.

'Volunteer *Jæger*' Units Outside of Copenhagen

Besides the regular *jæger* and light infantry regiments, there were a number of different 'volunteer *jæger*' units. Most of them were first raised c. 1801 by local nobles, high-ranking officers or landowners, and mostly recruited from among foresters and other associated workers generally used to hunting. Normally they were dressed at the expense of the nobles who raised them, without much 'formal' organisation and with independent command structures. Most of these formations were organised as 'mounted volunteer *jægere*'.

On 21 December 1807 they were renamed 'volunteer *jægere*', and their organisation was now formalised with a regular command and organisation. The following units were raised in 1801, and re-raised in 1807:

De Ridende Herregårdsskytter fra Sjælland/ Sjællandske Ridende Jæger Corps (mounted foresters), raised 1801/formalised 21 December 1807

De Ridende Herregårdsskytter fra Fyen/Fynske Ridende Jæger Corps (mounted foresters), raised 1801/formalised 21 December 1807

De Ridende Herregårdsskytter fra Jylland/ Jydske Jæger Corps (mounted and foot), raised 1801/ formalised 21 December 1807

De Ridende Herregårdsskytter fra Sydsjælland/ Lolland og Falster/Lollandske Jæger Corps (mounted and foot) raised 1801/formalised 21 December 1807

On 28 January 1808 a general uniform rule formally set out the guide for the volunteer *jæger* uniforms, both foot and mounted. Previously 'proof uniforms' had been made which would then be sent out to each unit, and subsequently each series of uniforms would be made locally.

The following items of uniform would now be standard for a 'mounted *jæger*'. An M1808 black shako with a green plume and cords with a white rhombic shield M1804 on the front for some. A green coatee with one row of buttons (no lapels), a white waistcoat (to be fully covered by the coatee), a pair of long grey trousers and a pair of long grey riding overalls, a pair of short black cavalry boots with spurs and a grey cavalry cloak. Not clearly noted, but also a green shabraque, bordered.

The foot *jægere* were to be issued with a black M1808 shako with a green plume, but no front plate. A green coat with one row of buttons (no lapels) a white waistcoat (to be fully covered by the coatee), a pair of long grey trousers and a pair of shoes worn with short black gaiters and a grey infantry overcoat.

Danish Volunteer Foot *Jægere* 1801–1814

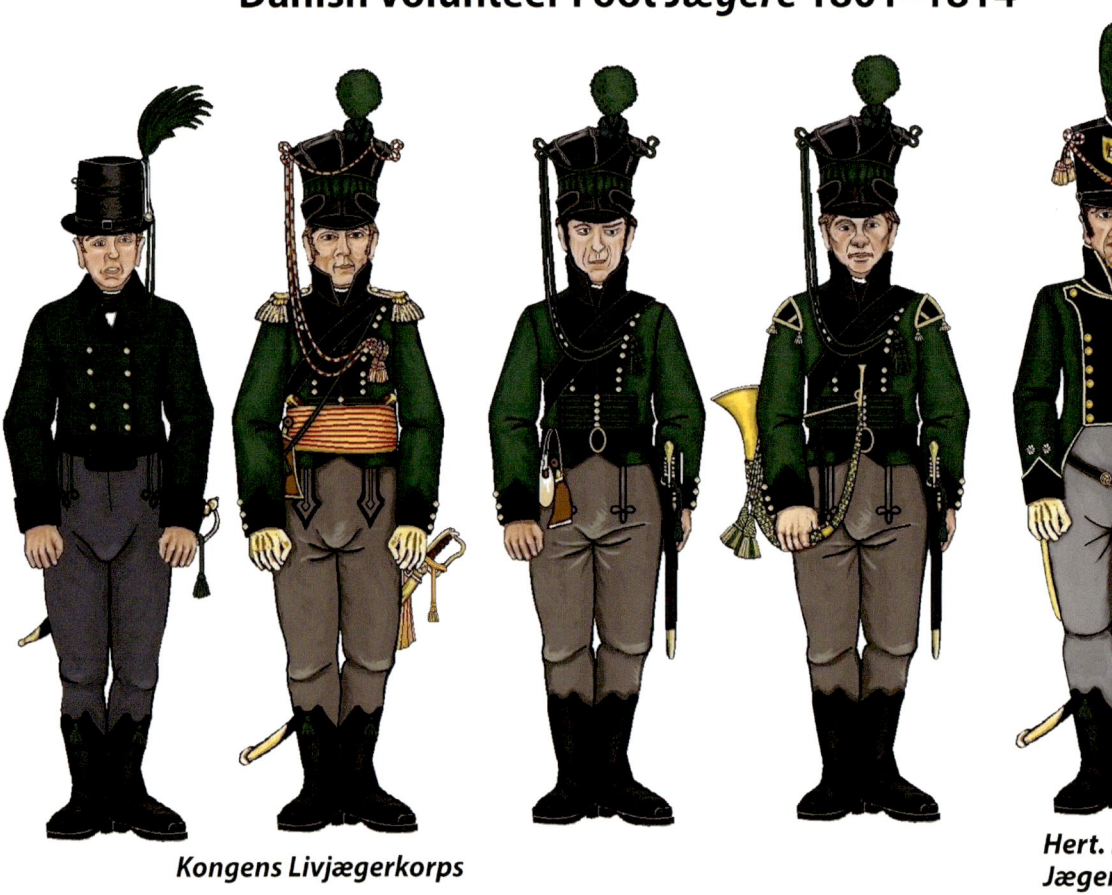

Kongens Livjægerkorps

Hert. Louise Jægerkorps

Hert. Louise Jægerkorps

Jyske Jægerkorps

Lollandske Jægerkorps

THE DANISH VOLUNTEER JÆGERE

> Facing page
>
> Plate 42. Danish Volunteer Foot *Jægere*
>
> Top row, left to right:
> 1. Kongens Livjæger Corps, *jæger c.* 1800
> 2. Kongens Livjæger Corps, officer
> 3. Kongens Livjæger Corps, *jægere*
> 4. Kongens Livjæger Corps, *halvmanblæsere* in field dress *c.* 1807
> 5. Hertuginde Louise Augustas Livjæger Corps, officer *c.* 1812
>
> Bottom row, left to right:
> 6. Hertuginde Louise Augustas Livjæger Corps, *jæger c.* 1812. He is shown with *jæger* equipment.
> 7. Jyske Jæger Corps, officer
> 8. Jyske Jæger Corps, *jæger c.* 1811
> 9. Lollanske Jæger Corps, officer
> 10. Lollanske Jæger Corps, *jæger c.* 1811

The units would be differentiated by the facings visible on their collar and cuffs, generally piped, and the colour of their buttons. Officers and NCOs used their usual distinctions adapted to the uniform.

The Volunteer Foot Jæger Corps

The Jyske Jæger Corps

Raised in 1807 and disbanded in 1814. The corps had only one company.

Uniform: *c.* 1808 they had a shako with brass chin scales, a diamond-shaped brass plate on the front, a black cockade, a green plume and green cords. The rhombic plate was unusual for foot *jægere*, being usually reserved for mounted troops, but as there was a mounted company as well it was obviously easier to produce a single model. Their single-breasted green coatee was closed by a single row of brass buttons. It had a red collar, red shoulder straps and cuffs with green cuff flaps, all piped white and white front turn-ups. Their fall-fronted breeches were grey and they had black belts and short black gaiters. Möller gives green faced red, piped white with yellow buttons.

The officers had a shako with a diamond-shaped brass plate and a green plume and gold and red cords. They wore a long-tailed single-breasted green coat with a red collar and red cuffs with green cuff flaps all piped white. They had a pair of fall-fronted white breeches and tasselled black Hessian boots. The coat had gold epaulettes with a red centre patch. Around the waist the wore a green and yellow sash (the red and yellow sashes were reserved for the regular forces only) and carried a steel-hilted hussar sabre with a red and gold knot.

Lollandske Jæger Corps

Raised in 1807 to help with patrolling the important coastline of the islands of Lolland, Falster and Møn, they were disbanded in 1814.

They had one foot company composed of a *premierelojtnant* (first lieutenant), *sekondlojtnant* (second lieutenant), *commandersergent* (sergeant major), eight *overjægere* (corporals), two *hornblæsere* (horn-blowers), and 100 *jægere* (riflemen). They also had a small staff consisting of an ADC, doctor and an armourer.

Uniform: a hat with a green plume and cords. A short double-breasted coatee made of very dark grey or black cloth with white upturned front corners; it had a green collar, shoulder straps and small round green cuffs, black or very dark grey lapels and cuff flaps, all piped white and white metal buttons. Their fall-fronted breeches were black or very dark grey and they had black belts and short black gaiters. They were armed with a *jæger* rifle and carried a M1791 *hirschfänger*. In 1810 Möller shows a green coatee with white piping and buttons with green breeches. From *c.* 1812 the men had a shako with a green plume and cords, green coatee, lapels and cuff flaps, three buttons all piped white. Green collar and cuffs piped white; the green appears to be lighter in colour.

Officer's full dress uniform 1810–1814: dark green coat, green collar and cuffs, white lining, one row of white/silver buttons, grey trousers (dark green for full dress), black bandoleer, green plume (*Hof og Stads Calender* 1810–1813).

THE DANISH ARMY OF THE NAPOLEONIC WARS VOLUME 3

Danish Mounted Volunteer *Jægere* (I)

Herregårdsskytterne c. 1807

Sjællandske Ridende Jægerkorps c. 1807

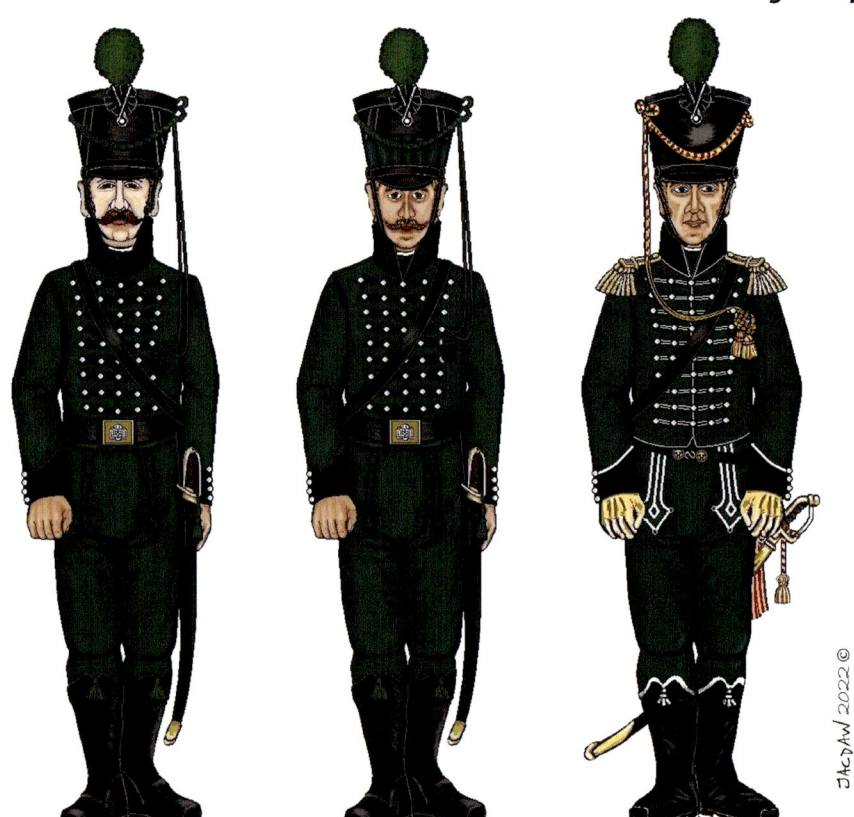

Sjællandske Ridende Jægerkorps c. 1811

> Facing page
>
> Plate 43. Danish Mounted Volunteer *Jægere* I
>
> Top row, left to right:
>
> - The Herregårdsskytterne (Mounted Foresters), shown dressed in the uniform they wore during the siege of Copenhagen in 1807
> - An officer of the Herregårdsskytterne
> - A Herregårdsskytterne soldier
> - A picture based on contemporary description of a free biracial servant, named Morgenstjerne ('Morning Star'), who served as a hornist with the Herregårdsskytterne in 1807.
> - A picture of a Herregårdsskytterne soldier from an estate close to Koege, painted *c.* 1807. We do not know if this was an official uniform, but the detachment serving with the Landeværn at Koege wore whatever uniforms they could find. They only had their own rifles, pistols and *hirschfängere*. They did not receive any arms or uniform equipment, like the Herregårdsskytterne during the siege of Copenhagen.
>
> Bottom row, left to right:
>
> - The Sjællandske Ridende Jæger Corps in December 1807. In *c.* 1811 Johannes Senn shows them wearing a completely new uniform with a light infantry/hussar-style jacket, but he shows same picture in two variations, and this first variation has the ammunition pouch worn incorrectly, over the right shoulder.
> - The other variation, shown with the ammunition pouch worn correctly and with a modified decorated shako, looking like the Danish-style *czapska*, worn by the Kongens Livjæger Corps. Again this is based on the illustration made by Senn. It is difficult to verify the details as there are so few illustrations in existence.
> - Author's reconstruction of an officer's uniform based on the portrait of Major Krogh, the company commander

Hertuginde Louise Augusta's Livjæger Corps

Raised in 1807 in honour of the Duchess Louise Augusta, the beloved sister of King Frederik VI. They were disbanded in 1816.

They had a regimental strength of three companies made up of a staff consisting of a major, ADC, doctor, armourer, and the regimental band. The companies were made up of three *captajner* (captains), three *premierelojtnanter* (first lieutenants), three *sekondlojtnanter* (second lieutenants), three *commandersergenter* (company sergeants), three *furer* (sergeants), 12 *underjægere* (corporals), six *halvmåneblæsere* (crescent horn-blowers) and 240 *jægere* (riflemen) who were divided into three companies. They also had a rather large band, some 20 musicians using brass wind instruments.

Although initially intended for the local defence of the island of Als, they were actively engaged during the campaign of 1813–14. At first they were part of the (small) 'reserve corps' formed by Field Marshal Prince Carl af Hessen, defending Schleswig and southern Jutland 1813–14. In December they were deployed to defend the different crossings of the *Eider Kanal*, and support the retreat of the Auxilær Corpset. By this time their strength was rather low with only 50–60 *jægere* to a company (the band and a guard detachment had been left behind on the island of Als, along with several sick men). One company joined during the retreat, later fighting at the battle of Sehested, losing one *jæger*.

On 9 December 1813 another detachment of half a company (one officer and 26 *jægere*) along with two 3-pdr field guns of a local defence battery of the Holstenske Artilleri Bataljon was guarding the bridge at Kluvensick just south of Sehested. They were attacked at dawn by 20 Hanoverian *jægere* and two Russo-German hussar regiments and a battery of two 6-pdr guns of the Russo-German legion.

The Danish defence was badly handled, and after losing four men wounded the force retreated north, only leaving the drawbridge of the channel pulled up. West of Sehested, the retreating Danish ran into the mobile part of three coastal batteries with 100 gunners, three 6-pdr and two 3-pdr guns, along with the battery commander with his wife and eight children in a coach trying to reach Rendsburg, guarded by 11 musketeers without any ammunition. The *jægere* formed a rearguard, as by now the enemy had managed to get the drawbridge down again, and with the enemy hussars leading they started the chase. Suddenly, out of the foggy morning light, the hussars charged and after a very short fight captured all of the Danes (helped by the battery commander crying for pardon, and ordering all to stop fighting to save his family).

This was probably the largest defeat single the Danish suffered during the campaign. In all they lost seven

Danish Mounted Volunteer *Jægere* (II)

Fynske Ridende Jægerkorps c. 1810

Jyske Ridende Jægerkorps c. 1810

Lollandske Jægerkorps, Squadron Til Hest

Langelandske Ridende Jægerkorps

> Facing page
>
> Plate 44. Danish Mounted Volunteer *Jægere* II
>
> Top row, left to right:
> - Officer *c*. 1808 (after the manuscript in the Danish Design Museum, In Rest Called KIM).
> - The Fynske Ridende Jæger Corps, *jæger c*. 1808 (after KIM)
> - The Jyske Ridende Jæger Corps, officer (after KIM and a contemporary portrait)
> - The Jyske Ridende Jæger Corps, *jæger* (after KIM) *c*. 1808
>
> Bottom row, left to right:
> - The Lollanske Ridende Jæger Corps, officer (after KIM) *c*.1808
> - The Lollanske Ridende Jæger Corps, *jæger* (after KIM) *c*. 1808
> - The Langelandske Ridende Jæger Corps, officer (after Res. nr. 85 1808, and Møller list 1810)
> - The Langelandske Ridende Jæger Corps, *jæger* (reconstruction from above) *c*. 1810

cannons, nine wagons, one man dead, four wounded and 120 men taken prisoner.

Uniforms: Around 1809 they wore a shako with a green plume and cords, and a short coatee in dark green cloth with straw yellow upturned front corners. The coatee had a black collar, lapels, shoulder straps and cuffs all piped yellow and brass buttons. They had a pair of fall-fronted grey breeches and short black gaiters. They were armed with a *jæger* rifle and probably carried an M1791 *hirschfänger*. Later they also received overcoats and straps to carry them, also *skydetasker* (special *jæger*-style knapsacks), with just one carrying strap, and in 1812 another 266 M1808 canteens.

In 1812 a new shield was approved for the shakos of the corps. We know from the text that this should be inscribed with L. I. C., but sadly the accompanying drawing is missing in the archives. However as rhombic shields were clearly only used by mounted units, the shield must have been of another form, and at this time this was probably of the same shape as the ones used by the Kongens Livcorps and Københavns Væbnings Felt Artilleri. Also Louise Augusta, the sister of Frederik VI, having her corps of troops imitating a shield of the same type as used by his corps, the *Kongens Livcorps* in his honour would seem rather natural.

Arms: In April 1808 they received 258 Hessian-style 16 *lødige*/17.5 mm *jæger* rifles (bought by Denmark, made in 1798 from the weapons factory in the German town of Suhl), together with 258 priming flasks, loose ball bags and a further 264 *hirschfängere* (six of which were for the hornists).

Colour: This corps was presented with a colour, obviously an honorary parade colour as *Jæger corps* did not carry colours and this unit was fairly dispersed, but it often paraded for the Duchess and her husband the Duke, whenever possible. It had a white field, and placed in the centre were the crowned arms of the Duchess Louise Augusta's husband, Duke Christian August of Augustenborg on a crimson and ermine mantle surrounded by a collar of the Order of the Elephant. The border was edged with a band of light blue interior and crimson exterior with a gold fringe. In each corner there was a gold crowned (red bonnet) gold monogram, on the top staff and bottom fly LA (Louise Augusta) and the bottom staff and top fly CA (Christian August). The finial was a special one which vaguely resembled a sceptre, the staff was painted crimson, the colour of the cords is unknown.

Jyske Jæger Corps

This corps was raised in 1807 to help with coastal patrolling, and the defence of the southern border. It participated in patrolling/defending Holstein in 1813, and fought bravely in the defence of the fortress Glückstadt. It had one mounted *jæger* squadron consisting of 30 to 40 *jægere* and one foot *jæger* company of 60. Staff: a *kaptain* (captain), ADC, *premiereløjtnant* (first lieutenant), *sekondløjtnant* (second lieutenant), *commandersergent* (sergeant), 11 *overjægere* (corporals), three *halvmånespillere* (hornists), 150 *jægeres* (riflemen), and a doctor and his aide.

Uniform: In 1810 these *jægere* had a shako with a black cockade, a green plume and green cords. It had a brass 'rhombic' plate, which was only used by the mounted 'squadron'. According to HS, in 1810 the officers had a black shoulder belt of the cavalry officers' model.

Following the list of abbreviations of *c*. 1813, the Jyske Jægercorps til Hest used the letters 'I. C.' and would probably also have used these letters on the shako plate shield. But according to Møller, in 1810 the uniform colours were a green coatee with a red collar, cuffs and lapels piped white, brass buttons and grey breeches.

Danish Mounted Volunteer *Jæger* Shabraques

Sjællandske Ridende Jægerkorps

Fynske Ridende Jægerkorps
Langelandske Ridende Jægerkorps

Jyske Ridende Jægerkorps

Lollandske Ridende Jægerkorps

The KIM plate shows the *jæger* wearing a single-breasted dark green coatee closed by a single row of brass buttons. It had a red collar, red shoulder straps and cuffs with green cuff flaps, all piped white and white front turn-ups. Their fall-fronted breeches were grey and they had black belts and short black gaiters. The officer had a pair of fall-fronted white breeches for full dress. The KIM plate shows the officer also had a short coatee, not a long-tailed coat.

The Mounted Volunteer Jæger Corps

De Ridende Herregårdsskytter fra Sjælland (The Forest Huntsmen), renamed the Sjællandske Ridende Jæger Corps in 1807. Disbanded 1814. This was a force of yeomanry-style volunteers from Zeeland, first raised in 1801 from men not having citizenship in a town and not obliged to serve in a citizen guard, or being peasants obliged to serve as soldiers. The corps was mainly recruited among the foresters from the large estates or from the King's forests, along with some innkeepers, millers, estate keepers and craftsmen not living in town. The corps was mounted on their own horses, but fought on foot. They supplied their own somewhat informal uniforms, but their arms were later supplied with uniforms by the state, these were the standard M1785 and M1791 rifles, both without a bayonet attachment. In 1807 the corps had 118 volunteer *jægere*. This was one of the tougher units, generally heavily engaged, in fact a lot of the credit which was later attributed to the Kongens Livjæger Corps was really theirs. In 1807, of the 118 men engaged during the siege of Copenhagen, they suffered 48 casualties. A 16-year-old boy called Hammer, who was a crack shot and became famous for wounding the British General Baring during the siege fighting, was a member of this corps. They also fought in a number of other skirmishes and some were also present at the battle of Koege.

Uniforms: Their first uniform is best described as 'civilian hunting dress', with 'military' elements. In 1807 the officers wore an old-fashioned civilian-style low gold laced black bicorn with a black Danish cockade and a gold knot at each. They had a green civilian-style three-quarter-length coat, with one row of brass buttons. It had a green collar and square cuffs with yellow flaps each with two brass buttons. The turnbacks and lining was buff yellow.

They had a pair of fall-fronted breeches and waistcoat which were buff yellow with brass buttons, yellow for others, possibly the officers and grey trousers for the rest. They had black riding boots, possibly with Hessian-style turn-downs, and spurs when mounted. Their waist belt

> Facing page
>
> Plate 45. Danish Mounted Volunteer *Jæger* Shabraques
>
> - The early model of the shabraque used by the Herregårdsskytterne is unknown, all that is known is that it would have been green.
> - In *c.* 1811 Johannes Senn depicted the Sjællandske Ridende Jæger Corps with a new shabraque.
> - The Fynske Ridende Jæger Corps shabraque *c.* 1810 is a reconstruction based on a written description. The Langelandske Ridende Jæger Corps shabraque appears to have been the same.
> - The Lollandske Ridende Jæger Corps shabraque *c.* 1810, is a reconstruction based on a written description
> - If the mounted *jaegere* had valises at all, they were probably grey, and strapped behind their saddle.

and cross belt, if worn, were made of blackened leather. The officers were armed with an officer's sabre, a pair of privately purchased pistols and possibly a rifle as well.

In 1807 the *skarpskyttere* received a new uniform consisting of an old-fashioned civilian-style low black bicorn with a black Danish cockade. They wore a long green civilian-style coat of the same cut as used by peasants and foresters, with one row of brass buttons. It had a green collar and square cuffs with yellow flaps each with two brass buttons. Their trousers and waistcoat were of civilian cut, normally grey or buff yellow. They had black Hessian-style riding boots and spurs when mounted. They had a white leather waist belt, with a belly box for their ammunition and shoulder belt. They were armed with a hussar sabre or *hirschfänger,* and either a privately purchased hunting rifle or a rifle supplied from the military stocks of Copenhagen. They would have carried a priming flask, bullet bag and bread-bag made of buff canvas. This was the official uniform, but as it was privately provided for there would probably have been a number of variations, for example the officers' uniforms coats could have two rows of buttons.

Nothing is known of the *hornblæsere* uniforms, but the reconstruction of a uniform can be based on a common livery as used by noblemen's private 'hunting buglers' *c.* 1800 in Denmark. In 1807 they wore an old-fashioned civilian-style low black tricorn with a black Danish cockade and a gold knot at each for the officers. They had a green civilian-style three-quarter-length coat with one row of brass buttons and gold laced wings. It had a green collar and square cuffs with yellow flaps. Each with two brass buttons on them. The turnbacks and lining were buff yellow. The fall-fronted breeches and waistcoat were buff yellow with brass buttons. He had long black riding boots, possibly with Hessian-style turn-downs and spurs when mounted. He carried a *waldhorn* with a green cord.

The shabraque was dark green with a black lace border piped straw yellow.

The name of one of the hornists has come down to us, a biracial man from the Danish West Indies called Morgenstjernes, in civilian life a nobleman's hunting hornist.

The Sjællandske Ridende Jæger Corps

This corps was raised late in December 1807 from the former Herregårdsskytterne. It consisted of one mounted squadron of four officers, a sergeant, 11 corporals, two horn-blowers, 150 *jægere*, a blacksmith and a surgeon.

They normally acted as the mounted squadron of the Kongens Livjæger Corps and saw themselves, and were seen by others as, an integral part of this corps due to their close relations in 1807.

Uniform: In 1808 the corps had a new uniform consisting of a shako with green cords and a green-tipped white plume, a green coatee with black cuffs, collar and lapels piped yellow with fall-fronted buff or green breeches and black Hessian-style boots in 1810 (Source: *Hof og Stads Kalender*). Möller shows dark grey fall-fronted overalls for 1810 as well, full dress and service dress perhaps. The shabraque was green with a large black dogtooth border piped straw yellow. They had buff yellow gauntlets. It is not clear whether this uniform was actually issued or was just a project, as the author has not found any other sources to confirm it.

By 1811–1812 the uniform had again changed for one which closely resembled hussar dress. It had a *czapska*-type hat or shako made of black leather had a green plume and cords like that worn by the Kongens Livjæger Corps. This uniform is confirmed, as there is a print by Senn and a portrait of the commander of the corps, Major V. Krogh *c.* 1812.

The uniform consisted of a short hussar-style coatee in dark green cloth with three rows of pewter buttons and black tape lace, with a black fur collar and cuffs. The fall-fronted breeches were green with a black lace trefoil on each thigh. Belts were black leather with a square brass buckle plate. The officers had black cloth collars piped silver and silver lacing and trefoils on the coatee. The shabraque was pale green with a large straw-coloured woollen lace border. It was piped white on the inside and red on the edge.

The waist belts were black leather with a square cavalry-style silvered or steel buckle and a shoulder belt and cavalry style cartridge pouch, also in black leather. (After Senn)

they were still armed with hunting rifles or rayed carbines, and a steel-hilted sabre carried in a steel scabbard.

In February 1808 the Sjællandske Ridende Jæger Corps received from the arsenal in Copenhagen some new weapons: namely 164 pairs of pistols, 164 sabres and 164 rifles. Here the rifles are again the M1791, as one found today is marked 'S. R. J. C 12' (rifle no. 12) and another 'S. R. J. C 66' (rifle no. 66). Again they were without bayonet attachments.

Fynske Ridende Jæger Corps
The corps was raised in 1807 with one squadron and disbanded in 1814. Strength: a *ritmester* (captain), a *premierløjtnant* (first lieutenant), a *sekondløjtnant* (second lieutenant), a *vagtmester* (sergeant), five *overjægere* (corporals), two *hornblæsere* (horn-blowers) 60 mounted *jægere* (riflemen), and a blacksmith.

In 1809, 22 *jægere* from this unit along with 54 regular *jægere* laid an ambush on the little island of Romsøe, owned by the unit's commander Hans Rudolph Juhl. Two English ships of the line had landed crews on the island and began looting all they could find, torching the houses and chopping down trees to carry the wood back with them. This was too much for von Juhl, so he planned an ambush. It went well, and he ambushed a company of between 150 to 170 British sailors, capturing the commander, two masters and 90 sailors. Around 20 seamen were left for dead or wounded and the survivors escaped back to their boats, probably some of them wounded as well. Because of the low water, the ships of the line could not bring their guns to bear and a seaborne attack was turned back by the presence of the Danish gunboats which had transported the *jægere*. The Danish only lost one man wounded.

Uniforms: From 1808 the corps had a shako with a green plume and a white metal rhomboid plate. The men wore a single-breasted tunic in green cloth with a red collar, cuffs and shoulder straps, closed by a single row of white metal buttons. They had a pair of fall-fronted grey breeches and black leather belts. Horse furniture was a green shabraque laced red.

For the Fynske Ridende Jæger Corps, no information is available, but they must also have received the M1803 rifle, without bayonet attachment (maybe as supplement to M1791), as one is today found in a collection marked 'FR 54' for Fynske Ridende Jæger Corps rifle no. 54. They would probably have received around 68 of these rifles, so this would correspond. Pistols were normally only marked with numbers, so we have no way at all of identifying the model which they used. They would, when mounted carry their rifles across the saddle or slung across the back (or front) of their body.

Langelandske Ridende Jæger Corps
Raised 1808 to strengthen the defence of the very important island of Langeland; disbanded in 1814. It had one mounted squadron. General Major Frederik Ahlefeldt-Laurwigen Greve af Langeland (Count of Langeland) was the official 'corps commander', but this was mainly an honorary title.

Originally the corps probably had around 60 *jægere*. The first known official organisation dates to 28 July 1810, when a formal organisation and list of effectives was given which gives the following strength: a *ritmester* (captain), *premierløjtnant* (first lieutenant), *sekondløjtnant* (second lieutenant), *vagtmester* (sergeant), *kvartermester* (supply sergeant), five *overjægere* (corporals) two *hornblæsere* (horn-blowers), 91 mounted *jægere* (riflemen), and a surgeon.

Uniforms: The men had a black shako with a green plume and cords. They wore a short coatee in grey cloth with upturned front corners; it had a green collar, shoulder straps, lapels and cuffs with brass buttons. They wore grey breeches and had black leather belts.

In 1808 the officers wore a rather elaborate uniform which consisted of a black shako with a dark green cordon, lanyard, badge and pompom. A dark grey coat/coatee, it had green lapels, pointed cuffs (again before the 1812 regulations) and collar with gold laced button holes with brass buttons, gold lace and epaulettes. Under the coat he had a straw yellow waistcoat with brass buttons and a black cravat. His shoulder belt was black with gold border and badge. He wore a pair of fall-fronted dark green breeches with elaborate gold Hungarian-style lacing. His foot wear consisted of a pair of black Hessian boots with gold lace border and tassels. The sword belt was made of black leather with a gilt buckle. They were armed with a hussar-style sabre, carried in a black leather scabbard with brass fittings. The sabre had a brass guard and hilt and a gold / crimson sword knot and strap.

The detail of their horse furniture is unknown, but probably it was a green shabraque edged in yellow.

Lollandske Ridende Jæger Corps
This was a small unit, raised in 1808 and disbanded in 1814. It had one company composed of a *sekondløjtnant* (second lieutenant), *vagtmester* (sergeant), three *overjægere* (corporals), a *hornblæser* (horn-blower), and 50 *jægere til hest* (mounted riflemen).

Uniform: A shako with a green plume and cords, and a short coatee made of grey cloth with white upturned front corners. It had a green collar, shoulder straps and small round green cuffs, grey lapels and cuff flaps, all piped white and white metal buttons. They wore a pair of fall-fronted breeches which were grey and they had black belts and short black gaiters. In 1810 they had a short coatee made of green cloth with white upturned front corners with a green collar, shoulder straps and small round green cuffs, all piped white and white metal buttons.

Jyske Ridende Jæger Corps
This was originally just a small unit of 30 or so *jægere*, but the request for rifles below means we can safely assume it had risen to a little over 70 officers and men by 1808. Strength: a *ritmester* (captain), a *premireløjtnant* (first lieutenant), a *vagtmester* (sergeant), five *overjægere* (corporals), two *hornblæsere* (horn-blowers), 60 *jægere* (mounted riflemen).

The corps wase raised to help with coastal patrolling and the defence of the southern border. It participated in Holstein 1813, and fought bravely in the defence of the fortress of Glückstadt.

Uniform: The uniform was similar to the Jyske Jæger Corps, green coatee with red collar and cuffs piped white, brass buttons and a pair of fall-fronted grey pantaloons or overalls.

In 1808 the Jyske Ridende Jæger Corps sent in a request to the arsenal of Rendsburg for the following weapons: 68 pairs of pistols, 68 sabres and 68 'cavalry rifles to hang from a carbine belt'. Cavalry rifles were in rather short supply, as only 400 M1791 had been made and all had already been issued for active service. But there is a clear indication that the arsenal found a technical solution for this request. The arsenal of Rendsborg was large and well equipped, with a number of fine gunsmiths attached. Apparently the corps received some of the new M1807 rifles, with the new inside *khyls* (locks).

Concerning the shako plates, there is doubt if the mounted *jægere* ever received rhombic shields for their shakos: here are none in existence, and there is no mention of them in the orders regarding the 'proof uniforms' (except that they are specified as 'cavalry shakos', which do not exclude that they had a rhombic shield of the standard 'rytter model'). There is no mention of them in the clothing regulations, and only the Jyske Ridende Jæger Corps are mentioned as wearing a 'yellow rhombic shield' in the *Hof og Stads Calender*. Also remember they were mostly very small companies. So this mostly points to only the Jyske Ridende Jæger Corps actually having them. They were made of yellow metal and probably stamped with the letters J. C. But as Voigt does show them in his proposed uniforms it is possible they did have them.

12

The Defence of Bornholm, Including Colours and Standards

(All the information here was kindly supplied by Jørgen Koefoed Larsen, who hails from the island of Bornholm and is the leading authority on the uniforms worn on the island).

The island of Bornholm is in a somewhat unique position, being so close to the Swedish shore and being fairly isolated in the Baltic from the rest of the kingdom. In 1614 King Christian IV decreed that 'The Island is to have its own Militia, to be served by the islanders themselves'. From the 1650s they had had a large of number of militia units covering all arms, of infantry, dragoons, artillery and coastal troops; in fact nearly every male on the island served in one militia unit or another.

Following a Swedish invasion they were strengthened in 1659, after the exiled Islanders, had on their own initiative attacked and liberated the island from the Swedish occupiers. From then on, they maintained a unique defence system, right up until 1868.[1]

During the Napoleonic Wars, with this system, together with some reinforcements of regular troops from mainland Denmark, they defended their island and the fortress of Christiansø for the Danish crown, fighting an effective war with long boats against passing British merchant ships, taking many prizes (in the real Viking spirit). Although the island had a population of only 10,000, it was said that everybody was armed, at least all the men.

The naval commander George Albrecht Koefoed, a hero of the battle of Copenhagen in 1801, had been born in Bornholm, and he was sent as commander to the island in 1807, but unfortunately, he died of a heart attack in 1808.

He was replaced by Commander Carl Adolph Rothe (1808–1816), another hero of Copenhagen and also a naval officer, once he had recovered from his wounds received in both in 1801 and 1807. He had lost an arm at the naval battle of Sjællands Odde against the British in 1808. He was a very capable and a much-respected officer, admired as much by the troops as by the population of Bornholm.

In 1803 and until 1808, the 'Bornholm Militia' had the following strength:

A Headquarters Staff
Two Nationale companies of dragoons
Four Nationale companies of infantry

There was one Nationale company of artillery, which was divided into two units, with one half of the company serving the 44 3-pdr M1687/59 regimental guns and the other half serving in the coastal batteries. Seven companies of town militia mostly manned the 121 guns in the coastal batteries. They were aided by four *herreds* companies, who also served in the coastal batteries. These latter were a form of *Landwehr* mostly composed of those who were too old or with some physical defect to serve elsewhere.

In all there were some 5,400 men. But this was only the theoretical full strength, for many of those enlisted were either too old, too young, too weak or were unable to serve for other health reasons. Their effective strength was probably closer to 4,000 men.

In 1808 up until 1813 the garrison was regularly strengthened and reinforced. All the troops were now commanded by the *guvernør*, assisted by a staff of 26 regular army officers. From 1806 the Nationale dragoons were augmented to four squadrons with 519 men, now more or less a complete regiment. There was one foot *jægere* company composed of 229 men and four companies of Nationale infantry, totalling 1,127 men (each company also had a platoon of *jægere* from the aforementioned *jægere* company attached to them) giving each company a fighting strength of 330 men.

---

1 The organisation of the military system of Bornholm (*Bornholms Milice*) was in many ways parallel to the Norwegian system of the same period, as both systems were based on a small core of professional officers and *geworbne* (enlisted) soldiers, with a large part-time Nationale (conscript) main force, only fully active in times of war. They were supported by the Landeværn (on Bornholm they were called *herreds kompagnier*), and the *borger kompanierne* (town militias).

By 1808 there were two companies of Nationale field artillery, with some 624 men responsible for 45 M1687/59 3-pdr regimental guns divided into 11 half batteries in four-gun divisions. Some of these artillerymen still also continued to serve in the coastal batteries.

The seven *borger* (town) militia companies had 670 men available for active duty, again serving the 141 guns placed in 41 coastal batteries. The four *herred*s (reserve) companies with 793 men on active duty also served in the coastal batteries.

The garrison was further reinforced with the grenadier company from the 1st battalion of the 3rd Jyske Regiment (152 men) and four musketeer companies from the 2nd battalion of the Dronningens Livregiment (458 men). Some further changes were made in 1806 when the possibility of war with France arose, and a number of surgeons were sent to the island to care for the sick and eventually the wounded.

Uniform

Due to their geographical position some distance from Copenhagen, at the start of the war the military personnel were still wearing uniforms of the style of the previous century including many 'hand-me-downs', including colours and arms. But due to their strategic importance they were eventually brought up to the same standard as the rest of the regular army.

The Bornholm Nationale *Dragoner*

The Bornholmske Dragoner Regiment were dragoons in the true sense of the word and were expected to move mounted, but to dismount and fight on foot, and so they continued to have drummers until around 1807 when they were replaced with trumpeters, so one may imagine that their mission had changed slightly as well. As in the infantry on Bornholm, only the ranks of *vagtmester* (sergeant) and corporal were used.

Uniforms

In 1789 the two dragoon companies had a black bicorn with a black cockade a white loop and plume. They wore a single-breasted dark blue tailed coat based on the M1785 model with a red collar, turnbacks, cuffs and cuff flaps. It had off white turnbacks, pewter or white metal buttons and straw yellow piping on collar and cuff flaps. They wore a straw yellow waistcoat and buff breeches with tall cavalry boots and white socks. By 1805 they had cut down their boots down in size to resemble the Hessian style.

In around 1805–1806 their bicorns were replaced with M1803 hats and they were authorised to use the same rhombic hat plate as the regular *ryttere*, made of yellow brass, but stamped with 'BD', for Bornholmske Dragoner, under a crown. It had a white plume with white cords and tassels.

About the same time they received a new M1796/1803 single-breasted dark blue coatee with a red collar and cuffs, blue cuff flaps, all piped white and white turnbacks.

In turn this was replaced in 1808 with a new uniform. They now received black shakos and appear to have kept their white plumes and did not adopt the black plumes with a red top as in the proposed uniform designs. The shako had a white metal scale chinstrap. Their uniform now consisted of dark blue coatee with a red collar, lapels and cuffs, blue cuff flaps, with straw yellow piping and white turnbacks. The buttons were pewter. Their fall-fronted trousers were now dark blue and were worn with short square topped boots of the specific Bornholm model. According to a contemporary 1808 water colour they also had a pair of dark blue overalls which had red piping and pewter buttons down the outside leg. They kept their buff yellow breeches for full dress.

In 1802 their cloak was red, rolled and carried behind the saddle. This was probably replaced with a grey cloak by 1808. The original saddle cloth was of the old square model of the previous century with separate pistol holster covers, which were red with a broad white woollen lace border. This was replaced in 1808 with a red and white shabraque, and if we do not know the exact model it was probably the same as the Prins Frederik Ferdinands Dragoner. An existing model dated 1819 confirms this model.

Arms and Equipment

They were armed with an M1785 *pallask*, a M1767 dragoon musket and a pair of M1772 pistols or a pair of older pistols, model unknown. Their waist belt, carbine belt and cartridge box belts were in whitened leather until 1809 and then replaced with black leather. The rather large cartridge box was made of blackened leather and a bayonet was carried on their waist belt.

Officers

In 1803 the dragoon officers wore a black bicorn with a black cockade, a silver loop and silver button; the bicorn also had gold tassels. Their uniform consisted of a dark blue long-tailed coat with a red collar, cuffs and lapels, piped yellow with red lining. They wore a pair of fall-fronted buff yellow breeches and wore Hessian-style black boots edged with silver lace and tassel. They were to use the same silver epaulettes, waist sash and sword knot as regular army officers.

Between 1805/1806 the officers received the M1803 hats to replace their bicorns and they were also authorised to wear the same rhombic plate as the other ranks with a white plume on the side with a black cockade and gold and red cords and tasselled flounders. In 1808 they replaced the hats with shakos, but they kept the same plume, rhombic plate and cords. The shako had a white metal scale chinstrap.

The officers had the same model saddle cloth of the old square model of the previous century with separate pistol

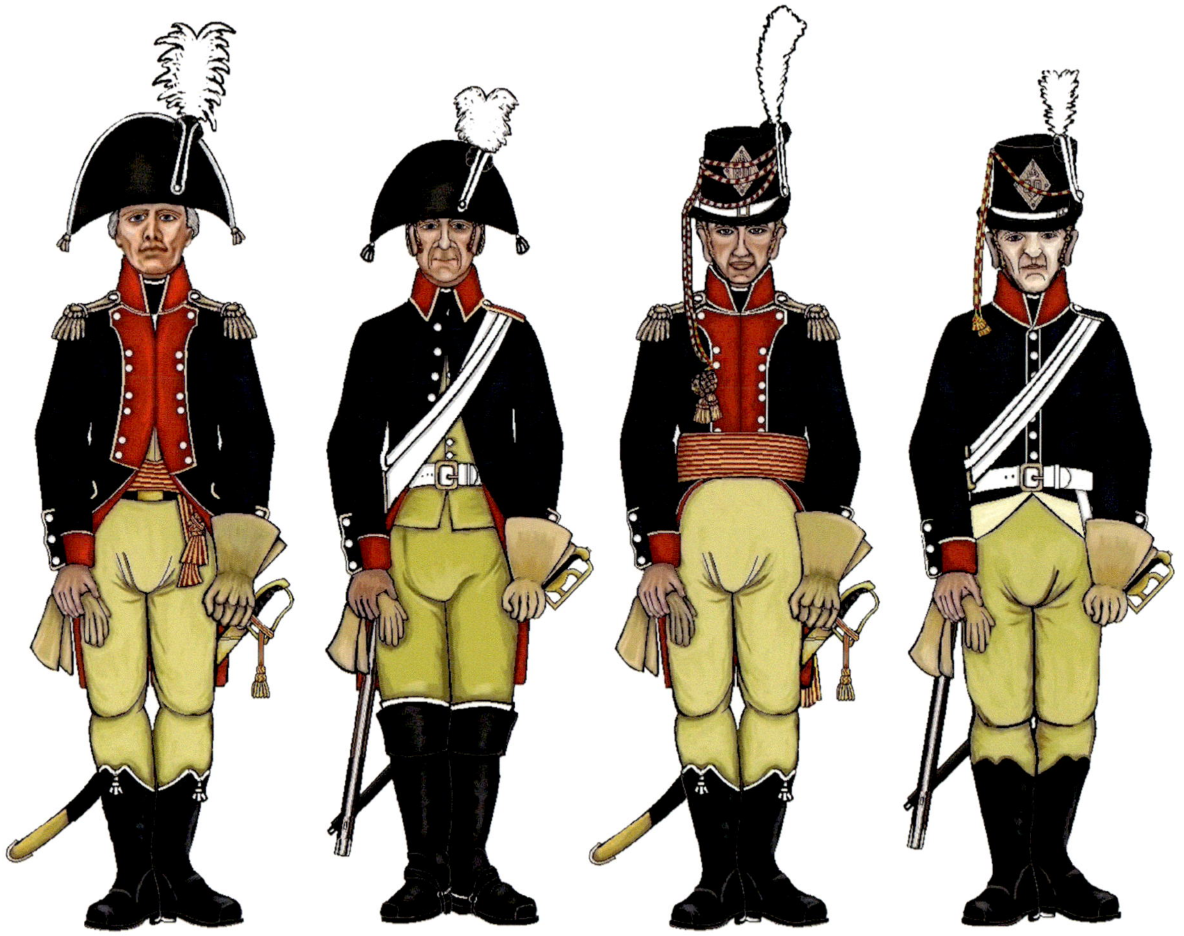

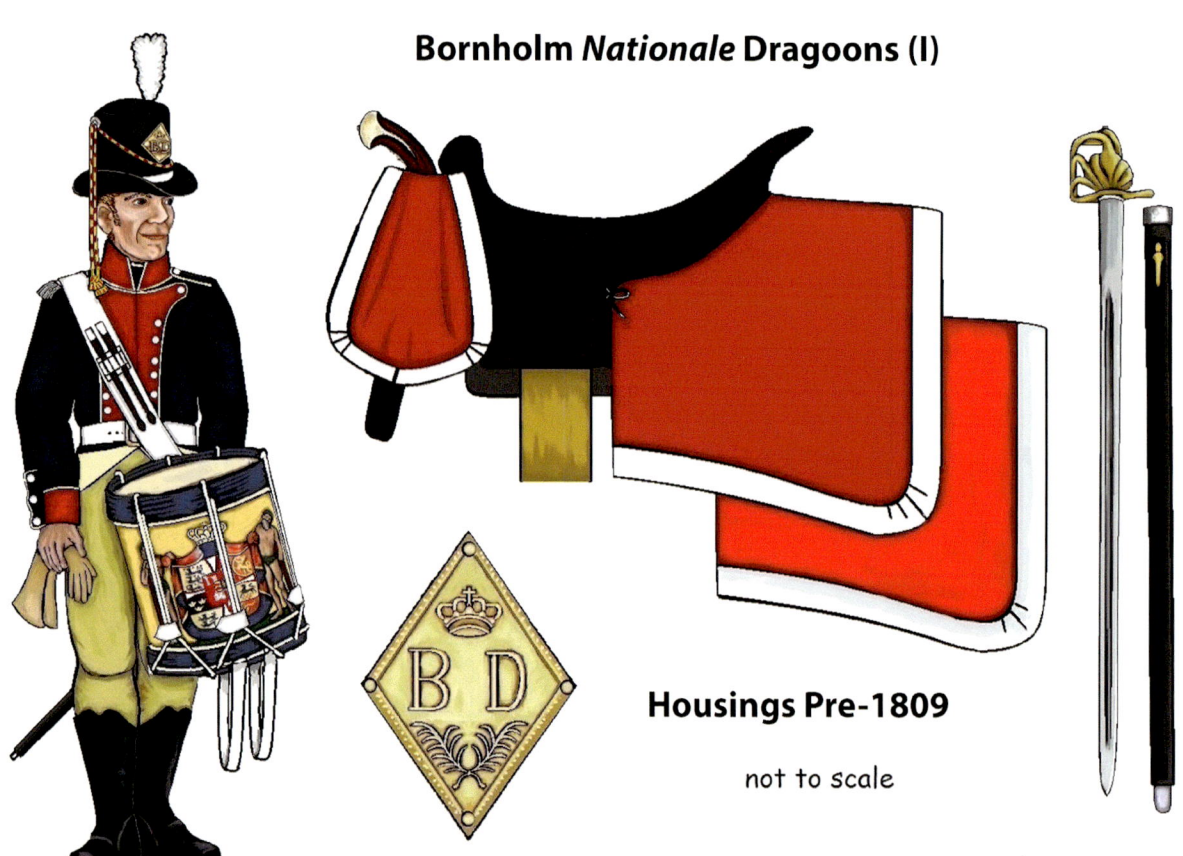

Bornholm *Nationale* Dragoons (I)

B D
Housings Pre-1809
not to scale
JACDAW 2022©

> Facing page
>
> Plate 46. Bornholm Nationale Dragoons I
>
> Top row, from left to right:
> - Dragoon officer *c.* 1803 wearing the M1796 uniform with M1801 epaulettes
> - Dragoon trooper wearing the M1785 uniform in 1803 carrying a M1740 dragoon *pallask*
> - Dragoon officer wearing new hat with rhombic hat plate *c.* 1806
> - Dragoon trooper wearing the single-breasted M1796/1803 coatee and hat with rhombic plate, carrying a M1740 dragoon *pallask*
>
> Bottom row, from left to right:
> - Dragoon drummer wearing the lapelled M796/1803 coatee. The illustration of the drum is drawn from an existing model now restored and conserved in the Military Museum of Bornholm.
> - The special Bornholm model hat plate stamped with BD (Bornholm Dragoons), confirmed by original M1804 plates conserved in the Museum of Bornholm
> - M1785 housings; trooper's red with white lace, and behind it an officer's housing made with brighter better quality guard's red cloth and a silver lace border, possibly with additional silver lace decoration.
> - M1740 dragoon *pallask*

holster covers, but theirs was in guard's red with a broad silver lace border. As for the dragoons they received new shabraques in 1808 of the same model as the Prins Frederik Ferdinands Dragoner. They were armed with a light cavalry sabre, normally the officer's sabre M1789 or a privately bought variation and a pair of pistols, also frequently privately acquired.

NCOs

The NCOs wore dark blue lapelled coatees and were they allowed to have their lapels piped yellow, and they had a fringed epaulette. The rest of the uniform was like that of the dragoons.

Drummers and Trumpeters

The dragoons used drums until 1807–1809 when they received eight trumpets, two for each company. Their hat had a white plume and white cords, and they were later received for the trumpeters as well. The drummers wore same dark blue coatees as the NCOs but without the epaulettes, but the rest of the uniform was like that of the dragoons. The drummers only acquired swallows' nests after 1810.

An original wooden drum case was found on the island in the 1970s, unfortunately in a very poor condition. The details of the discoveries made during the restoration are as follows. The drums, of the older wooden dragoon model, were much longer than the usual contemporary models, being some 60 cm high and painted pale (straw) yellow. In the centre were the crowned royal arms on a red mantle with wild men supporters. The rims were painted blue for the reign of Christian VII and later they would have been repainted red for Frederik VI.

Following a series of reforms a new uniform was prescribed for issue in 1808. For the trumpeters this new uniform consisted of a shako with the same attributes as before and a coatee with red swallows' nests with white lace and tassels. The rest of the uniform was as the NCOs. In 1812 the officers, NCOs and trumpeters uniforms would have been modified to conform to the new regulations for rank insignia. The officers and NCOs would have lost their epaulettes and the officers their sashes.

Between 1807 and 1812 several ships arrived with different stores to help equip the militia. Amongst the stores delivered were some blue M1800 fall-fronted cavalry overalls (although these may have been given to the *jægere*), M1808 shakos and a few trumpets, but although the exact date of the transition from drums to trumpets is unclear, 1809 would seem logical.

Horses

Until 1809 horse colours were not regulated, so horses of any colour from white/greys to piebald were pressed into service.

Standards

The standards carried by the dragoons were in fact standards from the Jyske Land Kyrasserer 1710–1720, and so bore the arms of Jutland, a fact not at all appreciated by all the islanders. The dragoons had two standards and from 1808, when they were enlarged to four squadrons, they were used as regimental standards and were now only carried on parades, when all four companies were reunited for the occasion. They were carried until 1818.

Bornholm *Nationale* Dragoons (II)

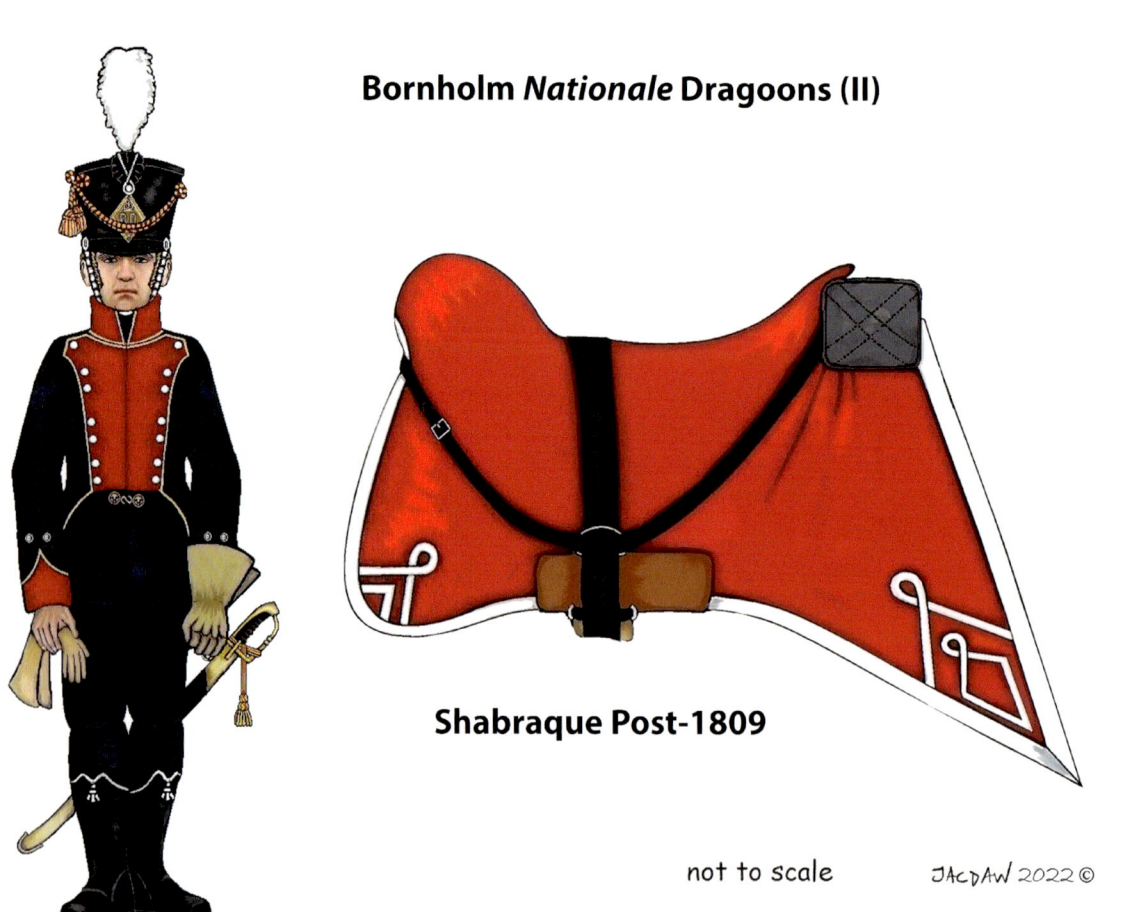

Shabraque Post-1809

> Facing page
>
> Plate 47. Bornholm Nationale Dragoons II
>
> Top row, from left to right:
> - Dragoon officer in uniform M1809 *c.* 1811
> - Trooper in uniform M1809 *c.* 1811
> - Trumpeter in new uniform M1809 *c.* 1811
> - Dragoon NCO in uniform M1809 with new rank distinctions post 1812, carrying an M1785 dragoon *pallask* which probably had been received as a new sidearm around this time
>
> Bottom row, left to right:
> - Dragoon officer in service dress, with new rank distinctions post 1812
> - Trooper's shabraque, as used from 1809 onwards. This year the dragoons received from Copenhagen 500 new saddles, 500 new *valdrapper* and 500 blue cavalry overalls.
> - Note: In full dress the officer would have worn yellow buff breeches.

The Bornholmske National Infanteri

The uniforms usually followed the same styles as on the continent, but as is the case for Norway, it was usually issued one to two uniform terms late, some three to six years at least. So when they were allowed to adopt the M1789/1801 uniform it was in a style unique to Bornholm.

In 1772 a suggestion was made that the whole Danish army should wear *halvstøvler* (half-length boots) for footwear, but this was only done with a few units. But in a description from 1805 of the organisation and uniforms on Bornholm, we know that the latest commander in chief, Colonel Ammon, had seen to it that this ordnance was applied on Bornholm and in 1805 all the infantry and gunners wore this type of footwear. Unfortunately none have survived (probably they were used as winter footwear by the population until they fell to pieces), but the official approval for the artillery has a drawing showing us that it was a plain short and probably quite practical black boot, reaching up to middle of the calf. It was cut straight at top, instead of the more elaborate 'V' cut in the later models.

All new reforms were always promptly applied on Bornholm, so from 1809/1810 a new uniform was prescribed following the reforms of 1808 in Denmark. The new uniforms and organisation were introduced after a resolution of 14 April 1809. So by 1810 the shako and new style of uniform were in general use by all Nationale *kompagnier*. Grey trousers and black short gaiters were never used on Bornholm by the Nationale *kompagnier*.

Infantry Uniforms

This comprised an M1789 hat with a white plume, hat band and loop with a black cockade and pewter button. Their uniform from 1802 was a single-breasted blue coatee with a white collar, cuffs and frontal turnbacks with blue cuff flaps (three buttons), all piped red with pewter or white metal buttons. The coat front had a line of red piping either side of the single row of pewter buttons. They had white shoulder straps piped red with a pewter button. Their trousers were white, and they wore short square-topped black boots. The cut of the uniform was the same as that adopted by the *Landeværnet*.

The new uniform of 1809 consisted of a shako with a white plume, a black cockade with a white loop and pewter button and red and yellow cords. They now had a standard double-breasted blue coatee with a red collar, lapels, cuffs and cuff flaps, all piped white, pewter or white metal buttons. The front turnbacks were red. They had a pair of dark blue fall-fronted breeches, and again they all wore short square-topped black leather boots. Möller confirms this uniform and gives blue with red collar and cuffs with blue breeches.

Arms and Equipment

Belts and bandoleers were white with a black leather cartridge box. They were armed with a M1774 musket with bayonet.

Officers

The officers had a black bicorn with a black cockade, silver loop and button with a white plume. They wore a standard dark blue long-tailed double-breasted coat with a white collar, lapels, lining, cuffs and blue cuff flaps (three buttons) all piped red with silver metal buttons. Their waistcoat was white, and their fall-fronted breeches were light buff yellow. Their boots were black. From 1801 they were authorised to use the same epaulettes, sword knot and waist sash as regular army officers. The officers had short Hessian boots edged with silver lace and tassel. From *c.* 1805 they were authorised to wear hats in place of their bicorn. Colonel Ammon notes that the new hat (M1789) was in general use

THE DANISH ARMY OF THE NAPOLEONIC WARS VOLUME 3

Bornholm *Nationale* Infantry

THE DEFENCE OF BORNHOLM, INCLUDING COLOURS AND STANDARDS

Facing page

Plate 48. Bornholm Nationale Infanteri

Top row, from left to right:

- An infantry officer before 1803, as from this year the waist sashes were to be worn over the coat
- An NCO in the new M1799 uniform. NCOs were allowed lapels on their uniforms
- A drummer also in the new uniform M1799. Considered to rank alongside an NCO, his uniform reflects this but without NCO distinctions. They did not have swallows' nests at this time. He carries a painted wooden drum.
- A private wearing the M1799 uniform, worn from 1801 until 1810. Note the resemblance in several details to the later uniform of the Landeværn, Samsøes Milits and others

Bottom row, left to right:

- A musketeer infantry officer in the new uniform M1809, worn from c. 1810–1811
- A musketeer private in the new service dress worn from c. 1810
- A *jæger* officer
- *Jæger* in the new service dress worn from c. 1810

- Note: In full dress the officers would have worn buff yellow breeches. The officers' and NCOs' uniforms would have been modified with the new rank distinctions post 1812. This uniform is confirmed by an original officer's coat c. 1815, conserved in the Museum of Bornholm.
- General notes to the new M1809 uniforms: They were introduced by a resolution on 14 April 1809, and we have found a drawing of their general appearance in the Danish Dress Museum's manuscript, and also have a general description in Møller's list 1810. The drummers and hornists wore the same uniform as the men in their company, but by now with swallows' nests, red with white tape for the musketeer companies and black with white tape for the *jægere*. By now the drummers would have received the standard brass infantry drum with red hoops.

by the infantry by 1804–1806 and some may have adopted the more modern M1803, but probably only by the officers and NCOs.

The new uniform of 1809 consisted of a shako with a white plume, a black cockade with a white loop and pewter button and red and yellow cords. They now had a standard double-breasted blue tailed coat with a red collar, lapels, lining, cuffs and blue cuff flaps (three buttons), all piped white, with pewter or white metal buttons. With this they had a pair of dark blue fall-fronted breeches.

In 1812 the uniforms were modified with the new rank insignia with pointed cuffs and the officers were to cease wearing the waist sash and epaulettes. They were armed with a light sabre normally an officer's M1789, or a privately bought variation, carried in a black leather scabbard with brass fittings and chape.

NCOs

The NCOs wore a dark blue double-breasted coatee with a white collar, lapels, lining, cuffs and blue cuff flaps (three buttons) all piped red with pewter metal buttons. Their trousers were white, and they wore short square-topped black boots. They had a silver NCO epaulette sewn on their right shoulder and a white shoulder strap piped red on their left shoulder. The sergeants had a short, fringed epaulette and the corporals had a simple double cord *dragon*. The new uniform of 1809 consisted of a shako with a white plume, a black cockade with a white loop and pewter button and red and yellow cords. They now had a standard double-breasted blue coatee with a red collar, lapels, cuffs and blue cuff flaps (three buttons), all piped white, pewter or white metal buttons. The front turnbacks were red. With this they had a pair of dark blue fall-fronted breeches. They all wore short square-topped black leather boots. In 1812 the uniforms were modified with the new rank insignia with pointed cuffs and the officers were to cease wearing the waist sash and epaulettes. Only the ranks of sergeant and corporal were used on Bornholm. They were armed the same as the men but with the addition of an M1753 infantry sabre.

Drummers

On Bornholm, only painted wooden drums were used until 1807–1809. All the infantry had one drummer for each company. In 1808 they received four M1753 brass drums with the red rims, as used in the reign of Frederik VI. The drum case was normally polished, so the brass shined bright.

From 1801 until 1809 the drummers wore the same uniform as the NCOs, but without distinctions or swallows'

159

Bornholm Militia

Herredskompagnier (Home Guard Companies)

Borgervæbningen (Town Militias)

Facing page

Plate 49. Bornholm Militia

Top row, from left to right:

- Herredskompanier (Home Guard), NCO from 1st Søndre (Southern) company; red collar and cuffs.
- Officer from 2nd Øster (Eastern) company; yellow collar and cuffs.
- Drummer from 3rd Vestre (Western) company; green collar and cuffs.
- Soldier/militiaman from 4th Nørre (Northern) company; orange collar and cuffs. They are shown in regulation dress, but there was a fair amount of variation in headwear. They could also wear long civilian waistcoats and breeches, which again could also be replaced with trousers.

Bottom row, left to right:

- Bogervæbningen (town militias), had a common uniform for all seven companies, approved in 1803. This is the officer's uniform. It had a bicorn with two gold tassels, and with the *port épée* M1801 of the citizen militia, the only official sign of their officer status.
- NCOs wore basically same uniform as officers, but without tassels to their bicorn and no *port épée*
- Town militiaman in the M1803 uniform, with hat and cross belt
- Officer with new model hat, feather with red top, and blue trousers as allowed from 1809. If they wanted, they were also allowed to privately purchase and wear the shako M1808.

nests. This was a standard single-breasted blue coatee with a white collar, cuffs and cuff flaps (three buttons), off white turnbacks piped red, pewter or white metal buttons, blue lining and white breeches. They all wore short square-topped black leather boots.

The new uniform of 1809 consisted of a shako with a white plume, a black cockade with a white loop and pewter button and red and yellow cords. They now had a standard double-breasted blue coatee with a red collar, lapels, cuffs and cuff flaps (three buttons), all piped white, pewter or white metal buttons with the addition of red swallows' wings piped white on each shoulder. The front turnbacks were red. With this outfit they wore a pair of dark blue fall-fronted breeches.

The Bornholmske Jæger Companie

Their original uniform is unknown; probably a hat with a green plume and a green single-breasted coatee with a black collar and cuffs. By 1809 they wore a shako with a green plume and cords, and they wore a standard dark blue coatee with a black collar, lapels, shoulder straps and cuffs, all piped white with dark blue cuff flaps (three buttons) and black turnbacks, pewter or white metal buttons, dark blue lining and a pair of fall-fronted dark blue breeches. They all wore short square topped black leather boots.

Arms and Equipment

They were armed with a *jæger* rifle M1791/03 and carried a *jæger hirschfänger* M1801 modified for use as a bayonet. They had black belts, cross belts and cartridge box. They also carried a powder horn and shot bag.

Officers

In 1809 they wore a shako with a green plume and gold and red cords, and they had a double-breasted tailed dark blue coat with a black collar, lapels, shoulder straps and cuffs, dark blue cuff flaps (three buttons), all piped white, off white turnbacks, pewter or white metal buttons, dark blue lining and a pair of fall-fronted dark blue breeches. The officers had short Hessian boots edged with black lace and a green tassel. From 1809 they were authorised to use the same epaulettes, sword knot and waist sash as regular army officers. In 1812 the uniforms were modified with the new rank insignia with pointed cuffs and the officers were to cease wearing the waist sash and epaulettes.

Hornists

Their early uniform is unknown. From 1809 they had a standard double-breasted blue coatee with a black collar, lapels, front turnbacks, cuffs and dark blue cuff flaps (three buttons), all piped white, pewter or white metal buttons with the addition of black swallows' nest wings piped white on each shoulder. They had a pair of dark blue fall-fronted trousers, and they all wore short square-topped black leather boots. There were five *halvmåne* (crescent horns) shipped to Bornholm between 1807 and 1809. So they had five hornists *halvmåneblæsere* as musicians, the best of which was called the *stabs halvmåneblæser* (staff hornist) who followed the company commander wherever he went. As a sidearm they carried an M1801 *jæger hirschfänger*.

Militia Uniforms

The 'Herreds' Bönder Compagnier (Home Guard)

Bornholmske *Nationale Artilleri* Companies 1802–1814

THE DEFENCE OF BORNHOLM, INCLUDING COLOURS AND STANDARDS

> Facing page
>
> Plate 50. Bornholm Volunteer/Militia Artillery
>
> Top row:
> - Officer *c.* 1802 wearing a bicorn, replaced with a hat *c.* 1804
> - NCO wearing regular M1802 uniform
> - Militia gunner 1802–1808. This rather outdated uniform was eventually replaced by the uniforms shown below.
>
> Bottom row:
> - Gunner *c.* 1804 in hat and new M1802 coatee
> - Gunner *c.* 1809 in shako and new M1809 coatee *c.* 1809
> - NCO in shako and M1809 uniform and M1802 sabre
> - The officers and NCOs wore the regular artillery uniforms.

Although these companies had a prescribed uniform it was probably in part civilian dress, so except for coats, the rest of uniform would be very different from person to person, even among the officers, due to both poverty and lack of materials.

There were four companies and each of the companies had different coloured facings. Their basic uniform was a long-tailed double-breasted bluish grey coat. The lapels were the same colour as the coat and the lining was light faded red (pinkish), and the facing colour was shown on their collar and boot cuffs. The buttons were made of pewter or white metal.

The 1st or Øster Herreds (Eastern shire) Companie had a red collar and cuffs.

The 2nd or Søndre Herreds (Southern shire) Companie had a yellow collar and cuffs.

The 3rd or Vestre Herreds (Western shire) Companie had an orange collar and cuffs.

The 4th or Nørre Herreds (Northern shire) Companie had a green collar and cuffs.

Uniforms

For headwear the ordinary soldiers used a mixture of styles, mainly simple unadorned tricorns, but also hats and other types of headwear were seen.[2] The privates wore a long-tailed double-breasted bluish grey coat, without lapels and the lining was light faded red (pinkish). The facing colour was shown on their collars and boot cuffs and the buttons were made of pewter or white metal. Their waistcoats were civilian models, so were quite varied and sometimes they wore more than one. The ordinary soldier was supposed to wear white breeches or trousers, but the colour would vary from buff yellow, blue or light grey. Their footwear could also vary from shoes to clogs or short boots.

Arms and Equipment

Their arms were equally disparate, generally an old musket M1748, without bayonet (also older models were used, as well as fowling pieces). Their sidearm was a *musketerkårde* (straight infantry sword) M1748 and some older models carried on a black or buff leather belt. They had an old black cartridge box on a black or buff leather bandoleer.

Officers and NCOs

The officers had unlaced black tricorn or bicorn hats, but were allowed to use unadorned shakos from 1810. Their uniform was a long-tailed double-breasted lapelled greyish blue coat, the lapels were the same colour as the coat and the lining was red. Their pockets, with three buttons, were piped in the lining colour. The facing colours were shown on their collar and boot cuffs and their buttons were made of silvered pewter or white metal. Their only distinction was a green and yellow sword knot. All the officers had privately acquired sabres normally based on the M1789 model or similar.

The NCOs had unlaced black tricorn or bicorn hats, but were also allowed to use unadorned shakos from 1810. Their uniform was a long-tailed double-breasted lapelled bluish iron-grey coat, the lapels were the same colour as the coat and the lining was red. Their pockets, with three buttons, were piped in the lining colour. The facing colour was shown on their collar and boot cuffs and the buttons were made of pewter or white metal. They carried a M1748 musket with a bayonet and they carried an M1748 musketeer's sword, the *musketerkårde,* on a black leather belt over their shoulder.

They were supposed to wear a white waistcoat, but again civilian garments would predominate. They wore trousers or more often old knee-length breeches in yellow,

---

2 *En Københavns Grosserers Ungdoms Erindringer* is the diary of a young artillery officer, in which he wrote that the ship he arrived in at Bornholm had a load of the new M1808 shakos, which shortly after were in use by the militia.

blue, white or even grey cloth. Their footwear could vary from black leather shoes to black turn down boots, which was preferred.

Drummers
The drummers wore the same uniform as the NCOs but their pockets were not laced, and they had no other distinctions.

The Bornholmske Borgervæbning 1803–1816
The town of Rønne had seven *borger* (burgher) companies; the 1st Rønne Borger Companie, the 2nd Rønne Borger Compani, the Hasle Borger Companie, the Allinge-Sandvig Borger Companie, the Svaneke Borger Companie, the Nexø Borger Companie and the Aakirkeby Borger Companie, each of which was permitted to have their own colour, which they paid for themselves, and they were all different.

Uniforms
The men wore M1789 hats with a white cockade, but without a plume. Their uniform consisted of a single-breasted medium brown long-tailed coat with a red collar and small round cuffs with pewter buttons. They had a double-breasted buff yellow waistcoat and a pair of fall-fronted buff breeches, white stockings and square-topped short black boots.

Arms and Equipment
Their arms were somewhat varied, mainly old M1748 muskets, together with private muskets and even some hunting rifles. Some may also have carried an old M1748 *musketerkårde* or even older swords, as a sidearm. They had a buff leather bandoleer and a black cartridge box.

Officers
The officers wore a bicorn with a black cockade and loop and gold tassels. The officers wore a similar uniform as the men but with the following differences; their coat was double breasted and lined brown and their red collar, small round red cuffs and leading edges were piped straw yellow. They wore short black boots. Hats were only officially sanctioned from *c.* 1806. In 1809 they were authorised to wear a red-tipped white plume. Those who could afford to buy them were allowed to wear the M1808 shako.

The officers had no epaulettes or any distinctions other than a yellow and green sword knot, but in 1806 several company commanders were allowed to adopt regular army epaulettes and sash, because of 'the responsibilities of their job'. Their uniform was slightly modified around 1809 and they were allowed to wear fall-fronted dark blue trousers for field service.

In 1810 Møller describes their uniform as a brown coat with red collar and cuffs, with white/straw yellow piping and brass buttons. The coat had red turnbacks and inside lining. Their waistcoat and trousers were yellow, but with blue trousers for field service. They had short black Hessian boots and an M1802 hat, probably later replaced with a shako, with a red-topped white plume. All the officers had privately acquired sabres; some also probably armed themselves with a pair of civilian or naval belt pistols.

NCOs
Between 1801 and 1814 the NCOs were allowed to wear the same uniform as officers, but with some differences; their bicorn did not have the gold knots and they carried a sabre without a knot on a black leather waist belt. They do not appear to have carried muskets.

Drummers
The uniforms are unknown, but were probably the same as the NCOs but without distinctions. They had wooden drums. An original drum has been conserved in Bornholm. It belonged to the citizen militia of the main town of Bornholm, Rønne. It bears the official arms of the town, 'three silver blue herrings on a white field, (now faded beige in colour) under a crown and a border decorated with a red mantle and a pair of helms'. The rest appears to be straw yellow. The rims are painted red, which shows us that they were still used after 1808, when Frederik VI became king. The rims would have been painted blue during the reign of Christian VII. This tells us that the other company's drums would probably also have born their civic arms.

The arms of the town of Halse were 'a cross botonny *argent* on a blue field'.

The arms of the town of Aakirkeby are based on the oldest known seal of the town from 1584. The arms show 'St John in a red robe holding his golden cup with a green snake on a white field'.

The arms of Nexø are based on the oldest known seal of the town, also from 1584, but the design might possibly be older. The symbol is unidentified but is officially described as a 'blue boat hook on a white field'.

The arms of the town of Svaneke are also based on the oldest known arms of the city from 1584. The arms are '*Gules*; a swan argent holding a golden ring in its beak' as *Svaneke* means the 'bay of swans'.

The Bornholmske Artilleri
The gunners were called *håndlangere* (gun handlers) until 1809.

Uniforms
The gunners adopted a uniform based on the 1789 model in about 1795, but in their case, it was pointed out 'That as they are among the poorest on the Islands, they are to be allowed to make their uniforms out of any cloth available, as long as it is blue', with a plain red collar and cuffs with pewter or white metal buttons. They were allowed to wear a pair of old fall-fronted knee-length trousers or any other

type of civilian trousers, generally of a dark colour and black boots. There were even some old pre-1789 uniforms including dark blue tailed coats with red facings which were pressed into service. They wore old bicorns, which had a white plume with a blue top.

By 1804 they now wore some M1789 hats which had a white plume and a blue top, a white hat band and yellow loop with a black cockade and brass button.

Their uniform from 1802 was a single-breasted blue coatee with a red collar, cuffs and frontal turnbacks with blue cuff flaps (three buttons), all piped red with a single row of brass metal buttons. They had a red shoulder strap with a brass button on the left shoulder. Their trousers were very dark blue or black and they wore short square-topped black boots. In 1809 shakos started to replace the hats, and it had a white plume topped blue and yellow and red cords. Otherwise the uniform remained the same until the end of the war, only the coatee became a little shorter and the trousers had a higher waist.

Arms and Equipment

Until 1802 they all carried muskets, but as in the rest of army, they were returned to stores and the only side arms carried was the M1756 infantry sabre on a white leather belt. There were also a few M1754 sabres in use as well.

Officers

The artillery officers were all regulars and as a consequence, they all wore the standard artillery uniforms of a crimson red double-breasted tailed coat with a blue collar, lapels and cuffs, brass or gilded buttons, crimson red cuff flap (three buttons) and blue lining. They wore a pair of dark blue fall-fronted breeches, and they wore black Hessian boots. They used the standard epaulettes, sword knot and waist sash of regular army officers. Initially they wore a bicorn with a blue-tipped white plume with a black cockade and a gold loop, button and tassels. Although not mentioned, this was probably replaced with an M1802 hat with a blue-tipped white plume with a black cockade, a gold loop and button and gold and red cords by 1806. From 1809 the hats were replaced with shakos which also had a blue over white plume with a black cockade and a gold loop and button and gold and red cords and tassels. In 1812 the uniforms were modified with the new rank insignia, with pointed cuffs and the officers were to cease wearing the waist sash and epaulettes. They carried the standard officer's sabre already described.

NCOs

The NCOs were enlisted men (from Denmark), and as a consequence, they all wore (and received) the standard artillery uniforms. This consisted of an M1789 black hat with a blue-tipped white feather, yellow loop with a brass button and a white hat band. They wore a red double-breasted coatee with a blue collar, lapels, front turnbacks and cuffs, red cuff flaps (three buttons) and blue lining with brass buttons. They had a yellow/gold NCOs epaulette sown on their right shoulder and a simple red shoulder strap on their left shoulder. Their fall-fronted gaiter trousers were dark blue.

In 1812 the uniforms were probably modified with the new rank distinctions and pointed cuffs, and they lost their epaulettes.

In 1809 the artillery was enlarged and divided into two companies. They were now allowed to be called *underkonstabler*, the title of the regular artillery gunners. They were also issued with a pair of fall-fronted long blue trousers and a shako with a blue-tipped white feather. The artillery companies do not appear to have had any musicians.

Arms

Until *c.* 1805 they were armed with *faskinekniv for artilleriunderofficerer* M1777 after which they were rearmed with the *artilleri sabel* M1802.

Artillery Pieces

The basic piece of field artillery used on Bornholm were the 88 old regimental cannons of 16 calibre 3-pdr M1687/1748/57 System Harboe which had been used until 1800.[3] Then the best of the remaining guns (45) were shipped to the isle of Bornholm for use by the militia. The remainder were put in store, and some were later reused by the Landeværn artillery in 1807 and by some other militias later.

All the different models appear to have been used on Bornholm. They were basically all the same except for the decoration on the barrel. Frederichsværk were notorious in the first years of its production for repeatedly changing small details of the decoration on the barrel on each series of castings, which often irritated the artillery board, as they were not always kept informed!

Before these pieces were shipped to Bornholm, a new elevating device was mounted on them. Each gun had a two-horse limber and a two-wheel ammunition cart attached, with two drivers. Note that originally, they had

---

3 In a casting period of only four years (between 1757 and 1761) they made at least five different versions of the monogram and other details. In the Swedish army museum they have a number of these guns, mostly captured in the fortress Glückstadt in 1813, and from their archives one can find the five different versions, but there may have been more that we are unaware of. The first of these has Arabic numbers, but from 1759 they began a new casting run, and they were now numbered with Roman numbers beginning with number one (I). The earlier models had the reversed double cypher of Frederik V while the later models had a simpler cypher. Most of the earlier models were shipped to Norway, but they were also sent some of the later models as well.

Danish 3-pdr 16 Calibre M1687/1748/1757 System *Harboe* Field Gun

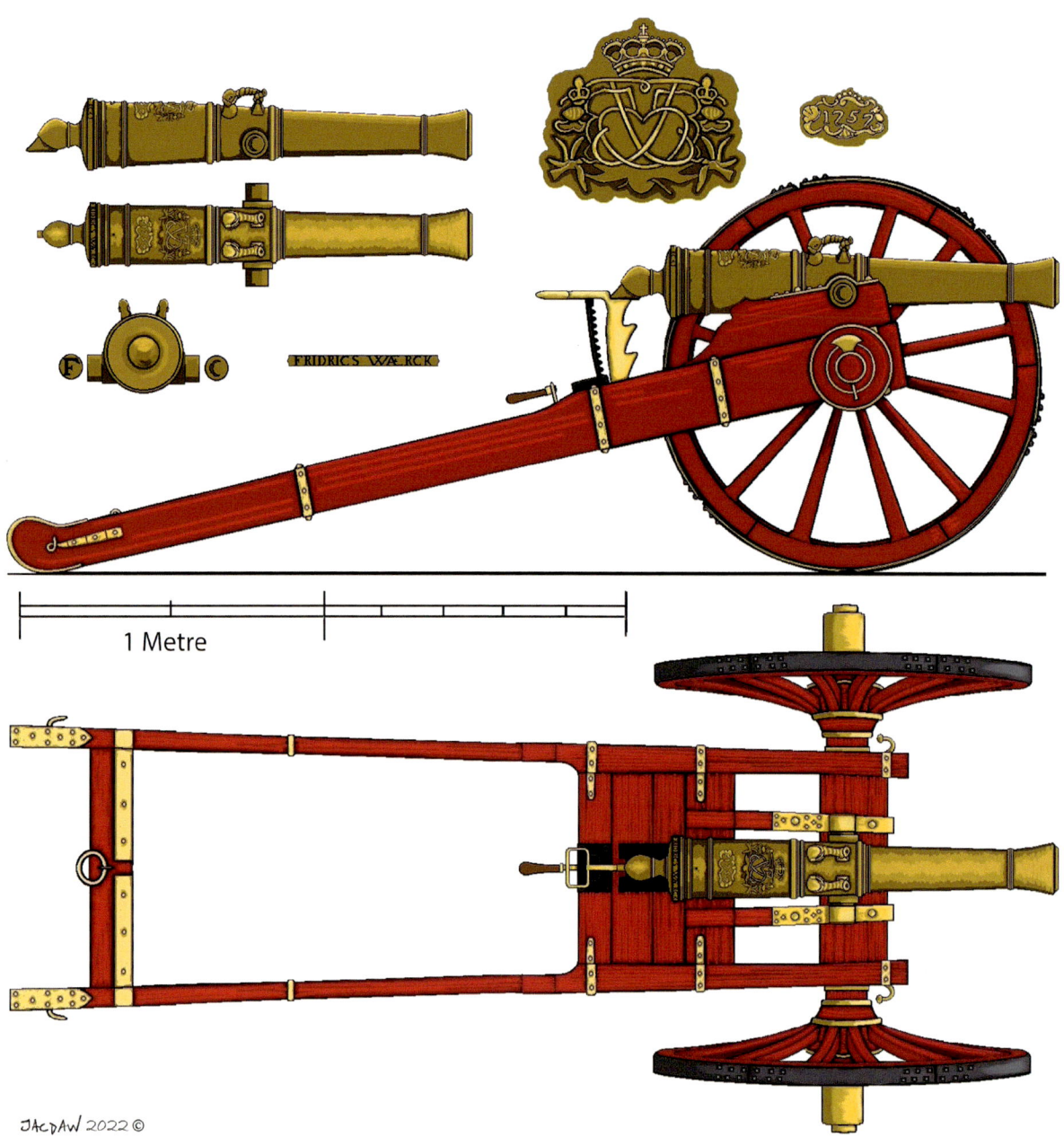

Plate 51. 3-pdr 16 calibre M1687/1748/1757 *Harboe* System Field Gun

The 3-pdr M1687/1756 field gun, which had previously been used by the Danish regimental artillery, had since been withdrawn and replaced with a more recent model. In around 1800 some 45 of these pieces were transferred to Bornholm for use by their artillery companies, and the last ones were only taken out of service as late as in 1868. One gun barrel dated to 1759 is preserved in the collection of the Defence Museum of Bornholm.

Before they were shipped to Bornholm, a new elevating device was mounted on them. Each gun had a two-horse limber and a two-wheel ammunition cart attached, with two drivers. Originally they had been pulled with a horse between the shafts, but as this was found to be unstable a trail transom and a towing ring were added, and a simple limber used for towing the piece.

At top left is the earlier model of the Frederik V cypher breech decoration, and on the right the later model with the simpler cypher.

been towed with a horse between the shafts, but as this was found to be unstable, they added a traverse and towing ring and used a simple limber for towing the piece.

On the island of Bornholm the largest coastal pieces were 12-pdr and 18-pdr iron pieces, of which only the last model was mounted on four-wheeled truck carriages which were placed on pintle-mounted wheeled casemate ramps. The rest of the coastal guns used a slightly smaller gun carriage with four large same-size wheels, and without a sledge, but instead they stood directly on a stone floor or a wooden floor of heavy beams, often at an angle, so the gun could roll back after firing. (See *The Danish Army of the Napoleonic Wars 1801–1814, Organisation, Uniforms and Equipment Volume 2: Cavalry and Artillery*, David A. Wilson).

The Colours and Standards used on Bornholm (by Jørgen Koefoed Larsen)

Until the middle of the 1700s, troops on Bornholm mainly had to do with old, captured colours or disused Danish colours, in the same way as did some Norwegian part time Nationale regiments at the same time. But in Copenhagen nobody had much interest in these colours and standards, and nobody wrote anything down regarding their history when they were put into storage. When the idea of creating a military museum on Bornholm was raised and the Tøjhusmuseet was contacted, the town militia colours were found, and as these colours were named, they clearly had a connection with Bornholm. But the dragoon, infantry and *herreds* company colours could not be found as they had not been properly catalogued. Thankfully, thanks to a lot of research and hard work by Jørgen Koefoed Larsen they have now been found and identified as the colours used on Bornholm between 1720 and 1820.

The Bornholmske Nationale Dragoons

They carried two standards as company colours and when they were expanded to four companies they were designated as regimental standards. These were in fact the old standards of the Jyske Land Kyrrasserer Regiment c. 1710, which they had received in 1722. The standards were of crimson red damask with a silver fringe and embroidery within the centre the silver crowned arms of Jyske, which were on a field or, a lion *azure* over nine hearts *gules*, supported by two golden lions. In the centre of the crown there was the double mirror monogram of Frederik IV in silver. The text was in gold thread.

The text on the first standard, embroidered on both sides was, at the top TAPPER OG RETFÆRDIG WÆRE ('Brave and Righteous to Be'), and at the bottom: GIFVER SEYER OG FØER TIL ÆRE ('Will Give Victory and Lead to Honour You See').

The text on the second standard was, (top) FOR DANNERKONGEN GOED ('For Our Good King'), and bottom JEG WOFVER LIF OG BLOED ('I will give my life and Blood').

The standards were the same on both sides, but note that the lion on the coat of arms always looked towards the staff. The dimensions are unknown, but they were probably around 60 cm square. The gilt finial was the Frederik style; it showed his cypher, doubled in mirror image. The cords and tassels were probably gold, or gold and red.

The Krigsmuseet has conserved three standards previously used by Jydske Land Kyrraserer between 1710 and 1722. This was a Nationale regiment raised for service in the Great Northern War, after which they were then disbanded, and their standards put into store. Most were lost to time and age, but one (the white 'life standard') was preserved in the arsenal of Rensburg and was shipped with all other stores to Tøjhusmuseet after the Schleswig-Holstein rebellion in 1848–51. The Tøjhusmuseet already had at that time two red standards of the same model in their collection for which they have no information.

In fact what they had were the two standards used on Bornholm between 1722–1820, where they can be found in the register of the arsenal of Rønne, where they were stored when they were not in use. In 1818 the dragoons were to receive four new standards and the two old ones, together with all the other old remaining colours of the infantry, those of the *herreds* companies and those of the town militias were to be returned to Copenhagen, which happened in 1819–1827, and where they were stored.

Nationale *Infanteri* Company Colours

Contrary to what some authors have affirmed, not all of the companies carried a colour, as the Bornholmske Nationale Infanteri only received two. This was according to the rules from 1785 which called for one colour for each two infantry companies, and this also applied to the Bornholmske Nationale infantry. There was one white and one red colour, with the Dannebrog in the top hoist, in the top centre the crowned arms of Bornholm, *gules* a dragon *or*, with a wreath, a light blue ribbon with the order of the elephant over an elaborate trophy of arms in natural colours, above which there was a light grey/white scroll bearing the device of Christian VI DEO ET POPULO ('For god and the People') in gold lettering. They were carried up until 1818. The island of Bornholm's official arms is officially (at least today) a golden dragon, but originally it was a Lindorm, on blue field, but in those days all the small islands were given a golden dragon on red field by the central government (that is, the island of Fyen, who continue to use these arms to the present day). It was then the colour of the field which showed from which part of Denmark they were from (Fyen traditionally had green colours until 1785).

As Christian VI ruled from 1730 to 1746 the colour must have been made and shipped to the Isle of Bornholm

Bornholmske Nationale Dragoner/Dragoon Standards and Infantry Colours

not to scale

THE DEFENCE OF BORNHOLM, INCLUDING COLOURS AND STANDARDS

> Facing page
>
> Plate 52. Bornholmske Nationale Dragoner, Dragoon Standards and Infantry Colours
>
> - These two standards were issued to the Bornholm Dragoons c. 1722 and again were recycled standards. They were originally made for the Jyskeland Kyrasserer Regiment in 1709 and these two standards were carried until 1818. A white colonel's standard also exists, but it was never issued to Bornholm. They were already nearly 100 years old by 1800–1814 so were already quite faded.
> - These standards were embroidered onto a crimson damask cloth, but have been shown on a simple crimson field for clarity. The obverse and reverse were identical.
> - The Nationale infantry colour, of which there were two, one in the first *liv* (life) companies and one in the 4th company. They were carried until 1818. They had been shipped to Bornholm c. 1790 following the reforms of colours carried out in 1785, but were originally from the former Bornholmske Geworbne Infanteri Regiment (1741–1785), a mainly German enlisted infantry regiment stationed in North Jutland, so except for its name it had no other connection with Bornholm. The obverse and reverse were identical.
> - Inset: a finial from the time of Christian VI of Denmark

after his death, probably after the general colours reform in 1785.

This flag had previously been identified as the colour of the enlisted Bornholmske Geworbne Regiment. This unit had no relationship to Bornholm at all (the regiment had been recruited mainly from Germans), and served for most of its existence in garrison in Jutland. It was formed from the former 'marine regiment' in 1741 and existed until 1785, when it changed its name to Det Aalborgske Regiment. Its last two colours, made in 1769, were taken into store in 1785 when that regiment was disbanded, and then shipped to Norway in 1788 together with another set from c. 1747, where all four are conserved.

It has been suggested that the four colours used on Bornholm could have been the colours originally made in 1741 for the Bornholmske Geworbne Regiment, and then shipped to Bornholm when they received new ones in 1769, but this is highly unlikely. First of all these Bornholm colours don't resemble those of any other contemporary line infantry regiment and they do not have the royal cyphers in the corners of the colour as all line regimental colours would have had.

They were carried up until 1827 when they received new colours. The arms on the new colours were also changed to the new arms of Denmark. Only part of one (probably the by then best preserved), is shown in the Danish *Fanebogen*.

The *Herreds* Companies

Each of the four the *herreds* companies also had old square red colours. The remains of these colours are so scarce that they are difficult to identify, but they may originally also stem from the beginning of the 1700s, but some of the details that have survived also point towards 1730–1746. They had a white Maltese Cross (*Dannebrog*) in the corner, and in the centre was the double mirror royal monogram of Frederik IV within a wreath of green oak leaves over which there was a motto and underneath the name of the company.

There is simply too little left of the original to be sure of looks and text. In 1800 they were probably 60–80 years old, and so already faded and strongly worn. Experts believe the colour was originally red, but not how deep a shade. But again in 1800–1814 it would also have faded, and be worn and torn. The facts imply that the flag was the property of the company, so were probably stored by the company commander, and not in the arsenal.

It is highly probable that these colours were in fact the old colours of the Nationale infantry companies, used until the colour reform after 1785.

The *Borger Compani*

Until 1778 the town militias, the Bornholmske Børgervæbning, had apparently used old colours which had probably been captured in Holstein-Gottorp in 1714 and then shipped to the isle of Bornholm together with the dragoon standards around 1720.

In 1728 the two companies in Rønne probably had two new rectangular colours made locally, paid for by the unit. This was followed in 1772, with another new privately financed colour made for the Nexø Borger Companie (Neksø town militia).

The 1st Rønne Borger Companie (Rønne town militia), probably not to be outdone by the new colour of *Nexø*, in 1779 they also had a new more elaborate colour made paid for by the members privately.

The colour made for the 1st Rønne Borger Companie was rectangular, not square, and the other companies were then allowed to make their own colours, but they were also paid for privately by the individual members of the companies. Soon after Svaneke (1785), Hasle (1787) and finally Allinge (1791) bought and designed by themselves new locally made rectangular colours. The partial remains

Bornholmske Borger and *Herreds Company* Colours

not to scale

THE DEFENCE OF BORNHOLM, INCLUDING COLOURS AND STANDARDS

> Facing page
>
> Plate 53. Bornholmske Borger and *Herreds* Company Colours
>
> Top: The colour of the 1st Rønne Borger Companie, made in 1777 for the 1st Company of the Rønne town militia. Each of the seven companies had their own flag, which were all different in colour and design. They were made specially for and paid for by the company. See main body of the text for full details.
>
> Bottom: Reconstruction made from the remains of a colour from one of the *herreds* companies. The original was probably red or deep crimson, with the crowned cypher 'FIV' in mirror image within a floral wreath. There were a number of inscriptions painted on the colour, and underneath the cypher was the name of the company, now illegible. Either side of the crown the partial surviving text probably reads '… Kongen tro' ('Faithful to the King') and '…reds Companie'. It is possible that these colours originally belonged to the Nationale infantry companies. As Frederik IV of Denmark died in 1730 this was already a very old colour in 1800, at least 70 years old, so obviously already faded and worn.
>
> Inset: a finial of Christian VI of Denmark.

of five are known today and a fragment of an unknown colour is possibly the sixth. Only the small company in Aakirkeby is known to have not made a new colour, but it is known that in 1742 the Commandant asked for 'an old colour to be sent from Copenhagen for their use, as they only had the flagpole left of its previous colour'. This unknown old colour was probably used until after 1820, when it was returned to Copenhagen, and so was lost in the arsenal.

As noted above, each of the seven companies had a colour, which had been paid for by the company and they were all described as being different, but to what extent is not clear. The only more or less complete one that has survived is that of the 1st Rønne Borger Companie which was made in 1777. It has a red field with a blue scroll with the gold text GUD KONGEN LANDET TROE, VI VORES FANE SVINGE BREED HIMMEL OVEROS DIN VARETÆGTES VINGE ('God king and country, faithfully we wave our flag with care in the sky over you') on two lines over the gold crowned double cypher of Christian VII on a pair of crossed swords. The cypher was flanked on the left with a blue shield with a bishop above the arms of Rønne, and on the right a blue shield with the text *Forferdiget Paa Compagniets Bekostning Anno 1777* ('completed at the company's cost 1777') painted in gold. On the base of the colour there was another blue scroll with the text RÖNNE BORGERSKABS FORSTE COMPAGNIE ('Rönne First Citizens Company') again painted in gold. The reverse and obverse were identical. The flags appear to have been rectangular and longer in the fly.

The finial was a gilt spearhead with the crowed double cypher of Christian VII cut out, and the staff was painted red. It had two sets of cords, the standard red and gold cords and tassels and a second short crimson red cord with a fringed tassel.

The few indications we have of the others is some fragments of the 2nd Rønne Borger Kompani which had a beige/straw yellow field with a Dannebrog (white cross lined red, not on the traditional red square). It appears to have had the same central device as the 1st company, a gold-crowned double cypher of Christian VII on a pair of crossed swords under a now illegible inscription.

The other survivor, preserved in the Bornholm's Forsvars Museum (BFM) is one which belonged to the Nexø Borger Companie. This colour is more or less complete but heavily faded and torn. It has a red field within the centre a crowned gold double cypher of Christian VII on a red shield surrounded by a trophy of arms over a large dark blue scroll with illegible text. In the top fly corner is a crowned shield with the town's arms all within a wreath.

The Garrison of Christiansø

There was also the island fortress of Christiansø some 18 kilometres to the north-east of Bornholm with its sister islands of Græsholm and Frederiksø, which were also fortified. The fortress was originally built in 1684, as part of the outer defences of Bornholm, and there were another 520 men with 107 guns garrisoned there.

The garrison rose to 811 men serving the 114 guns and mortars (including one 'regular' company from the regiments on Bornholm and 200 militia men, the youngest able and unmarried men from Bornholm, took turns by rotation to help defend the fortress).

In 1808 the fortress was bombarded by British warships and the garrison replied and they managed to inflict a lot of damage to the British ships. The garrison suffered only seven dead and ten wounded. Following this attack the defences of Christiansø were significantly reinforced. The giant ramparts, bastions and powder magazines that give Christiansø much of its distinctive appearance today were all built during this time. Thousands of tons of rocks were needed to expand the fortress, and the archipelago of Ertholmene was extensively quarried for the necessary stone.

The basic garrison of Christiansø was composed of three elements. Firstly there were the regular garrison troops, secondly an invalid company and lastly the local population, including fishermen, seamen and any other able-bodied male, not including the company of regular troops.

In 1807 there were 446 people living at the fortress, not just soldiers, gunners and petty officers, but also seamen, fishermen, their women, children, pensioners and a sizeable number of alms persons. Alms persons and pensioners were often former employees or widows of soldiers who were allowed to continue living there.

The commander in chief of the garrison was generally a naval officer sent from Copenhagen and was always known as 'the Commander' and for most of the war it was Johan Henrik August von Kohl, a native of Christiansø, who was a naval officer and something of a local hero.

He had two uniforms, a double-breasted scarlet red coat with dark blue facings gold lace and buttons. The coat bore gold epaulettes up until 1812 when they were abolished with the new rank distinctions. This was the official uniform of the commander.

His service dress was a naval uniform, and he was the only one of the fortress personnel who was allowed to wear this uniform, which showed that he had authority over naval personnel/naval officers visiting the island fortress as well as the soldiers. In consisted of a black bicorn which had a black cockade and a gold loop. It had gold tassels. His double-breasted coat was dark blue with red cuffs and collar his breeches were white, worn with black Hessian style boots.

The fortress company was a *geworbne* (enlisted) force, which in 1808 had a strength of one officer, a sergeant, three corporals, a fifer, a drummer and 34 soldiers.

The Fortress Infantry Uniform 1808
They fortress infantry had a black hat, with a white plume, hat band and cords. Their coatee was red with a black collar and cuffs and it had brass buttons, together with a dark blue waistcoat, black neck stock, blue or white trousers and black short gaiters.

The Fortress Artillery Uniform 1808
There was a small artillery detachment of one *overkannoner* (sergeant), four *underkannonere* (corporals) and eight *konstabler* (gunners). They had a black hat, with a white plume, hat band and cords. Their coatee was red with dark blue facings, collar and cuffs. It had brass buttons. It was worn with a dark blue waistcoat, black neck stock, blue or white trousers and black short gaiters.

The *overkomplet* or 'extra' soldiers of the garrison troops were former old or handicapped soldiers, now helping and doing different jobs on the island (there were 18 of them in 1808). Their uniform was a simple blue jacket, simple blue or white trousers and a simple black hat.

The naval personnel naturally wore naval uniforms. These were a black hat and a dark blue coatee with red cuffs and collar, and their trousers were white, worn with black shoes. In 1810 they manned their four gunboats, called the *Svaneke*, *Allinge*, *Rønne* and *Gudhjem* (named after the towns of Bornholm). These were giant rowing boats armed with single cannon on the bow.

In 1809, Christiansø saw a major mutiny by 200 enlisted soldiers from the Marine Regiment. The mutineers stabbed the Commander with a bayonet (he survived), arrested the officers and took over control of Christiansø. After several days of chaos, drunkenness, violence and killing, the mutiny ended with the rebels fleeing to Sweden on a couple of boats.

13

The Citizen or Town Militias (I)

The *Borgervæbninger* of Denmark and Norway, and of Copenhagen

The majority of these citizen militias never actually fought, except for those in and around Copenhagen during the siege of 1807, and some of the coast militia units. These units were quite numerous with differing strengths, depending on the size or importance of the town concerned.

Most were referred to as *borgervæbning*, literally 'armed citizens'. Although many groups of society were not eligible for military service, because of their status or trade (mainly those found in towns) it was still expected that they should 'do their bit'. Normally, service was part of the obligations of citizenship and was regulated by the government, but it was not a very rigid organisation, and in fact in peacetime, many a citizen militia was more of a kind of social club rather than a tough service unit.

When the war suddenly erupted in 1807, the grim reality soon made itself felt and now they were really needed. The English blockade and raids against shipping and coastal towns together with the war with Sweden in 1808–1809 forced them into action, generally with good results, but a lack of training and arms limited their efficacy if not their enthusiasm and this influenced what it was possible to do, and the presence of regular forces was often necessary. In some few known instances (the father of the famous writer H. C. Andersen), some few were paid by wealthy peasant families to take the place of their enlisted sons, and volunteer for the field army. Some though did enlist for service in a number of volunteer units.

As nearly all the citizen militias were found in coastal towns and cities, their main official role would be manning coastal fortifications and city defences. In reality they were used more as a police force and watch force, thereby freeing regular soldiers to serve in the field armies. This was their major contribution to the war, principally hunting spies and smugglers and general law enforcement.

In some towns the bourgeois citizens raised small, mounted citizen guards of honour (only 10 to 20 men for some of the mounted ones) which were funded and raised by the most influential and wealthy citizens. Their principal service before the war was to escort the king and other dignitaries when they visited the towns and possibly performed some service towards crowd control. As they had been formed from among the upper classes, they often wore splendid uniforms, but most had little real military training or the will to do anything else other than defend their hometown if necessary.

As already noted above some local defence organisations had been in existence since the seventeenth and eighteenth centuries, but the first formal structure was only created in 1801–1802 and centralised under the crown prince and at same time the uniforms were regulated. The citizen militia was to be formed the following way, occasionally divided into two wards or *avdelinger* based on social standing.

The 1st Avdeling: Here all the bourgeois citizens were to serve (merchants, shop-owners and craftsmen and their sons). They were allowed to supply their own uniforms, but only after agreement with the king. With the king being far away in Copenhagen, the interpretation of this agreement could be flexible.

Often within these social groups a small *friviligt jæger corps* was raised, normally found among the youngest men. The best fighting formations were found here and was often perceived as a kind of elite formation, but generally they were still inferior to regular formations. Their weapons were partly supplied by the state, the rest privately bought. They served (sporadically) in peacetime as a local police force. In wartime they had to guard and garrison the local defences in a system of rotation. They were not expected to serve outside their own towns and cities.

Danish Militia Units of Copenhagen

THE CITIZEN OR TOWN MILITIAS (I)

> Facing page
>
> Plate 54. Danish Militia Units of Copenhagen
>
> Top row, left to right:
>
> Københavns Borgervæbning infantry officer and private *c.* 1807; the gunners had the same uniform minus the epaulette. Private in uniform *c.* 1810.
>
> Københavns Borgervæbning Artilleri NCO and officer *c.* 1807. The gunner would be dressed and equipped the same as the NCO, minus the epaulette.
>
> Bottom row, left to right:
>
> Københavns Borgervæbning Artilleri officer *c.* 1810
>
> Kronprinsens Livcorps, became the Kongens Livcorps in 1808. Private/student and officer *c.* 1807. Uniform for the private and officer dated 1810, after a contemporary watercolour by Senn.

The 2nd Avdeling: here the rest of the fit but poorer male population was expected to serve (employees, workers, labourers, sailors etc.), but normally they did not train or serve outside times of war. Sometimes members of the upper classes could be found amongst them as well and they were expected to support the 1st Avdeling. Although they were allowed uniforms, they were only used very sporadically and weapons were often also lacking for them as well, and usually they had to make do with pikes and very old muskets.

Another interesting detail is that a number of fire brigades were included in this structure, as many were embodied as a semi-military unit, much like today's Paris Fire Brigade which is under military command and its members are classed as armed soldiers.

In the majority of these units the officers wore a civilian style of double-breasted long-tailed coat with large falling collars as did the NCOs and the drummers, but rarely the men, who generally only had single-breasted tailed coats or short coatees. This detail is not always clear and can lead to some confusion.

Another detail, whilst most officers wore bicorns in 1803 as did many NCOs, the men generally had M1789 round hats as did many officers in the *jæger* units. After 1804 they were all supposed to wear hats, although this took time particularly among the more isolated units. The hats began to be replaced with shakos (mainly by officers) by 1810 in the richer units. Another detail which has been taken into consideration is, whilst the uniforms of the officers are generally clearly described as are those of a number of NCOs, those of the men are more rarely described or illustrated so sometimes we have had to interpret the descriptions and cross-referencing these details with other sources. Also, some of the NCOs continued to carry a halberd as a sign of their rank up to 1808 at least, if not longer. Officers all bought their own swords and sabres, and they were in a lot of different models. The men also had theirs from several different sources, many private, others bought by the town, and finally some often surplus from military stores. Visible on many contemporary illustrations is a thin stripe of gold 'cords' at their waist: in fact this is a watch fob, a sign of their status as 'citizens'.

At first they only had the green and gold sword knot and strap (*port épée*) and the *borgervæbnings* epaulette M1801, and this was an unofficial sign of their special status. No officers except those who were former regular officers (and only very few were), were allowed to wear a sash.

Most had black neck stocks, but not all. Unfortunately, little information on the uniforms of the drummers or hornists has been found.

Many if not all of these units had a colour of some description; most have not been recorded and have since been lost, but where possible a brief description has been added. Units known to have had a colour were Nyborg, Aalborg, Rønne, Borg, Westerstad, Østerstad, Nørrestads, Klædebo, Køge and Strand. This list is not exhaustive and probably many more could be added eventually.

The Citizen Militia Companies of Copenhagen

The citizen militia of Copenhagen had its origins in the Middle Ages. They had fought well during the siege of 1659, and from that time on the citizens were given a number of privileges in recognition of their service. This came with a number of obligations, one of which was to serve in the militia, but by 1790 the militia had become neglected and disorganised, and this was evident following their ineffectiveness during the British attack of 1801. This caused the Prince Regent to decide to carry out a major reform to render them more efficient. They were divided into an infantry division and an artillery division.

The Københavns Borgerlige Infanteri (Copenhagen Citizen Guards 1801–1814) was reconstituted in 1799 and between 1801 and 1807 was formed into the 1st Avdeling, with 4,500 men formed into 12 companies, and a 2nd Avdeling, acting as a reserve, with around 5,500 men also formed

THE DANISH ARMY OF THE NAPOLEONIC WARS VOLUME 3

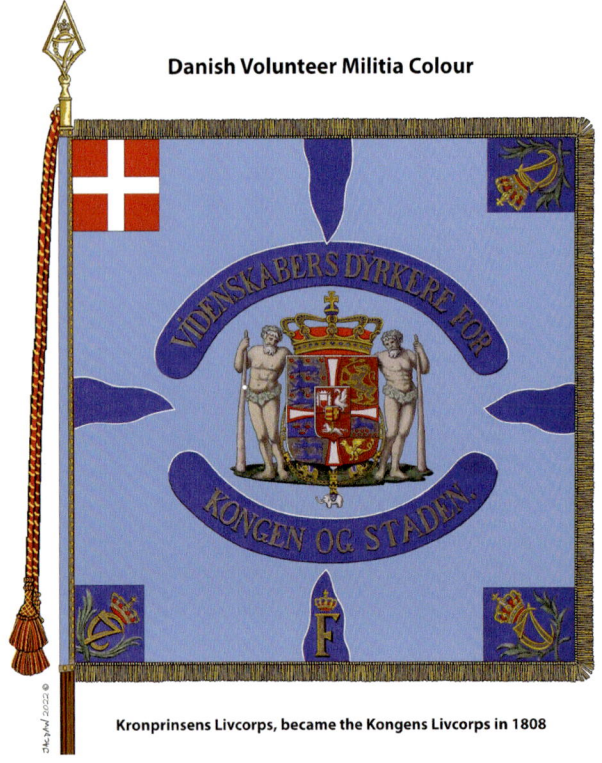

Plate 55. Danish Volunteer Militia Colour

The Kronprinsens Livcorps, which became the Kongens Livcorps in 1808, had two identical colours and the obverse and reverse were the same. The colour was issued in 1801.

into 12 companies. They were independent and they only had some basic training in manning the fortifications.

The Københavns Borgerlige Artilleri was formed 1789, mainly from the city's craftsmen and was originally composed of three fortress artillery companies, but it was slowly enlarged and by 1807 there were eight fortress artillery companies. They served or helped to serve most of the guns in the fortress defences during the siege of 1807.

In 1808 the whole force was renamed, reorganised and reuniformed. From now on it was to be called the Københavns Væbning (the armed forces of Copenhagen) and both the infantry and artillery was now part of a centrally organised command.

The infantry companies (still named Københavns Borgerlige Infanteri) were now formed into three active battalions, each of four companies, and three reserve battalions; with four companies in each. Both training and command were strengthened and formalised.

The artillery companies (also still called Københavns Borgerlige Artilleri) were also formed into three artillery battalions, with one 3-pdr *felt artilleri* companies and three *fæstnings artilleri* (fortress artillery) companies.

At the same time the volunteer Københavns Infanteri Regiment was formed mainly from the youngest and ablest men from the Københavns Borgerlige infantry and artillery companies and they became part of the permanent garrison of the town of Copenhagen.

The Københavns Borgervæbning Infanteri Regiment

Uniforms before 1808. They wore a carmine red coat with tails (Møllers 'liste 1810' gives crimson red), which had a light blue collar, cuffs and lapels, yellow piping and brass buttons. Earlier they had worn white breeches but by 1807 they had a pair of blue fall-fronted trousers. They wore a bicorn at least up to 1809, which had a white plume with a red tip. This was later replaced with an M1810 shako hat (made from old M1789 hats), with the same plume. They used the older militia distinctions for the officers and NCOs. When they were reformed in 1801, the ordnance stated that 'swords are to be carried by those without a bayonet for their muskets', so it is possible that not all carried a sword before 1808–1810. The M1756 sword was carried on a baldric which bore an oval stamped brass shield bearing the crowned monogram CVII, which was still in use around 1809–1810 after the death of King Christian VII. At a later date this was changed to the crowned lesser arms of Denmark with two shield bearers.

Uniforms Post 1808
Soldiers now wore the M1810 shako, and it is very likely that they were the very first to receive this model of headwear, as all those shown for this period are based on the 1789 model. All later issues shown were based on the 1803 issue (Johannes Senn 1809–1810). It had a thin yellow gold hat band. A new red over white round style of plume, common on the M1808 shakos, was placed at the front with yellow gold cords and a white cockade. The coat was now red. Their colours are unknown.

Københavns Borgervæbnings Artilleri Corps
In 1807 the gunners still had bicorns with a large white plume and a yellow loop. They wore a M1803 style red coatee with a blue collar, cuffs and lapels. Möller's 'list 1810' gives crimson red. It was lined and piped a pale straw-yellow and had brass buttons. The cuffs had a red cuff flap with three buttons. They had a pair of fall-fronted grey trousers and black Hessian boots.

Based on a contemporary illustration, the NCOs coatee was made of a brighter scarlet red with a small gold epaulette on the left shoulder and blue fall-front trousers. Both the men and NCOs had a black waist belt, and they still carried the ventral cartridge box, but now it was only used for tools, prickers and possibly fuses as they did not have muskets. A large number of priming flasks were made for the fortress artillery in Copenhagen in 1807, as loose powder was still used to load the heavy fortress guns. The officers were dressed in a similar uniform to the NCOs, but frequently with a crimson coat (which faded to a light crimson rather quickly) a gold loop on the bicorn, pre-1803-style gold epaulettes with the hanging tassels/balls, a carmine red long-tailed coat with gold buttons and they wore a sash around their waist. They carried a brass mounted sabre, model unidentified.

After the reform of 1808 they were issued with a shako M1810, which had a white plume on the front. The officers and gunners of the *felt artilleriet* (field artillery) had a shield-shaped brass plate embossed with 'F .A.' placed on the front of their shakos. The officers of the fortress artillery, serving the batteries of guns, had a large gilt metal button and cord on the front of their shako.

Their coat was now red with dark blue cuffs, cuff flaps, collar and lapels and the trousers were also dark blue. The officers had a cavalry-style cartridge pouch on a shoulder belt.

Their strength before 1801 consisted of two companies. From 30 January 1801 the artillery was increased with another company, and it now consisted of three companies. On 18 September 1801 another company was raised. In the *Borgervæbningen i Danmark og Norge 1803* it can be read that the artillery, which was divided into four companies, consisted of a commander, two majors, four captains, four staff captains, four premier lieutenants, eight second lieutenants, a surgeon, a correspondent and a bookkeeper, eight fire workers, four commanding sergeants, 40 bombardiers, 40 corporals/senior constables, 360 gunners/sub-constables, 12 drummers and pipers. This gave the unit total strength of 489 men.

The *Kongelig Resolution* of 29 April 1803 ordered that the corps be increased to 900 men and divided into six companies. On 20 November 1807, Det Borgerlige Artilleri was increased by two second lieutenants in each company, and on 28 January it was increased by two more companies, so that there were now eight companies. On 1 June 1808 a new organisation and regulations were drawn up, whereby the Københavns Borgerlige Infanteri and Københavns Borgerlige Artilleri were united as Københavns Borgervæbning, organised into two divisions. The artillery now consisted of three battalions, divided into 12 companies, with four companies in each battalion. In 1817, 12 company commanders are mentioned.

Studenter Korpset, renamed Prinsens Livcorps, became the Kongens Livcorps in 1808

This corps was raised in 1801 and were disbanded in 1842. They were renamed the *Kongens Livcorps* in 1808 when the Prince Regent became the King. Originally, they were composed of eight companies, each of 100 men. They were recruited from the students and staff of the University of Copenhagen. By 1812 the corps had dwindled to 140 men and was threatened with disbandment. So, service and participation were later made mandatory by Frederik VI if students were to pass their final exams. They were never considered to be a real military unit (unlike the Kongens Livjæger Corps) only a semi-military uniformed light infantry unit with basic training. They were only intended for guard duties and to help defend the walls and defences of the city if needed.

Uniforms
From 1801 to 1808 they wore a round black felt hat with a black plume over a white cockade with a black loop. Some contemporary illustrations show red and white cockades. They wore a double-breasted black civilian coat which had a red collar, black shoulder straps piped red and black buttons. Under their coat they had a white vest, and they wore a pair of fall-fronted grey breeches embroidered with black Hungarian knots and black Hessian-style boots. The NCOs had a black over red plume and the officers had the same plume and black arrow-headed embroidery on their breeches. The officers were allowed two epaulettes. NCOs were also allowed two epaulettes. Studying the few available contemporary pictures, they apparently did not wear them very often.

The men were armed with a musket and carried a M1753 infantry sabre on a black leather belt and a cartridge box on a black leather cross belt over the other shoulder. Officers and NCOs carried their sabre on a shoulder belt. Until 1808 officers and NCOs were only distinguished by having a red base on their plume, and officers did not carry muskets. C. W. Eckersberg does show a slight variation for the officer in a contemporary pen and ink sketch, where the officer has acquired cords for his hat which he has looped over a button on his coatee. He has also acquired what appears to be a dragoon style sabre with a two-branched hand guard.

No information exists regarding any musicians, but that they had the civilian musicians of the Royal Music Chapel playing at a couple of parades. They had no hornists as far as is known but maybe they did have some drummers as it is mentioned in the regulations, that 'when the Drums beat, everybody shall dress and arm themselves and stand too in front of the University, ready for action'.

The Kongens Livcorps (1808–1814) wore a black uniform coat and black trousers. The uniform was based on the standard dress of a university student, (as it was the required uniform in 1801–1808), with added collar, cuffs and turnbacks. But to give some fashionable appearance to the unit as some students requested, an officers' model shako M1808, with a rather classy shield was allowed. The students themselves had wanted far more elaborate and

THE DANISH ARMY OF THE NAPOLEONIC WARS VOLUME 3

Danish Volunteer Militia Rank Distinctions 1801–1812

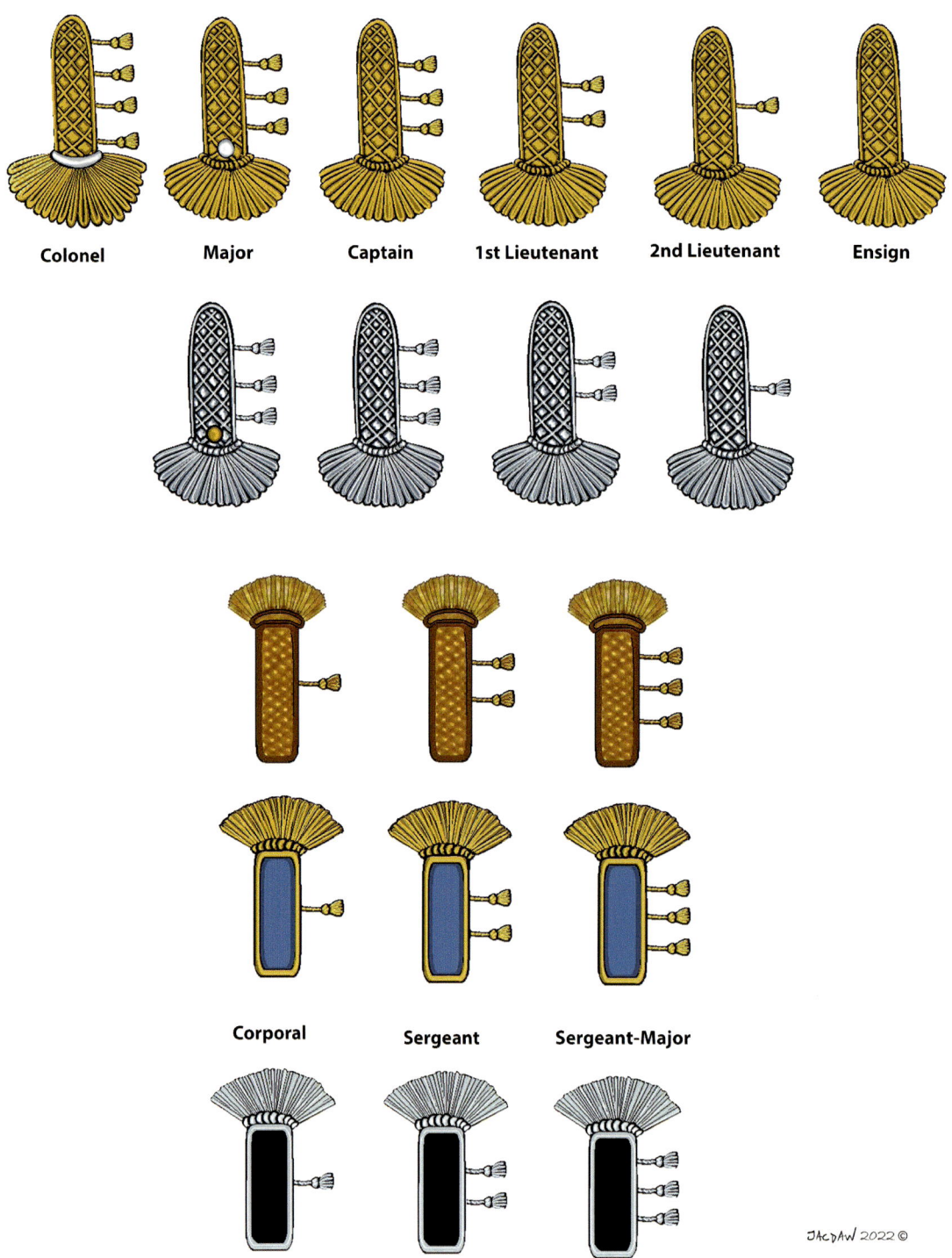

Plate 56. Danish Volunteer Militia Rank Distinctions

Top two rows, officers with the two versions for uniforms with gold or silver buttons.
Bottom three rows, three variants for NCOs, the bottom one specifically for *jægeres*.

expensive uniforms, like the ones used by the Kongens Livjæger Corps.

But the uniform authorised in 1809–1814 was again a uniform based on the ordinary student uniform, but as they had wanted a more 'dandified' uniform, it was 'militarised', and they were finally allowed to wear the officer's model shako with a rather splendid white metal shield with the figure of Minerva the goddess of learning in yellow metal riveted onto the plate. It had a black plume with a red tip and red and yellow cords. This was probably the most expensive item of the uniform, but the original idea, was that once made, the graduating students would be allowed to sell their uniform to new students when they left.

But soon the students began losing interest in the formation. They were now expected to train and stand guard more, and the prices to get a uniform made had quickly become rather expensive. So, from a corps of two battalions in 1801 with around a 1,000 members, they had only been able to raise 700 members in 1807, and by 1812, they were down to only 120 active members. Then the King stepped in and ordered that all students allowed a place at the university also had to serve in the corps and that (in theory) helped with numbers.

From 1808/1809 they received a new uniform, or more likely their original dress was retailored for economic reasons. They now had a black, officers' model shako bearing a white metal shield plate stamped with figure of Minerva, the goddess of learning, in yellow metal on the plate. It had a black plume with red tip and red and yellow cords.

They now had a black coat in a military cut with a red collar, red closed lapels, pointed red cuffs and turnbacks, all piped white and the buttons were made of white metal. They wore a pair of fall-fronted dark grey/black breeches, and black Hungarian boots completed their uniform. They had black shoulder belts for a black leather cartridge box and carried an infantry sabre and musket. The officers wore a green and yellow waist sash and sword knot. (Sources: C. W. Eckersberg, Johannes Senn).

Apparently, they had a colour from 1801. The field was light blue with medium blue flames. On the bottom flame there was a crowned 'F'. In the top shaft quarter, there was a Dannebrog and in the other three a medium blue square with the crowned monogram of Christian VII within a green wreath. In the centre there were the full crowned arms of Denmark surrounded by a collar of the Order of the Elephant with their supporters on a green ground. Above the arms there was the text VIDENSKABERS DÿRKERE FOR ('The sciences worshippers') in gold lettering on a medium blue crescent, and below the arms there was the text KONGEN OG STADEN ('King and City') in gold lettering on a medium blue crescent. It had gold cords and a standard gilt Christian VII finial. Strangely for an infantry colour, this standard had a gold fringe. Dimensions are unknown.

In 1808 the officers adopted the same epaulettes as the Københavns Borgerlige Infanteri but in silver, and the waist sash and *porte épée* of the regular army model. In 1812 they also adopted the same cuff rank distinctions as Københavns Borgerlige Infanteri but in silver.

Brandkorpset i København (Copenhagen Fire Brigade)
This was not a fighting corps as such, but it was a militarily regulated unit and an important part of the defence of Copenhagen. After the official approbation order dated 1809 in the Rigsarkivet (National Archives) in full dress the officers wore a white coat which had a black collar, cuffs and lapels with brass/gilt buttons and epaulettes and a double-breasted white waistcoat and breeches. They wore a black bicorn with a white plume with a yellow tip with a black cockade with a gold loop, button and tassels. He carries a brass mounted officers or cavalry sabre with a gold knot in a black leather scabbard with brass mounting.

In service dress they wore a double-breasted light grey coat with a black collar and cuffs, and their buttons were brass and epaulettes gold. Another contemporary print shows the coat with grey cuff flaps. Their double-breasted waistcoat was white, and their trousers/breeches were blue. The bicorn was unchanged. They all carried sabres. Their strength is unknown.

The contemporary illustration by Johannes Senn shows a slightly different uniform. The officer of 1807 is shown in a light grey double-breasted tailed coat, lined straw-yellow, and it has a black collar, lapels and pointed cuffs. The collar, cuffs and the centre of the coat are piped yellow. The buttons are brass, and the breeches are blue. Headgear is a bicorn with a yellow plume with a blue or black base (this may be the plume holder), yellow cockade with a gold loop, button and tassels. Boots were black piped white or silver with gold tassels. They carried a brass mounted officers or cavalry sabre with a gold knot in a black leather scabbard with brass mounting.

The illustration of the fireman shows him in what appears to be full dress about 1810–1812. The fireman wears a M1789 or early version of the M1803 hat with a yellow plume with a blue or black base, this maybe the plume holder, white cockade with a yellow loop, brass button and a yellow hat band and cords and tassel. On his hat he has a stamped brass plaque which consists of the King's monogram (Frederik VI) over a crescent shaped plaque. His jacket has square cuffs with black cuff flaps, three buttons and the flap were piped yellow.

He carries an M1802 artillery sword on a black leather waist belt with a brass buckle and over his shoulder a black cross belt with a black leather cartridge pouch, but since they did not carry firearms, one must presume it held some basic tools. His boots were black piped silver, without tassels. In foul weather or on winter service he could wear a grey double-breasted overcoat with brass buttons.

THE DANISH ARMY OF THE NAPOLEONIC WARS VOLUME 3

Samsøe Landevaern became *Samsøe Landmilits*

1. 2. 3. 4.

Danish Citizen Militias (I)

5. 6. 7. 8.

THE CITIZEN OR TOWN MILITIAS (I)

> Facing page
>
> Plate 57. Samsøe Landeværn and Danish Citizen Militias (I)
>
> Top:
>
> The Samsøe Landeværn became the Samsøe Landmilits in 1808. The Samsoe were in fact part of the Landeværn, but when they were reformed in 1808, they were renamed the Samsoe Landmilits.
>
> 1. Samsoe, infantryman *c.* 1810
> 2. Samsoe *feltartillerist* (field gunner) of the mobile battery, *c.* 1810
> 3. Samsoe, trooper of the Land Rytter *c.* 1810. They had a brown leather shoulder and waist belt of the old *rytter* model. They carried a heavy cavalry *pallask* and an M1805 *rytterskilte* rhombic cavalry plate on their hats with 'RR' stamped on the shield.
> 4. Samsoe, infantryman *c.* 1811 in the new uniform and a shako hat.
>
> Bottom:
>
> Danish Citizen Militia I (*Borgervæbninger*)
>
> 5. Aarhus, a *jæger* officer of the Borgerlige Jæger Corps
> 6. Aarhus, a *jæger* of the Borgerlige Jæger Corps
> 7. Aalborg Borgervæbning Infanteri, officer of the 1st Avdeling, 1st company (Ward)
> 8. Aalborg Borgervæbning Infanteri, private of the 1st Avdeling, 1st company (Ward). Note the 2nd company had same uniform, but with they had a white plume with a yellow tip.
>
> Note: The watch-chain hanging from their waists was an informal sign of a citizen and his rank.

The men of the Copenhagen Fire Brigade were still wearing these hats in 1812. The hat had a brass badge, and the officers wore bicorns with a cockade and loop and a white plume with a red tip.

Aalborg Borgervæbning Infanteri

In 1803 the officers of the 1st Avdeling (ward) wore a red double-breasted coat with a large green falling collar and round cuffs, brass buttons and gold epaulettes. Their waistcoat and breeches were straw-yellow. The first company had a white plume with a red tip on their bicorns and the second company had a white plume with a yellow top. The adjutant had a yellow plume with a red tip.

They had three colours, one per company. These had a pale-yellow field with a Dannebrog in the top stave quarter, and in the centre was a crowned double monogram of Christian VII with gold lion supporters over an order of the elephant on a blue ribbon. The date was marked on each side of the crown '18' on the left and '01' on the right. The company number was painted on each side of the supporters, for example 'det 2 det.–Comp' in gold lettering. The cords and tassels were red and gold mixed.

Aalborg Borgerlige Jæger Corps

In 1803 the officers had a short double-breasted green coat with black lining, collar, lapels and cuffs, piped yellow, white metal buttons, straw-yellow waistcoat and grey trousers. Their hats had silver cords, a black cockade and a green plume with a yellow tip. The men had a hat with a green plume, and they wore a green coatee with black lining, collar, narrow lapels and cuffs, piped yellow, white metal buttons, yellow waistcoat and grey trousers. They had three companies armed with muskets.

Later, in about 1810, the *jæger corps* had a shako with a green plume, and they wore a green coatee with black lining, collar, lapels and cuffs, piped yellow, white metal buttons and grey trousers. They had three companies armed with muskets.

Aalborg Borgerlige Artilleri

From 1803 they had an artillery company, the corps consisted of only 34–35 men besides three senior and five junior NCOs.

Their uniform was a single-breasted dark green or black coatee, and the round cuffs and falling collar were piped yellow, with yellow buttons. Their headwear was a round hat with a green feather. The waistcoat is not shown, but their breeches/trousers were grey. It is recorded that at this time the corps did not have any hand weapons/sidearms, but the officers and possibly the NCOs carried a gold-hilted sabre on a black leather shoulder belt.

They were issued with four cannon, each under command of a bombardier, according to the rendered muster roll which was supervised by the Prefect von Pentz on 17 August 1803.

The artillery was officially disbanded by ordnance on 4 August 1809, but nevertheless references to officers from the corps continue to appear in different contemporary sources up to 1842.

Aarhus Borgerlige Infanteri

The 1st Avdeling (ward), Østre (Eastern) Companie. In 1803 the officers had a scarlet red double-breasted coat with a dark green collar and round cuffs, brass buttons. Their waistcoat and fall-fronted breeches were grey blue. They had a bicorn without a plume. Officers had gold epaulettes. The NCOs had the same uniform, but their coat was a dark red and they had an NCO's epaulette.

In 1810 they had a red coatee with a green collar and cuffs, their buttons were yellow/brass. Their waistcoat and fall-fronted breeches were blue.

The 1st Avdeling (ward), Vestre (Western) Companie. In 1803 they had a red double-breasted coat with a dark green collar and round cuffs, brass buttons. Their waistcoat and fall-fronted breeches were straw-yellow. They had a bicorn without a plume. Officers had gold epaulettes. The NCOs wore the same uniform, but their coat was a dark red and they had an NCO's epaulette.

In 1810 they had a red coatee with a green collar and cuffs, their buttons were yellow. Their waistcoat and fall-fronted breeches were yellow.

In 1810 the 2nd Avdeling (ward), had a blue coatee with a red collar and cuffs, brass buttons. Their waistcoat was white, and their fall-fronted breeches were blue.

Aarhus Jæger Corps

In 1803 they wore a double-breasted dark green coat with a black collar and cuffs with brass buttons. Their fall-fronted breeches were dark grey blue. The officers' M1789 hat had a black cockade, a green plume and a gold loop and gold epaulettes. Both the officers and the men were only armed with a musket and bayonet carried on a black belt, but no sword or sabre. But the paintings in the Queen's Library show the officers carrying sabres and the men with hats and a ventral cartridge box on a belt, all belts were black leather.

In 1810 the uniform was simply described as a green coat and grey breeches/trousers.

Aarhus Borgerlige Artilleri Corps

In 1803 the officers had a medium grey coatee with a black falling collar, narrow lapels and round cuffs piped white with a double yellow piping on the collar and cuffs. The coat had black turnbacks on the front of the coat brass buttons and gold epaulettes and their fall-fronted trousers were dark blue. Their round hat had a dark grey plume. The men were dressed the same if less elaborate with cords on their round hats.

The uniform in 1810 was a grey coatee with a dark blue collar and cuffs with white metal buttons and a pair of dark blue fall-fronted breeches. Their plume was now black.

Aarhus Borgerlige Ridende Corps

In 1803 the dragoons had a black bicorn with a black cockade with a silver loop and tassels and no plume. They wore a double-breasted carmine red coat, the collar, round cuffs and narrow lapels were all the same colour, piped straw-yellow with white metal buttons, straw-yellow waistcoat and fall-fronted breeches.

The uniform in 1810 was a carmine red coatee lined yellow with white metal buttons, straw-yellow waistcoat and fall-fronted breeches. Their head wear and their housings or shabraques are not specified. Their strengths are unknown.

Assens Borgerlige Infanteri

In 1803 the officers had a red double-breasted coat with a black collar and round cuffs with brass buttons and gold epaulettes. They wore a straw-yellow waistcoat and straw-yellow fall-front breeches. They had a round hat without a plume.

In 1810 the 1st Avdeling (ward) wore a single-breasted carmine red coatee, green collar and cuffs with brass buttons, yellow waistcoat and yellow fall-front breeches.

The 2nd Avdeling (ward) wore a single-breasted red coatee lined yellow with a black collar and cuffs and a yellow waistcoat and yellow fall-front breeches. Their strength is unknown.

Bogense Borgervæbning

In 1803 the officers wore a long-tailed double-breasted crimson red coat with a medium blue collar and round cuffs piped white and gilt buttons. They had white breeches and waistcoat and their headwear was a round hat M1789 which had a white plume with a blue top.

In 1810 the 1st Avdeling (ward) wore a carmine red coatee lined white with a light blue collar and cuffs piped white with brass buttons and a white waistcoat and a pair of fall-fronted white breeches.

The 2nd Avdeling (ward) wore a blue coatee with a light red collar and a pair of fall-fronted blue trousers. Hat plumes not specified. Their strengths are unknown.

Ebeltoft Borgervæbning

In 1803 the officers wore a long-tailed double-breasted red coat with a black or dark grey collar and round cuffs and gilt buttons without epaulettes. They had dark blue breeches and waistcoat and their headwear was a bicorn without a plume. Their strengths are unknown.

Fredericia Borgerlige Infanteri

In 1803 the officers of the 1st Avdeling (ward), 1st company, wore a double-breasted carmine red coat with a straw-yellow collar, round cuffs with red cuff flaps piped straw-yellow and lining with gold buttons and epaulettes, straw-yellow waistcoat and breeches. Their headwear was a black bicorn with a white plume and gold loop.

In 1810 they had a carmine red coatee with a yellow collar and cuffs lined yellow and yellow piping with brass buttons. A yellow waistcoat and fall-front pantaloons completed their outfit. No details of headwear are known.

In 1803 the officers of the 1st Avdeling (ward), 2nd company, wore a double-breasted carmine red coat with a dark green collar, round cuffs with flaps piped white and white lining with silver buttons and epaulettes, and a straw-yellow waistcoat and breeches. Their head wear was a black bicorn with a white plume and silver loop and button.

In 1810 they had a carmine red coatee piped white, green collar and round cuffs and white lining with white metal/silver buttons, a white waistcoat and pantaloons. No details of headwear are known.

In 1803 the officers of the 2nd Avdeling (ward) wore a carmine red double-breasted coat with a dark blue collar and cuffs with flaps piped straw-yellow with yellow metal buttons. A yellow waistcoat and fall-front pantaloons. Their head wear was a black bicorn with a light blue plume and gold loop and tassels.

In 1810 they had a carmine red coatee piped white, blue collar and round cuffs and yellow lining with gold brass buttons, a yellow waistcoat and fall-front pantaloons. No details of head wear.

Fredericia Borgerlige Jæger Corps

In 1803 the officers of this *jæger corps* had a black M1789 hat with red and gold cords, a white plume and a yellow/gold hat band. They wore a dark green double-breasted long-tailed coat which was piped white on all leading edges, and it had a crimson red collar and cuffs piped white, silver buttons and epaulettes with knots. Finally, they wore a pair of fall-fronted grey trousers decorated with simple black Hungarian knots and black boots.

Officers carried a brass-hilted sabre with a gold sword knot carried in a black leather scabbard with brass mountings on a black belt edged silver with a gilt buckle.

The NCOs had a black M1789 hat with a white hat band, white plume with a green tip and a white loop. They wore a dark green double-breasted short-tailed tunic with a red collar and cuffs, silver buttons and a silver epaulette with knots and a pair of dark grey trousers. They were armed with a musket and a brass-hilted sabre with a white/silver sword knot in a black leather scabbard with brass mountings on a black belt with a brass buckle. Over the shoulder was a black cartridge box on a black leather belt which had an oval brass badge.

The men had a black M1789 hat with a white hat band, white plume with a green tip and a white loop. They wore what appears to be a short, dark green double-breasted tunic, with a red collar and cuffs, white metal buttons, and a pair of blue and white ticken trousers. He was armed with a musket and a brass-hilted sabre with a white/silver sword knot in a black leather scabbard with brass mountings on a black belt with a brass buckle. Over the shoulder was a black cartridge box on a black leather belt which had an oval brass badge.

Fredericia Artillerikorpset

In 1803 the officers had bicorns with blue-tipped white plumes and a black cockade with a gold loop and button. There was a gold knot on each side of the bicorn. They wore a dark blue double-breasted long-tailed coat with red cuffs and collar, piped light blue. The coat was piped light blue on the leading edges and the buttons were gold. They had epaulettes with knots. Their breeches were dark blue and white stockings were visible above their boots. They carried a brass-hilted sabre with a white/silver sword knot in a black leather scabbard with brass mountings on a black belt with a rectangular brass buckle.

The men had an M1789 round hat with a yellow hat band with a blue-tipped white plumes, black cockade and a gold loop and button. They wore a single-breasted blue tunic with a red collar piped light blue and red cuffs (no piping) and light blue piping all around the short tunic/coatee and brass buttons. They had blue trousers with simple light blue Hungarian knots, black boots and white stockings. Other ranks carried a brass-hilted M1759 infantry sabre in a black leather scabbard with brass mountings on a black belt with a rectangular brass buckle.

In 1803 the corps consisted of three officers, six NCOs and 64 citizens, a total of 73 men (another report in the same year gives 49 men, perhaps understood to be the privates). Everyone was in uniform and had side arms (sabres), but no one had muskets. The function of this artillery corps was to work the naval battery in the Oldenborgs Bastion.

(Fredericia) Kronprinsens Ridende Korps

This was more of a small, mounted guard than a real corps. In 1803 the officers wore a single-breasted light-yellow tunic with a blue collar and round cuffs, brass buttons and gold militia epaulettes with knots. The officers had a black M1789 hat with a yellow gold hat band and cords and a white plume. They wore a pair of light-yellow fall-fronted breeches and white stockings which were visible above black Hessian-style boots. A brass-hilted sabre was carried in a brass mounted scabbard on a black leather belt with a gilt buckle.

The troopers wore the same uniform minus the epaulettes, but their hat had a blue-tipped white plume and they wore black pouch and waist belts with a steel buckle.

Their white stockings were visible above his Hessian-style boots. Troopers also carried a brass-hilted sabre in a brass mounted scabbard on their belt and they were armed with carbines. The colour of their shabraques is unknown. Their strength in 1803 was four officers, a trumpeter and 12 troopers. They were popularly known as the 'Canaries' (*Kanariefuglene*).

Frederiksund Borgerlige Infanteri

In 1803 the officers wore a double-breasted carmine red coat with a dark blue collar, narrow lapels and round cuffs with gold buttons and epaulettes. They had a dark blue waistcoat and breeches. Their head wear was a black M1789 round hat with a medium blue/black plume and gold loop.

Frederiksvæks Frivillig Bevæbnede Korps

The Frederiksværks Frivillige Bevæbnede Corps, the volunteer armed workers of Frederiksvaerk were the first official citizen militia, formed in 1801, and served as the basis for all that followed. Also, it had a special status, as they protected the most important arms factory in Denmark. The planned strength from the start was to be 1,500 men, but this level was never reached and only 600 to 800 could be raised, mainly workers from the gun foundry at Frederiksvaerk.

But in 1807 because they proved themselves incapable of stopping the British from capturing the factory and carrying away their weapons and stores – they practically offered no resistance – this Frederiksværks Frivillige Bevæbnede Corps were disbanded. A new reorganised force was raised which was called the Det Frederiks-værske Corps (1808–1816). This had a Frivillig Artilleri Division (volunteer artillery company) of four officers 22 NCOs, two trumpeters and 100 gunners. The *sødivision* (sailors' company) was retained with three officers, 26 NCOs, two horn blowers and 64 sailors. They received pay for their service, but were disbanded after war ended in 1816.

In 1801 the uniforms of the officers and NCOs of the infantry of the Frederiksværks Frivillige Bevæbnede Corps was a single-breasted brown coatee with a black collar and cuffs with red piping on the collar, cuffs and on both sides of the brass buttons and red frontal turnbacks. This was worn with a black hat with a black cockade and light grey trousers. From 1801, they received gold *borgerlige* epaulettes M1801. The ordinary citizens/workers had basically same uniform, but without epaulettes. There were infantry, *jægere* and cavalry, all basically wearing the same uniform.

Their colour had a dark brown field, with a Dannebrog in the top corner and the King's crowned cypher (Christian VII) in gold on a red square, shown vertically. In the centre there was a circular red field with a gold frame, in the centre of which there was a crossed hammer and scythe in natural colours. The central design is strangely reminiscent of a more recent flag. It had a CVII finial and red and yellow gold cords and tassels.

Frederiksvæks Frivillig Bevæbnede Korps, Artilleridivisionen (Frederiks Works Volunteer Artillery)

As a royal artillery corps, the artillery officers had a single-breasted carmine red coat, but with a row of large brass buttons, and it had a dark blue collar and cuffs. They wore a pair of fall-fronted dark blue breeches and a bicorn with a plume.

Frederiksvæks Frivillig Bevæbnede Korps Sødivisionen (the Sea Division)

In 1810 they had a blue coatee with a red collar and cuffs and brass buttons. They had a dark blue waistcoat and breeches. They wore a round hat without a plume. Their strength is unknown.

Faaborg Borgervæbning

In 1803 the officers wore a double-breasted dark blue coat with a red collar and round cuffs and blue lining, brass buttons, white waistcoat and blue breeches or pantaloons. They had a round hat with a blue plume with a white tip. Some of the men were dressed in a similar fashion but were designated as a *jæger corps*.

According to a contemporary naive water colour found in the archives of Faabourg, in 1810 they had a dark blue coat lined blue with a red collar and round cuffs, two buttons and medium blue lapels, brass buttons, white waistcoat and trousers. They had a shako with white cords and a white plume with a blue tip. Their strength is unknown.

Grenå or Grenaae Borgervæbning

In 1803 the officers wore a double-breasted red coat lined and piped yellow, with a dark green collar and cuffs, brass buttons, yellow waistcoat and a pair of dark blue fall-fronted pantaloons. They had a round hat without a plume. In 1810 they had red coat lined yellow with a light green collar and round cuffs and yellow piping with brass buttons, yellow waistcoat and blue breeches or pantaloons. They had a shako with a white plume with a blue tip. Their strength is unknown.

Haderslev Borgervæbning

The uniforms and strength of this company are unknown.

Helsingør Borgerlige Infanteri

In 1803 the officers wore a double-breasted red coat which had a dark blue collar, round cuffs and narrow lapels with gold buttons and epaulettes. This was completed with a dark blue double-breasted waistcoat and a pair of fall-fronted dark blue breeches and short black Hessian boots. Their bicorn had a black cockade, gold loop, button and tassels under a blue plume. Originally, they had two companies. The colour of this citizen militia was originally made for the infantry and had a dark blue field with a Dannebrog in the top hoist. On each side there was a red flame and the gold crowned cypher of Christian VII in the other three corners. In the centre there were the crowned grand arms of Denmark surrounded by the collars of the order of the Dannebrog and the Order of the Elephant and with the 'wild men' supporters. A white scroll is hung from the ground of the wild men, but the text is now faded. There is a gold fringe around the colour, but this looks like a recent addition. After 1803 the colour was refurbished by the artillery companies.

Helsingør Borgerlige Artillerikorps
In 1803 the officers wore a double-breasted carmine red coat which had a dark blue collar, round cuffs and narrow lapels piped yellow with gold buttons and epaulettes. This was completed with a white double-breasted waistcoat, a pair of fall-fronted blue breeches and short black Hessian boots. Their bicorn had a black cockade, gold loop, button and tassels under a white plume with a blue tip.

In 1810 they wore a carmine red coat which had a dark blue collar, round cuffs and thin lapels piped yellow with gold buttons and epaulettes. This was completed with a pale yellow/buff waistcoat, a pair of fall-fronted blue breeches and short black Hessian boots. Their hat or shako had a black cockade, gold loop, button and tassels under a white plume with a blue tip. Their strength is unknown.

Brandkorpset i Helsingør (The Helsingør Fire Brigade)
Again, this was a military regulated firefighting unit as were most of the Danish Fire Brigades. In 1810 they wore a blue coat which had a black collar and lapels, red cuffs and piping. They had a red waistcoat, and their fall-fronted trousers were blue. Their hat had a white plume with a yellow tip.

Hillerød Borgerlige Infanteri
In 1803 the officers wore a double-breasted dark green coat which had a black collar, round cuffs and narrow lapels with gold buttons and epaulettes. This was completed with a dark grey double-breasted waistcoat and a pair of fall-fronted dark grey breeches and short black Hessian boots. Their M1789 hat had a black cockade, gold loop, button cords and tassels under a green plume. They carried a sabre with a gold knot and tassel carried on a black leather belt with a square plate buckle. Their strength is unknown

Hobroe Borgervæbning
In 1803, an image of an officer shows a long-tailed double-breasted scarlet red coat with red lining with green or blue cuffs and brass/gilt buttons. He wears a black bicorn with black cockade and gold loop. His breeches and waistcoat are buff yellow, and he has black Hessian boots. The men probably had a single-breasted red coatee with green or blue cuffs and brass buttons and an M1789 round hat. This description is taken from an approbation order conserved in the Rigsarkivet (National Archives) and a contemporary watercolour conserved in the Dronningens Håndbibliotek (Queen's Library).

Holbæk Borgervæbnin
In 1803 an officer of the 1st Avdeling (ward) was shown wearing a double-breasted red coat with a dark blue collar, narrow labels and cuffs piped yellow, brass buttons, a dark blue waistcoat and a pair of fall-fronted dark blue breeches. They wore a black bicorn without a plume. In 1810 the 1st Avdeling had a green coatee lined white with a black collar, cuffs and lapels piped white and yellow buttons. Their waistcoat was white, and their breeches/pantaloons were grey. Their hat had a white plume with a green top.

A 2nd Avdeling officer of 1803 was shown wearing a single-breasted dark green coatee lined and piped white with a black collar, lapels and cuffs, brass buttons, a white waistcoat and a pair of fall-fronted grey breeches/trousers. His round hat had a dark green plume. In 1810 the officer was shown wearing a single-breasted dark green coatee lined and piped white with a black collar, lapels and cuffs, brass buttons, a white waistcoat and a pair of fall-fronted grey breeches/trousers. His shako had a dark green plume. Their strengths are unknown.

Holsterbroe Borgervæbning
In around 1810 they had a dark blue coatee with a red collar with blue lining, brass buttons and a white waistcoat and a pair of fall-fronted blue pantaloons or breeches. The officers carried a sabre with a lion's head on the hilt; the model was particular to this unit. Their strength is unknown.

Horsens Borgerlige Infanteri
In 1803 the infantry officers wore a long-tailed double-breasted red coat with a dark green collar and round cuffs, brass buttons and a straw-yellow waistcoat and breeches/trousers and white stockings. Their bicorn had a green plume. By 1810 the officers now had a long-tailed crimson red coat lined red with a green collar and cuffs piped buff yellow. Their waistcoat and breeches/pantaloons were yellow buff, and they wore short black Hessian boots. They wore a black hat with a red topped white plume and gold loop and tassels

Horsens Borgerlige Jæger Corps
In a description taken from an approbation order conserved in the Rigsarkivet (National Archives) and a contemporary watercolour conserved in the Dronningens Håndbibliotek (Queen's Library).

It can be seen that in 1803 the officers of the *skarpskyttere* company had a long-tailed double-breasted dark green tunic with a dark green collar and round cuffs, silver buttons, but no epaulettes and wore a pair of fall-fronted white pantaloons or breeches. Their M1789 round hat had a white plume with a green tip. In 1810 their officers are depicted wearing a short green coat with black collar and cuffs, piped buff yellow with brass/gilt buttons. Their waistcoats were yellow, and their breeches/pantaloons were grey, and they wore short black Hessian boots. Their M1798 round hat or shako had a white plume with a green tip. They carried a sabre with a lion's head on the hilt. Their strength is unknown.

Kallundborg Borgervlige Infanteri (Callandborg)
In 1810 the infantry wore single-breasted red coatee lined yellow with a yellow collar, lapels and cuffs with brass buttons. They had a yellow waistcoat and a pair of fall-fronted breeches or trousers. Their hat had a white plume. Their strength is unknown. The *jægere* wore a double-breasted green tunic with green collar and cuffs piped black, a pair of grey, fall-fronted trousers and a green plume and cords on their hat. Möller gives brass buttons but does not show the black piping in 1810. Their strength is unknown.

Kierteminde Borgervæbning
In 1803 the officers wore a double-breasted long-tailed dark green tunic with a black collar, narrow lapels and round cuffs and brass buttons. They had a straw-yellow waistcoat and a pair of straw-yellow fall-fronted breeches or trousers. They had a black bicorn with a bushy yellow plume with a green top. From 1810 their uniform changed, and they now had a light green coatee with a black collar, lapels and round cuffs and brass buttons. They had a straw-yellow waistcoat and a pair of straw-yellow fall-fronted breeches or trousers.

The 1st Avdeling had a green cockade and a yellow plume with a green tip and the 2nd Avdeling had a yellow cockade with a yellow tipped green plume. This was worn on a round hat, possibly replaced with a shako. Their strength is unknown.

Kolding Borgervæbning Stadshauptmann
In 1803 the city governor wore a long-tailed double-breasted red coat with a black collar and round cuffs piped straw-yellow, brass buttons and gold epaulettes with a medium blue waistcoat and breeches or trousers, worn with short black Hessian boots. His black bicorn had a white plume.

Kolding Borgervæbning Infanteri
These companies were all dressed as *jægere*. In 1803 the officers of the of the 1st Avdeling wore a long-tailed double-breasted dark green coatee, lined buff yellow with a black collar and cuffs piped straw-yellow and brass buttons and gold epaulettes. They had a straw-yellow waistcoat and had a pair of straw-yellow, fall-fronted breeches or trousers and black Hessian boots. They wore a black bicorn with a white plume and gold loop, tassels and knots. The 2nd Avdeling wore a double-breasted green coatee, lined buff yellow with a black collar and cuffs piped white and brass buttons and had a pair of fall-fronted white trousers and black Hessian boots. They wore a black round hat with a green, red and green cockade with a yellow loop and the plume was green with a red tip. They were armed with a musket and bayonet.

These companies possessed at least one colour. An original colour conserved in Koldinghus museum, which also has their drum, has a red field, and in the centre under a gold open crown, a blue oval field with the following text placed on three lines: KOLDING BORGHERVAEBNING 1803. It is surrounded by a wreath of green palm fronds. In each corner there is a gold flower or rose and it has a gold fringe.

Kolding Borgervæbning Jæger Corps
The *jæger* company wore a double-breasted green coatee with a black collar and cuffs piped yellow buff and brass buttons and had a pair of fall-fronted grey trousers with simple Hungarian knots stitched on them and black Hessian boots. They wore a black round hat with a green plume and cockade with a yellow loop and yellow and green cords and were armed with a musket and bayonet. Their officers wore a long-tailed double-breasted green coat, lined buff yellow with a black collar and cuffs piped buff yellow, and brass buttons. The coat had gold epaulettes. With this they wore a pair of fall-fronted grey breeches or pantaloons with simple Hungarian knots stitched on them and black Hessian boots. They had a round M1789 hat with a gold hat band, gold cords, tassels and loop with a white plume.

Descriptions taken from an approbation order conserved in the Rigsarkivet (National Archives), contemporary watercolours in Koldinghus Museum and a contemporary watercolour conserved in the Dronningens Håndbibliotek (Queens Library).

Kolding Ridende Corps
Based on descriptions taken from the aforementioned approbation order conserved in the Rigsarkivet (National Archives), and a contemporary watercolour conserved in the Dronningens Håndbibliotek (Queens Library), officers of the mounted corps had a long-tailed double-breasted blue coat lined white with a red collar and cuffs, piped white with pewter buttons and silver epaulettes. Their breeches/pantaloons were yellow buff, and they wore short black Hessian boots. They wore a black bicorn with a white plume and silver loop and tassels. The volunteers had the same uniform but with a blue shoulder strap piped white and a rather odd red, white, red and white cockade. And they had a pair of fall-fronted yellow breeches and black

Hessian boots. The Hungarian-style shabraque was light blue. The strength of this unit is unknown.

Korsør Borgerlige Infanteri (Corsöer)
In 1803 the officers had a dark blue double-breasted coatee with red round cuffs and collar with yellow lining and red piping, brass buttons and a straw-yellow waistcoat and a pair of fall-fronted straw-yellow breeches. Their bicorn had a blue plume with a red tip. In 1810 they had a dark blue single-breasted coatee with red cuffs and collar and yellow lining, brass buttons, a straw-yellow waistcoat and a pair of fall-fronted straw-yellow breeches. Their hat had a white plume with a red tip. Their strength is unknown.

Korsør Borgerlige Brandkorps (Fire Brigade)
Their uniforms and strength are unknown.

Køge Borgervæbning (sometimes written as Kjøge)
This unit had rather ancient origins, first raised in 1554 with 275 men by Christian III of Denmark. They were recruited from among the tradesmen and craftsmen as an obligation. They carried firearms from the start. They could be called out by the mayor for different tasks, mainly policing. They were reorganised in 1801, when the Slaget på Rheden (battle of Copenhagen) brought a renewed will to defend the country which spread throughout the kingdom. In 1807 the *borgervæbningen* consisted of approximately 250 men.[1]

The uniform of the 1st Avdeling in 1803, which composed of the richest, youngest and fittest citizens, was a black tricorn with a yellow cockade, a long-tailed dark blue coat with a red collar, lapels and cuffs with brass buttons. Their waistcoat and trousers were white with a white belt and black boots. They were armed with a musket, a sabre and a cartridge box on a white bandoleer.

The uniform of the 2nd Avdeling, composed of the rest of the inhabitants and so not reckoned as being anything but a reserve, was a black hat, a dark green coatee with dark green cuffs and collar and white trousers.

They had a colour which was rather complicated and pretentious. It had a deep yellow field with two vertical carmine bands, one on the fly and one by the hoist, and a white one along the lower edge. In each angle there was a flaming grenade in natural colours. In the centre top there was the gold crowned double cypher of Frederik V within a ribbon of the order of the elephant in turn surrounded by a green wreath. Below this there was white scroll bearing the text 17 KIOGE BUES FAHNE 47 over a scene of a blue sky with a hand emerging from a cloud over a gold cross, a crown, a hose and a bridge in the sea over a trophy of arms colours and a mortar surrounded by a wreath of laurels and palm fronds.

The artillery company wore a blue tunic with a black collar and cuffs, brass buttons and blue or white waistcoat and a pair of fall-fronted drill trousers, but other sources say the artillery officers wore the same uniform as the infantry. In 1810 they had a red coatee lined white with light blue cuffs, collar and lapels and brass buttons. They wore a light blue waistcoat and breeches with short black Hessian-style boots. Their headgear is not known.

Mariager Borgerlige Infanteri
In 1803 the officers had a black bicorn with a black cockade and a gold loop, button and tassels. The plume was dark blue with a red tip. They wore a long-tailed double-breasted dark blue coat with dark blue collar and round cuffs piped white with gold buttons and epaulettes. They had dark blue breeches and a white waistcoat with short black Hessian-style boots. Their strength is unknown.

Mariboe Borgervæbning
In 1803 the citizens wore a long-tailed double-breasted dark green coat with a red collar and cuffs piped light blue with brass buttons. They had white breeches and a white waistcoat with short black Hessian-style boots. They had a black bicorn with a black cockade and a yellow loop and button. The plume was dark blue with a red tip. Their strength is unknown.

Marstall Borgerlige Infanteri
Their uniforms and strength are unknown.

---

1 On 24 August 1807 an English force of only 25 cavalrymen came to Køge to disarm the *borgervæbningen*. This militia unit suffered the same problems as many others. Like in other towns, the people of Køge were happy with their fine militia titles and uniforms, but in spite of the fact that they were threatened by war, a lot of the troop excused themselves from the preparatory weapon exercises on the Sundays of 26 June and 2 July 1807. The two butchers, Busch and Daldorff were busy marking lambs. Hansen the blacksmith was fixing a stove for a priest in a nearby village of Valløby. The merchant Permin had undergone a blood-letting, so he could not wear boots. Another merchant Thronsen, had a nail through his foot. Yet another, Ottosen was making his confession at the church. Peder Pedersen had dislocated his leg the night before when he jumped off the cart at the Hårlev Inn and Schiøtt the merchant had a bad knee. The miller Danielsen was at a market in the nearby borough of Slagelse, Meyer the glove maker's wife was in labour, and a merchant called Boserup had to take care of a traveller (as he had no servant at the time). The point here is that when you read the reasons why the men could not attend the drill training, it seems like they used every excuse possible to avoid it. So, this probably explains the reason why around only 25 cavalrymen were able disarm a whole town as well as their rather poor performance at the battle of Køge. After being disarmed in 1807 an artillery corps was created instead.

Middlefart Borgerlige Infanteri

There are two versions of the 1803 uniforms the officers of the *borgerkompagniet* (citizen company). In one they wear a long-tailed double-breasted red coat with a red collar and cuffs lined red and piped straw-yellow with gold buttons and epaulettes. They had a straw-yellow waistcoat and fall-front breeches, and a black bicorn with a black cockade and a yellow loop and button. The plume was white with a green tip. They carried a sabre on a black belt with a rectangular brass plate buckle.

In the other, from an approbation order in the state archives, the infantry officers wear a long-tailed double-breasted crimson red coat with a black or dark green collar and cuffs piped straw-yellow, gold buttons and epaulettes. They have a straw-yellow waistcoat and fall-front breeches, and a black bicorn with a black cockade and a yellow loop and button. The plume was white with a black or dark green tip.

In 1810 the infantry officers wore a crimson red coatee lined yellow with a green collar and cuffs piped yellow, gold buttons and epaulettes. They had a yellow waistcoat and yellow fall-front breeches. Their headwear is not specified.

Middlefart Jæger Corps

In 1803 the *jaeger* company officers wore a long-tailed double-breasted dark blue tunic lined blue with a crimson red collar and round cuffs, gold buttons and epaulettes together with a white waistcoat and wore a pair of fall-fronted dark blue pantaloons or breeches. Their round hat had a green plume with a red tip.

In 1810 the *jaeger* company officers wore a dark blue tunic lined blue with a crimson red collar and round cuffs, gold buttons and epaulettes together with a white waistcoat and wore a pair of fall-fronted dark blue pantaloons or breeches with red piping, probably down the outside leg seam. Their round hat or shako had a green plume with a red tip. Their strengths are unknown.

Nakskov Borgerlige Infanteri

In 1803 the officers of the 1st Avdeling had dark blue double-breasted long-tailed coats with red round cuffs and collar piped white, brass buttons and gold epaulettes and a straw-yellow waistcoat and a pair of fall-fronted yellow pantaloons or breeches. Their bicorn had a gold loop, black cockade and a blue plume. In 1810 they had a dark blue coatee lined white with red collar and round cuffs brass buttons and gold epaulettes and a straw-yellow waistcoat and a pair of fall-fronted yellow pantaloons or breeches.

The 2nd Avdeling had a dark blue double-breasted long-tailed coat with a white collar and round cuffs piped white with brass buttons and gold epaulettes. They wore a white waistcoat and white fall-front breeches or trousers. Their hat plume was blue. The men probably had single-breasted coatees and round hats. Their strength is unknown.

From 1810 they had a dark blue coatee with a red collar and cuffs piped white with brass buttons. Their waistcoat was white, and their breeches/trousers were blue.

These descriptions are taken from the previously mentioned approbation order conserved in the Rigsarkivet (National Archives), and a contemporary watercolours conserved in the Dronningens Håndbibliotek (Queen's Library).

Nyborg Borgerlige Infanteri

In 1803 the officers had a double-breasted crimson red coat with a blue collar and round cuffs, piped yellow, brass buttons and gold epaulettes. They wore a straw-yellow waistcoat and a pair of fall-fronted straw-yellow breeches and black boots. Their bicorn had a gold loop, black cockade and a white plume with a blue tip. In 1810 they wore a crimson red coatee with a light blue collar and cuffs piped and lined yellow, brass buttons and a straw-yellow waistcoat and a pair of straw-yellow fall-fronted breeches. They had shakos and their strength is unknown.

This unit had a white pennon with a silver fringe, painted on the obverse was a gold crown over a green wreath in the centre a gold monogram 'F' and below the wreath there was a '31' on one side and 'Julie' on the other written in gold. On the reverse there was a gold crown over green wreath, in the centre a gold monogram 'MIF' and below the wreath there was a gold number '17' on one side and '90' on the other.

Nykøbing på Falster Børgervæbning

In 1803 the officers had a double-breasted dark green coat with the lapels, round cuffs and collar the same colour, piped light blue, brass buttons and gold epaulettes. They wore a white waistcoat and a pair of fall-fronted white breeches and black boots. Their bicorn had a gold loop, black cockade and a green plume.

In 1810 the 1st Avdeling had a blue coatee with green cuffs and collar with white lining and piping, brass buttons and a white waistcoat. They wore a pair of fall-fronted blue pantaloons or breeches.

The 2nd Avdeling had red cuffs and collar for difference, otherwise the same. Their strength is unknown.

Nysted Borgerlige Infanteri

In 1803 the officers had a double-breasted dark green coat with white lining, narrow straw-yellow lapels, round cuffs and collar piped light blue, brass buttons and gold epaulettes. They wore a straw-yellow waistcoat, and a pair of fall-fronted short straw-yellow breeches and white stockings and black boots. Their bicorn had a gold loop, green cockade with a white border and a green plume with a red tip. In 1810 they had a green coatee with yellow lining, yellow lapels, cuffs and collar, brass buttons and a yellow waistcoat and breeches/trousers. Their strength is unknown.

Næstved Borgerlige Infanteri

In 1803 the officers had a double-breasted red coat with a medium blue collar, narrow lapels and round cuffs, piped yellow, brass buttons and gold epaulettes. They wore a medium blue waistcoat and a pair of fall-fronted medium blue breeches and black boots. Their bicorn had a gold loop, black cockade and a blue plume. In 1810 they had a red coatee with white lining and a light blue collar, cuffs, lapels and piping, brass buttons and a light blue waistcoat and breeches/trousers. Their strength is unknown.

Odense Borgerlige Infanteri

The Odense Borgerlige Infanteri was composed of three companies. In 1803 the officers and probably the NCOs of the 1st Avdeling had a double-breasted crimson red coat with straw-yellow lining and piping with a medium blue collar, crimson red round cuffs, brass buttons and gold epaulettes. They wore a straw-yellow waistcoat, and a pair of fall-fronted short straw-yellow breeches, with white stockings and black boots. Their bicorn had a gold loop, black cockade and a white plume with a medium blue tip. The officers and probably the NCOs of the 2nd Avdeling had the same uniform with the following differences; a double row of piping on the collar, long buff breeches and a white plume with a dark blue tip. The officers and probably the NCOs of the 3rd Avdeling had the same uniform with the following differences; long straw-yellow breeches and a blue plume with a white tip. The uniforms of the men are unknown, but were very mixed to say the least, and few had anything but scraps of uniforms. Also, their weapons were rather old and worn at best.

Odense Ungkarlekorpset

The Ungkarlekorpset or 'Young Bachelors Corps' was the best equipped and uniformed unit in Odense, and was an independent company recruited from young unmarried skilled workers, living in Odense.

In 1803 the officers had a single-breasted dark green coat lined green with a dark green collar and round cuffs, dark green buttons, red turnbacks and pocket piping, three buttons and silver epaulettes. With this they wore a white waistcoat, and a pair of fall-fronted medium grey breeches or pantaloons which had simple black knots on them and black boots. They had a bicorn with a silver loop, black cockade and a black falling plume with a red tip. The privates or centre company men and probably the *jægere* had a single-breasted dark green coatee lined green with a red collar and dark green round cuffs, dark green buttons and silver epaulettes. The cuffs, pockets and coat front were piped red. With this they wore a pair of fall-fronted medium grey breeches or pantaloons with a simple knot picked out in black and black boots. They had an M1789 round hat with a falling black plume with a red tip and white cords.

The grenadier company wore a single-breasted long-tailed dark green coat lined dark green with a dark green collar and cuffs and dark green buttons. With this they wore a white waistcoat, blue neckstock, short dark grey breeches, white stockings and black boots. Their headwear was an old-fashioned M1785 bronze-faced mitre cap stamped with the Danish Royal Arms. The cap was red with straw-yellow piping and the band was green piped gold with a large brass grenade, and it had a yellow and green tassel. This is a magnificent original cap is conserved in the Museum of Odense. The grenadiers had a black cartridge box on a shoulder belt which had a brass match case.

In 1802 they had a strength of 13 officers, 20 NCOs, three drummers, one fifer, two sappers, 48 *grenaderer,* 30 *jaegere* and 120 *gemene* (soldiers). All the officers and NCOs had steel-hilted sabres. Another 100 steel-hilted sabres were also distributed to the *grenaderer, jaegere* and the rest to some of the soldiers. The corps had no less than 250 muskets with bayonets, but by 1801 they were all very old and worn. In 1801 the town made 200 black cross belts with ammunition pouches. The *jaegere* and ordinary soldiers all had hats with a green plume with a red top.

Odense Borgerlige Ridende Jæger Corps

There was also a mounted unit, strength unknown. We know of two uniforms after a pair of small contemporary watercolours from around 1803. The officer has a black bicorn with a white plume and what appears to be a green cockade with a silver loop and pewter button. The bicorn also has a silver tassel on each side. He wears a dark green double-breasted tailed coat with the black collar is piped white, the buttons are dark green, and the cuffs are black. His leg wear is a pair of buff breeches with a knot picked out in black or dark green thread and a pair of Hessian-style boots. He is armed with a steel-hilted sabre carried in a black scabbard with steel fittings on a black belt with a silver buckle.

The trooper has a black M1789 style hat with a white plume and loop on the side and crossed white cords. He wears a dark green jacket or coatee, with a black shoulder strap piped white and a pewter button. The collar is black piped white and the cuffs black. His legwear is a pair of dark green riding overalls with pewter buttons down the outer leg seam, and black boots worn under the pantaloons with steel spurs. He is armed with a steel-hilted sabre carried in a black steel mounted scabbard on a black belt with a silver buckle. The trooper also wears a black pouch belt with a pewter badge. They all had a pair of pistols carried on the saddle. The colour of the housings or shabraque is unknown, but we can reasonably assume it to have been dark green. Their strength in 1803 was eight officers and

THE DANISH ARMY OF THE NAPOLEONIC WARS VOLUME 3

Danish Citizen Militias (II), *Borgervæbninger*

THE CITIZEN OR TOWN MILITIAS (I)

> Facing page
>
> Plate 58. Danish Citizen Militias (II), *Borgervæbninger*
>
> Top:
>
> 1. Faaborg Borgervæbning Infanteri, officer
> 2. Fredericia Borgervæbning. Officer of the 1st Avdeling (ward) of the 1st company.
> 3. Fredericia Borgervæbning. Officer of the 2nd Avdeling (ward)
> 4. Fredericia Artillerikorpset, gunner
>
> Bottom:
>
> 5. Helsingør Borgervæbning, officer
> 6. Helsingør Artilleri Corps, officer
> 7. Kolding Borgervæbning Infanteri officer of the 1st Avdeling and 2nd Avdeling (ward)
> 8. Kolding Ridende Corps, officer.
>
> Note: The watch-chain hanging from their waists, was an informal sign of a citizen and his rank.

NCOs, two trumpeters and 42 troopers. Note that as these uniforms were made individually there may well have been some variations. (Source: *Borgervæbninger 1550–1870* Søren Bitsch Christensen & *Borgervæbningen i Danmark og Norge 1803*, the Queen's Library).

Odense Borgerlige Jæger Corps
The uniforms and strength of this company are not recorded.

Præstø Borgerlige Infanteri
In 1803 the infantry officers had a red double-breasted coat with narrow medium blue lapels, medium blue round cuffs and collar, brass buttons and gold epaulettes. They had a medium blue waistcoat and a pair of medium blue fall-fronted breech/trousers and black boots. Their headgear was a bicorn without a plume.

Randers Borgerlige Infanteri
In 1803 the infantry officers of the 1st Avdeling had a red coat with red lapels, medium blue round cuffs and collar, all piped straw-yellow and brass buttons and gold epaulettes. They had a straw-yellow waistcoat and a pair of straw-yellow fall-fronted breeches/trousers and black boots. Their head wear was a bicorn without a plume. In 1810 the infantry had a red coatee with light blue cuffs and collar, yellow piping and lining, white metal buttons and a yellow waistcoat and trousers/breeches. Headwear not specified but they had either a hat or later a shako.

Randers Borgerlige Jæger Corps
In 1803 the *jæger* officers had a black M1789 hat with a green plume, black cockade with a gold loop and button had a dark green tunic with narrow deep olive-green lapels piped white, black cuffs and green cuff flap, both piped white and a black collar piped white, and they wore a pair of white fall-fronted gaiter trousers. The tunic had a pair of gold epaulettes. Armament was a brass-hilted sabre with a gold sword knot in a black leather scabbard with brass mountings on a black belt with a large rectangular brass buckle.

The men wore the same uniform minus the epaulettes and were armed with a musket and a brass-hilted sabre in a black leather scabbard with brass mountings on a black belt with a brass buckle.

In 1810 they had a green coatee, black collar, cuffs and lapels, piped white and brass buttons, grey trousers and their hat had a green plume.

The strength of the *jægere* company in 1803 was one captain, one first lieutenant, one second lieutenant, one sergeant, four *overjæger* (*jæger* corporals) 44 *hægeres* and five *hornblæsere* or hautboys. In 1808 they received 200 old rifles from the Fredricia Arsenal.

Ribe Borgervæbning
In 1803 the officers wore a long-tailed double-breasted red coat lined straw-yellow with black round cuffs and collar piped straw-yellow with brass buttons, gold officers' epaulettes. This was worn with a straw-yellow waistcoat and a pair of straw-yellow fall-fronted breeches, and they wore short black Hessian boots. They had a round hat with a red cockade with a gold loop and tassels and a white plume. They carried a lion's headed sabre on a black belt with a rectangular brass plate buckle. The NCOs wore the same uniform, but with just an NCO's epaulette on the right side.

The men wore a completely different uniform; a double-breasted dark green coat, including the collar and cuffs, brass buttons and a straw-yellow waistcoat and blue and white striped or ticken trousers worn with short black

THE DANISH ARMY OF THE NAPOLEONIC WARS VOLUME 3

Danish Citizen Militias (III)

THE CITIZEN OR TOWN MILITIAS (I)

> Facing page
>
> Plate 59. Danish Citizen Militias (III)
>
> Top:
>
> 1. Odense, officer of the Ungkarlekorpset (Young Bachelors Corps). The braiding on their trousers may have been dark green.
>
> 2. Odense grenadier Ungkarlekorpset
>
> 3. Private, Odense Ungkarlekorpset. The braiding on their trousers may have been dark green.
>
> 4. Trooper, Odense Borgerlige Ridende Jæger Korpset
>
> Bottom:
>
> 5. Ribe, officer of the Borgerlige Infanteri
> 6. Ribe, private of the Borgerlige Infanteri
> 7. Svendborg Borgerlige Jæger corps, officer
> 8. Varde Borgerlige Infanteri, officer
>
> Note: the watch-chain hanging from their waists, was an informal sign of a citizen and his rank.

boots. Their round hat had a white plume with a green tip. Their belts and straps were black leather.

In 1810 they had a crimson red coatee with red lapels, black cuffs and collar, yellow piping and lining, brass buttons and a yellow waistcoat and trousers. They had shakos. Their strength is unknown.

Ringkøbing Borgervæbning
In 1810 they wore a blue coatee with a red collar with white lining and piping, brass buttons and a white waistcoat and a pair of white fall-fronted breeches or trousers. Their strength is unknown.

Ringsted Borgervæbning
In 1803 the officers wore a medium green coatee with a red collar, narrow lapels and round cuffs, piped yellow with brass buttons and gold epaulettes and a straw-yellow waistcoat and a pair of fall-fronted straw-yellow breeches. They had a round hat without a plume.

From 1810 they wore a green coatee lined straw-yellow with a red collar and cuffs piped yellow, and a straw-yellow waistcoat and a pair of fall-fronted straw-yellow breeches. Their strength is unknown.

Roskilde Borgerlige Infanteri
In 1803 the officers wore a long-tailed double-breasted red coat with dark blue round cuffs, narrow lapels and collar with brass buttons and gold epaulettes which was worn with a dark blue waistcoat and a pair of dark blue fall-fronted breeches. They also wore short black Hessian boots. They had a bicorn with a black cockade with a gold loop and tassels but no plume. They carried a lion's headed sabre on a black belt with a rectangular brass plate buckle.

From 1810 they wore a red coatee lined white with blue lapels, cuffs and collar and a blue waistcoat and blue trousers or breeches. Their hat had a white plume with a red tip. Their strength is unknown.

Rudkøbing Borgerlige Infanteri
In 1803 the officers wore a long-tailed double-breasted dark blue coat with red round cuffs and collar with brass buttons and gold epaulettes worn, with a white waistcoat and a pair of dark blue fall-fronted breeches, and short black Hessian boots. They had a round hat with a black cockade with a gold loop and tassels and a blue plume with a red tip. They carried a lion's headed sabre on a black belt with a rectangular brass plate buckle.

From 1810 the infantry of the 1st Avdeling had a dark blue coatee lined white with blue lapels, red cuffs and collar with blue lining, brass buttons and a white waistcoat. They wore a pair of fall-fronted blue pantaloons or breeches and their hat had a blue plume with a red tip.

The 2nd Avdeling had a blue coatee lined white with a red collar, cuffs and lapels brass buttons and a white waistcoat. They wore a pair of fall-fronted blue pantaloons or breeches and their hat had green plumes with a white tip. Their strength is unknown.

Rødbye Borgerlige Infanteri
Based on a description taken from an approbation order conserved in the Rigsarkivet (National Archives) and a contemporary watercolour conserved in the Dronningens Håndbibliotek (Queens Library) we know that in 1803 the officers wore a long-tailed double-breasted dark blue coat with red round cuffs and collar short black Hessian boots. They had a bicorn with a black cockade with a gold loop

and tassels and a white plume with a red tip. They carried a lion's headed sabre on a black belt with a rectangular brass plate buckle.

From 1810 the infantry had a dark blue coatee with crimson red cuffs, lapels and collar piped and lined white, brass buttons and a white waistcoat and they wore white trousers/breeches. Their strength is unknown.

Saxkiøbing Borgerlige Infanteri
In 1803 the officers wore a long-tailed double-breasted dark blue coat with red round cuffs and collar, piped white with shiny black buttons, no epaulettes, a dark blue waistcoat and a pair of straw-yellow fall-fronted breeches and short black Hessian boots. They had a bicorn with a black cockade with a gold loop and tassels and a blue plume with a red tip. They carried a lion's headed sabre on a black belt with a rectangular brass plate buckle.

From 1810 the infantry had a dark blue coatee with crimson red cuffs, lapels and collar piped and lined white, brass buttons and a white waistcoat and they wore blue trousers/breeches. The hat of the 1st Avdeling had a blue plume with a red tip while the 2nd Avdeling had a white plume with a blue tip. Their strength is unknown. These descriptions are again taken from an approbation order conserved in the Rigsarkivet (National Archives) and a contemporary watercolour conserved in the Dronningens Håndbibliotek (Queen's Library). Confirmed in 1810 by Møller.

Skagen Borgerlige Infanteri
In 1803 the officers wore a long-tailed double-breasted blue coat with crimson red round cuffs and collar with brass buttons, gold epaulettes and a pair of dark blue fall-fronted breeches and black boots. They had a round hat with a black cockade with a gold loop and tassels and a blue plume with a crimson red tip. They carried a lion's headed sabre on a black belt with a rectangular brass plate buckle.

From 1810 the infantry had a dark blue coatee with crimson red cuffs and collar, brass buttons and a red waistcoat and they wore blue pantaloons/breeches. Their hat had a white plume with a blue tip.

Skagen Borgerlige Artilleri
From 1803 the artillery officers wore a single-breasted medium grey coatee with a dark blue collar and cuffs piped yellow, brass buttons and gold epaulettes. Their waistcoat was blue, and they had a pair of fall-fronted blue breeches and black boots. They wore a round hat with a black cockade with a gold hat band, loop and tassels and a grey plume. They also carried a lion-headed sabre on a black shoulder belt with an oval brass plate.

In 1810 they had a single-breasted medium grey coatee with a dark blue collar and cuffs piped yellow, brass buttons, gold epaulettes and a blue waistcoat and a pair of fall-fronted blue breeches. Their hat or shako had a blue plume. Their strength is unknown.

Skanderborg Borgerlige Infanteri
The uniforms and strength of this company are not recorded.

Skielskiør Borgerlige Infanteri
In 1803 the officers wore a long-tailed double-breasted blue coat with red round cuffs and collar with white piping, brass buttons, no epaulettes, a straw-yellow waistcoat and a pair of straw-yellow fall-fronted breeches and black boots. They had a round hat with a black cockade with a gold loop and tassels and a blue plume with a red tip. They carried a lion's headed sabre on a black belt with a rectangular brass plate buckle.

Slagelse Borgerlige Infanteri
In 1803 the officers wore a long-tailed double-breasted blue coat with black round cuffs, narrow lapels and collar with white piping, brass buttons, gold epaulettes, a white waistcoat and a pair of white fall-fronted breeches and black boots. They had a bicorn with a black cockade with a gold loop and tassels and a blue plume. They carried a lion's headed sabre on a black belt with a rectangular brass plate buckle.

In 1810 the infantry had a blue coatee with black cuffs and collar with white lining and piping, brass buttons and a white waistcoat and white or light blue grey breeches.

Slagelse Skarpskytte Corps
In 1803 the officers of the sharpshooters had a dark green coatee with a green collar and cuffs, white metal buttons and a pair of fall-fronted grey breeches, no epaulettes and a round hat with a green plume. In 1810 a green coatee with pewter buttons and grey trousers is mentioned. Their strength is unknown.

Sorøe Borgerlige Infanteri
In 1803 the officers wore a long-tailed single-breasted red coat with dark green round cuffs and collar with straw-yellow lining and piping, brass buttons, no epaulettes, a straw-yellow double-breasted waistcoat and a pair of straw-yellow fall-fronted breeches and black boots. They had a bicorn with a black cockade with a gold loop and tassels without a plume. They carried a lion's head sabre on a black belt with a rectangular brass plate buckle.

By 1810 they had a red lapelled coatee with red lapels lined straw-yellow with light green cuffs and collar, piped yellow and a straw-yellow waistcoat and a pair of straw-yellow fall-fronted breeches. Their strength is unknown.

Stege Borgerlige Infanteri
In 1803 the officers had a double-breasted red coat with dark blue round cuffs, narrow lapels and collar with brass

buttons and gold epaulettes, a dark blue waistcoat and they wore a pair of fall-fronted dark blue pantaloons or breeches. They had a red plume with a blue tip on their bicorn.

In 1810 they had a red coatee with red lapels lined blue with blue cuffs and collar piped blue, brass buttons and a blue waistcoat and a pair of fall-fronted light blue grey breeches. Their hat had a white plume with a blue tip. Their strength is unknown.

Stubbekiøbing Borgerlige Infanteri
In 1803 the officers had a double-breasted dark green coat with dark green round cuffs and collar with brass buttons and gold epaulettes, a straw-yellow waistcoat and they wore a pair of fall-fronted straw-yellow pantaloons or breeches. They had a round hat with a green plume. Their strength is unknown.

Svendborg Borgerlige Infanteri
In 1803 the officers had a double-breasted red coat with dark blue round cuffs, narrow lapels and collar with brass buttons and gold epaulettes, a straw-yellow waistcoat and they wore a pair of fall-fronted dark blue pantaloons or breeches. They had a white plume with a blue tip on their bicorn.

In 1810 the 1st Avdeling had a red coatee with blue lapels and collar, brass buttons and straw-yellow lining and waistcoat and they wore a pair of straw-yellow fall-fronted pantaloons/breeches.

In 1810 the 2nd Avdeling had a blue coatee with a red collar and white lining, brass buttons and a white waistcoat and they wore a pair of blue or white fall-fronted pantaloons or breeches. This militia company had shakos with a white plume and a blue tip.

Svendborg Ridende Jæger Corps
In 1803 the *jæger* officers had a round hat with a green plume and gold loop and hat band, green and gold cords with a green cockade, a double-breasted dark green coat with dark green cuffs and collar with white piping and dark green buttons, gold epaulettes, straw-yellow waistcoat and a pair of fall-fronted grey pantaloons or breeches.

The troop wore a hat with a black band, green cords and plume with a green cockade and their uniform was the same, but with brass buttons and a white waistcoat. All carried a brass-hilted sabre. Horse furniture unknown, but they probably had a green shabraque.

In 1810 they had a double-breasted dark green coat with black lapels and yellow piping and brass buttons, white waistcoat and they wore a pair of fall-fronted grey pantaloons or breeches. They had a green plume on their shako. Their strength is unknown.

Sæbye Borgerlige Artilleri
In 1803 the officers wore a long-tailed single-breasted medium grey coat with medium grey cuffs and collar with yellow piping, brass buttons, gold epaulettes and a pair of fall-fronted blue breeches and black boots. They had a round hat with a grey plume. They carried a lion's headed sabre on a black shoulder belt with a rectangular brass plate buckle.

Thisted Borgerlige Infanteri
The uniforms and strength of this company is not recorded.

Varde (Warde) Borgervæbning
In 1803 the officers wore a long-tailed dark blue coat lined straw-yellow with crimson red cuffs and collar, with white piping, brass buttons, gold epaulettes and a straw-yellow waistcoat and a pair of fall-fronted straw-yellow breeches and black boots. They had a round hat with a white plume and a red and white cockade. They carried a lion's headed sabre on a black belt with a rectangular brass plate buckle.

The men wore a double-breasted dark blue coatee with crimson red cuffs and collar, no piping, with brass buttons. They wore a pair of fall-fronted straw-yellow trousers and black boots. They had a cartridge box on a brown leather bandoleer and a brown leather waist belt with a brass buckle. They had a round hat with a white plume and a red, white and blue cockade.

From 1810 they wore a dark blue coatee with crimson red cuffs and collar piped yellow and yellow lining with brass buttons. They had a straw-yellow waistcoat and a pair of fall-fronted straw-yellow breeches. Headgear is not specified. Their strength is unknown.

Vejle Borgervæbning
In 1803 the 1st Avdeling officers wore a double-breasted long-tailed red coat with straw-yellow lining, round red cuffs and collar, brass buttons and a straw-yellow waistcoat and a pair of fall-fronted straw-yellow breeches. Their bicorn had a white plume with a red tip.

In 1810 they wore a red coatee with straw-yellow lining, round red cuffs and collar and brass buttons, with a straw-yellow waistcoat and a pair of fall-fronted straw-yellow breeches.

In 1803 the 2nd Avdeling officers wore a double-breasted long-tailed red coat with dark blue round cuffs and collar piped straw-yellow, with brass buttons and a gold epaulette. They wore a straw-yellow waistcoat and a pair of fall-fronted straw-yellow breeches. Their bicorn had a white plume.

In 1810 they had a red coatee with straw-yellow lining, red cuffs and collar, brass buttons and a straw-yellow waistcoat and a pair of fall-fronted straw-yellow breeches.

Vejle Borgerlige Jæger Corps
In 1803 the *jæger* officers wore a double-breasted long-tailed dark green coat with a black collar and round cuffs piped straw-yellow with brass buttons. They wore a pair of

fall-fronted grey pantaloons/breeches and a grey waistcoat. They had a round hat with a green plume.

In 1810 they had a green coatee piped and lined yellow, brass buttons and grey trousers.

The strength of these three companies is unknown.

Viborg Borgerlige Infanteri
In 1803 the officers wore a double-breasted long-tailed red coat with a dark green collar and round cuffs piped yellow, with gilt buttons and gold epaulettes. They had a straw-yellow waistcoat and a pair of fall-fronted straw-yellow breeches. They had a black round hat with a white plume.

Vordingborg Borgervæbning
In 1803 the officers wore a double-breasted long-tailed crimson red coat with a dark blue collar, narrow lapels and round cuffs with gilt buttons and gold epaulettes. They had a dark blue waistcoat and a pair of fall-fronted dark blue breeches. Headgear was a black bicorn without a plume.

In 1810 this company had a red coatee lined blue with blue lapels, cuffs and collar, brass buttons and a blue waistcoat and pair of fall-fronted blue breeches or trousers. Their hat had a white plume with a red tip. Their strength is unknown.

Ærøskøbing Borgervæbning
They had a blue coatee with crimson red cuffs and collar, brass buttons and a straw-yellow waistcoat. Their strength is unknown.

14

The Citizen or Town Militias (II)

The *Borgervæbninger* of Schleswig-Holstein

Altona Gardekorpset

In 1803 the mounted officer of the Altona Grüne Corps wore a dark green coat with a grass green collar, cuffs and lapels, lined yellow with brass buttons, gold epaulettes and aiguillettes, a yellow waistcoat and a pair of fall-fronted yellow buff leather breeches. They had a black bicorn piped gold, gold knots and a gold badge under a green plume. They carried their sabre on a buff shoulder belt. They had square green housings and pistol covers edged straw-yellow or gold and two thin rows of straw-yellow or gold lace and Danish knots in the rear angle and pistol covers.[1]

In 1814 the mounted Altona Grüne Corps other ranks had a green coat with a black collar, cuffs and lapels, lined yellow with brass buttons, a yellow waistcoat and a pair of fall-fronted yellow buff leather breeches. Headwear was a shako with a white plume. They had a black pouch belt on a black leather bandoleer and the sabre was carried on a black leather waist belt. The horse furniture was of the same cut as previously mentioned, but with a simple straw-yellow border.[2]

Altona Borgerlige Infanteri

In 1803 the officers had a hat with a gold hat band and gold cords and flounders. In 1810 the infantry wore a single breasted blue coatee with a black collar and black cuffs. The coatee had brass buttons. The waistcoat was white, and they had a pair of blue fall-fronted trousers. Their hat had a white plume with a red tip. Their strengths are unknown.

Femern (or Burg) Frivillige Jæger Corps (Volunteer Foot Jaeger Company)

This was a unit raised to strengthen the defence of the important island Fermern, now called Fehmarn. Referred to as a foot company in 1810 and it is mentioned in 1813 as part of the forces taking part in the guarding of the island, and here they are described as mounted.

Strength in 1808 was a *kaptain*, a *premierelojtnant* (first lieutenant), a *sekuntlojtnant* (second lieutenant), eight *overjægere* (corporals), two *halvmånespillere* (horn-blowers) and 100 *jægere* (riflemen). They were active from 1808 to 1814.

Uniform

Very little information is available of their uniforms and subsequent history, probably because they were considered more as a kind of active citizen militia, rather than a formal volunteer jæger corps. However, based on a portrait of their commanding officer of 1810 and a letter from the chief of staff von Bülow of 24 April 1808 they originally wore a hat, later replaced with a shako, with a green plume. They wore a dark green short coatee, black collar, facings and cuffs, yellow (white?) lining, yellow (white?) buttons, and grey trousers. Their bandoleer was black (edged gold for officers). They had same distinctions as citizen guards with a gold/green sword knot. The NCOs were allowed one epaulette. The jaegers wore green coat with black collar, cuffs and narrow lapels piped white, white lining with white metal buttons, a pair of fall-fronted white or brown pantaloons with green lace.

The officers' full-dress uniform in 1810 consisted of a dark grey jacket, black collar, facings and cuffs, white lining, white buttons, white or dark brown trousers with green lining. They had a black pouch on a black leather bandoleer and a black shako with a green plume.

---

1   Source: contemporary watercolour dated 1802 and titled *Altonner Bürger Garde, Grüne Corps*.
2   Source; contemporary watercolour dated 1814 and titled *Altona ridene grønne garde corps*.

THE DANISH ARMY OF THE NAPOLEONIC WARS VOLUME 3

Schleswig and Holstein Citizen Militia

THE CITIZEN OR TOWN MILITIAS (II)

Facing page

Plate 60. Schleswig and Holstein Citizen Militia

Top:
1. Altona, Altona Grüne Corps, 1803
2. Altona, Altona Grüne Corps, 1810
3. Altona Borgerlige Infanteri, 1808
4. Femern, Frivillige Jæger Corps, 1813 (author's reconstruction)

Bottom:
5. Flensborg Borgervæbning; officer of the Frederiksgarden, 1803
6. Flensborg Borgervæbning; commanding officer of the Christiansgarden, 1802
7. Flensborg Borgervæbning; private of the Christiansgarden c. 1810
8. Rendsborg Borgerlige Artilleri, officer 1808

Note: the watch-chain hanging from their waists, was an informal sign of a citizen and his rank.

Burg på Femern Borgervæbning

The mounted corps wore a double-breasted light blue coatee with narrow red lapels, yellow metal buttons and their hat had a white plume with a blue top. A portrait of the first commander, Christopher Conrad Greve Holck, (1775–1810) is preserved in the Rewentlow Museum. This shows the commander in a light blue coat with black cuffs and lapels edged with gold lace, small gold lace 'Brandenburgs' and a black shoulder belt also edged in gold lace, and gold fringed epaulettes. Unfortunately, it does not show his headwear or breeches.

Flensborg Borgervæbning

These troops were not originally military units, but parade units formed by rich burghers. The officers of the Frederiksgarden troop wore a ponceau red coatee with straw-yellow collar, cuffs and lining with brass buttons, straw-yellow waistcoat, blue trousers, gold lace on the uniform, a carmine red sash, black cockade and a cartridge pouch.

In the Christiansgarden troop in 1803, the captain wore a short double-breasted tailed coat green coat with black collar, cuffs and green lining with brass buttons with gold epaulettes, a white waistcoat with a pair of fall-fronted buff yellow breeches and a cartridge pouch with a brass 'CG' on the flap. He had a hat with a gold hat band, a yellow, green and black cockade and a white plume. The other officers wore a short double-breasted green coatee with black collar, cuffs and green lining with brass buttons with gold epaulettes, a white waistcoat with a pair of fall-fronted grey trousers and a cartridge pouch with a brass 'CG' on the flap. The officers of the Christiansgarden troop were allowed a special waist sash in 1801, coloured black, yellow and green. They wore a hat with a gold hat band, a yellow, green and black cockade and a white plume.

The men wore a hat with a white plume, and they had a short green coatee with black collar and cuffs with brass buttons, a white waist coat, grey trousers and black short boots. They all carried a brass hilted sabre in a black leather scabbard with brass fittings. They had a green colour with a black lozenge in the centre which bore a silver crown over an indistinct central motif with silver cyphers in each angle, probably the King's, and they also had a large brass band. Their strengths are unknown.

Husum Børgervæbning

In 1810 they wore a single-breasted blue coatee with a red collar, cuffs and lining, brass buttons with a pair of fall-fronted blue or white trousers or breeches. Their hat had a white plume with a green tip. The *skarpskyttere* had a single-breasted dark blue coatee with a red collar and lining, brass buttons worn with a pair of fall-fronted grey breeches. Their hat had a white plume with a green tip. Their strength is unknown.

Itzehoe Ridende Borgergarde

Although they existed in the period covered by this book, it has not been possible to find any uniform details for this unit before 1842. Their strength is unknown.

Kiel Borgervæbning

In 1810 the infantry wore a red coatee with black collar, lapels (and probably the cuffs) and brass buttons. They had a straw-yellow waistcoat and a pair of straw-yellow fall-fronted breeches or trousers. They had a *Freikorps* whose members wore a green tunic with green facings, piped white with brass buttons and a yellow waistcoat, and a pair of straw-yellow fall-fronted breeches or trousers. Their strength is unknown.

Borgerlige Artillerikorps i Rendsborg, 1st and 2nd Companies
In 1810 they wore a carmine red coatee lined yellow, which had a medium black collar, cuffs and lapels, yellow piping and brass buttons, yellow waistcoat and blue trousers. Their shako had a white plume with gold and red cords. They had a sealskin cartridge pouch on a black leather shoulder belt.

Brandkorpset i Rendsborg (The Rendsborg Fire Brigade)
Their uniforms and strength are unknown.

Slesvig Borgerlige Infanteri
The uniforms and strength of this company are not recorded.

Tønningen Børgervæbning
In 1810 they had a dark blue coatee with black cuffs and collar, narrow dark blue lapels, piped and lined white, brass buttons and a white waistcoat. They wore a pair of fall-fronted light blue grey pantaloons/breeches. Their hat had a white plume with a blue tip. Their strength is unknown.

15

The Norwegian Citizen Militia

In Norway (as in Denmark and Holstein) beside the regular army there were a large number of volunteer militia units raised for home defence with a semi-permanent status. They were mainly found in the major towns and ports, as these were the centres of trade, as well as the coastal militia (Kystværnet). Some of these units were quite ancient in origins, with many having been in existence since the middle ages at least. But the most important for the structure and organisation, as basic for all the rest, were Det Kongelige Frivillige Røroiske Bergjæger Corps, formed in 1788, and this unit was used in both Denmark and Norway as the basic guide for the new volunteer militia units formed from 1800 and onwards.

Although many groups of society were not eligible for military service, because of their status or trade, (mainly those found in towns) it was still expected that they should do their bit.

Normally service was part of the obligations of citizenship and was regulated by the government, but it was not a very rigid organisation; in fact in peacetime, many a citizen militia was more of a social club rather than a tough active service unit.

When the war suddenly erupted in 1807 the grim reality soon made itself felt and now, they were really needed. The English blockade and raids against shipping and coastal towns together with the war with Sweden in 1808–1809 forced them into action, generally with good results, but a lack of training and arms limited their efficiency if not their enthusiasm, and this influenced what it was possible to do, and the presence of regular forces was often necessary. As nearly all the citizen militias were found in coastal towns and cities, their main official role was manning coastal fortifications and city defences, hunting down spies and smugglers and general law enforcement.

Rørås. Det Kongelige Frivillige Røroiske Bergjæger Corps (see also Appendix 4)

This was a specialist unit, composed of workers at the copper works at the Rørås copper mine as a local volunteer defence force for the important mines. The workers had previously done some volunteer service in times of war 1710–1720, and even received two colours[1] in 1778. The first official volunteer formation of workers at Rørås was formed on 10 October 1788 as Det Kongelige Frivillige Røroiske Bjerg Corps.

Before 1799 they wore a black cap with a pointed front flap with a motif (probably a yellow or brass crossed double-headed axe and a pick) on it and a green-tipped white plume on the side. They had a black velvet smock with lapels, buff or pale yellow breeches and white gaiters. Around their waist they had a grey/brownish leather belt with an apron of the same colour, which was pushed around their back when not in the foundry. The apron worn by miners was always worn turned to the back. It was a traditional miner's equipment to protect the backside of his trousers when working in the mines.

On the 30 March 1798 the corps was renamed Det Kongelige Frivillige Røroiske Bergjæger Corps, and reorganised as a volunteer *jæger* corps. From 1799 it had the following organisation and strength:

> 1st company had three officers, 11 NCOs, two *waldhornister* (hornists), 74 *underjægere* (*jaegere*)
>
> 2nd company had three officers, 10 NCOs, two *waldhornister*, 74 *underjægere*
>
> Artillery: one officer, two NCOs and 17 *underjægere* who served two iron 6-pdr cannon from the Trondheim arsenal.

As a reserve were 211 *bergværnere* (home guard) of older workers. In 1799 it was planned that they should, when available, receive the following weapons from the arsenal in Trondheim: 200 rifles, 200 *krudthorn* (powder horns), 200 M1774 *korte carabiner* (shortened muskets), 200 *hirschfänger* M1791 and five *halvmåner* (crescent

---

[1] In 1778, when a more formal organisation and training were started, two very splendid colours were made, one red and one blue and on these colours there is an illustration of a *jæger* showing him wearing a cap with the crossed axe and pick. They are still suspended today in the church of Rørås.

THE DANISH ARMY OF THE NAPOLEONIC WARS VOLUME 3

Norwegian Citizen Militia (I)

Facing page

Plate 61. Norwegian Citizen Militia (I)

Top:

1. Officer, Christiania Ridende Borgergarde in dismounted service uniform *c*. 1803.

2. Officer, Christiania Ridende Borgergarde mounted service uniform *c*. 1803. Note the silver reversed lion of Norway badge on pouch belt strap. Following new regulations in 1806 this uniform changed to a braided hussar/light cavalry-style coatee.

3. Officer, Christianias Borgerlige Infanterikorps

4. Officer, Christiania Frivillige Jæger Corps. Note the gold crossed sabres badge on pouch belt strap.

Bottom:

5. Det Kongelige Frivillige Røroiskebjerg Corps (author's reconstruction)

6. Arendal Borgerlige Jæger Corps, officer. His coat had black hussar-style braiding down the front

7. Arendal Borgerlige Jæger Corps, *jæger*. His coat also has black hussar-style braiding down the front.

8. Officer, Bergen Borgerlige Infanteri.

Note the watch chains hanging from their waists; this was an informal sign of a citizen and his rank.

horns). But it seems that they just received the shortened muskets M1774 for training and the five *halvmåner*. Most of the older equipment was apparently used until 1808/1809, and the rifles were first issued when available. In 1798 a new jaeger uniform was allowed for the officers, which would also be adopted by all the others later.

Uniforms
The first uniform which was authorised for the officers of the Det Kongelige Frivillige Røroiske Bergjæger Corps, according to a *Kongelig Resolution* made on 19 July 1799. They were described as a dark green coatee with a black collar, cuffs and turnbacks piped light yellow, dark green cuff flaps and gold buttons. They wore buff yellow breeches and a round M1789 hat, with a green plume. They had the same general uniform colours in 1810, as shown for the officers in *Møller's List 1810*, but now with grey trousers, also for full dress and his book implies that they now had lapels on their coats as well. In the same resolution, it is stated that the soldiers will at a later date adopt uniforms of the same general model. Also, that there would in the near future drawings be made of this model. As we have so few contemporary pictures and very few other sources for uniforms of this unit many mistakes and myths have arisen.

Research of all known contemporary and official sources presents a clear but also surprising picture. One important and well-known source for many years been Johannes Senn's colourised etchings *Norske Klædedragter* originally published 1811. But what is not so well known is that his work is really just a copy, made after the Norwegian painter Johan Fredrik Leonard Dreier's older original water colours painted *c*. 1799–1801. A copy of this probably exists in the Norwegian army archives. The original, copied by Senn, no doubt shows the Røroiske Bergjæger Corps' first uniform. As they always had a close connection with Nordenfjeldske Skiløber Corps and even had same commander (C. G. von Bang), they also had access to uniforms from the same sources, as official letters also show, written during the years of 1798 to 1814.

So, as can be seen on Dreier's original/Senn's copy in 1800 the *jaegere* wore a M1789 cap, but with a new white, green-topped, feather, green uniform, probably based on the M1793 *skiløber uniform*, but with M1789/95 lapels and collar. White trousers M1791 were worn, with older white belts from *c*. 1788, and what probably is a *Bjergmand sabel* M1788, and as stated in the *Kongelig Resolution*: 'just issued for this occasion, new black musket straps, long cloth trousers [see above] and black shoes'. Clearly from Dreier's painting, they also received the new shortened M1774 muskets 'to use for the yearly exercise'. (Johannes Senn's copy was first made in 1811 after the original by J. F. L. Dreier 1799–1801). The grey trousers must at some point between have been adopted by all, as Dreier shows another jaeger of the corps in another painting from *c*. 1809/1810, again in the M1799 uniform, but now in grey overalls, a short red hussar-style jacket, probably from the stocks of Nordenfjeldske Skiløber Corps, armed with a rifle and *hirschfänger*, which they must also have received at this time. Also worthy of note, they are again shown with skis. This was probably the uniform worn *c*. 1808/1814 by the active *jægere* of Det Kongelige Frivillige Røroiske Bergjæger Corps. (The sketch was probably made by J. F. L. Dreier *c*. 1810 and is now in a private collection). Most of the details in both paintings are confirmed in other written sources.

As late as 1814, it is clear from the correspondence of the commander of 1st Trondhjemske Nationale Regiment, General Major C. G. von Bang,[2] which clearly states that, both the 2nd Nordenfjeldske Skiløber Bataljon, as well as the 1st Nordenfjeldske Skiløber Bataljon, 'Have enough green uniforms available, of two models, to equip them both and even enough left to supply some to the Det Kongelige Frivillige Røroiske Bergjæger Corps. The Bergværnere home guard of older workers wore the old black pre-1799 uniform, with red collar, cuffs and facings, yellow breeches, black gaiters and a black workers cap.

In 1814 Det Kongelige Frivillige Røroiske Bergjæger Corps, had six officers, 14 NCOs, four hornists and 390 *jægere*.

Prins Christian's Frivillige Jæger Corps

Originally this corps was in fact raised in 1807 as an extra regular unit, but it was found to be more expensive to maintain than a normal regular unit. Volunteers were few and of variable quality, so this force never really grew as it intended. The planned strength should have been four officers, 13 NCOs, nine *waldhornister* and 150 *jægere*. But in 1809 their real strength was said to be only 20 *jægere*.

A nineteenth-century reconstruction gives the proposed uniform as a black hat with a long green plume worn fore and aft and a black cockade on the side. They wore a green coatee with black collar, cuffs and lapels, piped white and pewter buttons. It had pale yellow turnbacks at the front. Their trousers were grey, and they had black gaiters, a black waist belt with a square brass buckle and they were armed with *jæger* rifles and *hirschfängers*.

Grev Herman Wedels Bogstads Livjæger Corps

The Grev Wedel-Jarlsbergs Frivillige Jæger Corps were also known as the Bærumske Jæger Corps and Grev Wedel-Jarlsbergs Frivillige Jæger Corps. In Norway this was the only volunteer unit that was officially raised outside a town, and they had a strength of 150 men. Although a fine corps, serving and patrolling alongside the main army, they only had one armed encounter, taking one prisoner, and their main contribution was guarding and escorting Swedish prisoners of war during hostilities. The *jæger* unit wore all grey uniforms with green facings and a sash and a Bavarian Rumford-type leather helmet with a green caterpillar over the top and down the back. An original hat is actually preserved in the Forsvarmuseet in Oslo.

Arendal Borgerlige Infanteri og Artilleri

In 1803 both the infantry and artillery officers wore a black bicorn with a blue plume and a black cockade, and a gold loop and tassels. They had a double-breasted long-tailed dark blue coat with a black falling collar and black cuffs with gold epaulettes and gilded brass buttons, and a double-breasted white waistcoat, dark blue pantaloons and short black boots.

They carried a brass-hilted sabre in a black leather scabbard with brass fittings on a black waist belt with a rectangular gilded plate buckle. The uniform was changed with the addition of narrow lapels and a little before 1810 the bicorn began to be replaced with shakos; at the same time white piping is also mentioned. The men do not appear to have had a uniform.

Arendal Frivillige Jæger Corps

In 1803 officers had a M1789 round hat with a black hat band, green cockade, gold cords and a green-tipped yellow side plume. They wore a single-breasted dark green coatee with a black collar and round cuffs, 10 black buttons and 10 rows of black hussar-style frogging with tufts on each side, like a dolman. They wore a black and yellow hussar barrel sash around their waist over the coatee. Their pantaloons were light beige yellow with simple black embroidered Hungarian-style knots and short hussar-style boots with black tassels. They carried a steel/silver hilted sabre with a gold sword knot in a black leather scabbard with brass fittings on a black waist belt with a rectangular silvered plate buckle.

The men wore the same uniform, but with the following differences. Their hat cords and tassels were green, and they did not have a barrel sash, but they had a black leather belt with a black leather ventral cartridge pouch. They were armed with a fusil with a black leather sling, and they carried a steel-hilted M1753 infantry sabre or *hirschfänger* in a black leather scabbard with brass fittings. By 1810 the pantaloons were now grey, and the cut of the coat had changed slightly to conform to the new styles.

Bergen Borgerlige Infanteri og Artilleri

In 1807 both the infantry and artillery officers wore a black bicorn with a cockade and a gold loop and tassels. They had a single-breasted long-tailed dark blue coat with black velvet collar laced gold, with black velvet round cuffs, gold epaulettes and gilded brass buttons, white pantaloons and

---

2   Major, later General Major Carsten Gerhard von Bang (1756–1826), who is a much undervalued figure in Norwegian history. He was a strange man, the son of a bishop, educated as a lawyer, he was director of the works at Rørås, but also a soldier, commanding Det Kongelige Frivillige Røråsiske Bergjæger Corps, later becoming commander of 1st Nordenfjeldske Skiløber Bataljon, later commander of 1st Trondhjemske Nationale Infanteri Regiment, which included both 1st Nordenfjeldske Skiløber Bataljon and 2nd Nordenfjeldske Skiløber *Bataljon*. At the same time with the title of *Kommerceconsulent/ Commercial Consultant*, he was a leading citizen in Trondheim. And he was probably responsible for the supply of green uniforms to Det Kongelige Frivillige Røråske Bergjæger Corps, 1st Nordenfjeldske Skiløber Bataljon, 2nd Nordenfjeldske Skiløber Bataljon, and also for the Trondheim Frivillige Jæger Corps.

short black boots. There are indications that the coat was changed for a double-breasted one at some point.

The men wore a dark blue coatee with a black collar and round cuffs, white waist coat and blue pantaloons with a round hat and a cockade. The individual companies were only differentiated by the colour of their cockades; red, white or blue.

Christiania Ridende Borgergarde

The first (and probably the finest corps) was the *Gule Cor* (the Yellow Company). It was raised and paid for by the richest and most influential members of society in Christiania. In 1812 it was organised with one commander, two lieutenants, two trumpeters and 18 volunteers. This was an officer grade unit, used mainly for parades and internal security. In 1808 new uniforms of a 'hussar style' were adopted.

In 1803 the officers had two uniforms, one for mounted service and another for service on foot. For mounted service they wore a pale yellow double-breasted coatee with a dark blue, high falling collar and round cuffs piped with blue and silver/white lace. The coat had dark blue turnbacks on the front. Their buttons and epaulettes were silver. On these the commander would have had two rosettes and the lieutenants one. They had a dark blue waistcoat and straw yellow leather riding breeches. They wore a round hat with a white plume with a blue tip with blue and silver cords and gold tassels. They had a black shoulder belt with a reversed silver Norwegian Lion badge and black cavalry boots. Their sabre was a model specific to them; the steel hilt had a three-branch guard engraved with a floral design on the guard plate and the sword knot was red and gold. It was carried in a black leather scabbard with steel fittings on a black belt with a silver buckle.

For foot service they wore a pale yellow double-breasted long-tailed coat lined pale yellow with a dark blue collar and round cuffs piped with blue and silver/white lace. The coat had dark blue turnbacks on the front. Their buttons and epaulettes were silver. They had a dark blue waistcoat and pale yellow breeches with short Hessian-style boots. They wore a black bicorn with a black cockade, silver loop, gold tassels and a white plume with a blue tip with blue and silver cords and gold tassels. After a modern reconstruction by Bloch the officer is shown with a double-breasted long-tailed yellow coat and a black bicorn with the same plume and cockade.

The men only had one silver/white epaulette on the left shoulder and their buttons were pewter. The shoulder belt was black leather with a stamped reversed silver Norwegian Lion on the breast and a cartridge pouch. The company had a trumpeter who wore the same uniform, but without an epaulette. After a contemporary print dated 1803 and a near contemporary painting by Vogt dated 1817.

They were all to be armed with a steel-hilted hussar-style sabre with a red/orange/yellow sword knot, carried in a black leather scabbard with steel fittings and a pair of pistols. The shoulder belt was black leather and had a shield stamped with the Norwegian lion on the breast and 'FR VI' on the flap of the cartridge pouch. The saddle cloth was to be blue, edged with two white lines of lace, which were silver for the officers.

In 1808 their uniform was changed to a pale yellow hussar dolman, but with five rows of buttons, and with light blue lace between the pewter buttons. The collar and cuffs were blue; this was now a lighter medium blue and was piped white for the men and silver for the officers.

The officers had silver shoulder belt with a black leather cartridge pouch. The men had a black leather shoulder belt with a black leather cartridge pouch, and it had a shield stamped with the Norwegian lion on the breast and 'FRVI' on the flap of the cartridge pouch.

Their headdress was now a casque (cavalry helmet) with a 'Danish' brim, yellow turban and chains with a caterpillar similar to the English-style Tarleton. It had a blue-tipped white plume over a black cockade.

Christiania Borgerlige Infanterikorps

In 1803 the officers wore a black round M1789 hat with a pale yellow, green-tipped side plume, a gold hatband, cords and a black cockade and a gold loop. They had a double-breasted long-tailed dark green coat with a black falling collar and black cuffs with gold epaulettes and gilded brass buttons, a double-breasted, light-yellow waistcoat, grey pantaloons and short black boots. They carried a brass-hilted sabre in a black leather scabbard with brass fittings on a black waist belt with a rectangular gilded plate buckle. In 1808 the officers received a black leather pouch on a black leather bandolier. The men had the same uniform, but their hat cords were yellow. They had a black leather bandoleer with a cartridge box and a black leather waist belt, and they were armed with a musket.

Christiania Frivillige Jæger Corps

This *jæger* corps was made up of the youngest and richest men from the militia. They served with the main army in 1809, although they mustered only 67 *jægere*. In 1801 the officers uniform was a bicorn with an upright, red-tipped white plume, black cockade with a gold loop, button and tassels, a double-breasted long-tailed dark blue coat with a red collar piped or laced gold with gold epaulettes and gilded brass buttons, a white waistcoat, dark blue pantaloons and short black boots. They carried a brass-hilted sabre with a gold knot.

The men wore the same uniform with an M1789 round hat with a red-tipped white plume bent back over their hat, no piping on their collar and brass buttons. They had a black leather cross belt with a cartridge box and a black leather waist belt suspended a sabre or *hirschfänger*. Their uniforms were changed in 1808 when the officers adopted the same uniform as the infantry officers and the men

Norwegian Citizen Militia (II)

> Facing page
>
> Plate 62. Norwegian Citizen Militia (II)
>
> Top:
> 1. Officer, Strømsøe Borgerlige Infanteri Corps
> 2. Private, Strømsøe Borgerlige Infanteri Corps
> 3. Officer, Bragernes Frivillige Jæger Corps
> 4. *Jæger*, Bragernes Frivillige Jæger Corps
>
> The town called Drammen was founded on 19 June 1811 by joining the two smaller towns of Bragenæs and Strømsøe into one, under the new name of Drammen. The uniforms were probably standardised at the same time.
>
> Bottom:
> 5. Captain, Kongsberg Ridende Jæger Corps
> 6. Officer, Øster-Riisører (Risør) Borge Corps
> 7. Officer, Stavanger Borgerlige Infanteri
> 8. Officer, Trondheim Borgerlige Artilleri Corps. Illustration based on an original watercolour, but even though not shown, they most likely had the standard gold officer's epaulettes.
>
> Note: the watch-chain hanging from their waists, was an informal sign of a citizen and his rank.

received a single-breasted dark green coatee lined yellow with yellow piping and brass buttons.

Christiania Borgerlige (Ridende) Artilleri Corps

They were formed and commanded by Captain Ludvig Mariboe. They were volunteers from mainly the Christiania Borgervæbnings Jæger Corps. In 1807–1808 they had five officers, six NCOs and 95 gunners, but by 1809 there were 68 officers, NCOs and gunners with the army. They served as a light horse artillery company, under the command of *Oberstløjtnant* von Ohme, taking part during the fighting at Onstadsund and Grønsund and earning a fine service record. As a horse artillery battery it was a force the army could and did employ. They were equipped with twelve 1-pdr 22 calibre M1766 *amusettes*, which were surplus guns from the regular horse company who had been re-equipped with 3-pdr guns. They were delivered in 1807, from the arsenal at Aggeshus according to the arsenal records. This unit also appears to be listed within the regular artillery companies, so their status may have changed.

We have very little information on their uniforms, just a portrait of Captain Mariboe and an order of 88 brass-hilted M1756 infantry sabres. Captain Ludvig Mariboe's uniform was a dark green short jacket with a high black collar, cuffs and narrow lapels. The coat had two rows of brass or gilt domed ball buttons on the front. He wore a green waistcoat with one row of brass buttons, under his open short jacket, as is visible on his portrait. The officers in general had M1801 militia epaulettes with three hanging tassels. Captain Ludvig Mariboe had a black leather shoulder belt and pouch with an oval brass badge on his breast bearing two crossed cannon barrels. Probably these were also worn by the other officers. A black leather waist belt with gilded brass lions head bosses and an 'S 'clasp buckle. In his portrait he is wearing what are probably green trousers. The gunners wore a simpler version of same uniform as the officers.

Christiansand Borgerlige Infanteri og Artilleri

In 1803 both the infantry and artillery officers wore a black bicorn with a blue plume and a black cockade and a gold loop and tassels. The infantry officers wore a long-tailed double-breasted dark blue coat with a black collar, round cuffs and narrow lapels, all piped white with gold buttons and epaulettes. Although the coat was supposed to be dark blue, but it was probably black due to scarcity of blue cloth. The artillery officers wore the same coat, but with a dark blue collar and cuffs but no lapels. They wore a pair of dark blue breeches and a double-breasted white waistcoat worn with short black boots and white stockings. Their sword was carried on a black leather shoulder belt worn under their coat.

The infantrymen were dressed in a dark blue double-breasted civilian coat with brass buttons, dark blue breeches, white stockings and square topped short boots and had round hats with a black cockade, but no plume. The artillerymen had a short double-breasted jacket. The infantry was armed with a musket and had a cartridge box carried on a red shoulder belt with white laced border and they carried a straight sword with a brass hilt.

After 1804 they were divided into two divisions, the Eastern *Østlig* and Western *Vestlig* wards, they continued to wear the same uniforms except the uniforms of the Western division were now piped red. The men did not have a uniform, so the dark blue coats really were civilian coats. Little is known about the *jægere* except that they had a green coatee with black facings, brass buttons and grey trousers.

Christiansund Borger Corps
1st Avdeling: In 1803 the officers wore a long-tailed double-breasted dark blue coat lined white with a red collar, round cuffs and narrow lapels all piped white; the pockets were also piped white with gold buttons and epaulettes, worn with a double-breasted white waistcoat. Their dark blue trousers had red tape on all seams including their inside leg and front vents and fly. They had a black bicorn with a black cockade and a gold loop and tassels. No plume was worn. They carried a brass-hilted sabre in a black leather scabbard with brass fittings on a black waist belt with a rectangular gilded plate buckle.

2nd Avdeling: The same uniform as the 1st Avdeling, but their coat had a dark blue collar and round cuffs all piped white and their trousers had white piping. No details of the men's uniform are known, and the unit appears to have been disbanded by 1810.

Drammens Borger Corps
Originally formed in two separate towns, Bragernes and Strömsö, until their units were merged in 1811.

Strømsøe Borgerlige Infanteri Corps
In 1803 the officers wore a long-tailed double-breasted dark green coat lined white, and their collar and round cuffs were piped yellow, with double piping on cuffs. The pockets were piped yellow gold with gold buttons and an epaulette on the right shoulder only, worn with a double-breasted, light-yellow waistcoat. Their dark green trousers were piped yellow including front vents and short black boots. They had a black bicorn with a black cockade, a yellow-tipped green plume and a golden loop and tassels.

The men wore a long-tailed double-breasted dark green civilian cut coat without piping, a double-breasted yellow waistcoat, dark green trousers and short black boots. They wore a black round hat with a black cockade, a yellow-tipped, green plume and gold or yellow cords and hat band. They had a cartridge box on a white leather shoulder belt and a white leather waist belt.

Bragernens Borgerlige Infanteri Corps
In 1803 the officers wore a long-tailed double-breasted dark green coat lined white, and their collar and round cuffs were piped yellow, double piping on cuffs. The pockets were piped gold with gold buttons and epaulettes. The details are not clear, but it is possible that the collar and cuffs were black. They had a double-breasted white waistcoat and trousers with short black boots. They had a black bicorn with a black cockade, a green-tipped white plume with a gold loop and tassels. The NCOs wore the same uniform as the officers minus the gold piping and epaulettes.

The men wore a long-tailed double-breasted dark green civilian cut coat without piping, with black buttons worn with a double-breasted white waistcoat, white trousers and short black boots. They had a black round hat with a black cockade, a green tipped white plume and white loop, cords and hat band. They had a cartridge box on a white leather shoulder belt and a white leather waist belt.

Bragernes Frivillige Jæger Corps
They were composed of 50 *jægere*. In 1803 the officers wore a long-tailed double-breasted dark green coat lined black, with black collar and round cuffs, green cuff flap with three buttons piped white, silver buttons and gold epaulettes. They had a double-breasted white waistcoat and trousers with short black boots. They had a black bicorn with a black cockade, a green tuft plume with a gold loop and tassels.

The men had a black hat with a black and green plume and a black cockade on the side. They wore a single-breasted short green jacket with black collar and cuffs, with double white piping down the front of the jacket, on the cuffs and collar, and pewter buttons. The coatee had white turnbacks. They had white gaiter trousers and black shoes, a cartridge box on a black shoulder belt and waist belt. They were armed with *jæger* rifles and *hirschfängers*.

Drammens Kongelige Borgergarde
They were known as the Det Grønne Korps i Bragernes (the Green Corps of Bragernes). In 1803 the officer wore a black bicorn hat with a white plume with a green tip and a black cockade and a gold loop and tassels. They wore a double-breasted dark green coat lined dark green with a black collar, the coat, collar, coat front and the cuffs were piped gold/yellow with gold buttons and epaulettes. They had a white double-breasted waistcoat, and buff breeches wore black Hessian boots, a black waist belt with a rectangular brass plate buckle and carried a gold-hilted sabre with a gold knot. The details of the housings/shabraques are unknown, but were probably green.

Frederikshald (Halden) Borgerlige Infanteri Corps
In 1803 they wore a black round hat with a green-tipped yellow plume and a black cockade. They wore a single-breasted dark green coat lined dark green with a black collar. The coat, collar, coat front and round cuffs were piped yellow with gold buttons. They wore a buff double-breasted waistcoat and buff breeches. The officer had gold epaulettes, black Hessian boots, and a black waist belt with a rectangular brass plate buckle and carried a gold-hilted

sabre with a gold knot. The men had a cartridge box on a black shoulder belt and a black waist belt.

Prins Christian's Frivillige Jæger Corps
This unit was a small unit of only 20 men. Very little is known about their uniforms, just a brief contemporary written description and a reconstruction made by A. Bloch around 1900 from now lost documents.

The written description gives a green jacket, black collar and lapels piped yellow, grey trousers and a green plume. Bloch shows them with a black round hat with a black cockade on the side and green caterpillar crest fore and aft on the top of the hat. They wore a dark green coatee with a black collar, lapels and round cuffs, piped yellow with brass buttons. The coat had yellow turn-ups on the front and black shoulder straps piped yellow. They wore a pair of grey breeches with a strip of black tape down the outside seam and black embroidered Hungarian knots, short black gaiters and shoes. The officer had gold epaulettes, black Hessian boots, and a black waist belt with a rectangular brass plate buckle, and carried a gold-hilted sabre with a gold knot. The men had a cartridge box on a black shoulder belt and a black waist belt with a *hirschfänger*, and were armed with a rifle.

Frederikstad Borgerlige Infanteri Corps
A short-lived corps disbanded in 1811. In 1803 they wore a black round hat with a green-tipped yellow plume and a black cockade. They wore a single-breasted dark green coat lined dark green with a black collar. The coat, collar, coat front and round cuffs were piped light yellow, with light yellow turnbacks and brass buttons. A buff double-breasted waistcoat and buff breeches completed their attire. The men had a cartridge box on a black shoulder belt and a black waist belt. The officer had silver epaulettes.

Holmestrand
In 1807 they were dressed as *jægere*.

Kongsberg Ridende Jæger Corps
This unit was also known as the Det Grønne Ridende Corps. In 1803 the officers wore a black bicorn hat with a white plume with a green tip, and a black cockade and a gold loop and tassels. They wore a green coatee with a buff collar, cuffs and lapels, all piped white, and a green cuff flap and gold buttons. The coat had gold epaulettes. Breeches and waistcoats were buff. Black Hessian boots were worn, with a black waist belt with a rectangular brass plate buckle and they carried a straight sword (a *pallask* like the *Bornholm* dragoons). Horse furniture is unknown, but they probably had a green shabraque.

Kragerø Borger Corps
Another short-lived unit which consisted of infantry and artillery, and it was probably disbanded before the end of the war. Only the officers were uniformed.

In 1803 the officers wore a long-tailed double-breasted dark blue coat lined dark blue with a black collar and round cuffs all piped white with gold buttons and epaulettes (captain two epaulettes, lieutenants only one), worn with a double-breasted white waistcoat. They had a pair of white trousers and short black boots. They had a black bicorn with a black cockade and a gold loop and tassels with a yellow plume. They carried a brass-hilted sabre in a black leather scabbard with brass fittings on a black waist belt with a rectangular gilded plate buckle.

Larvik Borgerlige Infanteri Corps
This corps had ceased to exist by 1812. The uniform details are taken from a contemporary watercolour conserved in the Dronningens Håndbibliotek in Copenhagen. In 1803 the officers wore a black round M1789 hat with a green-tipped yellow plume and a black cockade and a gold loop on the side. They wore a long tailed double-breasted olive-green coat with a black collar, piped white, with turnbacks, buff lining and gold buttons. Grey breeches and a buff waistcoat were worn. The officers wore short black boots with tassels, a black waist belt with a rectangular brass plate buckle and carried a hussar-model sabre.

Molde Borger Corps
From 1801 to 1814, and based on a modern reconstruction, in 1802 they wore a black round hat, with a black cockade and a white plume on the side. They wore a long-tailed double-breasted dark blue coat with gold buttons. The coat had a dark blue collar, cuffs and lapels, all piped white, and white turnbacks. The cuffs had cuff flaps with two buttons. They wore grey breeches and a double-breasted white waistcoat and short black gaiters. Möller gives a blue coatee with dark blue facings piped white, and brass buttons. They also had light grey trousers.

Moss Borger Corps
In 1803 they had two officers, five NCOs, a drummer and 44 militia men. The following year this had risen to three officers, five NCOs and 65 men. They were not uniformed before 1807. All that is known is they had green jackets/coatees and black hats.

Øster-Riisører (Risør) Borger Corps
In 1803 the officers wore a black bicorn with a black cockade, dark blue plume with gold loop and tassels. They wore a long-tailed double-breasted dark blue coat with a dark blue collar and cuffs piped white, with gold buttons and epaulettes. They wore a pair of dark blue breeches and a white waistcoat, short black boots, a black waist belt with

a rectangular brass plate buckle and carried a sabre with a brass gilt hilt. Later changes were made and by 1804 the piping had gone and the plume changed to green and white.

In 1803 the men wore a black round hat, with a black cockade on the front. They wore a long-tailed double-breasted dark blue coat with a dark blue collar and cuffs and gold buttons. They wore a pair of dark blue breeches and a white waistcoat, short black boots over white socks, a black waist belt with a rectangular brass plate buckle and carried a straight sword with a brass gilt hilt. Artillery officers wore the same uniform as the infantry officers minus the plume and piping.

Möller gives a green coat with black facings, pewter buttons and blue grey breeches in 1810.

Sandefjord Borgervæbning
The officers wore a black bicorn hat with a green-tipped yellow plume and a black cockade and a gold loop and tassels. They wore a long-tailed double-breasted green coat with a black collar, piped white, and cuffs with green lining. Coat tails were lined pale yellow and had gold buttons. In 1803 the officers wore a black round hat with a white plume with a green tip and a black cockade and a gold loop on the side and gold cords. The officers had gold epaulettes. The collar, cuffs and cuff flaps pockets and all leading edges were piped pale yellow. Breeches were grey and the vents had black embroidery, and a double-breasted buff yellow waistcoat. They wore black Hessian boots, a black waist belt with a rectangular brass plate buckle and carried a gilt-hilted artillery model sabre. Other ranks wore the same costume, but without the gold cords and epaulettes and were armed with a *jæger* rifle and a *hirschfänger*.

Skien Borgerlige Infanteri (Telemark)
In 1803 the officers wore a black bicorn with a light-yellow plume with a green tip and a black cockade with a gold loop and tassels. They wore a long-tailed double-breasted dark green coat with dark green lining and cuff flaps with two buttons, a black collar and round cuffs, all piped yellow with gold buttons. The turnbacks were buff. They wore buff breeches and waistcoat, with short black Hessian boots and a black waist belt with a rectangular brass plate buckle, and carried a straight sword with a brass or gilded hilt. In 1810 the officers are listed as having a green coatee with yellow lining, a black collar, yellow piping, brass buttons and straw yellow trousers.

Stavanger Borgerlige Infanteri
In 1803 the officers wore a black bicorn with a blue plume and a black cockade with a gold loop and tassels. They wore a long-tailed double-breasted dark blue coat with black collar, round cuffs and narrow lapels piped white, with gold buttons and epaulettes. They wore dark blue breeches and a white waistcoat, short black Hessian boots and a black waist belt with a rectangular brass plate buckle. They carried a sabre with a brass or gilded hilt. Another contemporary illustration shows them with their sabre on a black shoulder belt.

The infantrymen were dressed in a dark blue double-breasted civilian coat with brass buttons, dark blue breeches, white stockings and square-topped short boots. They had round hats with a black cockade on the front, but no plume. The infantry was armed with a musket and had a cartridge box carried on a red shoulder belt with a white-laced border and they carried a straight sword with a brass hilt. By 1810 they were wearing a lapelled blue coat with a dark blue collar, cuffs and lapels piped white, blue lining and brass buttons and epaulettes. They wore black breeches and a white waistcoat. The artillerymen had a short, double-breasted jacket.

Stavanger Borgerlige Artilleri
In 1803 the officers wore a black bicorn hat with a blue plume, a black cockade and a gold loop and tassels. They wore a dark blue coat with a black fall down collar, cuffs and lapels all piped red, blue lining with gold buttons and epaulettes. They wore a pair of fall-fronted blue breeches and a white waistcoat, short black boots and carried a hussar-style sabre on a black leather waist belt with a rectangular brass plate buckle.

The NCOs had a black hat with a red cockade. They wore a blue coat with red piping on the collar, cuffs and lapels, with blue lining and gold buttons. A pair of fall-fronted blue breeches and a white waistcoat were worn; together black boots and the men carried an artillery-model sabre on a black leather shoulder belt with an oval brass plate. The men did not have a uniform as such, but they wore dark blue civilian coats and a round hat.

Tromsø
In 1809 they received a new uniform of a dark blue jacket or coatee with a red collar and cuffs, all piped white with yellow buttons. Their waistcoat was white and the trousers were dark blue. They had a round hat with gold cords and a red and white cockade.

Trondheim Borgerlige Infanterikorps
Originally, they had two companies, but in 1801 the unit was expanded to four companies, each divided into two sections or wards. In 1798 the 1st company of the 1st Avdeling ward had blue coats, yellow buttons and black trousers. The officers and men all wore a black bicorn with a blue cockade and plume; later the men exchanged their bicorns for round hats. They had a brown leather cartridge case with the royal cypher carried on a brown leather cross belt, all edged with light yellow lace. This cartridge case and cross belt were black by 1803. The 2nd company of the 1st Avdeling had the same uniform and equipment, but with a

green cockade and plume and no cypher on the cartridge case.

In 1803 the officers had a bicorn with a green cockade and plume, gold buttons, epaulettes, ties, loop and tassels. They wore a dark blue coat with a black collar, lapels and cuffs, all piped white, with a white waistcoat and trousers. The men had a bicorn with a green cockade and plume, gold ties and loop. They wore a double-breasted coat dark blue coat and cuff flaps with a black collar and cuffs, all piped white with a white waistcoat and trousers. Their cartridge case and cross belt were dark green/black by 1803, piped white.

For the 2nd Avdeling we have the uniform for the 4th Company. The officers wore a dark blue coat and cuff flaps with a black collar, lapels and cuffs all piped white, gold buttons and epaulettes with a white waistcoat and trousers. They had a bicorn with a black cockade with a white centre and black plume, gold loop and tassels.

The men wore a double-breasted coat dark blue coat with a black collar and round cuffs all piped white, brass buttons and epaulettes with a white waistcoat and dark blue trousers, white stockings and black boots. Their cartridge case and cross belt were dark black. They had a round hat with a black cockade with a white centre on the side. The 3rd company were dressed the same but their cockade was black.

In an 1810 work Möller gives them a blue coatee with light blue facings, pewter buttons and grey trousers, but this is an error as what is shown is the commanding officer's uniform, a unique uniform worn only by them.

Trondheim Frivillige Artilleri
In 1803 the officers had a black hat with a red tipped black plume which fell from front to back, and a red cockade on the side. The officers wore a dark blue coat and cuff flaps with three buttons and a red collar, cuffs and lapels all piped white, including the pockets and gold buttons. The coat tails had white turnbacks. They had a pair of dark-blue, fall-front trousers and a double-breasted white waistcoat. They had short black boots; a brass-hilted sabre carried on a black waist belt with a rectangular brass plate buckle. The captain had gold lace on his collar.

The men had a short double-breasted blue coat with a red collar, dark blue lapels and round cuffs piped white, dark blue, fall-front trousers and a double-breasted white waistcoat. The coat tails had white turnbacks. They also had short black boots; a brass-hilted sabre carried on a black waist belt with a rectangular brass plate buckle. They had the same hat as the officers.

Möller gives us the same uniform colours in 1810 in a description taken from a contemporary watercolour conserved in the Dronningens Håndbibliotek in Copenhagen together with a contemporary portrait of the commanding officer in 1812.

Trondheim Frivillige Jæger Corps
In 1803 they had a black hat with a green plume and white or grey cockade on the side. They wore a green coatee with black collar, round cuffs and narrow lapels piped white and six brass buttons. The coat had white frontal turnbacks. They had a pair of grey fall-front trousers and a white waistcoat. They had short black boots, a black waist belt with a rectangular brass plate buckle and they were armed with *jæger* rifles and *hirschfängers*. This information is taken from a contemporary watercolour conserved in the Dronningens Håndbibliotek in Copenhagen.

Some have suggested that by 1812 the men had a M1808 coatee with lapels with seven brass buttons and pointed cuffs in the same colours and a hat with a green plume and cord. Also the *hornblæser* had black shoulder rolls with thin yellow piping around them and five stripes across them. But this was more likely to be the M1809 *skiløber* uniform, produced in Trondheim between 1809 and 1811, and after 1814 were used also by some members of Trondhjemske Frivillige Jæger Corps.

An original coat is conserved in the Trøndlag Folkmuseum, and a *hornblæser*'s coatee and a pair of trousers are both conserved in the NTNU Vitenskapsmuseet, Trondheim. Möller's list of 1810 gives them a completely different uniform in 1810; a blue coat with black facings piped white, brass buttons and grey trousers, but he is probably wrong, as they were dark green. This is confirmed by the written description of an officer's uniform between 1810 and 1814, in the *Kongelig Hof og Stads Calender*.

Tønsberg Borgerlige Infanteri og Artilleri Corps
In 1803 officers wore a black round hat with a yellow tipped green plume and a black cockade with a gold loop. They wore a long-tailed double-breasted dark green coat with black collar, dark green round cuffs all piped white with gold buttons and epaulettes. They wore buff breeches and waistcoat, and short black Hessian boots. They were equipped with a black waist belt with a rectangular brass plate buckle, and carried a sabre with a brass or gilded hilt.

The men wore the same uniform minus the epaulettes and sabre. They had a black cartridge case and cross belt piped white. The artillery wore the same uniform, but their plume was all green and their trousers were grey.

Tønsberg Ridende Borger Corps
This was just a mounted Guard of Honour. In 1803 the officers wore a black bicorn with a light blue plume and a black cockade with a blue and gold loop and gold tassels. They wore a long-tailed double-breasted dark blue coat and cuff flaps with black collar, narrow lapels and round cuffs all piped gold with gold buttons and a gold epaulette. They wore buff breeches and a double-breasted waistcoat and short black boots, a black shoulder belt with an oval brass

plate with the arms of Tønsberg and a sabre with a brass or gilded hilt.

The Norwegian Kystværnet (Coastal Defence Force)
The defence, patrolling and guarding the coastline between larger towns and cities was performed by a *Kystværn*. They were principally recruited from among the local fishermen, craftsmen and farmers living along the coast.

Because of the British blockade and raiding along the coast and shipping and foraging for supplies, no part of the coast was secure. Already in 1801 the first steps had been taken to create a force, in Norway built on an old common 'defence pact' where all freemen were obliged to arm themselves with a weapon of some description, and serve with their kinsmen to defend their homeland against attack.

This system was formalised in July 1807 and was organised along the same lines as in Denmark. The main arms were to be pikes and spears and only the first rank should have a musket. Many men only had an old sword or the old traditional 'Norwegian axes' used since the Dark Ages. Few were uniformed and in most cases just had a red wooden cockade with the white cross of Dannebrog stitched onto their coat or hat. Officers were allowed a uniform, but they did not wear it all the time, and even when worn it was not always complete. Training was normally a couple of hours every Sunday, but systems of watch and beacons for alarm were made and kept. According to the regulations:

> Those who had a gun at front, trained in shooting are in battle to take first rank, firing at enemy softening him up before attacking. Rest to gather in two or three ranks behind with 'pikes' all formed 'arm to arm' looking enemy in eyes, move against him, and at right moment and signal, to in a short run, storm the enemy and overwhelm him.

But in fact, many didn't or couldn't take things seriously, and in most cases this was never more than a look out force, never a true 'fighting force', but their presence no doubt helped keep the British at some distance.

The officers of the coastal militia in 1808 wore a dark blue uniform. The uniform was made and delivered by the State to the locally appointed 'officers' and they were probably the only ones in uniform as such.

In theory an impressive force was thus organised. In Bergen, for example, 12,500 men were, in theory, part of the force. They were organised into four 'divisions' subdivided into 'sections', all of different sizes and varying organisation.

Appendix I

Norwegian Cavalry Active in 1808–1809

The following Norwegian cavalry units were part of the forces active from late 1808 to early 1809.

Søndenfjeldske Division:

General-Major Staffel's Brigade:
One officer with 33 NCOs and dragoons from the *Oplandske Dragonregiment*

General-Major Lowzow's Brigade:
Two officers with 82 NCOs and dragoons from the *Smålenske Dragonregiment*

General-Major Holst's Brigade:
The *Geworbne* company of the *Akershusiske Dragonregiment* of two officers with 48 NCOs and dragoons (who were sent home on furlough by March 1809)

Chain of couriers of the *Ordonnans Kæde* for the general staff numbering 130 dragoons who were drawn from all three regiments

Detachment on foot to guard Swedish prisoners in the main city of Christiania:
One officer with 150 NCOs and dragoons

The rest of the dragoons were either in garrison, at their depot or at home on furlough.

Nordenfjeldske Division:

A number of small detachments from the *Trondhjemske Dragonregiment*, details unknown.

Appendix II

Norwegian Horses

The fjord horse or Norwegian fjord horse (Norwegian: *fjordhest*) is a relatively small but very strong horse breed originating from the mountainous regions of western Norway. It is an agile breed with the build of a light draught horse. It is also one of the world's oldest breeds. All fjord horses are rather dun in colour. They have been used for hundreds of years as farm horses in Norway, but also by the army, from the Vikings to modern times. They were used by the dragoons during the Napoleonic wars, a small but sturdy transport horse for dragons and as a pack and draught horse, particularly in the north. Despite its small size, between 130 and 150 cm height at the withers (12.3 to 14.3 hands) this hardy breed is fully capable of carrying an adult human as well as pulling heavy loads. Their coat becomes particularly thick and heavy in the winter, very practical in the Norwegian climate.

Another, more common, breed of Norwegian horse was the *Gudbransdalske Heste/Dølehest* (the Dole Gudbrandsdal horse), which was favoured by the southern dragoon regiments, as it was a larger 145 to 160 cm high at the withers (14.1 to 15.3 hands), and usually bay, brown, or black, occasionally grey. More common 'Danish' horse breeds could be found during 1800–1814, mainly as riding horses for officers. Also some Swedish horses were pressed into service.

Appendix III

Norwegian Orders of Battle

Battle of Trangen 1808
Overall commander: Colonel Bernhard Ditlef von Staffeldt

The grenadier battalion of the 2nd Trondhjemske Nationale Infanteri Regiment (Major von Ræder)

The Sønnenfjeldske Skiløber Bataljon (technically part of the Norwegian Jægerkorps) with three ski companies (Aamodtske, Elverrumske and Hoffromske ski companies (Major Von Stabell)

The Lærdalske Lette Infanteri Companie (Captain von Jürgensen)

Two *skarpskytte* platoons, drawn from the 1st and 2nd Trondhjemske Nationale Infanteri Regiment and another *skarpskytte* platoon from the Bergenhusiske Nationale Infanteri Regiment, who fought as a combined company uni (Captain Sigholt?)

30–70 dragoons from the Oplandske Dragonregiment.

Battle of Lier 1814
Overall commander: Lieutenant Colonel Andreas Samuel von Krebs

1st battalion (Ullensakerske) from the Akershusiske Skarpskytte Regiment

Søndenfieldske Skiløber Bataljon: Aamodtske, Elverrumske and Hoffromske ski companies

2nd Trondhjemske Nationale Infanteri Regiment: Field battalion Stang

2nd Company (Eidsvoll/Nesiske) from the Akershusiske Ridene Jægercorps (70 light cavalrymen)

1 Pundigt Regiments Artillerie with four 1-pdr artillery pieces

½ of 3rd (formerly 12th) 3 Pundige Fodartilleri Kompani. Half company foot artillery with four 3-pdr artillery pieces (Lieutenant von Meidell)

The total strength was approximately 2,500 soldiers

Appendix IV

Det Kongelige Frivillige Røråske Bergjæger Corps

The official formation of the *Det Kongelige Frivillige Røråske Bjerg Corps* dated from October 1788, and was renamed *Det Kongelige Frivillige Røråske Bergjæger Corps* in 1798. This was really the first formally organised volunteer militia formation, created outside of the normal military system. There were some citizen militias before that, but they were in practical terms more social clubs, to show their status as citizens, independent of any military command or common structure. Following the first attacks on the coast of Denmark and Norway, Crown Prince Frederik knew the British would come again, and he now began to search for the means to protect the coast from attacks from the sea so he would be able to concentrate the main army on the border and in Copenhagen. Permanent batteries and defences were needed, but most of all, troops to man them and the surrounding countryside. It was in this context that the volunteer units and *Borgervæbninger* (Citizen Guards) were formed throughout the Danish–Norwegian kingdom.

The whole basis for this was a proposal to form a voluntary all-arms force of the workers at the gun foundry at *Frederiksværk*. The proposal was submitted by War Commissioner A. S. von Hasler, who wanted to create a force based on the organisation of *Det Kongelige Frivillige Røråsiske Bergjæger Corps,* and so form a local defence force at this important place, under the command of the factory officials. The workers themselves had to pay for the uniforms and the State delivered weapons and equipment. The Crown Prince fully supported the idea and on 9 January 1801 the *Frederiksværk Frivillige Bevæbnede Corps* (the volunteer armed workers of *Frederiksvaerk*), was officially formed. But the Crown Prince, after discussions, decided 'That the example of the *Rørås Frivillige Bergjæger Corps* will be the formal basis of the following reorganisation of the defence'. Shortly after 19 January 1801, plans for a Landeværn (inspired by the Norwegian Landeværn) and also a volunteer *Kystmilits* were ordered. Then on 28 February 1801 the citizen militia of Copenhagen were reorganised, and new volunteer formations formed there, and on 17 February 1801 orders for the same basic organisation were written for all larger market towns and cities in Denmark, Schleswig-Holstein and Norway, but it took until 1803 before they became formally adopted.

But *Det Kongelige Frivillige Røråske Bergjæger Corps* was the basis for all the subsequent militia forces, in particular the organisation and the way that the men served, were equipped and armed. But in Norway *Det Kongelige Frivillige Røråske Bergjæger Corps* was only composed of common workers, never really seen as deviating very much from Norwegian citizen society, and was not of equal social status. But the army always considered them as part of the regular army, something the citizens never were.

Glossary

Danish–English Ranks

Auditør	Military Judge Advocate
Commandersergent	Sergeant Major
Constable(r)	Lance Corporal(s) or Gunner(s) First Class
Corporal(er)	Corporal(s)
Dragon(er)	Dragoon(s)
Feltkommissariatet for den Danske hær	Quartermaster General
Fourer	Staff sergeant
Generalintendandt	General of Intendance
Geworbne	Regular Infantry
Grenader(er)	Grenadier(s)
Hoboister	Bandsmen, literally oboe player
Hofmarskal	Lord Chamberlain
Hornblæser(e)	Hornist(s)
Husar	Hussar
Jæger(e)	Jæger(s)
Kaptajn	Captain
Major	Major
Musketeer	Musketeer/Private
Oberst	Colonel
Oberstløjtnant	Lieutenant Colonel
Overconstable(r)	Corporal(s) / Bombardier(s)
Piber	Fifer
Premiereløjtnant(er)	First Lieutenant(s)
Regimentsjæger(e)	Regimental Jæger(s)
Repetent(er)	Cadet Teacher(s)
Ritmester	Captain of Cavalry
Rytter(e)	Cavalryman 'rider'(s)
Sekondløjtnant(er)	Second lieutenant(s)
Sergent(er)	Sergeant(s)
Skiløber(e)	Ski soldier(s)
Statholder	Governor
Stykkuske	Artillery train drivers
Skarpskytter(e)	Sharpshooter(s)
Tamboure(r)	Drummer(s)
Tambourmajor	Drum major
Tænkuske	Waggoneers
Tømmermand	Sapper, literally woodsman / carpenter
Trommekorporal	Drum corporal

Other Terms

Halvmaane	Half moon

Regimental Names

Kongelige Norske Landkadet Corps

Active Regiments
The 1st Akershusiske Nationale Infanteri Regiment
The 2nd Akershusiske Nationale Infanteri Regiment
1st (Nordre) Trondhjemske Nationale Infanteri Regiment
2nd (Søndre) Trondhjemske Nationale Infanteri Regiment
The 3rd Trondhjemske Nationale Infanteri Regiment (disbanded in 1789)
The 1st Smaalehnske Nationale Infanteri Regiment (disbanded in 1789)
The 2nd Smaalehnske Nationale Infanteri Regiment (disbanded in 1789)
The 1st Oplandske Nationale Infanteri Regiment
The 2nd Oplandske Nationale Infanteri Regiment (disbanded in 1789)
The 1st Bergenhusiske Nationale Infanteri Regiment
The 2nd Bergenhusiske Nationale Infanteri Regiment (disbanded in 1789)
The 1st Westerlehnske Infanteri Regiment
The 2nd Westerlehnske Infanteri Regiment (disbanded in 1789)

Søndenfjeldske [Southern Division] Geworbne Infanteri Regiment
Nordenfjeldske [Northern Division] Geworbne Infanteri Regiment
Telemarkske Nationale Infanteri Regiment

Fribataljoner: levy battalions

Norske Geworbne Jæger Corps
Nordenfjeldske [Northern Division] Skiløber Bataljon
Søndenfjeldske [Southern Division] Skiløber Bataljon
Lærdalske Lette Infanteri Compani
Norske Lette Infanteri Bataljon
Walderske Skarpskytte Bataljon
Bergenhusiske Skarpskytte Bataljon
Akershusiske Skarpskytte Regiment

Akershusiske Ridende Jæger Corps
1st Søndenfjeldske [Southern Division] Dragonregiment
2nd Søndenfjeldske [Southern Division] Dragonregiment
Akershusiske Dragonregiment
Smaalehnske Dragonregiment
Oplandske Dragonregiment
Søndenfjeldske Dragonregiment.
Trondhjemske Dragonkorps
Nordenfjeldske Artilleribataljon
Nordenfjeldske Nationale Artillery Companie
Fodartilleri Companie
10th Norske *Ridende* Artilleri Companie

Sappør companie: sapper company

Names of Old Regimental Colours / Fanen

Oldenburgske Infanteri Regiment
Møenske Infanteri Regiment
Danske Livregiment til Fods
Sjællandske Regiment
Kongens Regiment til Fods
Falsterske Infanteri Regiment
Dronningens Liv Regiment
Prins Frederiks Regiment
Holstenske Infanteri Regiment

Bibliography and Sources

Original Sources I: Contemporary Iconography

Anonymous artist, a series of contemporary watercolours of the Danish and Norwegian *Børgerkorps* made in 1802–1803. *Hendes majestæt Dronningens (Private) Håndbibliotek,* Christian VIII's Palæ, Amalienborg slot, DK-1257 København K, Denmark.

Brockdorff, Schack von, *Den Danske Armées Uniformer c.* 1806 (Copenhagen: Krigsmuseet)

Köller, Frederich Ludwig von, a series of watercolours (Kiel: Darmstadt University and Federal State Library)

Ljunggren, Carl Johann, *Minnes-Anteckningar under 1813 och 1814 årens kampagner uti Tyskland och Norge* (Stockholm: 1855)

Möller, *Fuldstændige Tabeller over alle den Kongelige Danske og Norske Armee tilhörende, regimenters, corpers, bataillioners, borgervæbningers og frivillige etc, corpers Corpser Uniform* (Kiöbenhavn: C. Steen forlag, 1810) Not to be confused with Waldemar Moller of *c.* 1892

Senn, Johs, Eckersberg C. W. Wilhelm Heuer & J. Reiter, *Danske Klædedragter* (København *c.* 1808–1812)

Suhr Brothers, *Abbildung der Uniformen aller in Hamburg seit den Jahren 1806 bis 1815 einquartiert gewesener Truppen.* (Berlin: Staatlicher Museum Kunstbibliothek). These illustrations were published in the 1820s in a book called *The Danish Army in Hamburg (1812-1814) Uniform Plates*. They were drawn and painted by Christoph and Cornelius Suhr. Only four copies are known to exist. Glückstadt, *c.* 1809–1810 (Hamburg-Altona, Das Altonaer Museum)

Danske Fanebogen, ref. CR7. FR6. A series of watercolours of Danish flags and standards conserved in the Tøjhusmuseet, *c.* 1860.

Original Sources II: Manuscripts

Kierulf, Herman, *Kalender over samtlige officerer ved den kongelige Danske og Norske Armée ansatte Officeerer og øvrige Beetiente, saavelsom over Borgervæbninger og frivillige corps No. IV.* (København: Kongelig og Universitets Bogtrytter, 1811)

Rosenstan, Goiske P. (1670–1800) og Hedegaard J. C. (1801–1816) *Ordrer, Resolutioner og Collegial breve den danske Krigsmagt til lands angående* (Copenhagen 1790–1815).

Schouboe, Oberst O. B, *Bornholms Værns Historie.* (Unprinted manuscript conserved in the central archives of the Island of Bornholm *c.* 1820).

Uniformsmanuskriptet or more correctly *Forslag til den Danske armees uniformer 1808.* Painter officially unknown, but most research points to *Feltjæger* Diederich Heinrich Wilhelm Voigt, who painted these originally for use by the Crown Prince Frederik's general staff (where he worked as an illustrator), and they were made between 1806 and 1811. The Kunst Industri Museet, Copenhagen.

Kongelig Danske Hof og stats calender i årene 1810 –1814, (Copenhagen 1810 to 1814)

Borgervæbninger i Danmark og Norge 1803 Hendes Majestæt Dronningens håndbibliotek, Christian VIII's Palæ, Amalienborg slot, DK-1257 København K, Denmark.

Printed Sources

Aagaard, Erik, *Den Norske Hær I Dansketiden-et billedheft* (Oslo: Forsvarsmuseet Småskrift nr. 10, 1992)

Aagaard, Erik, *Uniformene til den Norske Hærs Lette Infanteri-Del I 1786–1814* (Oslo: Norsk Våpenhistorisk Selskap Årbok, 1996)

Aagaard, Erik, *Det Norske kavaleris standarter* (Oslo: Norsk Våpenhistorisk Selskap Årbok, 2016)

Aagaard, Erik, *Det Norske infanteri faner.* (Oslo: Norsk Våpenhistorisk Selskap Årbok, 2017)

Aagaard, Erik, *Tilføyelser og debatt: Krigsskolens faner* (Oslo: Norsk Våpenhistorisk Selskap Årbok, 2018)

Aagaard, Erik, *Andreas Bloch Publiserte tegninger av uniformer* (Oslo: Norsk Våpenhistorisk Selskap Årbok, 2021)

Barstad, Oberstlieutant H.J, *Bergenhusingerne i Felten 1808-1811 1. Bergenhusiske Nationale grenaderbataljon* (Kristiania (Oslo): S & Jul Sørensens Bogtrykkeri 1908)

Barstad, Oberstlieutant H.J, *Bergenhusingerne i Felten 1808–1811 1. 2. Bergenhusiske Nationale Musketerbataljon* (Kristiania (Oslo): S & Jul Sørensens Bogtrykkeri 1909)

Barstad, Oberstlieutant H.J, *Bergenhusingerne i Felten Krigen mod Sverige 1813–1814* (Kristiania (Oslo): S & Jul Sørensens Bogtrykkeri 1918)

Blom, Otto, *Ældre danske metal og jern stykker* [Older Danish Metal and Cast Iron Cannons] (København: Krigsministeriet, 1891)

Bruhn, Helge, *Dannebrog og danske faner gennem tiderne* (København: Jespersen og Pios Forlag, 1949)

BIBLIOGRAPHY AND SOURCES

Cassin-Scott, Jack, *Scandinavian Armies in the Napoleonic Wars.* Osprey Men at Arms No. 60 (London: Osprey Publications, 1976)

Elting, John R., *Swords Around a Throne, Napoleon's Grande Armée* (London, Weidefeld and Nicolson, 1988)

Eriksen, E. & Frantzen, O. L. *Dansk Artilleri I Napoleonstiden* (København: Tøjhusmuseets, 1988)

Feldbaek, Ole, *The Battle of Copenhagen 1801* (original title *Slaget på Reden* 1985). English translation by Tony Wedgewood (Barnsley: Pen & Sword, 2016)

Glover, Gareth. *The Two Battles of Copenhagen, Britain and Denmark in the Napoleonic Wars.* (Barnsley: Pen & Sword, 2018)

Johansen Hauerbach, M. W, *Fanekatalog over Hærmuseets samling* (Oslo: Utg. Hærmuseet, 1956)

Johansen, Oberstløjtnant Jens, *Frederik VI's Hær 1784–1814* (København: Udgivet af Generalstaben, Heydes Bogtrykkeri, 1948)

Jonsgaard, Moen Ola *Regimental Distinctions of Norwegian Regiments 1807–14* (Oslo: Elverumske Skiløber Compagnie, 2014)

Juel, Major Anders, *Den nye sommer og vinter affutasje laget i Trondheim i 1809–10* (Hærmuseet årbok, Oslo, 1962)

Kannik, Preuben, *Military Uniforms of the World in Colour* (London: Blandford, 1968)

Knötel, Richard, Knötel H. & Sieg, H., *Uniforms of the World* [Handbuch der Uniformkunde] (London: reprint, Arms & Armour Press, 1980)

Krogh C.C. *Meddleelser om Kongelige Livgarde til hest.* (København: Andr. Fred. Høst & sons, Kongl. Hof-Bogandel, 1886. Ex Konliege Garnisonsbibliotek Københavnn)

Lange P.H.W. *Den danske generalstabs historie* (København: Unknown Publisher, 1889)

Lindeberg, Lars. *De så det ske – Englandskrigene 1801–14* (Copenhagen: Lademann Forlagsaktieselskab, 1974)

McIntyre, James R., *Johann Ewald, Jäger Commander* (New York: Knox Press, 2020)

Nielsen, Kay S, *Danske blankvåben* (Copenhagen: Forlaghet Sixtus, 1978)

Petersen, Karsten Skjold, *Kongens klaeder. Hærens uniformer og udrustning I Danmark- Norge* (Copenhagen: Tøjhusmuseet, 2014)

Petersen, Karsten Skjold, *Faner og Estandarter I den Danske Haer* (Copenhagen: Tøjhusmuseet, 2016)

Richter, V., *Den danske landmilitærestat 1801–1894* (København: bd. 1–2, 1934–1935)

Salchow, U., *Militærbeskrivelser over øen Bornholm 1813* (Bornholm: Bornholms Historiske Samfund, 1954)

Sandstedt, Fred, *Between the Imperial Eagles, Sweden's Armed Forces during the Revolutionary and the Napoleonic Wars 1780–1820* (Stockholm; Armémuseum, 2000)

Saxtorp, Niels M. *Hærens Blankvåben på Napoleonskrigens tid* (Oslo: Norsk Våpenhistorisk Selskap, 1974)

Skovgaard, P.N., *Bornholms beskrivelse 1804* (Copenhagen: 1804)

Strøm, Knut Erik. *Norges borgervæpinings-uniformer* (Oslo: Norsk Våpenhistorisk Selskap, 2016)

Strøm, Knut Erik, *Norske Borgervæpingsuniformer et Billedhefte* (Oslo: Forsvarsmuseet Akershus, 1992)

Thaulow, Th. *Samsø i krigsårene 1801–14* (Samsø: Boghandler Henri Neble, 1934)

Vaupell, Otto, *Den danske Hærs Historie til Nutiden og den norske Hærs Historie indtil 1814* (København: Forlagt af den Gyldendalske Boghandel, 1872–76) 2 volumes

Walberg, Erik, *Vapenlexikon Artilleri 1350–1880* (Stockholm: Sveriges militähistorika arv SMHA 2017)

Wise, Terry, *Flags of the Napoleonic Wars (3)* Osprey Men at Arms No. 115 (London: Osprey Publications 1981)

Wolter, Hans Christian, *Den Danske Hær I Napoleonstiden 1801–1814. Håndbog om uniformer, faner, udrustning ogkrigshistorie* (Copenhagen: Tøjhusmuseets skrifter 12. Tøjhusmuseet, 1992)

Magazines and Periodicals

Bruun, Daniel, *En ung Rytterofficers Erindringer fra felttoget 1813* Militært Tidsskrift, 43.årg. (1914) pp.1–30

Hoff, An, *Ridende og kørende artilleri*, Danske Artilleri Tidsskrift, 1970, pp.185–194

Hoff, An., *Det ridende artilleri i Danmark*, Danske Artilleri Tidsskrift, 1970, pp.222–227

Wolter, Hans Christian, *Danish Infantry of the Line and Light Infantry 1803–1814, the Perry Achievement*, Chakoten, December 2016, No. 71 årgang nr.4, pp.10–17.

Thureholm, Ole & Larsen, Jørgen K, & Wolter, Hans Christian, *Danish and Norwegian Cavalry and Artillery 1803–1814, the Perry Achievement*, Chakoten, September 2018, No. 73 årgang nr.3, pp.4–10.

Web Sources

Uniformserie Suhr http://napoleon-online.de/suhr.html (Last accessed 9 January 2020) for the plates by Suhr.

Arma-Dania. The Virtual Museum of Danish Arms and Armour

<https://www.arma-dania.dk/public/timeline/_ad_blankvaben_list.php> (last accessed 9 January 2020). Website containing details and photographs of Danish weapons.